On the Wrong Side
of the Track?

On the Wrong Side
of the Track?

EAST LONDON AND THE POST-OLYMPICS

Phil Cohen

Lawrence and Wishart London 2013

Lawrence and Wishart Limited
99a Wallis Road
London
E9 5LN

Cover: Graphic © Peter Kennard and Tarek Salhany

ISBN 9781 907103 629

British Library Cataloguing in Publication Data.
A catalogue record for this book is available from the British Library

Contents

Preface and Acknowledgements

I would like to thank Donald Nicholson Smith for his friendship, professional advice and support in helping see this book through to publication. Jean McNeil read some of the material and was, as ever, my best critic. Nick James prepared the index with exemplary thoroughness and Elizabeth Adams did the same with the proofs. Sally Davison and colleagues at Lawrence and Wishart gave dedicated support at every stage of the production process from copy editing to final publication. Many colleagues have supported the research presented here over the past few years and I would specially like to thank Toby Butler of the Raphael Samuel Centre for Social history at the University of East London for his constant encouragement and support. My greatest debt is to the people of East London and to the Olympic Park workforce who agreed to take part in the research and whose stories I have tried to tell. The photographers and artists whose images feature in the book have added an important dimension to the text; further information about their work can be found in 'Notes on Contributors' at the end of the book.

Thanks to Peter Kennard and Tarek Salhany for the cover; Aldo Katayanagi for his illustration 'Welcome to the Post-Olympics'; Jason Orton for his photographs of Thames Gateway and Olympic Park; Jake Humphries for 'Rise and Fall of Thames Gateway' from his portfolio and Ed Frith of Greenwich University for facilitating this project; John Claridge for permission to reproduce his wonderful photographs of East London; Adam Dant and the Museum of London for permission to reproduce his New East London map; John Wallett for designing the special narrative map to help readers unfamiliar with the area; Julian Wood for his cartoon; Jock McFadyen for permission to reproduce 'Piggy Back'; Loraine Leeson and Peter Dunn for permission to reproduce an image from the Docklands Community Poster Workshop series; Ian F. Rogers for permission to reproduce two photographs from his book *From Old to Newham*; Ben Crofts for help with map of Thames Gateway and DCLG for permission to reproduce it. Jenni Munro-Collins of the Newham Local Studies Centre and Michelle Johansen of the Bishopsgate Institute generously allowed me to draw on their historical research; thanks to Winning Words for permission to reprint extracts from the poems by John Burnside and Carole Anne Duffy. I am grateful to Lavinia Greenlaw for permission to reproduce an extract from her poem 'River History' and to Ahren Warner for his poem 'Dionysus'; also to the LLDC and the Olympic Delivery Authority for images of the Olympic Park. CABE for permission to reproduce an image/text from their report *New Stuff happens*. Tate Images for permission to reproduce Graham Sutherland, 'Devastation in an East End street'. Finally short extracts from the book appeared in *Soundings 50*, *Agenda* April 2012 and Open Democracy. An earlier version of the 'Ode to the Also-Rans' appeared in Agenda Poetry on line.

List of Illustrations

Online galleries

There are three visual essays in the form of powerpoints designed to supplement the book and which include images discussed in the text. These can be downloaded from my website: www.philcohenworks.com.The references to specific images are given in the text as follows:

* 1-169 *East London, a journey through the ruins*

Overviews – The gothic imagination – The old East End – Maps and territories – Apocalypse then: the Blitz – Apocalypse now: the transition to modernism and beyond – The nay-sayers

> 1–192 *Olympic dreams and nightmares*

Mix n Kitsch – Scenes from the Tempest – The Naysayers: images of protest – The anti-industrial machine – The ceremonies – Inter-ludology – Carrying the torch – Ideal worlds and imaginary cities – Dialectics of the Enlightenment

^ 1–122 *Body politics*

Elemental Labour – Mummers, miners and sweeps – Time and motion studies – Automata – Youth culture and extreme sport – Physical culture and the dream of the collective body – Masculinity and manual labour in a post industrial world.

Note

Every effort has been made to trace the source of images and quotations in this book. We would be grateful if anyone with information on the very few cases in which we have not been able to find the source would contact the publishers.

Abbreviations

DCLG	Department of Communities and Local Government
DCMS	Department of Culture, Media and Sport
GLA	Greater London Authority
IOC	International Olympic Committee
LDA	London Development Agency
LLDC	London Legacy Development Corporation
LDDC	London Dockland Development Corporation
LTGDC	London Thames Gateway Development Corporation
LOCOG	London Organising Committee of the Olympic and Paralympic Games
ODA	Olympic Delivery Authority
ORN	Olympic Road Network

DEDICATION

Ode to the Also-Rans

To Ritsos, the commis chef,
who, knowing the backstreets of Athens
as well as his onions,
took a shortcut through the main course
and won the first Marathon of modern times.
Those who cook the books
know the proof of the pudding
never survives its eating.

To the doves of Seoul
who, scorched, but unconsumed
by the Festival of Flame, carried
the torch of Hope
back to the Olympic dovecot
where it was devoured
raw, not cooked,
by the assembled vultures
hungry for pigeon pie.
Luck not fate decides
which birds of passage survive.
The outcome is not always what the Gods intend.

To Titos Patrikios,
Chief of the Athens Games,
who, *with bunches of bats hidden
in the empty dome of his heart*
was unable to write the statutory ode
and resigned his commission.
And to all poets who refuse
winning words; let them make praise songs
with cunning rhymes, graceful lines
mischievously scanned
against the iambics of official verse.

To Socrates' sweetheart, Asopichus
winner of the boy's footrace
and to all athletes, whose bodies
are parables of passions
that dare others to speak their name.
Of all the sweet and delightful things
belonging to men,
reticence and modesty
are most to be prized.

To Hermes, who needs no toast,
Shape shifter, man of many parts:
Courier of dreams and the dead,
Patron of poets and boxers,
Champion sprinter turned getaway artist,
Trickster, rap master, psychopomp, thief.
Your lyric is no simple panegyric.
Above the door of the gymnasium
we read your caution to the watching fans
'Admiration Makes All Things Beautiful
Yet belies the truth'.

We know the race is not to the fastest,
the strongest or the highest minded
but to those whose will to triumph
is driven by a bitter thought:
There is no truce. The crowd is fickle.
It roars for the victors, not the also-rans.

July 29 2012

LIGHTS ON
FOR THE TERRITORY
TOGETHER WITH AN
EAST END HALL OF FAME

 DOCKS

EX-INDUSTIAL

PARKS

MARKETS

IAIN SINCLAIR
WUZ ERE

INSTITUTIONS

DISASTERS

CONFLICTS

HACKNEY WICK...

Located on the edge of Hackney marshes, the area housed many factories, including chemical and dye works, Clarnico's sweets and Bryant and May's where in 1888 Annie Besant, a famous feminist, socialist and Theosophist, helped organise a match girls strike. The area went into decline in the 1980's but in recent years has become home to a thriving community of young artists. Future plans are to turn the area into a creative industry hub which will accelerate its gentrification.

RIVER LEA

Victoria Park

6

HACKNEY WICK

OLD FORD RD

ROMAN RD

BOW QUARTER

3

Shoreditch

Bethnal Green

BETHNAL GRN RD

Mile End Park

5

1

PETTICOAT LN.

WHITECHAPEL

BRICK L.

COMMERCIAL ST

BISHOPSGATE

1

3

4

WHITECHAPEL RD

2

Stepney Green

BURDETT RD

DEVONS RD

CRISP ST.

WATNEY MKT.

1

2

CABLE STREET

THE HIGHWAY

TOWER BR.

Wapping

E. INDIA DOCK
Poplar

4

(A13)

Canary Wharf

2

5

Isle of Dogs

BILLY BRAGG

DIZEE RASCAL

SID VICIOUS

CHARLES BOOTH

BEN TILLETT

CHARLIE CHAPLIN

ARNOLD WESKER

BARBARA WINDSOR

BOW QUARTER...

No-one is quite sure if the famous 'Bow bells' whose sound was supposed define the extent of Cockney London were ever actually located here but the area has long been a stronghold of local working class community pride. It also has a well established cosmopolitan tradition. Gandhi stayed here. Dizzee Rascal was born here. In the last ten years a new cultural quarter has been established with many galleries and restaurants and parts of the area have become property hot spots.

STRATFORD...

Stratford was a railway town and home to many 'dirty' industries that could not be located within the boundaries of the city. This industrial legacy produced the heavily polluted area that has now been transformed in the Olympic park. The construction of Westfield Shopping City, and the proposed new International Quarter with office blocks and luxury housing will complete the transformation of the area into a new commercial and transport hub plugged into the global information economy.

KEY:

INSTITUTIONS
1 Toynbee Hall
2 Wilton's Music Hall
3 Whitechapel Library
4 East London Mosque
5 The People's Palace
6 Eton Manor Boys Club
7 Theatre Royal Stratford
8 Upton Park Stadium

CONFLICTS
1 1936 The Battle of Cable Street
2 1911 Seige of Sydney Street
3 1888 Bryant & May Match Girls Strike
4 1911 Railway Gas & Dock Workers Strike
5 1911 Poplar Rates Strike
6 1911 Railway Gas & Dock Workers Strike

DISASTERS
1 1943 Bethnal Green Tube Disaster
2 1940 'Black Saturday' (first day of the Blitz)
3 1916 The 'Big Bang' Silvertown Munitions Factory
4 1968 Ronan Point Flats Disaster

CARPENTERS RD

HIGH STREET

Olympic Park
STRATFORD

GREEN ST.

7

Upton Park

East Ham

'COCKNEY DIASPORA' TO ESSEX & PARTS EAST

NORTHERN APPROACH

BOW CREEK

(A13)

(A13)

Canning Town

4

RD

BLACKWALL TUNNEL

3

VICTORIA DOCK RD

Beckton

Royal Docks

LONDON CITY AIRPORT

Silvertown

RONNIE LANE

GEORGE LANSBURY

IAIN DURY

DAVID BECKHAM

SYLVIA PANKHURST

JACK 'KID' BERG

CLEMENT ATLEE

JOAN LITTLEWOOD

John Wallett

PLEASE NOTE: THIS MAP IS NOT INTENDED TO BE EITHER CARTOGRAPHICALLY ACCURATE OR TO BE A COMPREHENSIVE MAPPING OF ALL THE SIGNIFICANT SITES AND PERSONALITIES IN EAST LONDON

Introduction:
welcome to the Post-Olympics

As evening drew on we went to what was left of Tower Bridge to watch 'The Para-Olympic Dream', marvelling at the flickering figures as they vaulted over the sandbagged parapets in their giant wheelchairs. Our gaze was inevitably drawn downriver to the famous motto *Amplius, Charius, Colossicus*, written in neon lipstick against the city's darkening rim. It was time to visit the Olympic Park and sample the remaindered glory of the games. We hired a gondola at the Isle of Dogs and as we approached the site were overwhelmed by the awesome spectacle of the Orbital Tower, now leaning more crazily than ever Pisa's did, with noxious weeds from foreign parts clinging to its superstructure creating a veritable hanging garden of London Babylon.

We disembarked at a pontoon where in happier days the late Sir David Beckham had handed the Olympic torch to Bradley Wiggins, fresh from his triumph in the Tour de France. Little did either of them dream of the disaster to come. As we made our way across the deserted walkways toward the tower we were dismayed by the signs of neglect and decay all around: broken railings, park benches vandalised, drought-withered gardens, a derelict open air café where only a few tables bolted to the ground remained as mute witness to the conviviality they had once entertained. And everywhere the hidden hand of the graffiti artist mocking the ambitions the 2012 tag had once evoked – 'Live the nightmare' … 'Everyone's a loser' … 'Betray a generation' – and other, cruder, slogans were blazoned in dayglow colours on wall after crumbling wall.

The stadium itself, abandoned by the ill fated 'Hammers', after they were relegated to the lower divisions of our once famous football league, now served as a travellers' encampment; from time to time this community organised a horse fair or produce market to which the remnants of the Cockney tribe flocked from the outskirts of the city where they now eked out an existence on their allotments. As we skirted the settlement the smell of cooking and the shouts of children playing amidst the ruins of the velodrome sent a welcome message that at least there was some human life in this bleak, Allah-forsaken, place.

At last we approached the Tower itself, that monument to the shared hubris of a steel magnate, a famous sculptor and a London mayor. The building was now officially classified as a dangerous structure since the death of two visitors

Aldo Katayanagi, Welcome to the Post-Olympics

from falling debris. As we looked up at it in some apprehension we were accosted by what we took to be two desperadoes intent on robbery. But then, when we looked more closely, to our amazement they turned out be Wenlock and Mandeville, the Olympic mascots, who wanted not our money but a sympathetic ear. And what a hard luck story they had to tell!

It seems that for a few years after 2012 they had made a good living posing for photographs with visitors to the Park. But then the collapse of the Chinese economy and the Second Great World Recession meant that the flow of tourists dried up. They applied for jobs as security guards, who were then much in demand due to frequent attacks on the venues by disgruntled Hammers' fans, but they were turned down on the grounds that walking around with sub-machine guns would spoil their public image as cuddly children's toys. This was the beginning of a long and fruitless search for alternative work. No-one wanted to employ someone with only one eye instead of a nose, and a track record in dodgy PR, despite all the talk of equal opportunities. They had been invented for the Olympics, how could they possibly reinvent themselves now the games were over? Wenlock took to drink and joined the local winos who congregated in the Hackney Wick end of the Park, while Mandeville – or Mandy Rice Davies as she now styled herself – hung around Stratford Shopping City offering her services to the passing trade. At present, Wenlock told us, they spent most of their time scavenging for scraps of food and cadging money from the odd autograph hunter – mostly Olympophiles desperate for some special trophy to show off to the folks back home. As we gave the hapless pair some spare change and the remnants of our picnic, we pondered how this tragedy had been allowed to happen. How did a couple who embodied the hopes and aspirations of a whole generation turn into such feral creatures, the very kind of people we warned our children against becoming?

○○○○○

That it is so easy to conjure up an apocalyptic vision of the Post-Olympics tells us something about the nature of the beast: the facile optimism of Olympophiles who think the games can do no wrong invites a rejoinder which encourages worst case scenarios to flourish.[1] But if the optimism of the will so evident in the official Olympic discourse provokes a pessimism of the intellect as its necessary counterweight, this should not tempt us to join the nay-sayers, for whom the Olympics can do no right. In the event 2012 signally failed to live up to the prophecies of the doom-mongers, neither did it justify the official predictions of a bonanza for London. 2012 produced no economic miracle nor did it usher in a new dawn in which the body politic was magically healed of its social afflictions. It was never very likely that a generation of couch potatoes were going to be sufficiently inspired by the successes of team GB to cast aside their IPods and take to the streets or cycle tracks in their thousands. Nor was a population divided so deeply by social inequalities going to start singing from the same hymn sheet, even if the tune was composed by Sir Paul McCartney.

London's response to the games needs to be understood in the context of a history of long duration. From the Great Exhibition of 1851 to the Festival of Britain on the South Bank a century later, and from the pomp and circumstance drummed up by municipal pride to the processional pageantry of the labour movement on the march for social justice, the metropolis has often been host to the nation's hopes for economic and social renewal; many generations of Londoners have had to carry that particular burden of representation. The staging of grand spectacles and public divertissements is a London thing. And so are the demonstrations, strikes and riots provoked by the all too visible social inequalities etched into the city's fabric.

Even in the 1960s, the West End's transition from glittering hub of Empire to heart of 'swinging London' did little to disturb its longstanding unequal relation to East London as the home of immigrant 'low life', where the Empire might just strike back. There were some connections: Bohemian London and the demi-monde built social bridges, slummers patronised the pubs and music halls in search of rough trade, and drugs connected the drawing rooms of Mayfair with Limehouse dives; while East Enders went 'up west' on special occasions, when they wanted to celebrate or demonstrate. It is only since the 1980s that the tables have begun to be turned, and East London has come to be seen as a site of investment and wealth creation in its own right – even though in fact it has been at the heart of the capital's commercial and manufacturing economy for almost a century. Will 2012 really end the area's long legacy of poverty and deprivation? Will Londoners in future talk about going 'up East' when they want to have an expensive night out, and about 'going down west' when they want to see how those less fortunate than themselves are making out?

We had a preview of what such an outcome might feel like during 'games time', in the contrast between the thronged thoroughfares around Olympic Park and the deserted streets around Piccadilly. But was this a glimpse of a sustainable future or an ephemeral effect? Has everyone been a winner, as promised by the bid campaign? Or will 2012 come to be remembered as the story of two Olympics, of those for whom the Games were a cause for celebration, and those for whom its promises had a hollow ring?

This book takes a close look at the difference East London and the Olympics have made and still might make to each other. It insists that this is a two way process. The Olympics are often portrayed as a global juggernaut flattening everything in its way. They can often feel like that to those most directly in its path. But the Olympics themselves are also changed by their local circumstances and East London 2012 has made its mark on the Olympic movement, often in ways that are not officially recognised and which may take some time to be fully taken into account.

Part I sets the scene by exploring the seismic shift in London's social and cultural geography as its pathway of economic growth changed direction from west to east, and the impact this has had on the East End's working-class communities. It is only by fully appreciating this background that we can understand local people's responses to the arrival of the Olympics on their doorstep.[2]

The opening chapter examines how the area has been represented over the past century by and to outsiders – by writers, artists and social commentators who set out to colonise the area through the exercise of their gothic imaginations, and by architects, planners and urban reformers who have attempted to transform it into some approximation of a rationalised modernist city.

The following chapter looks at the impact these interventions have had on the stories East Enders currently tell themselves about who and where they are. Drawing on original research amongst communities on the Isle of Dogs, it looks at how issues of 'race' and class are being defined by the older generation as well as by young people as they negotiate the new social and urban landscape. Chapter Three sets this experience in the wider context of the eastwards turn in London's growth, and in particular the regeneration of 'Thames Gateway', in which the different visions of the future on the part of artists and planners, so often opposed, nevertheless here seem to coalesce in a common strategy of 'imagineering', making an otherwise disparate and often desolate environment culturally inhabitable for a new generation of middle class pioneers.

In the second half of the book the spotlight is turned on 2012 itself, focusing on the strategies that were used to present an 'Olympian' vision of London and Britain to the world, and the rhetorics and realities of Olympic style regeneration as experienced by East Londoners.

Chapter Four considers the dilemmas facing those who had to construct a plausible account of the city's past, present and future in bidding for the games. How could they do justice to both the local and global dimensions of London's identity whilst at the same time having to conform to the protocols of the Olympic ideal? The chapter looks at what being a Londoner means for those who live there, and its relation to the corporate brand image of the capital as an international financial centre. It goes on to look at how the notion of London as an 'Olygopolis' was materialised in special regimes of surveillance and spatial control, and concludes by analysing the peculiarities of 'Games Time'.

Chapter Five explores different aspects of the 'body politics' that were configured by the games. It starts with a photo-essay and series of ethnographic interviews documenting the manual labour process of the 'dig, demolition, design' phase in the construction of the Olympic Park. A commentary shows how this 'labourhood' became an important *lieu de mémoire* for its workforce. The chapter goes on to discuss the relation between manual labour and sport as physical cultures of masculinity, and the conditions and effects of their racialisation. It concludes by looking at changing regimes of athleticism, exploring the relation between athletic and youthful bodies in Olympic rhetoric ('Inspire a generation') and contemporary youth cultures.

The discussion then shifts from issues of delivery to those of legacy. Chapter Six develops a framework for understanding the complex and often mystifying relationship between market and moral economies as these are articulated in the Olympic compact, and compares the profiles of different Olympiads from Berlin 1936 to London 2012. It goes on to critique the conventional definitions of legacy and propose a new typology of gift and debt, endowment and dividend as a means of re-framing the post-Olympic debate. The chapter concludes by taking a long hard look at the audit culture that has been assembled around the evaluation of 2012 and arguing for an alternative notion of the Olympics as a 'values tournament'.

The next three chapters examine different aspects of the cultural politics of staging the London Olympics. Chapter Seven develops a theory of kitsch and carnival capitalism to offer a revisionary analysis of the contemporary spectacle that draws on and deepens the original situationist critique and applies it to an historical reading of official and popular cultures of celebration. The chapter discusses the Olympic torch relay as both ritual and performance, mascots as hyper-kitsch, and the jurisdictional role of the International Olympics Committee, as examples of the spectacle in both its operatic and bureaucratic modes. It concludes by considering the changing culture of sports spectatorship, not as an instance of 'post modernity' but of how carnival capitalism, as a specific mode of cultural production, has created its own regime of envisagement.

Chapter Eight focuses on the imaginative resources that were available to those who had the task of telling the nation's story to the world in the ceremonies, and the constraints which the Olympics aspirational agenda and spectacular idiom placed on their use. The choice of the 'Isle of Wonders' theme from *The Tempest* is discussed in relation to current debates about British identity, the popular-national, and the meaning of Shakespeare's play. The chapter provides a historical overview of the 'island story' and the changing uses to which it has been put in the imagination of Englishness, putting in question the concept of multiculturalism. It concludes by returning to *The Tempest* and some of its contemporary readings in search of a strategy which might enable the narrative legacy of 2012 to include both the tragic and comic aspects of the event.

Chapter Nine applies the concepts and arguments developed in the previous two chapters to a close reading of the 2012 ceremonies. The analysis concentrates on Danny Boyle's 'Isle of Wonders' and the Paralympic 'Enlightenment' scenarios; it discusses the aesthetic and political choices that were made, and the ways in which they negotiated the constraints of the 2012 agenda and the audio-visual ideology of the spectacle, with its techniques of ethno, retro and techno-kitsch. The chapter concludes by discussing the uses of surrealism and humour in the ceremonies.

Up until this point we have been examining the points of view of those who were charged with delivering, reporting or evaluating 2012. Chapter Ten looks at how the working-class communities described in the first part of the book responded to the advent of the Olympics on their doorstep. It draws on research conducted over a five year period to investigate how far East Enders owned the Games, and identified with the aspirations it represents. The chapter examines the patterns of stake-holding that emerged as the grand project unfolded, and how these were affected by its vicissitudes. It looks at how 'bonders' and 'bridgers' responded to the regeneration agenda and to the ceremonies, and concludes by drawing out the implications of this evidence for longer-term legacy issues.

A good enough legacy is one that can be owned by the host community. The concluding chapter looks at the plans for the post-games development of the Olympic Park and considers the vision of city and community which it proposes. It discusses the gentrification effect, the fate of the Olympic stadium and the process of place-making, and draws on the current debate on the renewal of participatory democracy to propose a radical framework of governance for this new part of London. The chapter ends by discussing the culture of hospitality, both official and unofficial, generated by the Games, and its role in creating London's post-Olympic reputation.

A Para-Olympic perspective

The analysis of the Olympics must match the narrative scope of its subject. For this purpose we need a framework in which different measures of value or worth can be assessed for their relevance. In developing such a framework I have tried to move beyond a simple 'pro' or 'anti' Olympic position – which does not mean sitting on the proverbial fence, but rather considering what kind of conversation may be possible across it. That is why I have used the term 'Para-Olympic' in some places in the text. It is, of course, partly to insist that the Paralympic Games can well claim to best represent the Olympic spirit in holding to its original amateur ethos and in exemplifying the struggle to overcome adversity that is at the heart of the Olympic movement's aspirational agenda. But it is also to indicate that I am trying to work across traditional demarcation lines in how the Olympics are debated.

'Para' is an interesting little prefix, which in attaching itself to bigger and apparently more important words fundamentally changes their orientation. Its core meaning is 'beyond', 'outside', 'beside' or 'to one side'. Hence it suggests a supplement which offers an additional perspective not otherwise given, as good a prescription for 'left field thinking' as you can get; and it therefore signifies the standpoint of critical engagement with the Olympics which this book is concerned to develop.

'Para' also holds the connotation of an accessory or ancillary, as in 'para-medic', and by an all-too-easy-slippage can be taken to imply a position of subordination, of being pushed aside. At the very least this alerts us to the fact that the hierarchy of values entailed in the Olympic mission might sideline what are more urgent priorities from the point of view of its host communities. Finally 'para' can also be used to indicate that which is regarded as irregular, dysfunctional or just plain wrong. A paralogism is an illogical argument and a paradox is a self-contradictory statement. And as we will see there are plenty of those in the Olympic discourse. There can also be an imputation of deviance: a paraplegic is someone whose limbs don't work as they should, and a paramour is an illicit lover.

This book is concerned to put such constructs under pressure both politically and conceptually. Sections of the media in 2012 drew some very firm lines in the sand between visitors whose presence was welcome and those regarded as interlopers or threats. The *Daily Mail* led a moral panic about an epidemic of street crime, featuring gangs of professional pickpockets and prostitutes from abroad 'flooding' the capital, thus providing unfair competition to our home-grown informal economy, which had been expecting a shot in the arm from the Olympics. The *Mail* focused on Romanians as the main folk devils, following through on an earlier press campaign against immigrants from Eastern Europe taking 'British jobs from British workers' on the Olympic Park. Now, though, it was 'gypsies' who were once more the target of popular prejudice – because, as everyone knows, all Romanians are Romani, an irony that was not lost on the traveller community who had been evicted from their legal campsite to make way for the International Broadcasting Centre and have spent the past five years in limbo.

One of my aims in writing the book has been to problematise the role of the Olympics in neutralising political conscience in the name of an abstract universalism of sporting competition. Perhaps it needs to be stressed that in political terms a Para-Olympic perspective is not a 'third way' in the Blairite sense. It does not involve an ideological mix and match, wanting to have the best of both capitalism and socialism. Nor is it a liberal position, seeing all points of view and trying to reach some kind of compromise between them. It is closer to what standpoint epistemologists call a 'third space', a position that is properly dialectical and moves beyond either/or both/and types of argument. In the case of Olympic Studies this involves putting in question the familiar distinction between hard and soft legacy, and insisting that material and symbolic assets (or liabilities) cannot be considered separately but only in their interplay. It also means rejecting the 'Olympian' standpoint of panoptic/ forensic social science, in favour of a more grounded approach to understanding what is going on.

A Para-Olympic perspective thus requires an active dialogue between disciplines. Although such an approach is officially encouraged, the prevailing academic division of labour means that it is difficult to sustain in practice. Collections of articles by different specialists around a common theme may be multidisciplinary but they do not add up to a properly inter-disciplinary approach.

In some ways the human sciences have created a Frankenstein's monster, a hybrid made up of many disparate parts, none of which fit, but whose tissues have been stitched together into the semblance of a more or less functioning simulacrum of a human being. There is a part of this creature that works and a part that plays, a part that plans and another that dreams, a part that thinks and a part that is preoccupied with bodily functions. The problem is that each of these parts has its own exclusive interpreters, who act as if this creature did nothing but work, or play, or solve problems, or make rational choices, or have sexual phantasies, or tell stories, or make things happen. But in the case of sport all these things are going on at once.

So in this book you will find discussions of buildings and poems, bodies and texts, technologies and landscapes, institutions and narratives, and the various processes through which they become interconnected as they become 'Olympified'. But here perhaps a caveat lector needs to be issued. One of the occupational hazards in writing about the Olympics is that you become obsessionally preoccupied with the most trivial intricacies of Olympic history and policy. I have tried to avoid this temptation. There are already a number of detailed histories of the Olympic movement, and the academic journals are full of specialised articles about every aspect of the games. Instead I have used

2012 as a lens through which to look at some of the deeper trends in contemporary culture, just as East London is treated as symptomatic of the economic and demographic changes that have taken place in other major cities, not only in Britain, but across the western world.

The other, related, risk is that sporting metaphors burrow their way into habitual ways of thinking and writing. It is salutary to recognise just how far terms from cricket, football, sailing and athletics predominate in everyday language as sources of clichéd expression. If you don't play a straight bat, if you take your eye off the ball or sail too close to the wind, you are likely to find that your argument fails to get over the line.... Nevertheless sporting metaphors have their uses, especially if mixed into a cocktail of proverbial caution. In this case they forced me to recognise that this book is a game of two unequal halves, and might amount to a bit of a marathon for some readers. So I have organised the chapters into a series of short sprints. In order to assuage the loneliness of the long distance reader, I have also provided some companionable material in the form of online galleries containing visual essays related to some of the main themes, some resources for further study both on and off line, and also some material that might be regarded as light entertainment.

I recognise that there may still be readers who will want to cut to the chase, and skim or skip Part One so as to plunge straight into the Olympics. But the material in Part Two, especially chapter ten, will make much more sense if read against the analysis of the changes that have taken place in East London over the past half century, presented in the first three chapters.

At any rate in order to help readers to choose how best to navigate the text I am now going to run some of the key concepts and themes of the book past you, in what might be regarded as a warm-up for the main event; if you like, they are exercises in preparation for the mental gymnastics to come, each posing a question that requires further public debate, a debate to which this book hopes to make a contribution.

Key themes

Imagining community

Community, like culture, is one of the most over-used, ill defined and ideologically exploited words in the English language, especially by politicians; it is also, by no coincidence, a key point of reference for understanding the impact of East London and the Olympics on each other. East Enders' 'community spirit' was much invoked as a reason why the area should host the Games, and 'community engagement' was a buzz word for the Cultural Olympiad.

To use the same word to describe a religious sect, sufferers from asthma, the citizens of the United Kingdom, a street gang, poets, people who prefer their own sex, an internet forum whose members never meet except on line and an alcoholics anonymous group, indicates, at the very least, the plasticity of the human capacity for making associations. But the very fact that it has become a portmanteau word that can mean all things to all people indicates its importance, as does the sense that it is the loss or absence of community that characterises our so called 'post-modern' times.

Benedict Anderson in his book *Imagined Communities* added to our understanding of what is at stake in the notion.[3] Anderson is concerned with how national identities are created. He emphasises the multiplicity of circuits through which the nation is constructed as a narrative and as a country of the mind: the mass media, popular historiography and collective memory are all mobilised. To belong to a nation or a people requires a shared imagination of its past, as well as its present and future but that is not something that can ever be taken for granted.[4] Whether enacted through rituals of commemoration or supplemented by variously invented traditions, the aim is to create a cultural heritage whose transmission is controlled through a diversity of channels, from the state education system to the heritage industry.[5] The 2012 Olympic ceremonies were classic examples of how an imagined community of Britishness gets fabricated and relayed.

But imagined community does not only apply to nations. It applies to ethnicities and to what Hannah Arendt called 'nationalisms of the neighbourhood'. Local prides of place are often the basis for staking moral claims over public amenity and resource, and form the very stuff of community politics. But they can take on a sharper and more aggressive edge, for example in the rituals of territoriality through which street gangs assert symbolic claims to own and control 'their' areas; and these too have their archivists, their custodians of trophies.[6] This has for a long time been a marked feature of community relations in East London, and it became a key factor in understanding how the Olympics were owned or disowned by particular groups.

Similarly, a generation is an imagined community of people who share memories of certain formative moments, usually but not always in their youth; it is often associated with living through specific historical events or conjunctures – the 'lost generation' of the interwar period, the baby boomers, the generation of 'May 68' or the velvet revolutions of '1989'. It is in that sense that I have referred to the generation of 'twenty-twelvers', young people who have grown up with the Olympics, many of whom have tried to live its dream but who are also having to face austerity measures that are drastically reducing their life chances.

To imagine community is also to desire to belong to it. And in a second moment to desire that others do not. The quest for community often expresses a deep and diffuse longing to experience a sense of lost unity, a restoration of human solidarity in which all differences of status are temporally suspended or permanently erased. This is community as communion, as what anthropologists call 'communitas', the more or less ecstatic sense of togetherness created through particular rituals of sharing and gift giving. The Olympics, with their mission to promote youthful fraternity, peaceful competition and international understanding, and the ceremonial protocols which enact these values, are a prime site in which this is supposed to take place.[7] The festive crowd with its inclusive and infectious sense of conviviality is its most vivid embodiment. And yet its power of social combination threatens norms of public order designed to protect the space of flows – whether of people, or commodities – on which the economy and much else depends. The culture of hospitality required by the Games imposed its own constraints on the host city and called forth special measures of regulation. Ground control in London 2012 was an exaggerated, militarised, form of the routine regulation of the city's traffic with the world, literally built into its architecture, transport systems and public spaces.[8]

Crowds may be instant communities, but they can also turn nasty, or panicky, seeking scapegoats for the frustration of their demands in those whose faces do not fit. For 'community' is Janus-faced. Its inclusivity and internal democracy, its forms of caring and sharing are conditional on the fact that it encloses itself in rituals of recognition that regulate its boundaries and make them more or less impermeable to outsiders. The Other is now always just around the corner, just out of sight or reach, but the ever present focus of rumour and gossip, fear and loathing. The slightest and most trivial distinction can then become the basis of social animosities: living in the next street, supporting a different football team, belonging to a different school or gang, voting for a different political party, following a different faith. And while some of these rivalries may be more or less friendly and harmless, they can also escalate into deadly feuds. Ethnic cleansing is only nationalism of the neighbourhood become more toxic. This downside of community relations has also been much in evidence in East London.

So community is produced at the intersection of positive and negative reciprocities; it is where networks of elective affinity can reinforce patterns of enmity and vice versa: the enemy of an enemy is a friend. Above all it is where a moral economy built around mutual aid can be put to work to gain competitive advantage in the market. So this leaves us with a question: how far does the peculiar kind of gift that is an Olympic legacy work to mitigate these animosities and sustain a more generous cosmopolitan identity for Londoners? To what extent does its mixed economy of public and private interests underwrite the dual aspect of community relations?

London's turning

From the very outset London's bid for 2012 was to be about legacy, to involve the making over of what one of the bid campaigners described as 'a pretty terrible part of town' and Lord Coe in his auto-biography referred to as 'a centuries old blot on the physical and psychological landscape of the city'.[9] For those of us who live or work there, such descriptions were part of another legacy – they belong to a long history of misrepresentation in which the East End and East Enders have been either demonised or romanticised as belonging to the Capital's 'other scene'.

East London's long history of immigration includes both hostility and welcome to newly arrivant communities.[10] This is not simply a continuing game of the established versus outsiders – a pattern that has been described by urban ethnographers as invasion, succession and dominance, and has been repeated over and over again – as Huguenots, Irish, Jewish, and more recently Asian communities have moved in and then moved on.[11] History does not actually repeat itself, even though the way it is represented often does. It would be more accurate to say that different kinds of travelling story have put down roots to form part of the local memoryscape, and this has supported recurrent patterns of ambivalence in the response of host communities to new arrivals.

A story told to me by a woman who grew up in Whitechapel in the 1930s when it was the heart of London's Jewish community illustrates the complexity. Next door to her there lived a family who were notorious for their anti-semitism. When in 1936 Mosley and his gang tried to march through the East End, they climbed onto the roof of their Jewish neighbours and started ripping the slates off, chucking them down on the Blackshirts shouting 'they may be Yids, but they're our bloody Yids'. In this way they managed to simultaneously attack Jewish property while also protecting the owners from attack by what they regarded as an alien force of outsiders who were trying to invade the area.

The double-edged nature of community and its patterns of ambivalence need to be factored in to any account of Olympic legacy. In the official version of 2012, East London and the Olympics were made for each other, an area in desperate need of regeneration working in partnership with a project that needed to find an economic justification. But it was always a somewhat hastily arranged marriage, and divorce still remains a possibility now that the honeymoon period is over. What would have to be put in place to secure a lasting and mutually beneficial relationship?

A values tournament

The uniqueness of the Olympics comes not just from their scale but from their scope. By scope I do not simply mean the bizarre array of sports that are assembled under its umbrella, from archery and clay pigeon shooting to curling and Graeco-Roman wrestling; or even the fact that it brings together athletes from all the nations of the world. What is unique about the Games is the scope of their *narrative*. Other mega sporting events may be about who is best in the world at football, or cricket, athletics or swimming, but the Olympics are on a mission to change the world, to promote international solidarity through the fraternity of Youth; sport and sporting competition is supposed to be the means to this end, and not an end in itself. The critics of the Olympic movement are quick to point out how far the reality falls short of the ideal, and how the values of professionalism and global commerce have not only undermined the Olympic ethos but have also been actively embraced by the International Olympic Committee. But the criticism, however justified, also bears witness to the singular ambition of the Games. No-one is going to accuse FIFA of having failed to promote the 'nobility of the athletic body' through their staging of the World Cup. Thus, if the post-Olympic debate cannot but be about the future of East London, it is also one whose terms of reference are, inevitably, far wider. For any discussion on the Olympics inevitably must also be a discussion about values.[12]

The Olympics has been called a 'values tournament', in that it provides an arena in which different ideologies or value systems compete. According to some accounts that contest is all over. The Olympics are a global 'mega event' featuring professional athletes, a sporting spectacle orchestrated by the corporate media; and capitalism in whatever version, East or West, is the only game in town. But perhaps after all the values of commerce and community, capitalism and carnival, are not so easily reconciled.[13] Indeed what makes each Olympiad unique is the ways in which specific conflicts and contradictions internal to the host society are stage-managed so as to give an impression of national unity and pride, and to project a positive image to the world. From this point of view what really counts is the narrative legacy of the Games, the reputational status of the host city, and the way the post-Olympic identity measures up in comparison to previous Games.[14]

Body politics

In the advanced economies of the West, the industrial regime that throughout most of the twentieth century provided a metaphor and model for the measurement of sporting achievement has become all but obsolete. The time and motion studies pioneered by Fordism are largely redundant in the era of the open-plan, open-necked work cultures of the knowledge economy. But they have been retained in the sphere of sports science, where success is still largely motivated and measured by bio-energetic principles of performance. In contrast to all this stands the popular multiculture of urban athleticism that has emerged over the last quarter century in the metropolitan heartlands, and which has evolved its own highly stylised aesthetic. Hip hop, skateboarding and BMX biking are now the main field and track events on the streets and playgrounds of East London – as they are in the barrios of Rio. Even the traditional Olympic sports such as boxing, swimming and athletics, which historically formed a core element in popular narratives of aspiration, especially amongst immigrant and working-class communities, are declining in terms of their levels of participation and spectatorship. At the same the majority of people in the West no longer work with their bodies, and increasing numbers, especially the young, are growing fat on a sedentary consumerist life style, creating a major new health problem.

In the rest of the world it is a very different story. Here millions of bodies continue to be broken by poverty, hunger, famine, disease, wars, lack of basic facilities and terrible working conditions. Yet popular participation in sports like football that require little in the way of equipment and facilities is growing exponentially in these countries. Most of them, however, lack the economic infrastructure that would enable them to host the Olympics as presently constituted. There is a growing polarisation between two quite distinct body politics and so we are left with a question about knowledge transfer and how the experience of 2012 can help the Olympics movement to find a way of creating a level playing field.

The architecture of narcissism

The Arcelor Mittal Orbital Tower, Anish Kapoor's architectural folly cum observation platform for the Olympic Park, well illustrates the cultural politics of the Games. The Tower strikes a garish in-your-face attitude, with its writhing spiral form evoking a surreal funfair helter skelter as well as Tatlin's and Eiffel's efforts at the genre. Cecil Balmond, its chief engineer-designer, has likened it to an electron cloud, propping itself up, its instability creating a form of stability – a pretty accurate metaphor for how global capitalism works these days. Architectural critics have variously described it as 'an electricity pylon designed by Isambard Brunel on acid', 'a drunken party animal of a building' and 'pink entrails', but it has been a hit with the public, who know a good piece of bad taste when they see one.

'Orbital' is perhaps best read as the last will and testament of a now widely discredited form of urbanism that attempts to regenerate the working-class city by parachuting grand cultural projects into its midst. The leaning tower of Stratford will at any rate be a lasting monument to the steel magnate and professional plutocrat, friend of Tony Blair and the Labour Party, who paid over £30 million for it to be built and named after him; renowned for his extravagant life style, ruthless asset-stripping and dodgy business deals, Mr Mittal somehow got to carry the Olympic torch as one of the country's 'unsung heroes', while modestly proclaiming his affinity with Olympian athletes because they too are inspired by the principles of perseverance and hard work that have made him Britain's wealthiest man.

Various attempts have been made to Olympify the Mittal Tower, for example to claim it incorporates the five Olympic rings, or represents the continuous asymptotic orbit of the 'Olympic journey'. Kapoor himself describes the experience of ascent as 'going up and up and in on oneself' – as accurate a description of what happens when you get high on the dream of 2012 as can be hoped for. And when you get to the top you not only find the whole of London spread out like Lilliput at your feet, but huge convex mirrors that reflect back your suddenly giant Brodingnagian self as part of the panoramic spectacle. It all adds up to an ironic comment on Marx's oft-quoted observation that 'men can see nothing around them that is not their own image, everything speaking to them of themselves'. So it raises the question: is there another architecture available that makes human scale the measure of its achievement while *not* dominating the environment?

Lost in translation: poetry @ the Olympics

2012 offered an unparalleled opportunity to bring the worlds of art and sport into closer conversation. It may be the case that European poetry came into existence with the Olympics and Pindar's odes in praise of its athletes – and the te tum te tum of the iambic is only a heart beat away from the athlete's metred stride – but in modern times they have existed on different planets. C.P. Snow talked about the two cultures of the humanities and sciences, but arts and sports have also gone their separate ways. Brain and Brawn, Bohemian and Body Builder, Aesthete and Athlete, Wimp and Jock, until very recently these binaries and the stereotypes they underwrote prevailed. I well remember as a teenager in the late 1950s, who was into existentialism, beat poetry, jazz and CND, sneaking off to the White City to watch Gordon Pirie, Chris Brasher, Chataway and the other great British long distance runners take on the world and win, all the while feeling that I was somehow betraying my rebel cause.

The Cultural Olympiad was an opportunity to bridge this Great Divide. It was the largest and most costly programme of its kind ever organised by a British government.[15] Artists are normally part of the awkward squad, but those who went into serious training to carry the torch for art in the Olympics have, on the whole, adopted its 'can do' agenda. Their work stressed the power of creativity and self inventiveness to overcome adversity and heal the hidden wounds of social disappointment. So, as in wartime, art put its shoulder to the wheel to help improve national morale at a time of crisis. Artists who in an earlier conjuncture would have explored the political or personal dynamics of the anger and frustration experienced by those living at the sharp end of the recession were now concerned to use the platform of the Cultural Olympiad to communicate gentler and more positive structures of feeling. The argument goes that people who are having a difficult time do not want to be upset or shocked, but supported. So a new kind of cognitive art therapy has emerged in which the public are encouraged to engage in positive thinking. It is a 'care-full' art that is meant to work like an anti-depressant, and help us look on the bright side of life.

As an example of the creative and political dilemmas this can pose, I want to consider two poems commissioned from the poet laureate, Carol Ann Duffy, as part of the 'Winning Words' project for the Olympic Park.[16] The first poem explores the East End's heritage as a source of Olympic inspiration and is preoccupied with questions of aspiration, disadvantage and their long legacy; for, as she says in the opening line, 'the past is all around us, in the air', and, she later reminds us 'still dedicates to us/its distant, present light'. The poem is about a now defunct youth club that had a sports ground on the site used for Paralympic tennis and hockey. The Eton Manor Boys' club has an interesting history (*126).[17] It was founded by a group of Old Etonians in the 1880s as part of a broader civilising mission on the part of the upper classes to establish community settlements and youth clubs in the most deprived areas of the East End, a place where:

> ... boys are yearly turned loose, without aid, without sympathy, without exercise, without amusement, into the burning fiery furnace of the streets of our growing and densely-crowded cities. When they fall into sin and ruin, as so many of them do – when they pass from betting and gambling (a sin fearfully on the increase) into dishonesty and crime, or when they pass from levity and godlessness into the abyss of yet more misery and destruction, there is no-one to offer them help or social encouragement.[18]

The founders saw themselves as pioneers entering an 'unknown country'. One of them recorded in his diary: 'Having searched diligently through "Mogg's Guide to London and the Suburbs" for the correct geographical position of Hackney Wick, and all the Metropolitan timetables for a suitable train to Victoria Park Station, I duly started off one evening in search of adventures in the Wild East...'. These new colonisers of the working-class city quickly settled in and turned the area into 'their manor'. As urban slummers with a social mission, their main charitable aim was to inculcate their public school ethos amongst the lower orders, through various forms of rational recreation and self improvement, including sport; in particular, as the club's historian Michelle Johansen puts it, 'they wanted to change the clandestine street gang into a well-organised, highly visible and socially responsible presence in the community'. To this end Eton Manor members were organised into 'houses' to encourage team spirit and healthy competition; regular attendance was required and the highest standards of behaviour. The club bought a large derelict site in Hackney Wick and transformed it into the most lavishly equipped sports facility in London, which they called, without a trace of irony, 'the Wilderness'. The club excelled in boxing and athletics, producing a bevy of Olympic medallists, and it certainly succeeded in tapping into the role which sport can play in deprived communities whose access to social mobility by other means is blocked. It offered other perks too – if you were unemployed the guvnors might find you a job. It is a classic case study in the way sport has been used as part of a 'civilising process' , promoting a form of moral hygiene - clean minds in clean bodies- in which working class youth are empowered through learning the 3 D's : Discipline, Deference and Docility.

Eton Manor closed its doors in 1967, although it still leads a vigorous afterlife in the form of an old boy's network of East Enders who remain loyal to its traditions. But that is not the end of its story. Eton Manor now has a very contemporary message, since David Cameron and his Old Etonian chums came up with the jolly wheeze of reinventing upper-class philanthropy and Tory paternalism under the populist rubric of the 'Big Society'.[19]

This then is the complicated history which our poet laureate chose to explore. How did she go about it? Largely, it has to be said, by ignoring or glossing over its more problematic aspects. The poem begins promisingly enough with an evocation of its chosen mise en scene. Hackney Wick is all: 'fleas, flies, bin-lids, Clarnico's Jam; the poor/enclosed by railway, marshland, factories, canal'.

We are in the City's edgelands, that in-between space where the planners writ no longer runs, and whose surreal ecology has been lyrically described by Paul Farley and Michael Symmons Roberts in their recent book as 'England's true wilderness'.[20] Recently the area has become home to a fringe festival of creative dissenters and the focus of a vibrant Olympic counter-culture.[21] But Duffy's Wilderness, for all that it is a landscape of exclusion, is going to be reclaimed for other purposes. Thanks to the Old Etonians she names, it becomes a 'glorious space' connecting 'the power of place to human hope'. The response of the locals is one of amazement and gratitude, in the one line in the poem where their voice is directly heard: 'Blimey, it's fit for a millionaire'.

I kept listening for a tinge of irony in the poem but it is all grace notes: 'translated poverty to self-esteem/camaraderie, and optimism similed in smiles'. Her definition of legacy is equally soft-centred: 'young lives respected, cherished, valued, helped/to sprint, swim, bowl, box, play, excel, belong/ believe community is self in multitude'. It reads more like a paraphrase of the Club's mission statement, or even a manifesto for the Big Society, than an engagement with the complex poetics of working-class aspiration; while the redefinition of community in such individualistic terms begs an important question about its rhetorical use. Perhaps it is not surprising that the 'past all around us' has melted into 'air' that rhymes in the next but one line with 'millionaire'.

The poem's closing lines, celebrating the continuity of this tradition of sponsored aspiration, contains its most powerful but also most questionable imagery:

> The same high sky,
> same East End moon, above this reclaimed wilderness,
> where relay boys are raced by running ghosts.

The sudden appearance of a spectral geography does not disturb the elegiac sense of a wilderness reclaimed. Nor does it point to another possible and better world where the poor would not have to depend on charitable handouts from the rich to get by. These ghosts are not about to haunt the Games with their uncanny presence, or spoil the Olympic dream with their message of lives unredeemed by private philanthropy. They have been recruited to run for Team GB; they are simply there to spur the athletes on and persuade us that we too can be superhuman.

In her post-Olympic poem 'Translating the British', Duffy moved onto surer, or at least less treacherous, ground. She set out to capture the mood of public euphoria that attended team GB's medal successes and translate it into the demand for creating a more level playing field in British society. She begins quite bullishly, though not in a John Bull kind of way:

> We speak Shakespeare here,
> A hundred tongues, one voiced;

The national bard, having furnished a common language and even a sense of organic community, is here set to work in voicing a collective celebration of the country's new-found certainty in an Olympic identity:

> We say we want to be who we truly are,
> Now we roar it. Welcome to us.

In the next verse Duffy makes clear her purpose is not to merely echo a popular triumphalism but to refocus it, by proposing a quid – or rather several million quid – pro quo:

> We've had our pockets picked,
>   The soft white hands of bankers,
> Bold as brass, filching our gold, our silver;
> We want it back.
>
> We are Mo Farah lifting the 10,000 metres gold
> We want new running-tracks in his name ...
> For every medal earned
> We want school playing fields returned.

Given the actual demographic of the Olympic crowd, which was hardly a cross-section of the British population, the rhetorical 'we', which reverberates like a mantra through the poem, is more than somewhat ambitious in its claim to inclusiveness. Whoever 'we' are, we are symbiotically identified with a string of 'people's champions', and by virtue of that fact are entitled to a legacy that will include more sports facilities and cycle lanes – a modest enough demand to be sure, which may give David Cameron and Boris Johnson some momentary qualms of conscience but is unlikely to cause them many sleepless nights.

The best lines in the poem attack the corruption of language by its Olympification, with a velopedic side swipe at Norman Tebbit's notoriously smug advice to the unemployed, and a possible advertisement for the present Mayor of London's contribution to reducing traffic congestion:

> Enough of the soundbite abstract nouns,
> *Austerity*, *policy*, *legacy*, of tightening metaphorical belts;
> We got on our real bikes ...

The central trope of the poem, its equation between Olympic champions and champions of the people ('we are Bradley Wiggins, side-burned, Mod, god;/ We are Sir Chris Hoy, Laura Trott ...) is premised on the notion that when it comes to the Olympics 'everyone is a winner' (^181). In other words it simply underwrites the pseudo-democratic 2012 message that elite athletes are both Superhuman and Just like Us. But is such a 'translation' possible? Mod may rhyme with God, but even the Who's quadrophenic celebration of the subculture did not try to invest scooters and parkas with a theological mission. As for Our Bradley, he may have turned sideburns into a must-have fashion accessory for twenty-twelvers, but beating the French at their own game in the Tour de France is still likely to be the victory for which he will most want to be remembered.[22]

Following in the steps of Pindar, Duffy's proposition is that in admiring athletes we are worshipping the shadow cast by our own ideal selves; but things have moved on a bit since Plato's Cave, and Freud is on hand to remind us that in all such identifications, the narcissism of minor differences is ever present. Bigging up Team UK is perhaps not the best way to cut national sporting rivalries down to size. Moreover the opposition the poem conjures up between the Bankers (boo), with 'their soft white hands', and the People (cheers), presumably with their hard black ones, pulls on an all too easy political rhetoric that begs all the important questions. Are bankers the only baddies? What about the CEOs of Dow Chemicals, Adidas and Coca Cola, not to mention Mumbai's and now London's very own plutocrat Lakshmi Mittal? Hardly paid up members of the clean hands brigade, just good – or bad – old- fashioned corporate capitalists wearing their smiley Olympic sponsor faces.

The poet laureate glosses over these more problematic aspects of 2012. Although superficially the syntax of 'Translating the British' is oppositional, its semantics are fully complicit with the populist aspirational agenda that underwrote the London bid. The Olympified version of multiculturalism has one simple proposition: it does not matter what colour an athlete is, *as long as it is gold*. Duffy's Hall of Fame – both poems contain a roll call of honour, in the first case of rich philanthropists, and in the second of about-to-be-rich elite British athletes – leaves no room for doubt; no room either for the have-nots and the also-rans, the state pensioner who donates ill afforded money to help send local children to the seaside for a week's holiday, or the runner who suffers the anguish of failure or defeat but still manages to summon up the good grace to applaud the winner. Yet these are the real unsung heroes, far closer to embodying the altruism of the Olympic ideal than the posturing antics of some of the medal-winners, who cash in on their success through lucrative sponsorship deals with Adidas, Coca Cola et al.

Our poet laureate will not let any such pessimism of the intellect leak in to her poem to dent its optimistic winning words, and she ends on the same high note of collective self congratulation as she began, echoing David Cameron's honeyed phrase about the spending cuts, in an attempt, no doubt, at irony, but one which falls rather flat in the overall context of the poem's upbeat message: 'We sense new weather./We are on our marks. We are all in this together.'

Certainly the post-Olympic debate, in so far as it looks forward as well as back, has to be part of a larger and more inclusive conversation about the direction in which British society is moving, as it struggles to lift itself out of social as well as economic recession. The Games themselves offered a brief, and for many a welcome respite from the rancorous debates that characterise the political discourse of a deeply divided society. Yet despite all the talk of 'maintaining the momentum', the truce did not outlast the closing Festival of Flame, which celebrated nothing but the culture of celebration itself.

The simple truth is that rhetorics of 2012 aspirationalism begged a whole series of questions. Do we want to live in cities whose economies are dependant on cultures of consumption rather than production, on the provision of services rather than the making of goods, on the accumulation of private assets rather than development of public amenity? And if we do, what new balance between work and leisure, individual and collective interest, needs to be struck? Do we have to make a choice between the values of commerce and community, or can we have the best of both worlds? Is sport, like art, the secular religion of affluent, post-industrial societies? And if so, is this new 'opiate' of the people any less harmful than the old one? It is certainly no less mind-numbing in promoting a version of 'high' culture in which there is no place for the tragic, or any come-down from the heights of peak performance or sublime athleticism to engage with the real problems of the world. These questions, raised by 2012, will not be answered by sticking our heads in the sands of time or surrendering to nostalgia for a future in which they no longer need to be asked. The coming of the Olympics to London forced us consider such matters as part of the immediate pragmatics of its occasion rather than as a topic of abstract philosophical speculation or academic debate. The Olympics are good to think through, if not always to run with. And we should be grateful for the chance they present to do just that.

PART I

East London in transition:
an everyday story of 'race', class and imagined community

East London lay hidden from view behind a curtain on which were painted terrible pictures: starving children, suffering women, overworked men; horrors of drunkenness and vice; monsters and demons of inhumanity, giants of disease and despair. Did these pictures truly represent what lay behind, or did they bear to the facts a relation similar to that which the pictures outside a booth at some country fair bear to the performance or show within? This curtain we have tried to lift.

Charles Booth, East London Life and Labour (1899)

Visitors to the Olympics will be able to join the locals in a 'knees up' or singalong in one of the many friendly pubs, see the funny side of life with stand-up comedians whose jokes are part of the area's traditional cockney sense of humour, be challenged by the visual wit of East End's street artists whose fringe Olympic festival is happening at Hackney Wick, strike a bargain while taking in the ethnic vibe at the famous Green Street market, and round off the day by enjoying an authentic Bengali curry in Brick Lane. With all these hotspots no wonder they call it a world in a city!

Guide to East London and the Olympics (2012)

People using Bank Machine's ATMs can opt to have their prompts and options given to them in rhyming slang. They will be asked to enter their Huckleberry Finn, rather than their Pin, and will have to select how much sausage and mash (cash) they want. The rhyming slang prompts will be available from cash machines throughout East London. Ron Delnevo, managing director of Bank Machine, said: 'Whilst we expect some residents will visit the machine to just have a butcher's (look), most will be genuinely pleased as this is the first time a financial services provider will have recognised the Cockney language in such a manner. On our cash machines in Wales less than 1% of people opt for the Welsh language, whereas between 15-20% opt for Cockney when given the chance'.

BBC Report 2012

It is possible to see one crucial aspect of modernity as an ongoing crisis of attentiveness, in which the changing configurations of capitalism continually push attention and distraction to new limits and thresholds, with an endless sequence of new products, sources of stimulation and streams of information, and then respond with new methods of managing and regulating perception.

Jonathan Crary, Suspensions of Perception

John Claridge, East London Gasworks

1. London Goes East:
the gothic imagination and
the capital's 'other scene'

History, Marx liked to remind us, usually proceeds by its bad side. But he could not have envisaged, in his wildest dreams, that a tourist industry would develop based on turning scenes of public nightmare into popular visitor attractions. Yet if most of the visitors to East London for the Olympics in 2012 knew anything at all about the area's history, it was probably to do with Jack the Ripper, the Kray Twins and the Blitz.

Beginning in fiction a practice that has continued in fact up to the present day, one of the earliest commentators on the area, Pierce Egan, focused on the East End's role in attracting the aristocracy from the West End to witness boxing contests (then illegal), and possibly to engage in sexual adventures with the 'rough trade'; his 'Tom and Jerry' characters as depicted by George Cruickshank (*9) pioneered the art of urban slumming, as they follow a rake's progress amongst East End 'lowlife'.[1] And despite the recent efforts of civic imagineers to promote a sanitised, happy-clappy version of its past, the East End's ill reputation continues to precede it; indeed, suitably glamorised, its turbulent history of violence and lawlessness was exploited during the Olympics to add a little frisson of excitement for visitors to the '2012 experience'.[2] Updated with a media panic about Stratford as a hotspot of street crime, it may also have frightened some people away.

W.T. Snead was another early explorer of the East End, 'that strange inverted world that is the London labyrinth' as he called it.[3] Drawing on the imagery of the Book of Revelation, with its vision of the apocalyptic destruction of cities, he portrayed the dreadful consequences of allowing a great part of the capital to become a den of iniquity. Other Victorian explorers joined in to establish a narrative template which sealed the East End off as a site of urban dereliction from the rest of London: it was either a mysterious underworld entirely enclosed within its own densely impenetrable meanings, or else it was surreptitiously infiltrating the overworld through trafficking in drugs, sex, and subversive ideas.

The question of how East London and its inhabitants have been represented to, by and for outsiders over the past century and a half forms the substance of this chapter. We look at a tradition that belongs, primarily, to writers and artists who have explored the more shadowy aspects of London's history and geography and focused on the East End for this purpose.[4] Their interest has been in the hidden layers of meaning that have been deposited in the urban landscape by long-vanished cultures and communities, as well as by those currently drawn into its local/global space of population flow. This approach creates a vantage point that disrupts the surface density of the city's traffic with the world in order to gain greater perspectival depth and bring to light its 'other scenes': scenes that have been erased by the city's continual pursuit of modernity, or deleted from its official memoryscape, but whose traces remain to haunt it.[5] And in unearthing them, another, more disquieting picture of London emerges in which the very ideals which have animated the city's growth have also made the city unreal to itself.

This is a tradition more concerned with losers than winners: those who have been drawn in by the capital's promise of fame and fortune but discovered to their cost that these are evanescent dreams. Yet it is not just about celebrating unsung heroes who have been banished from the picture of 'swinging London'. There is a darker, more troubling aspect to the story in which everything that has been repressed by the drive to construct a metropolis built upon principles of rationality and order returns to disrupt it and make history 'by its bad side'. In what follows I have focused on one particular strand of this history, in which the East End of London has become a privileged object of the gothic imagination.[6] To introduce the reader to this imaginative history, each section in what follows is prefaced with quotations from some of the key texts which will then be discussed.

The internal Orient

By the time we reached the street there was blood everywhere. The muffled crash we heard while we were talking in the Golden Lion Social Club must have been the bottle breaking on his head. Under the street lights the bloodied glass was being ground into the pavement by the boots that came again and again, pounding at the stranger's body. They were about twenty of them and they all ran off together, melting into the night. Their victim looked like he had blundered out of a Tarantino movie. He was spitting out the blood trickling into his mouth. His companion, although unharmed, was clearly in shock. We were just walking back from the pub. It sounded like a pathetic bleat of protest. Why us? Such a question on a dark night in Cannon Street Whitechapel can only be rhetorical. He knew why and so did we. His friend, gathering his wits, dabbed at the blood in his eyes. He was in no doubt. It's because we're white, mate.

Evening Standard, 12 September 1995

At the beginning of 1995 the *Evening Standard* ran a series of special reports on the condition of East London, under the title 'The Betrayed'. The declared aim was to 'reveal how so many of its citizens live an underprivileged existence in the shadow of the success of this great capital'. The series rehearsed many of the key themes of a journalistic campaign run over a century earlier by Snead, whose 'The Maiden Tribute of Modern Babylon' (*10), a series of articles on juvenile crime, prostitution and urban decay, had done much to set the terms of public debate and intervention into the life of the East End.[7]

The *Standard* report examines what it calls 'the bloodstained face of race relations in East London, exacerbated by poverty and disease'. The front page shows a picture of white youth, under the caption: 'Cannon Street Whitechapel and the random victim of an Asian gang stumbles to safety, his head pouring with blood.'

This picture is used to introduce, and in a sense anchor, the main theme of the report, which is that Bangladeshi gangs are on the rampage, picking on innocent white people in a form of reverse racism, committing gratuitous acts of revenge for the harassment they have suffered over the years at the hands of white East Enders. This message is underlined on the inside cover, where there is a photograph of a group of Bangladeshi boys lined up across a street, in a gangsta 'they shall not pass' pose.

Of course this graphic realism is no less constructed than the meaning of the picture itself. But what seems so peculiar about the text which is supposed to authenticate it is that it is couched in such florid sensationalist terms, as if it were a piece of popular fiction, rather than a demonstration of sociological fact.

The introductory paragraph, quoted above, gives the flavour. We are back in the torrid world of Victorian melodrama and slum fiction, now made into a pulp fiction movie. As readers we are deliberately turned into the spectators of a piece of cinema or street theatre which has been staged for our benefit. The dramatic quality of the mise en scene is enhanced by not revealing the colour of victim and assailant until the last sentence. The holding back of the key racial descriptor (it's because we're white, mate') and its sudden revelation functions as a kind of denouement, a shock tactic designed to encapsulate the main point of the argument:

> Attacks, assaults, hatred – there is a mood of gothic barbarity amongst the poor and the angry encapsulated in this warning by the 21 year old posse leader in the Golden Lion Social Club. 'We are the majority, we are strong. If anyone gives us trouble we will hurt them.' Yes, that much is known. We have the picture that proves it.

The reference to the gothic has a double meaning in this context. It certainly evokes a return to a new dark age brought about by the advent of an alien, uncivilised anti-christian power in our midst. This is a well rehearsed theme. The Victorian urban explorers frequently used racial imagery to define the 'natives' of the East End as primitives, or barbarians; with the settlement of colonies of Chinese, Malays and Africans in docklands areas, and then the advent of Jewish immigrants from Eastern Europe, the non-christian, non-occidental character of the area became a topic of increasing public concern (*38-40). Just as the West End was sharpening its image as the glittering cosmopolitan hub of worldwide Empire, so it was felt to be increasingly menaced by the East End as a kind of Internal Orient, a dark mysterious continent whose dense localisms formed the heart of that Other England, where the Empire was already preparing to strike back.[8]

The first cartographer of this internal orient was Thomas De Quincey. In *The Confessions of an English Opium Eater* he discusses his experiences with the 'oriental drug' and his explorations as an East End flaneur in almost identical terms. His dreams are crowded with turbulent processions of Chinese and Malays, in street bazaars where he is forever lost and wandering in search of forbidden pleasures, pursued by the monstrous fauna and flora of the Ganges and the Nile. Then he describes himself walking in an East End:

> ... surrounded on all sides with a sea of myriad shapes in which everything fluctuates as I seek to find an individual human face within the indistinguishable mass of this surplus population so reminiscent of the swarming continent of Asia'.

De Quincey also observes in the language and gestures of these East Enders 'the subtle signs of subversion, the Jacobin influence'. He is both fascinated by the promiscuity of the urban crowd and fears its powers of social contagion and combination, and he locates both in an imaginary geography where the East represent what he calls the barbaresque – the negation of everything that the West stands for.

As John Barrell shows in his study, De Quincey's fear of being 'contaminated' by physical or social contact was also an important element in his anti-semitism.[9] In one notorious passage he writes of:

> men's natural abhorrence of the Jewish taint, as once in Jerusalem they had hated the leprosy and cholera (oriental diseases), because even while they raved against it the secret proofs of it could be detected amongst their own kindred.

In the portrayal of the East End as a centre of foreign immigration and cultural diversity, anti-semitism and orientalism increasingly converged in constructing an alien threat which is both global in scope and intensely local in effect. In the process Jews are increasingly confused with 'orientals'. For example one of the witnesses from a local community settlement cross-examined during the police enquiry into the Jack the Ripper murders described living conditions in the Jewish quarters in the following terms:

> There is something of the Oriental bazaar about the Jewish market, the swarms of unkempt children running hither and thither on countless errands, the women haggling with each other, shouting to make themselves heard over the general hubbub, the men scurrying in and out of dark alleyways, the whole effect is one of labyrinthine confusion which can scarcely fail to make a fearful impression on the casual visitor (quoted in Walkovitz, p76).

In the sober deliberations from the House of Commons Select Committee on Housing in 1901 we find the following exchange:

Lord Robert Cecil: What do you say about the inhabitants?
Lord Lupton: Most of the inhabitants are Jews and their habits are said to be clean so far as their persons go, but certainly the courts outside their houses are ...
Lord Robert Cecil: Eastern in character.
Lord Lupton: Yes that is so exactly (*Hansard*, 18.2.1901).

The Jews referred to were of course Ashkenazis from the shtetls of Eastern Europe, not Sephardis from North Africa or the Middle East, but this conflation is entirely characteristic of both popular and official perceptions of the period. At the same time moral panics around drugs and sexuality that became focused on the Chinese community of Limehouse in the late Victorian and Edwardian period included many features borrowed from anti-semitism. As Marek Kohn has shown, the theme of a criminal underworld organised by a secret oriental conspiracy, which was popularised by Sax Rohmer in his Fu Manchu novels, owed much of its logic to the Protocols of the Elders of Zion (*12).[10] Another point of convergence was the white slave trade (*13). If opium was a medium of seduction of white women by 'men of colour', their induction into oriental perversity was supposed to lead inexorably to their final falling into the hands of Jewish pimps, who shipped them out to the brothels of the Middle East. Finally the Asian and Jewish communities were accused of a similar duplicity; the outward appearance of respectability and even prosperity was only a cloak for hidden cruelty or corruption undermining both family and nation. Jewish money allied to Oriental vice was a channel linking the East End with the West End, directly injecting moral infection into the civilised heart of the metropolis.

This close articulation of orientalism and anti-semitism has been an important element in both literary and journalistic representations of the East End over the past century. But it is important to stress that the idea of the East End as an internal orient was not confined in its application to Jews. The Irish and English working class were also recruited – cockney urchins, for example, were routinely re-described as street arabs (*14).[11] What this form of orientalism drew on and racialised was a certain more general way of thinking and feeling about the city, and in particular its spectral geographies, its 'other scenes' in which the gothic has played a central role. And it is to this we must now turn.

Keepers of the ruins

I also stood in Satan's bosom and beheld its desolations:
A ruined man, a ruin'd building of God, not made with hands
Its plains of burning sand, Its mountains of marble terrible
Its pits and declivities flowing with molten ore and fountains
Of pitch and nitre; its ruin'd palaces & cities & mighty works
Its furnaces of afflicion in which his Angels and Emanations
Labour with blackened visages among its stupendous ruins

Arches, & pyramids and porches, colonnades and domes,
In which dwells Mystery, Babylon; here in her secret place,
From hence she comes forth on the Churches in delight
Here is her cup filled with its poisons in these horrid vales
And here the scarlet vale woven in pestilence and war,
Here is Jerusalem, born in chains, in the days of Babylon

William Blake, *Milton Book The Second*, lines 15-27

I should like to formulate what we have learnt so far as follows: *Our hysterical patients suffer from reminiscences.* Their symptoms are residues and mnemonic symbols of particular (traumatic) experiences. We may perhaps obtain a deeper understanding of this kind of symbolism if we compare them with other mnemonic symbols in other fields. The monuments and memorials with which large cities are adorned are also mnemonic symbols. If you take a walk through the streets of London, you will find, in front of one of the great railway termini, a richly carved Gothic Column – Charing Cross. One of the old Plantagenet kings of the thirteenth century ordered the body of his beloved queen Eleanor to be carried to Westminster. And at every stage at which the coffin rested he erected a gothic cross. Charing Cross is the last of the monuments that commemorate the funeral cortege. At another point in the same town, not far from London Bridge, you will find a towering, and more modern column, which is simply known as 'The Monument'. It was designed as a memorial of the Great Fire which broke out in that neighbourhood in 1666 and destroyed a large part of the city. These monuments then resemble hysterical symptoms in being mnemonic symbols; up to that point the comparison seems justifiable. But what should we think of a Londoner who paused today in deep melancholy before the memorial of Queen Eleanor's funeral instead of going about his business in the hurry that modern working conditions demand or instead of feeling joy at the youthful beat of his own heart?

Or again what should we think of a Londoner who shed tears before the Monument that commemorates the reduction of his beloved metropolis to ashes although it has long since risen again in far greater brilliance. Yet every single hysteric and neurotic behaves like these two impractical Londoners. Not only do they remember painful experiences of the remote past, but they still cling to them emotionally; they cannot get free of the past and for its sake they neglect what is real and immediate. This fixation of mental life to pathogenic traumas is one of the most significant and important characteristics of neurosis.

Sigmund Freud, *Five Lectures on Psychoanalysis 1909* (p78-9)

You find me today ensconced in my ultimate stronghold, a car wreckers yard. I'm certainly not short of space. The clearing I camp in is state property, a plot of land expropriated to give elbow room to the earth moving operations.

I am you see pursuing a project, that of tracing the geometry of the city with the skeletons of motor cars. Not therefore scattering them haphazardly in the first vacant space but arranging them, in order and in line, their skulls aimed in the appointed directions. In my dream town I already have a grid iron of zones with streets already christened Blue Simca street, Three Renaults Boulevard, Alfa Romeo alley, a main square is coming into being encompassed around with black limousines; in the centre is the carcass of a bus which impact has warped and fire blackened with leprous burns. Thus unconsciously with these aligned and lidded sepulchres I have been creating a replica of the country graveyards of my youth.

As I pace between the scrap metal hedges I try to imagine in each interior the forms of life which one time hovered there. I hearken to amorous whispers, words of wrath, fevered or fatuous stirrings of the heart. A people of the dead roams my domain from end to end, an invisible flock that dotes on me. Not without special regard for the showpieces: the Mercedes of a murder victim, its windscreen milky from bulletry; a massive hearse behind which it is hard not to conjure up a cortege.

J.G. Ballard, *The Keeper of Ruins* (p67)

What could an eighteenth century Romantic poet, the founder of psychoanalysis who saw himself as a scientific rationalist and man of the Enlightenment , and a contemporary science fiction writer possible have in common? The answer is a fascination with ruins and with the metropolis as a site of their installation. Ballard's hero is a new kind of post-industrial archaeologist. He scavenges amongst the detritus of modernity in search of clues as to how it got that way, but only in order to reconstitute out of these fragments of lost memory a new dream city of the dead. In his fixation on ruins, he seems to be suffering from reminiscences in the way described by Freud; he is trapped in a particular kind of morbid memoryscape because it provides a local habitation and name for his desires.

Freud frequently used his urban excursions as a pretext for reflecting on the topography of the human psyche.[12] In his 'Introductory Lectures on Psychoanalysis', he draws our attention to the paradoxical function of the memorial – which is to enable us to forget, or at least to get sufficient emotional distance from the painful memory so that we are not completely overwhelmed or immobilised by it. The memorial is both an evocation of past trauma and a defence against its return. Those who are unable to objectify trauma in this way are condemned to embody it all too concretely in their symptoms.

What Freud perhaps overlooked is the fact that the Charing Cross monument no longer functions as a mnemonic symbol because the historical moment it represents is not part of the living memory of Londoners; it is not a 'lieu de memoire', subject to any ritualised commemoration. It is not even the original relic, but a copy, and even its French name – *chère rene* – has been thoroughly anglicised, so that it no longer evokes an unwelcome chain of associations to the Plantagenets (*88). Finally, as part of this process of emotional disinvestment and symbolic erasure, the site has been reconstituted or re-centred as the pivot of an entirely modern metropolitan space of traffic flow. Since 1888 all distances to London are measured to Charing Cross – and this practice continues even though its function as central place (like that of the Strand) has long ago been taken over by Piccadilly Circus and nearby Trafalgar Square, not to mention Oxford Street. Many of the statues to the founding fathers of Empire which adorn the streets of Central London have undergone a similar fate. They are not commemorated or vandalised; they are largely ignored, except by a few foreign tourists, mostly Japanese and Chinese, who snap them to add to their collection of curios, perhaps out of a respect for ancestors which in their cultures at least survives. Londoners have on the whole moved on.

As for the Monument, its popularity with tourists largely stems from its role in providing panoramic views of the city (albeit one now largely usurped by the London Eye, and most recently the Shard and the Olympic Orbital Tower), rather than from the fact that its height measures the exact distance to the presumed spot where the Great Fire of London broke out (*89). As Freud points out, the view from the top measures how far the city has come in regenerating itself from its first great moment of ruination, and makes the fire itself a catalyst in that process, as later the Blitz was to become.

The panoramic prospect offers the spectator the illusion that the city can be comprehended in a single sweeping glance to the horizon, its identity reduced to its skyline and its topography to a few conspicuous landmarks; en route everything that is otherwise experienced as noxious (and human) about it – its noise, pollution, traffic jams, crowded thoroughfares etc – melts away; for a moment the city is reborn to our wondering gaze as a pristine presence untainted by bad memories, an unknown territory waiting to be explored and perhaps to reflect our own self regard (*90/91). The view from the Anish Kapoor's Orbital Tower draws the eye to the spectacular iconic buildings of the City and West End, to Canary Wharf and the Shard, or Stratford's new skyscrapers, not to the huddled streets of East London, or its bleak downriver hinterland. Yet if the panorama enables Londoners to locate themselves within a bigger picture of their city, to skim and get a measure of its surface density, it also compresses the memoryscape in a way that eliminates much of its perspectival depth.[13]

If the urban panorama is a device for composing the city into a harmonious visual totality, making it into the abstracted object of a panoptic vision, the ruin reverses the emphasis: its role is to ground our relation to the environment, give a local habitation and a name to what excites reminiscence, and help us remember what is dispelled by forgetfulness, whilst maintaining sufficient distance so that we are not overwhelmed by what is evoked. The paradox of the ruin is that it involuntarily conjures up the process or act of destruction, but also what survives to represent its effect – like a symptom, it is both a remainder and reminder of the past. If the creators of the early dioramas were so attracted to ruins as their subject matter it was because the technology permitted dramatic visual transformations of the mise en scene, and so could exploit gothic aesthetics to the full (*86/7).

As objects of contemplation ruins have been used for many different purposes, especially by artists and writers: to symbolise the transience of human existence, or the vanity of thinking that any structure could withstand the passage of time or the ravages of nature, as in the poem by Edmund Spenser; ruins have also represented the destruction of empires and the survival of ancient civilisations, acts of divine providence and human folly; they have served as memorials to atrocities, and also as monuments to the capacity of the human spirit to survive them (*16-28).[14] For William Blake the ruined palaces of London Babylon symbolise the broken lives and bodies of its inhabitants. But what happens when the city becomes subject to that form of space and time compression we have learnt to call modernity and, it would seem at first sight, makes the ruin redundant?[15]

In a study of the peculiarities of English modernism, Eric Hobsbawm has argued that its roots were paradoxically in the medievalism which so influenced William Morris, John Ruskin and the Guild Socialists.[16] He writes:

In the smoky workshop of the world, a society of egoism and aesthetic vandals, where the small craftsman so visible elsewhere in Europe could no longer be seen in the fog generated by the factories, the medievalism of peasants and artisans had long seemed a model of a society both socially and artistically more satisfactory.

For Ruskin and Morris the division of labour imposed by capitalism destroyed the unity of hand and brain embodied in the skills of craftsmanship which the artisans had employed in building the gothic cathedrals of the middle ages. There were others, though, who saw in gothic medievalism not so much a vision of an alternative and freer society made up of independent producers, but an organic society in which the rich man in his castle and the poor man at his gate each recognised and kept to their separate estate.

The gothic revival of the second half of the nineteenth century ushered in new memoryscapes and new keepers of ruins. For some, gothic medievalism was a means of preserving, at least in matters of public taste, the traditional influence and privilege of the land-owning aristocracy. In the mid-Victorian period these tastes were still largely associated with the eighteenth century – the Georgian town house and square, Palladian architecture, Arcadian landscape painting and gardens, to which a folly or classical 'ruin' might add an element of picturesque interest.[17] But after the Great Exhibition of 1851, which was housed in a specially constructed Crystal Palace made almost entirely of glass and ironwork, even the most traditionalist arbiters of taste sensed that a new response was needed to the scale of change (*29). They saw in the gothic cathedrals of mediaeval Europe a model for the great public buildings they wished to erect as monuments to the prosperity which Industry and Empire had brought to Victorian Britain.[18] St Pancras Station, with its turrets and elaborate gothic ornamentation, is a typical expression of this aesthetic, striking such a strong contrast with Kings Cross Station next door, built at around the same time, but along clean functionalist lines (*30-32).

The gothic novel gave to medievalism a more apocalyptic tone; it frequently featured half-destroyed structures, ancient buildings which had fallen into decay and disrepair, or had been subject to attack through vandalism or bombardment. These buildings contained secret chambers, subterranean passages, trapdoors, underground vaults, putrefying corpses, all of which had an important narrative function in evoking a past that has been forgotten or ignored, rather than cultivated or celebrated as a living heritage – and which returns as a threatening or disruptive force.

The gothic thus came to represent what had been repressed or made unrepresentable by modernity, but which returned to haunt it. If the gothic imagination sometimes had a political edge, it was because it provided both a language and a landscape in which the ghosts in the machinery of industrial capitalism – those whose livelihoods had been destroyed by its advent – could be summoned up and then, if not laid to rest, at least usefully re-employed with walk-on parts in scenarios of its ruination.

Marx frequently used gothic imagery in dramatising the class struggle. Capitalism is described as a vampire, sucking the blood of the working class, who nevertheless had a historical mission to become its gravediggers.[19] However he set little store by what he called the 'lumpen proletariat', the urban underclass who might on occasion form themselves into a mob, but whom he regarded as leading a disorganised and parasitic existence on the margins of capitalist economy, where they formed a reserve army of labour used by employers to break strikes and depress wages.[20] Yet for many reformers the unacceptable face of capitalism remained the all too visible destitution of the urban poor, and in so far as they could be portrayed as the denizens of an 'underworld', it was they who also continued to capture the gothic imagination of London.

This perspective on the capital city has a long provenance. William Blake called it Los or Babylon, and those who followed in his footsteps spoke of an outcast London whose grandest architectures were overshadowed by sepulchral ruins, and whose brightest thoroughfares haunted by an afflicted populace, bodies and minds ravaged by what the capital – or Capital – had made of them. These critics may have shared Blake's anti-urban and anti-industrial sentiment, but they were not always as anxious as their mentor to resist the assimilation of 'ruin sentiment' to the picturesque.[21]

Explorations of the uncanny, that twilight world in which the living and the dead, the animate and inanimate become strangely confused, has been an integral feature of the gothic imagination of London. It has given us a city whose traffic with the world follows mysterious lines of desire not to be found on any planners' map, and which the march of municipal improvement has tried in vain to sweep from the streets; yet whatever name is given to the places, practices and people connected by these means – the slum, the rookery, the bohemian quarter, where the residuum and the demi-monde mingled and created an 'underground' culture – their very survival pointed to the limits of the fully rationalised city, and even, in some eyes, signalled the impossibility of the project of modernity itself.[22]

Moreover, if the dynamism of the modern city, driven by the 'monstrous' productivity of capital, was to be its own downfall, its gravediggers had at least to be trained up as future keepers of its ruins. This was the task which bohemian artists and poets assigned to themselves, and which marked their ambivalent identification with the struggles of the oppressed; rejecting the picturesque rural scene in favour of the sublime terrors of the metropolitan abyss, it was not difficult for Poe or Baudelaire, or Hoffman, or even James Thompson or Arthur Machen, to discover the labyrinth, the secret passage, the dungeon and all the other characteristic gothic devices in the wastelands of the working-class city, with its maze of courtyards and alleyways, its cellars and dead ends. In their hands, the eighteenth-century gothic ruin with its, 'tottring battlements dressed with rampant ivy's unchecked growth', is both urbanised and modernised as it is relocated in the dilapidated tenements and 'dark satanic mills', where the dangerous, perishing and labouring classes were confined. The aim of their fascination was purely cartographic; as good bohemians they wanted to map the territory, to conserve its danger and its difference, not reform or translate it into some approximation of the 'bourgeois thing'.

James Thompson in *The City of Dreadful Night* (1874) made the link between the ancient and the modern view of ruins:

> The city is ruinous, although
> Great ruins of an unremembered past
> With others of a few short years ago
> More sad and found within its precincts vast (lines 67-70).

A promiscuous intermingling of ruins helped to create a spectral geography in which distinctions of wealth and poverty were magically erased. These connoisseurs of urban dereliction were too invested in ruin sentiment and what might still be excavated imaginatively from it to want to see the slums of the Victorian city demolished altogether.[23] Their view of London Babylon had little interest in the mundane reforms of street lighting, sanitation and new model dwellings, let alone the Clean Air Act. Such improvements would only have the effect of destroying the city as an aesthetic resource.

The capital city as envisioned by the Fabians and other municipal reformers who were to found the London County Council was neither mysterious, awesome, terrifying or sublime; its model dwellings for the working class, its public works and parks, its suburban streets and shopping precincts were as useless for entertaining the prospect of revolution as for contemplating the retrospect of civilisational decay. Instead the reformers were animated by a desire to refashion the city according to a rational design, rather than leave it to the tender mercy of market forces and to ensure that its public amenities operated for the benefit of all citizens and not just the privileged few.

In the 1860s and 1870s more of London was rebuilt than at any time since the first Great Fire of 1666. Large parts of the central and inner city were turned into a vast building site, as the Metropolitan Board of Works and the railway companies undertook the widening and straightening of roads, creating new thoroughfares, and levelling and tunnelling wherever they went.[24] These improvements were unevenly distributed. The main effect was to clear large areas of Holborn and Westminster of its residual rookeries, and drive 'outcast London' eastwards.[25] The Mile End Road and the People's Palace exemplified the new municipalism, but as for the rest, London became an increasingly visible tale of two cities. The West End was the glittering hub of Empire, home to the conspicuous consumption of a new leisure class; the East End provided the city's manufacturing base, where home grown workshop industries joined hands with international trade and commerce to support a large, almost exclusively working-class population and also to sustain a hidden economy which provided a major additional resource for the area's diverse immigrant communities.[26]

One response to this spatial re-alignment of leisure and labour was to apply the devices of romantic ruinology to the task of deconstructing the West End and the City, with its pretensions of wealth and power exemplified in its great public buildings. Hubert Robert had first popularised the genre by imagining the Louvre in ruins – sacked by a victorious proletariat, a visual polemic made by a disgruntled aristocrat shortly after the fall of the Bastille. Joseph Gandy depicted the newly built Bank of England as a classical Piranesi ruin; and the Compte de Volney, in his classic account of *Revolution and Empire*, produced numerous imaginary scenarios of the great cities of the world in ruins to illustrate his pessimistic thesis about the rise and fall of civilisations, which bears closely on Marx's argument about the mutual ruin of the contending classes (*16, 19, 20).[27]

In 1872 the French social realist Gustave Doré teamed up with Blanchard Jerrold to produce *London – a pilgrimage*, a visual tour of the city based on a geography of contrasts between high society and lowlife, West End and East.[28] Doré uses his skill with chiaroscuro effects to depict the tale of two cities – one of glittering light and the other of murky depths, associated here not so much with capital and labour as with the worlds of the rentier and the criminal (*6/7/11). His pictures of slum housing have been endlessly reproduced; and, for example, they provided the visual inspiration for Edgar Anstey's classic documentary on the subject which in turn had an important influence of post-war urban planning. Perhaps less well known in this context is an etching captioned 'A New Zealander contemplating the ruins of a once great and powerful city'. It shows an artist seated on a broken arch of London Bridge sketching a cathedral-like ruin (*15). On closer inspection this building turns out not to be a church but the brand new Cannon Street Station (completed in 1873), here imagined with the cast iron piers of the bridge rusting away in the tidal ooze. The railway, whose coming had done so much to transform London into a modern metropolis, is thus rendered into a piece of obsolete industrial archaeology.

This conceit gives a new twist to an old tale. The figure of the native from the new world contemplating the ruins of London was already well established by the time Doré came to depict his version of the scene. It was mentioned by Gibbon in his study of *Decline and Fall of the Roman Empire* and also in a throwaway comment by Macaulay. In *Archimago* by 'Jno', published in 1864, the scene is vividly described:

I sit upon the last crumbling stones of that bridge, erst the famous London bridge Pavement, footway, parapet abutment pillar, pier all, all are gone ... and I on the last few mouldering stones survey the ruin'd and desolate city (p34).

Recently Doré's picture, with its theme of the artist triumphantly surveying (and surviving) the destruction of modern technology has been taken up by Michael Moorcock, one of the key figures in the contemporary renaissance of urban ruin fiction. In 'Mother London' and in a series of science fiction stories written from the vantage point of the late twenty-first century, Moorcock has been concerned to construct an archaeology of the present in the form of a counterfactual history of London in which modernity is just a blip on the screen. His back to the future story imagines the city regressing to a medieval world of villages and primitive agriculture. His narrator follows in the footsteps of Volney in moralising about the fate of imperial cities, but, with a nod to Arnold Toynbee's theory of civilisations, manages to end on a more optimistic note:

We reached the ancient village of Suthuk which is on the edge of the river bed of the Thames, most of which is reclaimed land planted with cabbages, the export of which form the principle staple of the country ...

Our first destination was the vestiges of the once famous Lun-dun Bridge mentioned in many ancient accounts and in one folk lore ballad which has come down to us beginning, 'Lun-Dun bridge is falling down'. Several arches of this structure now span the intervening space between the village of Suthuk and the extremely picturesque ruins which are visible on the summit of an opposite eminence. These ruins are all that is left of the once famous Cockni cathedral of St Pauls.

... Several benighted peasants, who, we are told claim to be the last survivors of the tribe of the Cocknies now began to gather round us, and to offer for barter certain objects which they had dug up ... in the vicinity ... many of which possessed a certain archaeological interest ...

... Indeed there are few places which promise a greater attraction for a summer holiday than the ruins of ancient Lun-Dun.[29]

All that is solid melts into marsh and fog

I ... watched the sun
On lurid morns, on monstrous afternoons ...
Push out through fog with his dilated disk
And startle the slant roofs and chimney pots
With splashes of fierce colour. Or I saw
Fog only, the great tawny weltering fog
Involve the passive city, strangle it
Alive, and draw it into the void,
Spires, bridges, streets, and squares, as if a sponge

Had wiped out London, – or as noon and night
Had clapped together and utterly struck out
The intermediate time, undoing themselves
In the act. Your city poets see such things ...

But sit in London, at the day's decline,
And view the city perish in the mist
Like Pharaoh's armaments in the deep red sea
     ... Then surprised
By a sudden sense of vision and of tune
You feel as conquerors though you did not fight...

Elizabeth Barrett Browning, *Aurora Leigh, Book III*

Picture a land of mist and mud ... London as an immense, sprawling rain drenched metropolis stinking of soot and hot iron and wrapped in a perpetual mantle of smoke and fog ... ceaseless activity in warehouses and on warves washed by the dark slimy waters of an imaginary Thames in the midst of the forest of masts, a tangle of beams and girders piercing the pale lowering clouds. Up above trains raced by at full speed and down in the underground sewers others rumbled along occasionally emitting ghastly screams or vomiting floods of smoke through the gaping mouths of airshafts

J.K. Huysmans, *Against the Grain*, p38

The cloud looks partly as if it were made of poisonous smoke; very possibly it may be: there are at least two hundred furnace chimneys in a square of two miles on every side of me. But mere smoke would not blow to and fro in that wild way. It looks more to me as if it were made of dead men's souls – such of them as are not gone yet where they have to go, and may be flitting hither and thither, doubting, themselves, of the fittest place for them. You know, if there *are* such things as souls, and if ever any of them haunt places where they have been hurt, there must be many about us, just now, displeased enough!

John Ruskin, *Storm Cloud of the Nineteenth Century*

When the wind collects the miasma and as it were presses it together it becomes visible as a low cloud which hangs over the place. They say the sun is sometimes hidden when the vapour is thickest – it is plain there are no fishes in the water, all the rottenness of a thousand years is there festering under the water.

Vast marshes now cover the site of ancient London; through there is no doubt that in the days of old there flowed the River Thames. The river had become partially choked from the cloaca of the ancient city which poured into it through enormous subterranean aqueducts and drains ... when this had been going on for some time the river, unable to find a channel, began to overflow into the deserted streets and especially to fill the underground passages and drains, of which the number and extent was beyond all power of words to describe. The waters underneath built up and burst in, the houses fell in and the huge metropolis was overthrown. All those parts which were built on low ground are become marshes and swamps. There was nothing visible but trees and hawthorns on the upper lands, willows reeds and rushes on the lower. These crumbling ruins still more choked the river and almost but not quite turned it back – there is no channel through to the salt ocean – it is a vast stagnant swamp which no man dare enter since death would be his inevitable fate.

Richard Jeffries, *After London* (pp35-6)

At night, while he was working on the 'London Pilgrimage', Gustave Doré, accompanied by a minder, wandered the streets of Limehouse and Cable street with sketch pad in hand, part flaneur, part slummer, part artist in residence. But his days were spent at the Café Royal, mixing in what was then known as the 'haute bohème'. Oscar Wilde was a member of the circle, and so too were James McNeill Whistler and Claude Monet while they were in town to paint the Thames red, yellow, vermillion and green. Both artists has been attracted to London by a phenomenon which served both to blur the outlines of its divisive social geography and to obscure its municipal improvements – its famous fogs.

The smoke was Victorian and Edwardian London's second name. The 'Peasoupers' turned day into night, and rendered the most modern and familiar parts of the metropolis once more mysterious, and uncanny; as T.S. Eliot describes in *The Wasteland*, under the brown fog of a winter dawn even the most brightly lit and open thoroughfare suddenly becomes a spectral and unreal place; in reality traffic ground to a halt, and thousands of Londoners, especially the very young and the old, died prematurely of respiratory illness. In *A Mutual Friend* Dickens famously describes these two aspects:

It was a foggy day in London, and the fog was heavy and dark. Animate London, with smarting eyes and irritated lungs, was blinking, wheezing, and choking; inanimate London was a sooty spectre, divided in purpose between being visible and invisible, and so being wholly neither.[30]

The Thames was the prime attractor of fogs, but their cause lay principally elsewhere, in large-scale domestic and industrial coal-burning throughout the capital. But this association between metropolitan miasma and an increasingly polluted river, and the fact that the Thames was in effect an open sewer carrying both industrial and human waste, leading to what came to be known as the Great Stink of 1851, enhanced the scandal that was Babylon. Ruskin in his lecture 'Storm Cloud of the Nineteenth century' portrayed fog as a physical sign not just of industrialism but of its morally polluting effect on the human condition, while Huysmans elaborated a whole cartography of special landscape effects predicated on the spectral gloom.[31]

If Doré was concerned with the medical impact of London's fogs on the lungs of its people, Whistler and Monet were more interested in its aesthetic effects. Monet was concerned to explore how fog transformed light and colour, and in his London river paintings he uses broken masses of colour to create smudged surfaces and blurred outlines which give the canvas its layered painterly texture (*4). No wonder he went on record as saying that what he adored most about London was the fog, since in his eyes it made the city look ever more like one of his own impressionist paintings: Nature imitating art imitating the environment. In contrast Whistler's etchings of the Thames (the nocturne series (*5)) tried to made dockland look not so much picturesque as sublime; using a range of diffused tints to envelop each scene, he paints the river as if it were the further shore of some industrial Byzantium, and at dusk, thereby effectively vaporising the squalor which Doré invested with such fine graphic detail. The indeterminacy of form, and the uncanny reversals of figure and ground which fog gives to a landscape, was for Whistler, as for many urban romantic poets, an incitement to imagine another world; the Isle of Dogs really might be the Isle of Doges, the Greenwich Peninsula the Venetian shore. As Whistler put it in his diary:

And when the evening most clothes the riverside with poetry as with a veil and the poor buildings lose themselves in the dim sky and the tall chimneys become camapanili and the wharehouses were palaces in the night and the whole city hangs in the heavens and fairy land is before us (p34).

Elizabeth Browning castigates the city poets for their moral passivity in the face of urban degradation and the all too easy victories achieved by their aesthetic resolution of it into a metropolitan sublime; but the kind of subtle alchemy wrought by dusk or the painterly palette, the cosmetic makeover achieved by fog, the consoling melancholy of ruins – these devices of imaginative transformation offered a powerful symbolic substitute for the kinds of change achieved by social and political struggle – struggles for which the bohemian subculture inhabited by painters and writers had little real interest or material stake.[32]

The apocalyptic vision of the capital's ruin had one further resource. The vast cemeteries that were built in the Victorian period to provide a last resting place for London's growing population were often in the East, where land was cheap and, just as important, unfitted for any other purpose. This necropolis was Victorian London's edge city, drawing around itself a whole nexus of social, cultural and economic activity; in the twentieth century, as the city sprawled ever further eastwards into the Essex marshlands, turning them into the suburban badlands of Chingford, Romford and Dagenham, the romantic ruinologists used the movement of both the living and the dead to good effect to create a whole new space of representation for the urban uncanny.[33]

That space is also present in T.S. Eliot's striking image of office worker-zombies streaming across London Bridge, lost souls condemned to measure out their lives in coffee spoons:

Unreal city
Under the brown fog of a winter dawn
A crowd flowed over London Bridge, so many
I had not thought death had undone so many.[34]

The 'lost-soul' conceit pulls upon a rich vein of gothic imagery which, as we
have seen, portrays London in vampiric terms as sucking the life blood out of
its inhabitants. Eliot gives the image a characteristically modern twist, albeit
one whose ramifications his own conservative inclinations made it difficult for
him to pursue, if only because it related to changes in the composition of
London's labour force that required another kind of discourse, belonging not
to poetry but political economy, to make clear.

London has always relied on a large reserve army of casual labour to service
its economy, many of them East End immigrants, working in small sweatshops
and street trades, at the mercy of seasonal fluctuations in demand.[35] Its transition
to the Fordist machine age was slow and uneven and mostly concentrated in
smokestack industries located well downriver and downwind of the City. But
their advent did mean that that dead labour (the productivity embodied in
machines) rather than living labour (the trade skills of manual workers) became
increasingly regarded as a key factor of London's economic development (*60-
64). At the same time the growth of a new consumer culture, of bureaucracy
and of the professions meant that by 1900 London was making rapid strides
towards becoming a service-based economy. As a result, the proportion of
London's working population directly and fully engaged in skilled manual
labour, whether artisanal or industrial, declined during the interwar period,
while those whom dead labour had 'undone' or deskilled, or whose work was
essentially parasitic on the value created by productive labour, increased. In
London, by the late 1920s the 'ghosts' in the machinery of capitalism
outnumbered the 'hands' who operated it by a ratio of about 5 to 1.[36]

How was this shift to be represented? In the Victorian period fluctuations
in urban prosperity and population were represented as organic, or as cyclical
processes of decay and renewal, often imaged through bodily metaphors.[37]
London, like other great cities, was equipped with a heart, lungs, a circulatory
system and bowels. But with the advent of a fully fledged modernist discourse
of town planning after the First World War, mechanistic metaphors of
reproduction – of urban function and dysfunction – were increasingly the
norm (*95-99). Planners saw the city in terms of a spatial division of labour,
modelled into distinctive zones: a central business and commercial district, an
inner industrial ring or zone of transition, and outer residential suburbs. In
Patrick Geddes and Ebenezer Howard's 'retro-modernist' vision of the garden
city we can see both sets of influences at work in the way they tried to achieve
an organic sense of community through rigorous zoning policies.[38] This
vision, inspired by William Morris and the arts and crafts movement as much
as by Ruskin's critique of the machine age, was realised in Unwin's plan for
Hampstead Garden City, and subsequently became the model for much
working-class housing built in the expanding suburbs during the interwar
period. The Becontree estate in Barking, the largest of its kind in Europe, was

built in the 1920s and 1930s to rehouse East Enders from the slums and also to provide a residential workforce for Ford's new factory built on a marshland in nearby Dagenham (*65-7). Fordist mass production met the arts and crafts movement on ground of neither's choosing.

As the vision of a fully rationalised and regulated city took hold – in London largely under the aegis of the London County Council and the banner of municipal socialism – those places, populations and practices which fell through the grid found themselves confined to a new form of urban liminality – a twilight zone in the interstices of metropolitan modernity, where they morphed easily into the figures of an existing gothic landscape.

One site where this happened with particular power was in outer East London's 'badlands'. Marshes had long been a part of the gothic vocabulary – the home of pestilential fogs and solitary rumination, belonging neither to land nor sea, but where these elements enter into their most intimate dialogue. The vast muddy indistinction of sky, water and shore that is the Thames Estuary was host to endless speculations about the porousness or permeability of the nation's boundaries – as well as to doubts about the loyalties and residential status of those who lived there.[39] Cockney kids might be happy as mudlarks playing on the river's 'beaches', but anyone quite so at home in the tidal ooze was at the very least an anthropological curiosity, and not to be regarded as a fully-fledged member of the 'island race' unless proof positive was provided.

For the late Victorian ruinologist, the very indeterminacy of the habitat provided an ideal setting for the telling of cautionary tales about the transience of human existence and/or the vanity of the grandiose monuments to Industry and Empire which now dominated the capital's skyline. In *After London*, Richard Jeffries draws on one of the original uses of the gothic ruin – as a site for contemplating the triumph of nature over the follies of man – to paint a powerful picture of this new Babylon, a megalopolis strangled by its own monstrously destructive forces of production and reverting to the organic vegetative condition of marshland. Mud, slime and ooze become the symptomatic medium of destruction, carrying the trace elements of the ruined civilisation to a watery grave. The theme of the deluge clearly links to anxieties created by the great public works taking place in London at this time – and in particular the renewal of the sewers.[40] The metaphor of flood is also closely associated with the fear of uncontrolled flow of populations, just as the crumbling tenement evoked the crumbling of the Empire from within.

This network of associations stabilised a certain apocalyptic vision of London's future as its long imperial and industrial decline gathered pace during the 1920s and 1930s. But then history intervened to produce a ruination whose catastrophic scope and scale created a new and more dreadful city of the dead beyond the wildest nightmares of the gothic imagination.

Apocalypse now

Blitzkrieg has come to London in all its fury and brutality and filth ...
Death drops from the skies. It falls on the just and the unjust. It strikes

against the weak, the humble, the unoffending. Fire, ruin, explosion, murder stalk through our streets and work their will, not without impediment, but without any single restraint which humanity normally imposes on the devilry of man ... How can human frames parry such blows of metal? How can human brains withstand such endless pounding? The mighty machine rattles on and obliterates flesh and blood in its giant cogs and pincers.

Something flowers among the ruins, something so fine and noble that not all the powers of hell can destroy it – the courage of our people

Evening Standard editorial, September 1940

If Wren's most beautiful churches and some of the City's most noble and historic buildings are damaged irreparably, they have taken with them in their passing some of the dreariest and meanest stretches of Victorian office building. The hun is giving us a priceless opportunity to reconceive the city on a more rational and liveable plan.

McDonald Hastings, *London calling*, December 1940

Half masonry, half pain: her head
From which the plaster breaks away
Like flesh from the rough bone, is turned
Upon a neck of stones; her eyes
Are lidless windows of smashed glass,
Each star shaped pupil
Giving upon a vault so vast
How can the head contain it?

Mervyn Peake, *Shapes and Sounds* (lines 23-32)

　　　　　... In succession
Houses rise and fall, crumble, are extended
Are removed, destroyed, restored, or in their place
Is an open field, or a factory, or a by pass
Old stone to new building, old timber to new fires
Houses live and die: there is a time for building
And a time for living and for generation

T.S. Eliot, *East Coker* (lines 52-9)

The advent of aerial warfare, and in particular the bombardment of cities and other civilian targets from the air, was perhaps the main instigator of twentieth-century urbanism.[41] Since the advent of Charles Booth's great *Survey of London Life and Labour* at the beginning of the century, the search for panoptic strategies of urban planning and governance aimed to create standpoints from which it was possible not only to map the city's physical geography street by street, but to comprehend its social patterns and economic prospects as a meaningful whole.[42] It was never going to be easy to connect the local ethnographies produced by the urban explorers to a wider framework of conceptual and political control; the very complexity and scale of the territory resisted assimilation to some omniscient, all-embracing mental map or pictorial view. But with the advent of aerial photography the whole city could now be laid open to detailed inspection for the first time. And where the cameraman pioneered the military strategist was not far behind in exploiting this new regime of representation.[43]

Once the scope of the birds-eye view narrows to that of a bomber's gun sight, once whole neighbourhoods can be devastated, and their populations all but annihilated, the creation of a rational urban grid through the imposition of zoning regulations does no more than provide a template for the more efficient application of terror from the sky. Moreover once the explosive power and accuracy of the bomb on impact makes total destruction of the target possible, what is left behind to mark the moment of impact may not be a ruin at all but a heap of rubble and dust. The ruin works its magic by evoking the complete edifice of which it was once a part. Its role in the urban fabric is to celebrate the triumphant survival of form over the annihilation of function. But once reduced to formless rubble, the scene of devastation can no longer function as a *lieu de mémoire*. It signifies only the obliteration of all distinction between the human world and inorganic waste, an objective correlate of the state of numb no-thingness which overwhelms the sense of loss in cases of traumatic abreaction to catastrophe.

The blitzing of London, and in particular the docks, was the single most traumatic event on the home front during the Second World War.[44] Not because it was unexpected, or even because of the extent of suffering it caused, but because it upset the official calculus of risk and its geographical coding. The main target of German carpet bombing was not the heavily protected centres of wealth and power in the West End, but the dense concentration of working-class areas adjacent to main industrial arteries of trade and commerce. The engine of the British empire had to be destroyed (*72-81). The Thames Estuary lived up to its reputation for letting the enemy in through the back door by providing a clearly visible fix for German pilots to navigate by on their way in to bomb the East End. Fog however changed sides – no longer a treacherous dissembler of appearances – it provided a comfort blanket protecting a population whose faith in bomb shelters, let alone barrage balloons and anti aircraft, batteries was by June 1941 at an all time low.[45] But 'nature' could not be relied upon either, and when the skies cleared, the fog was replaced by the smoke and flames of the burning docks.

The second Great Fire of London posed as great a challenge to the resolution of the war artist as it did to the fire fighter, the air raid warden and the dockers themselves. And they responded in a remarkably similar way – by carrying on as usual, by denying the impact of the horror, and yet, at the same being awestruck by the scale of the destruction all around them.[46]

As far as English war artists were concerned, this meant trying to assimilate the landscapes of the Blitz to the pictorial conventions of the gothic ruin or the picturesque landscape as a way of asserting a sense of historical continuity with the national cultural heritage.[47] The National Gallery may have been bombed but the aesthetic code of Turner and Constable was indestructible – that was the message. Kenneth Clarke, the doyen of English art critics, indeed described the bombing of the East End as Picturesque. His protégé John Piper painted the remnants of Coventry Cathedral as if it were a replica of Tintern Abbey; his sketches of blitzed East End houses would not look out of place alongside Constable. In contrast, his contemporary Graham Sutherland explores the register of the gothic sublime. His Devastation Series shows the twisted girders of bombed buildings transformed into writhing organic forms as if to celebrate nature's final redemption of the terrible damage inflicted on the world by the hand of man (see illustration).

Writers at the time were also quick to exploit the aesthetic possibilities of the blitz, to manage, impressionistically enough, to convey the shock and the awe evoked by the spectacle of massive incendiary bombing, and also its picturesque qualities. In order to render what might otherwise be unpalatable to the reader into a palette of pleasurable sense impressions, it was enough to paint a word picture after Monet and Whistler, with a nod or two at the penny dreadful. Consider this piece of purple prose penned at the time by Mrs Gwendolyn Cox, viewing the blitzing of the docks from the safe prospect of her flat in Cholmley Gardens Hampstead:

It was a dark and moonless night, volumes of rose pink smoke and many coloured flashes from explosions pierced again and again the blood red cloud which, brooding and angry hung over the city.

Fifty years later David Johnstone in the *City Ablaze* recreates the scene like this:

A rainbow of shades, some almost delicately radiant, transfixed onlookers, deep crimson flecked with scarlet, blue tinted with yellowy green. Vermilion edged with orange and gold – all tossing in the north easterly gale. Each district was floodlit by its own distinct tincture. Everything seemed grotesque and unearthly – the overall effect was an otherworldly nightmare, a carnival night in hell (p12).

He cannot, unfortunately, resist recruiting other people, supposedly there at the time, to bear witness to his prosaic flights of gothic fancy:

To 15 year old Dorothy Haring the whole scene was like a dream, the fire and the smoke, the noise of the fire pumps and anti aircraft guns seemed too loud to be real. More than one fireman staring out at the daylight brilliant wall of flame suffered a sensory breakdown, some were literally hypnotised, others experienced mild hallucinations seeing weird forms and unreal faces in the windblown fires. Even other firemen when seen in that light looked like strange creatures from another world (p14).

Graham Sutherland, Devastation in an East End Street

John Piper, Project for a war memorial 1946

This invocation of the Blitz transforming London into an unreal city grounds its response in the frailty of the human form pitted against the monstrous new war machine. Mervyn Peake, the future author of the great post-war gothic novel *Gormenghast* also reinstates the body as the measure of the city's pain, imagining Blitzed London as a ravaged woman: 'Half masonry, half pain: her head /From which the plaster breaks away' (see above).

Elizabeth Bowen was another novelist who directly transposed her experience of London's bombed out streets into a gothic idiom – that of a city in which the dead come back to life, and whose presence renders the familiar strange. In her novel *Heat of the Day*, she writes:

> ... most of all the dead, from mortuaries, from under the rubble ... the dead made their anonymous presence – not as today's dead but yesterday's living – felt through London. Uncounted they continued to move in shoals through the city day, pervading everything to be seen, heard and felt. The wall between the living and the dead thinned ... (p45).

The mainstream response, however, was to attempt to free London from its haunting by re-inscribing its recent past in an organic, unifying image of community, city, nation and state. This not only runs like a red, white and blue thread through all the wartime propaganda narratives, but extends into the rhetorics of post-war reconstruction.[48] Divested of terror-laden imagery, this appeal to the reparative powers of the urban body politic served to assimilate the traumatic experience of the Blitz to a quasi-natural cycle of urban decay and renewal, which was traditionally seen to be integral to a thriving city. The war ruin is thus integrated into the harmonising compositional structures of the picturesque landscape as just another tumbledown building overgrown with ivy.

This is the burden of Eliot's response to the Blitz in *East Coker*: 'Old stone to new building/old timber to new fires'.[49] In fact his 'raid on the inarticulate' discovers a principle of eternal recurrence in London's wartime travails which owes as much, if not more, to his the interest in the cosmology of Eastern religions as it does to his sense of evolutionary urban history. Nevertheless it was to furnish a decidedly profane principle of hope for post-war reconstruction.

It was a short step from accepting the air raids as part of a higher purpose, to seeing them as a godsend to all those who wanted to rebuild London according to a more rational plan. The view that Hitler's bombers were clearing the East End of its slums more cheaply and efficiently than any municipal bulldozer was first enunciated by MacDonald Hastings in his wartime broadcast. Even if the planners at the LCC who were put in charge of London's post-war reconstruction did not dare to publicly voice such sentiments, it is clear from their memoirs that they privately more or less shared this view. They were inspired by Le Corbusier's vision of the dwelling as functional machine for living in, and of the city as a megastructure, a giant building, linked by pedestrian bridges.

The Abercrombie Report, published in 1948, was the first attempt at a comprehensive master plan for the whole of London. Perhaps its most significant feature was that in abandoning the piecemeal development which had hitherto characterised metropolitan growth it went back to Ebenezer Howard's model of organic community. The result was to turn London into a series of self-contained improvement zones, little islands of urban redevelopment – an unconscious mapping perhaps of the 'stand alone' island story so central to Britain's wartime image of itself (*101).

The clearing of the bomb sites not only deprived the blitz kids of their favourite adventure playgrounds, it put an end, for the moment, to the gothic revival. As Rose Macauley put it, the British have had enough of German 'ruinlust' to last several life times.[50] But not everyone was happy with the result. John Betjeman, the poet laureate of late Victorian Gothic, especially in so far as it had influenced the vernacular architecture of London's middle-class suburbs, saw in the new developments nothing but an act of vandalism which was completing the destruction already wrought on the capital by the Luftwaffe, as in his famously vitriolic poem, which starts with the famous line: 'Come friendly bombs and fall on Slough', the town representing for him the acme of modernist barbarism.

The new public housing estates, both low and high rise, brought the principles of modernist design to bear for the first time on everyday working-class life (*102,135-40) . The application of Parker Morris housing standards ensured that in principle the inhabitants of these new model dwellings could enjoy as much space for relaxed conviviality indoors as out. Although increased privacy was welcomed, the loss of public amenity was not. The architects talked loftily about building 'streets in the sky', which would encourage 'neighbouring across balconies', but it did not happen. In the East End the old street life was missed and the streets were increasingly abandoned to children and the territorial rivalries of male gangs, free from the watchful eyes of their mothers and grandparents.[51] Estates like Robin Hood Gardens, designed by Peter and Alison Smithson, the champions of 'brutalist' modernism, may have won lots of prizes, but for the working-class families who lived in them, the kudos of having your picture in an architectural magazine was no substitute for having your own front door and backyard.

There was little room in the new urban order for the kind of spectral geography which had made 'The Smoke', with its 'holes and corners hidden from the honest and the well to do' (Mayhew) such a popular haunt of the uncanny, not to mention the down and out. The clean air acts killed off the pea soup fogs, leaving the blacked up faces of London's public buildings and monuments to be washed and brushed up by a small reserve army of unemployed construction workers.

Yet, easily as the material signs of damage could be removed, the memory traces left by the blitz, the hidden wounds of war, resisted erasure.[52] The aftermath of trauma might be disavowed, but disavowal always leaves space for re-inscription. One of the more interesting examples of this was the design of the New Towns, and in particular Milton Keynes, modernism's flagship in Britain's post-war reconstruction. Victor Pasmore worked on the project and so organised the town's layout that from the air it looked a bit like one of his

John Claridge, Three steps to heaven

abstract paintings. The very turn to abstraction in British post-war art, in which Pasmore played a leading role, was a more or less conscious rejection of the aesthetics which had hitherto dominated English landscape painting – including much of its wartime art.[53] There was nothing picturesque or sublime about Pasmore's work – it was cool, hard-edged, architectonic – a kind of abstract impressionism in that it sought to give formal precision to the otherwise chaotic sensorium of experience. Interestingly enough, much of his work looked compositionally very like a plan view of the bunkers, emplacements and other military installations which British and German architects, inspired by Bauhaus principles, had built to defend the coasts of their respective countries from invasion during the war. This may be coincidence – a family resemblance between different instances of the modernist aesthetic.[54] But it may also bear the unconscious imprint of the blitz trauma. For here was an art that celebrated the indestructability of pure form, its ability to distil from the detritus of everyday life a transcendent sensibility of an enduring beauty. Translated into urban planning terms, this aesthetic conveyed a definite message which said, in effect, 'we can design and build new towns and cities that can never again be ruined, that are vandal proof and will survive everything that history can throw at them'. The brutalist architecture of the 1960s gave an aesthetic-political gloss to post-war reconstruction, celebrated the power of concrete to withstand the passage of time; the ambition was to build a New Jerusalem that would indeed last for a thousand years.

Yet history did not take long to prove otherwise. In the sterilised purity of its conception, brutalist architecture harboured the seeds of its own undoing. Tower blocks soon became the favoured target of vandals, and concrete surfaces did not fail to provide an urban canvas for the graffiti artist. They were what Robert Smithson has called 'ruins in reverse'.[55] Pasmore's design for a Pavilion in the new town centre of Peterlee was adopted as a hangout by local youth gangs, and quickly became the worse for wear. And in May 1968, as the students in Paris took to the barricades in protest against the attempt to modernise the French educational system, the inhabitants of Ronan Point, a council tower block in the misnamed Clever Road, East London, discovered to their cost that cut-price modernism – modernism without frills as one of its advocates put it – had its own inbuilt but unplanned principle of obsolescence, when a gas explosion caused part of the structure to collapse (*85-6). To cap it all, the construction of the vast downriver Thamesmead estate with its almost total lack of community amenities and indoor 'streets' – which quickly became a haunt of muggers – gave modernism a permanently bad name amongst the general public, as well as offering Stanley Kubrick an ideal location for *Clockwork Orange*, his dystopic movie about feral youth (*120).

These planning disasters also gave the post-industrial ruinologist a whole new a mise en-scène: vandalised tower blocks, abandoned factories, decaying shopping malls, flyovers and underpasses that housed cardboard cities for the homeless – all were pressed into service for a revival of the gothic imagination. Modernism, for so long having treated the city as a ruin waiting to be demolished, now had to contend with the fact that some of its own buildings were ready for the bulldozer. No-one was going to put a preservation order on a 1960s steel and concrete office block.

There were also reactions to post-war modernism amongst architects and town planners.[56] Amongst planners, master plans were out; piecemeal neighbourhood renewal with an emphasis on rehabilitating the urban fabric and community consultation was in. Amongst architects, 'post-modernism' made its appearance.[57] Architects rejected the notion that a building's physical and social function should be directly expressed in its form and fabric, and instead produced designs that quoted playfully from a range of architectural idioms, often drawn from different historical periods and cultures. Sometimes the results were more than somewhat kitsch, as in Terry Farrell's or Will Alsop's work, but for many people it was a welcome relief from the brutalist aesthetic of strict modernism (*152-3).

However the main professional reaction was to argue that the earlier version of modernism had failed because it lost its nerve. In the 1980s the advent of new construction technologies meant that it was possible to treat form and function as independent variables. Architecture could once more become sculptured space and a source of aesthetic delight, as well as meeting all the usual functional requirements.

Hypermodernism emerged in the 1990s as a worldwide response amongst architects and planners to the impact of globalisation on cities.[58] In a period when capitalism was enjoying an unprecedented period of expansion and profitability, there was a large international demand for prestige office blocks and corporate HQs, trade exhibition centres, tourist hotels, entertainment complexes and luxury apartments, all requiring a location in or near the city centre. In addition, thanks to capitalism's cultural turn, concert halls, museums, theatres, opera houses and art centres came increasingly to be regarded as an essential aspect of urban regeneration.[59] In response to this demand, a new wave of 'starchitects' emerged who were able to produce spectacular iconic buildings, buildings that dominated the skyline as well as their immediate surroundings.[60] Under their shadow, public place making became less about creating spaces where people could congregate and feel at home, and more to do with constructing a stage from which the building itself 'performs' to a remote global audience. These structures are the twenty-first century equivalent of the Victorian gothic revival – cathedrals made of glass and steel glorifying the power and/or the taste of their clients (*132-3). Yet in reaching for a new form of the sublime – and some of these new structures are truly awesome – they also attract the attention of the gothic imagination, if not the terrorist bomber. It is hard, from this standpoint, to look at Renzo Piano's Shard (*113), now so dominant a presence in the Central London skyscape and yet so fragile in silhouette, and not imagine it one day falling down across the line of its own shadow, a sublime piece of architecture brought to subliminal ruin by the hubris of its conception.

Hyper-modernism is a turbo-charged form of modernity which has wrenched free from the ideological programme of socialist renewal and any connection with working-class aspiration.[61] Whereas the modernists conceived of the city as a huge piece of architecture to house the urban masses, the hypermodernist wants to reverse the design process and put the whole city into a giant building, incorporating all its functions – economic, social, cultural, political – in a single mega-structure. The result is often a kind of architectural mash-up. Rem Koolhaas, an architect (*105-6) who many regard as one of its chief exponents, describes it thus:

> ... orphaned particles in search of a framework or pattern. All materialization is provisional: cutting, bending, tearing, coating: construction has acquired a new softness, like tailoring ... The joint is no longer a problem, an intellectual issue: transitional moments are defined by stapling and taping, wrinkly brown bands barely maintain the illusion of an unbroken surface; verbs unknown and unthinkable in architectural history – clamp, stick, fold, dump, glue, shoot, double, fuse – have become indispensable.

Koolhaas subsequently became disillusioned with this programme, which he described as creating 'junkspace':

> A fuzzy empire of blur, it fuses public and private, straight and bent, bloated and starved, high and low, to offer a seamless patchwork of the permanently disjointed. Seemingly an apotheosis, spatially grandiose, the effect of its richness is a terminal hollowness, a vicious parody that systematically erodes the credibility of architecture, possibly for ever.[62]

The excesses of hypermodernism have led some cultural critics to call for a return to the more sober principles of post-war modernism with its no frills architecture design to provide affordable public housing. As Will Self presciently pointed out, much of this re-evaluation is animated by a nostalgia for a political world we have lost, and is based on impressionistic surveys, whistle-stop tours through the ruins with no time for what residents themselves think and feel.[63] As Tony Parker showed in his painstaking ethnography of one large tower block council estate built in the 1960s, modernist architecture encourages people to withdraw from public space and cocoon themselves in private utopias built around hobbies and indoor pursuits.[64] Behind the monolithic facade of public housing he discovered a version of the hothouse society in which the most exotic blooms were flourishing; literally so in the case of one couple who had turned their front room into a greenhouse in which they were cultivating marijuana plants. The popular gothic imagination, whether fuelled by drugs or not, continues to subvert the modernist project. But it does not offer a viable alternative politics of space.

Today tower blocks may provide rooms with a view for young mobile professionals, niches for do it yourself enthusiasts, or haunted landscapes for connoisseurs of the urban uncanny, but for young children and the elderly, for the poor and those with mobility problems, their scale and lack of public amenity remain as oppressive as ever. When the Robin Hood Gardens estate failed to get listed as a historical building in 2007, and was threatened with demolition instead, starchitects like Zaha Hadid and Richard Rogers leapt to its defence, lauding it as one of the finest examples of post-war modernist architecture in Europe, but the residents wanted the building refurbished, or failing that, knocked down.

Meanwhile, at street level, the impact of globalisation has been registered in the urban fabric in quite another way, in the changing demographics of East London's communities, in new configurations of class and ethnicity that have profoundly changed its internal landscape, and its relation to the metropolis. In the 1980s, answering the call of Mrs Thatcher's 'property-owning democracy', East Enders moved to the outer suburbs or beyond in search of homes they could call their own, streets where the kids could play out safely, gardens and allotments they could cultivate, and fences that could be mended and neighboured over – in a word the very kind of environment that the modernists despised and had sought to replace with their version of urbanism for the masses. At the same time the rapid de-industrialisation of what was left of East London's traditional economy opened up new opportunities for architects, planners, property developers and entrepreneurs to build their own version of the New Jerusalem, a promised land to be occupied by the nouveau riche of the global knowledge economy. In the next chapter we shall look at how East Enders themselves have responded to the challenges posed by these changes.

*Peter Dunn and Loraine Leeson, Not a rhetorical question:
docklands campaign poster 1982–5*

2. Island Stories:
dreams and nightmares in a Docklands community

The docks and their immediate hinterlands were a central reference point for the iconography described in the last chapter. They were both a symbol of modernity and of its absence. Dockers formed an intensely local, almost closed community, which nevertheless controlled a key artery of global commerce; they were a potent force in the organised labour movement and the rise of industrial unionism but an equally significant presence in the East End's hidden economy which 'redistributed' goods from dockside to hearthside across the city; at once the backbone of the nation and a race apart, patriotic Cockney and congenital crook, heroic boxer and sexual rough trade, the figure of the docker came to focus all the ambivalent identifications which both bourgeois and bohemian entertained towards the East End and its diversely dangerous classes.[1]

The closure of the docks in the 1970s was not the end of the story. Until the coming of the Olympics to Stratford, Docklands, and in particular the Isle of Dogs, was the pivot of London's eastwards turn, the fulcrum of its social regeneration, and – according to your point of view – either the hinge or the hiatus between the old and new economies.[2] The commercial redevelopment of the area has in fact reproduced the spatial segregation of the former enclosed docks. Whereas the docks were once surrounded by a peripheral wall built for security, a six-lane highway and the cluster of corporate buildings around Canary Wharf has now effectively cut the site off from working-class Poplar to the north. It is a man-made peninsular, connected to mainland London by two swing bridges, and when these are disabled it literally becomes an island. But its insularities have not been confined to, or solely determined by, this fact.

If the dockers and their families who have lived there for generations formed such a close-knit community, where the primacy of kith and kin was strongly embedded in a shared pride of place, then it was because this was a way of asserting a form of symbolic ownership and control that was, in material terms, largely denied them.[3] Not only was dock work casualised, but the demand for their labour depended on fluctuations in world trade. Nevertheless, for the 'Islanders', as they called themselves, growing up working-class meant an apprenticeship to an inheritance entailed in the transmission of manual trade skill in the case of boys, or domestic skills in the case of girls, skills that were an enduring legacy passed from generation to generation. They may have been poor but they were rich in what sociologists like to call 'social capital'.[4]

The struggle to keep the London docks open is described vividly by Colin Ross, whose family had worked there for three generations:

> People don't realise the battles we had in our struggle to keep the docks open. We saw that containerisation was coming and we realised it was going to mash the East End to bits. There were 27,000 regulated dock workers, and for every one of them another two workers dependent on the docks. 100,000 people relied on the docks for a living. We negotiated with the Port of London Authority and they said, 'It's no good standing in the way of progress.' But what's the good of progress if it doesn't benefit everyone? Our argument was – You have the docks in place and the rail links and the workforce, why can't containerisation be done in the docks? Gradually, they weakened our cause with increased offers of severance pay and then, before we knew it, the asset strippers moved into the Royal London Docks – only they called them Venture Capitalists – they bought up the docks, closed them down and sold them as flats at half a million pounds each.[5]

The closure of the docks was a catastrophe for this community. Even a decade later it was not uncommon to see ex-dockers, now in middle age, staring out wistfully into the river, no doubt remembering a time when it was crowded with ships from the four corners of the world (*51-9;121/2) .

In her poetic history of the river, Lavinia Greenlaw vividly captures this moment of disjuncture:

> No ships, no work. The industry found itself
> caught in a net of passing time,
> watching mile after mile of dockland fill
> with silence and absence. Land changed hands
> in an estate agent's office, short lease premises
> with 'Upstream' and 'Downstream' carved above the doors.[6]

The closure coincided with the advent of a large new immigrant population from the Indian subcontinent, and also of Vietnamese-Chinese refugees. This dramatic transformation was accompanied by another. The building of a whole new business and commercial quarter on the site of the old West India docks meant that for the first time in the area's history it became both workplace and home to an affluent professional class.

In the 1980s the iconographies of 'Essex Man' and 'Essex Girl' came to symbolise the political project of Thatcherism, the enterprise culture and the advent of the 'home owning democracy'.[7] In particular, the dismantling of solidarities associated with the culture of manual labourism and its replacement by a more individualistic, mobile and suburbanised life style was the subject of much public comment.[8] Alongside this, a picture of an immobilised residuum or underclass was built up. Whether seen as refugees from globalisation at home and abroad, or as denizens of an ever-expanding hidden economy, all who failed to make the transition to 'post-modern times' found themselves lumped together and symbolically relocated into a slum version of the post-industrial 'edge city', where they furnished raw material for the gothic imaginations of novelists and journalists writing about 'Cockney Siberia', or 'Estuary Ethnics'.[9]

In the popular media, the TV soap *EastEnders* attempted a sentimental retrieval of the urban melting-pot thesis, albeit one which bore little relation to the lived realities of growing up in East London; whilst the songs of Ian Dury explored a less nostalgic style of reinventing East-Ender identities as they moved eastwards into the badlands of Romford, Billericay and Southend on Sea.[10]

As Ted Johns, the Dockland community's most dynamic and progressive leader, commented to us:

> There's been a lot of romanticising of the East End by people who never lived there, or who went on to became rich and famous and write all these books about their wonderful East End childhoods. They show it as an area full of colourful Cockneys, or full of dead beats and villains. It's all nonsense. But you also get a certain amount of romanticising from the inside. Take the villains like the Krays, who are right vicious bastards but who are sometimes treated like local heroes.[11]

Knowing the East End outside in

Since the 1980s, these discourses and the interventions inspired by them have been the object of an increasingly sophisticated re-reading by academics inspired by Marxist, post-structuralist and feminist critiques. The slum novel, urban ethnography and the popular press have all been grist to the mill of these various deconstructions; such texts have provided rich pickings for inquirers into the representations of class, gender and race that have dwelt in the Victorian city.[12]

In some recent accounts there has been a tendency to regard these outsider stories as pure hallucinations. The 'East End' of Besant and Gissing, Jack London and W.T. Snead, not to mention De Quincey and Oscar Wilde, is understood as a pure figment of the fevered bourgeois imagination; even the sociological investigations of Mayhew and Booth, it is argued, had little real bearing or impact on the actual inhabitants of East London.

Certainly Thomas De Quincey's description of East End street markets, where he sees the 'swarming masses of Asia' in the 'myriad of faces in the urban crowd', seems to owe more to opium-induced paranoia whipping up aristocratic terror of the working class than to any social observation![13] And Charles Booth's social survey of East London owed as much to his passionate concern about the underclass as his desire to construct a grid of scientific observation.[14] But to read the Victorian literature as simply a projection of bourgeois anxiety about 'the Other' is to be carried away by its own rather calculating rhetoric. It would perhaps be more precise to say that the urban explorers were horrified to discover the open drains and middens, the slum tenements with no water, heating or light, the physical evidence of lives so different from their own, and the very evident signs of distress which accompanied these conditions; but this phenomenology of poverty also excited their sociological imagination about its causes and consequences in a way which provided, in some cases, a space for the expression of more florid phantasies about the state of the body politic.

The hallucination model has the unacknowledged pay-off that it leaves the lives of real East Enders intact, if invisible, outside its written representation. East End cultures can therefore remain unpolluted by the perverse imaginations of the civilising missionaries, as resistant to the oppressive disciplines of capital as they are to the corrupting delights of cosmopolitan modernity. The 'inside story' continues to rule OK as an index of a purely proletarian authenticity. It follows that if there are 'impurities' – if, for example there is a pronounced local history of racism – then it has to be explained by factors which are purely intrinsic to the East End itself; we must be dealing with a natural home-grown peculiarity of this particular section of the English working class.

This is the view advanced by Charles Husbands in his seminal study of East End racism.[15] His work takes in a broad sweep of local racisms: from the popular anti-semitism which helped pioneer the Aliens Act of 1905 (Britain's first official immigration controls), through the Mosleyite agitations of the interwar years to the Dockers' support for Powell's Rivers of Blood speech in 1968, and the mounting harassment of the Bangladeshi community during the 1980s. He argues that underlying and linking all these instances is a common, and generationally transmitted, culture of racism, which stems from the persistence of an ethnically homogeneous and inbred working-class community, centred originally in Hoxton and Bethnal Green and subsequently diffused to other areas through white flight. He describes this community as exhibiting:

A profoundly materialistic culture, which implies a very limited and confused perception of social structure, and a corresponding readiness to apportion blame in inappropriate directions. Its political sophistication has been similarly limited; it was long resistant to sustained mobilisation by the left, and even in its more recent voting has had a narrowly pragmatic and poorly articulated ideological basis. A continual readiness to engage in right wing racial exclusionism suggests the persistence of a 'rootless volatility' which was also a feature of working class politics in 19th century.[16]

This characterisation seems to amalgamate Mayhew's model of 'wandering tribes' with a quasi-Marxist view of the 'lumpenproletariat' and its false consciousness. East End racism is put down to the persistence of an archaic, pre-modern and irrational streak in its inhabitants, consequent upon their 'inbreeding'.

There is however an alternative reading, which completely reverses the terms of Husbands's argument. It is suggested that, far from failing, the civilising mission was all too successful. From the 1880s onwards the mass of East Enders were transformed, slowly and unevenly, from dangerous revolutionaries or denizens of the underworld into cheerful patriotic Cockneys; this was achieved through the combined and cumulative influence of the labour movement, the church, state education, better housing and sanitation, and strategies of self improvement provided by settlements, clubs and missions. Even the music hall played its part. The emergence of a conservative, inward-looking and above all respectable culture of labourism in Docklands could be seen to epitomise a wider process in the remaking of the English working class in and through the late Victorian culture of imperialism.[17]

Race is again a key motif in this story, but now it is seen as something injected from outside, as part of the transition to modernity. The emergence of local support for little-Englander nationalism, or white supremacism, in the post-1945 period is put down to the fact that East Enders have internalised the aspirations for social mobility prescribed by Labour Party meritocrats, whilst being systematically deprived of the means to achieve these ambitions and have then made newcomers the scapegoat for their disappointment. According to this line of argument, these once-upon-a-time immigrants have learnt only too well how to defend themselves against the discrepancy between the official success story and the actual outcome of their lives by drawing a line under their own feet. By inventing a white ethnicity which excludes Asians and black people and blames them for a general failure of working-class expectations, they manage to sustain a 'one-up' position, at least in their own eyes. The fact that the indigenous working class may also be in competition with immigrants for scarce resources like housing and jobs provides an economic rationale for this 'false consciousness'.[18]

Underpinning these different theoretical perspectives is a split representation of the urban scene. For East London is also a tale of two cities. In the first case it is portrayed as a drab, soulless, single class monoculture. The most famous exponent of this view is Jack London. In *People of the Abyss* he writes:

> No more dreary spectacle can be found on this earth than the whole of the 'awful east' with its Whitechapel, Hoxton, Spitalfields, Bethnal Green and Wapping to the East India Docks. The colour of life is grey and drab. Everything is helpless, hopeless, unrelieved and dirty. Here lives a population as dull and unimaginative as its long grey miles of dingy brick.[19]

A somewhat similar, if less dramatic picture was painted by the sociologist Peter Willmott nearly seventy years later in his study of post-war Dagenham. As a general rule the further east you go the drabber the portrait becomes. In more recent reporting about the East End by the liberal press, this imagery was drawn upon to contrast the Isle of Dogs invidiously with Whitechapel, now portrayed as a vibrant multicultural society, as in this account from the *Independent*:

> Brick Lane perhaps offers one model of what the East End might become. One of the all-night bagel shops has a poster for a Gujarati dance company; the other has a poster asking for information about Quaddus Ali's stabbing. Through these shops move Bengalis, artists (the East End, and this part in particular, is home to the largest group of artists outside New York), whites, blacks, City executives and tourists, mingling happily over their smoked salmon and cream cheese rolls. But Brick Lane is different from the rest of the East End, and fashionable in its exoticism.[20]

This trendy hybridity – the post-modern equivalent of the compact between bohemian and bourgeois perceptions of the late Victorian city – is thus set up as constituting an essentially anti-racist environment. The *Guardian* extolled its virtues in the following terms:

> Today Brick Lane exudes the confidence of a community that no longer cowers in the face of hostility. Its marriage of Asian and English customs is unabashed and potent. Smells of coriander, cardamon and incense merge with that of steak and chips. On one corner stands a Fried Chicken Store marked Al-Halal. Brick Lane is as much of an oasis as the Isle of Dogs, with its own mores and loyalties. Yet, unlike the Island, its doors are not closed to outsiders. It has become a popular residence for successful artists like Gilbert and George, whose presence in Fournier Street, an adjoining terrace of ramshackle Georgian properties, has earned it the title of London's new Millionaires' Row.[21]

So here the East End is portrayed as the natural habitat of a cosmopolitan elite *and* a hive of popular multi-culturalism, the former providing the money to unslum the neighbourhood and the latter the 'local colour' that attracts them to the area. It is this model which the 2012 bidders drew upon in their imagineering of East London as a host for the games.

Inventing traditions of community: from the inside out

Given the massive burden of representation which the East End and its inhabitants have had to carry, how far have these images and narratives been absorbed, or invested with other meanings, or otherwise exploited, so that political or cultural capital can be made out of them by East Enders themselves?

One response is to be found in certain post-war romanticisations of the old East End in the autobiographies of professional East Enders like Dan Farson, Ralf Finn, Dolly Scannell, Gilda O'Neill and a host of others.[22] The picture of the slums as redeemed by warm, close-knit family and neighbourhood life, the cosy Cockney village, with its friendly pubs and markets spiced with a bit of

John Claridge, After horse power: Canning Town 1956

safe ethnicity, and naughty but nice sex, communities united against adversity, but not usually against class adversaries or ethnic minorities, the heroic stories of self help, self sacrifice and self improvement, all of this seems not only to have touched a chord amongst the incoming yuppies, but amongst working-class people as well. The defence of traditional East End values of solidarity and tolerance is as common a refrain in left-wing accounts of the local working-class culture as mourning for their passing is in the life stories of the older generation who grew up in the area in the 1930s and 1940s.[23]

What is notable about this genre is its resolute determination to conform to a 'triumph over adversity' school-of-life story-telling, whether in the traditional rag trade to riches story or – in more contemporary versions – in a focus inspired by identity politics on personal struggles to overcome various kinds of disability or discrimination.[24] Gilda O'Neill's *My East End*, for example, combines oral testimony with archival research to create a memoryscape in which the sense of belonging to a working-class community and its pride of place over-rides all differences of gender, ethnicity and status, even though these lines of distinction are so clearly etched in the patterns of everyday life. In her sequel, *Our Street*, centred on East Enders' reminiscences of the second world war, she is concerned to restate the Cockneyfied 'myth of the blitz', and East Enders once more become the sturdy backbone of an island race whose indomitable community spirit proved stronger than the might of the Luftwaffe.[25]

It is not that these stories do not convey, often vividly, the human solidarities engendered by difficult circumstances, but that, perhaps in unconscious reaction against the gothic imagination of their lives by the literati, these insider accounts of life on the 'wrong' side of the tracks censor the tropes of its 'other scene', figures which, as we will see, do in fact pervade the imaginative story worlds of young East Enders. Nothing of this is allowed to leak into these stories of resilience and fortitude, ambition and the courageous struggle to overcome disadvantage. In its place there is only a profound nostalgia for a world that has been lost due to the area's regeneration and the onset of gentrification.

Easy though it is to write off such narratives as simply sentimental idealisations owing their origin and power to the workings of collective false memory, it is important to recognise that this sense of imagined community also draws on material structures of life and labour that have been dismantled by the malign confluence of post-fordism and Thatcherism, but which are being remembered selectively to dramatise feelings of loss.[26] The histories of Jewish East End radicalism, or that peculiar fusion of trade union militancy and municipal socialism under the leadership of George Lansbury that was known as 'Poplarism', remained sedimented in a memoryscape that was not entirely erased, and in the case of someone like Ted Johns remained part of a political vocabulary that could still inspire.[27]

At the same time there were other, more insular, oral traditions to be drawn upon and it is these which were the focus of the research which is going to be reported here.[28]

When Elisabeth Riley moved onto 'The Island' in 1948, she was allocated a council house which locals had decreed as belonging to a neighbour's daughter who was an 'Island' native. She describes the reaction of her neighbours:

> I used to go into shops and people would be talking. They'd stop as I walked in and wait until I left. They couldn't understand us having the house and Mrs Bailey's daughter not getting it because she was an Islander. My two kids were the only ones in the neighbourhood not invited to the Coronation street party.[29]

This attitude extended to kith and kin, and in a way that could challenge aspects of working-class patriarchy, as in this story by a local woman about what happened when she 'married out':

> The other Islanders treated Jim alright, although he didn't really feel one of them at first. He was treated all right but not really accepted. It took a long time for him to be accepted. He was always someone that married Nellie Kohler. When he went round to Farmer's shop, Frank Farmer said 'Hallo Jimmy Kohler what do you want?' 'My name's not Kohler it's Prist', said Jim. We used to give all the boys the girl's name when they got married if they came from outside the Island (Joan Kohler).

It was not only endogamy and matrilocalism that ruled OK. Male territorialism was also very much in place, and reinforced a closed sense of community. Another Islander recalls:

There were often fights when our own gang turned on those from neighbouring streets and told them to get back to where they belonged. An Englishman's home may be his castle but the Cockney's street was his kingdom and not lightly trampled on by outsiders. Even we small girls felt this bristling pride of belonging (Elsie Rankin).

This highly territorialised sense of place informed a larger geography:

Southend was only thirty miles away from where we lived but it was like going to an outpost of Empire for us. We knew the natives were hostile but there was always enough of us so we didn't really have to mix with them. I preferred hop picking in Kent to Southend. The natives were just as hostile but there were less of them (Marge Kennet).

Quite early on in the interview we asked our informants whether they identified with being an East Ender, or an Islander, or some other description, and what they associated with these terms. Informants were virtually unanimous in associating the term Islander exclusively with white people living on the Isle of Dogs. The older generation of whites were proud to call themselves Islanders; they associated it with long-term residence in the area and keeping up traditional values. They also thought that Islanders were the true East Enders, a term which for most of them was also synonymous with Cockney. This was an equation which the under-25s rejected almost completely. Although quite a few of them strongly identified with being Islanders, they used the term simply as a racial synonym – a condensed statement of whiteness. In fact some of them took great pains to uncouple or dissociate the term Islander from that of East Ender or Cockney. These latter terms had in their eyes been appropriated by young Bangladeshis and hence had become racially contaminated or hybridised. That was a cue for a few of their peers to adopt these very descriptors in order to take their distance from the racist connotations of Islander. So whereas for their parents and grandparents to proclaim oneself a Cockney was to sign up to a little Englander position, for some of their children it was the nearest thing they could get to black 'attitude' – it meant to be cool, street wise, and in your face.

Those who preferred 'Islander' to 'East Ender' were not noticeably more tied to the immediate area; they travelled to other parts of East London and further abroad just as much or as little as those of the same age, gender and status who saw themselves first and foremost as East Enders. It was a question of cultural not physical geography, imagined not real community. This point was underlined by a major difference in the way our white informants talked about the Isle of Dogs. There were those who were primarily concerned to construct an insider account of what had happened to the area, and for whom Islander or East Ender meant not just a social description of a certain kind of people or place, but a deeply-felt source of autobiographical anchorage and personal identity. As we might expect, this orientation was most frequently found amongst the older, grandparent and parent generation, who had grown up in the area or lived most of their lives there; there were, however, a significant number of young people and newcomers who adopted a similar stance. They were often defensive about the area's public reputation, but dismissed such reports, especially those emanating from the national press or TV, as being ill-informed and prejudiced.

The second orientation was much more concerned with how outsiders saw the area, and the kinds of stories generated by outside sources which might give a wrong or bad impression to people who did not know it. From this perspective, East Ender or Islander were positional rather than personal terms of identification: they placed people in a wider social structure, and ascribed certain moral characteristics to them. For most of this group the terms also projected a largely negative image to the outside world, for example as being a yuppie area, or a hotbed of racial violence, or being full of yobs. A few dissociated themselves from the Islander/East Ender label altogether for that reason. Others still held to these localisations, but dealt with possible cognitive dissonance by adopting a strategy of narrative impression management – telling stories to us which would show up the area in a good light and hence convince us, as outsiders, that most of the media reports were exaggerated and untrue. For example they would tell us anecdotes designed to reassure us that there was little or no racist feeling amongst whites, citing examples of their own good neighbourliness, whilst at the same time portraying the Bangladeshis as ungrateful or unresponsive to these overtures, keeping themselves to themselves, and gaining unfair advantage in housing.

On the whole young people (under 25) were more highly sensitised to the area's public image and reputation than their elders, and they were correspondingly more likely to take these 'outside-in' stories directly into account in constructing their own versions. But there was one significant exception. Those with the most pronounced and unambiguous racist views were invariably committed to the insider view, and dismissed media and indeed all other accounts as examples of wilful prejudice on the part of ignorant outsiders.

Our Bangladeshi informants had a quite different set of orientations. Not surprisingly none of them identified with being Islanders; for most it held negative connotations, of being not only white but racist. Length of residence in the area was not seen by them as an enabling criterion. Some of the younger Bengalis felt more positive about the 'East Ender' label, which for them was a wider, more socially inclusive, term. Two were quite insistent that they were Cockneys – a term which they associated with being smart and streetwise. For young Bangladeshis who claimed these terms (and there were still a significant number who did not), East Ender and Cockney were quite compatible with being black, Asian, Bengali, Muslim, British, Silheti, or any combination of these terms. There was considerable variation in which of these descriptions were felt to be most self-defining. There were some quite marked generational differences, with the under 25s who had been born and/or grown up in the area being more likely to twin a local (i.e. East Ender) identity with a global one (i.e. Muslim), whereas their parents were less likely to use local descriptors and to prefer British and Asian as general terms of self reference. Black was not a popular category amongst the Bengali sample of any age, nor was it used by the whites to refer to them.[30]

Their accounts varied chiefly in the extent to which they explained the racism they or their children suffered in terms of the peculiarities of the Isle of Dogs or the East End, or how far they saw it as a local instance of a wider phenomenon affecting the whole of British society. On the whole the older generation took a more particularistic view, and felt that in other areas of London, or the country as a whole, things were not nearly so bad for Asian people. Their children tended to see racism as something more structural or inherent, although many also thought there were important exceptions to this rule.

The most obvious case where the particularisms of place took on a wider, media-generated resonance, in a way that was hard for 'locals' to ignore was, of course, TV's *EastEnders*. Here is the ultimate outside-in story, whose authenticity relies on its claim to portray vernacular cultures which in all their diversity remain 'home grown'. A large number (60 per cent) of the older Bangladeshis watched the programme on a regular basis, a much higher percentage than among the whites. One interesting reason for this, put to us by one of our informants, was that the programme showed that East End people could get along together, and that they weren't all racists or hooligans. If only the real East End were as good as it was shown on TV! It was the perceived 'utopianism' of the soap's successful multiculture which appealed to them.

Their children took the opposite view. They were much more critical of what they saw as the programme's patronising, tokenistic or stereotypical portrayal of ethnic minorities. They also thought that the programme ignored or downplayed the extent of racial tension, and, unlike their parents, were critical of its lack of realism on this score. Their white counterparts also criticised the programme, but on grounds of class stereotyping rather than race. 'It shows us all up as being thick, spending all our time in the pub, having rows, and working in street markets' was the gist of one frequent complaint.

Fictive kinships

We decided in a second phase of the research to look at how narratives were organised in the case of one particular group. We interviewed a small sample of white residents who supported a local campaign to promote the rights of the indigenous Islander over and against the claims of the Bangladeshi community. This campaign was entirely composed and led by self identified Islanders. It rejected overtures from the racialist organisations and was never affiliated to any political party, though it did for a time have the support of a local Liberal Democrat councillor. In what follows we have concentrated on the views of the older, parent and grandparent generations, rather than the voice of youth.

A refrain running through all these accounts was the decline in traditional or 'old' East End values associated with certain moral qualities of community. This old East End was always contrasted unfavourably with the new. Here is one very typical comment:

It used to be a nice place. I mean it wasn't very well known, but it was a warm and friendly place, where people looked out for each other and stuck together through thick and thin. If you said you came from the Isle of Dogs they wanted to know where it was. Other people thought it was a terrible rough sort of place, but now it's regarded as one of the best places, everyone knows about it because of Canary Wharf and you get all these notices 'welcome to the Isle of Dogs'. But I don't like it. We've had enough. Our houses have all been made dirty with the lorries coming by and all the building work. And people have kind of shrunk into their shells (John Coaker).

Public ignorance or bad impressions of the area, containing perhaps an echo of the 'drab wasteland' theme, is contrasted with its rich inner life, available only to those who live there. There is a double inversion at work here – a working-class area which used to be regarded as rubbish by outsiders, but which was prized by those who lived there, is now seen to have been transformed into a 'high-class' area for yuppies but ruined for 'the real insider'.

In the process the more negative aspects of the 'old East End' are glossed over, as in this comment, which contrasts the good old days of the Krays with the present state of local crime:

… we've always had villains on the Island. But the attitude was – don't shit on your own doorstep. So it was safe to leave your door open or the window open. But as the years have gone by the old Island people have moved off and it's got worse, and they've put in the new housing, especially where the Yuppies are, and people think if you live on the Island you must be well off and have something to take. So you don't feel safe going out as you used to. In the old days down our way if you saw someone who wasn't supposed to be there you'd ask them what they was doing. But now there's so many strangers in the area, people coming from outside, you don't know who they are (Harry Knoakes).

So even the villains observe local protocols of public propriety, and indeed police them. The general point being argued here is a Durkheimian one, that internal moral regulation exercised informally through social networks has given way to a state of anomie caused by rapid social change. The idea that what planners see as economic regeneration has in fact resulted in moral degeneration is a common refrain in many of the Islanders' interviews and part of a larger story about urban decline and social decay.

The Old East End is invested with an exclusive aura of cultural authenticity, which, by definition, newer habitats – and newer inhabitants – cannot possess. To some Islanders the very notion of 'Docklands' was a newfangled and suspect bit of urban imagineering. As Ted Johns put it:

Docklands is an industrial term, and increasingly it's an advertising term, used as a marketing device by the LDDC. There is no such place as Docklands. I mean people identify Docklands as being where they are. Beckton is not Docklands you know, 'cos Beckton is a very different sort of place from the Island. The term just doesn't recognise that Wapping, the Isle of Dogs, Surrey Docks, Shadwell, these are all distinct areas with their own histories and identities.

All white down our way

These accounts continually evoked the power of collective memory to landscape the area with personal meanings.[31] It was this sense of immanent belonging which allowed these storytellers to symbolically own the Island and construct it as the locus of a fixed, almost biological sense of identity.

> I'm an Islander and proud of it. It's in your blood. We were born here, we've grown up together, we all help each other, and we stick together. I mean you go to some places and no one wants to talk to you but if you're an Islander you know you're an Islander (Paul Desmond).

In the next quote, the sense of belonging to a distinctive historical generation, rooted in local custom and circumstance, furnishes what might be called a genealogy of place – the sense that one's social destiny is almost congenitally linked to one's place of birth and early life. This sense of identity could be extended to the East End as a whole:

> I think that Islanders have a sense of identity, a bit like being working-class – you identify with a particular group and a particular place – it's seen as a negative term by other people, but not by us. And with East End, again there is a certain affinity. I can't quite define it but it's there. It has something to do with the shared experience of being brought up during the Blitz and living through all the changes in the East End (Mary Thomas).

In many cases this kind of genealogy supported a nostalgic myth of origin, to the effect that once upon a time, in some golden age, Islanders and/or East Enders were one big family, where everyone was on good terms with their neighbours, and lived happily ever afterwards. But this myth is only mobilised in order to be counterposed to another in which this urban village idyll is shattered by the invasion of The Others – who are variously referred to as 'the immigrants', the 'ethnics', or the 'coloureds'.

Here is a typical statement in this vein:

> Our street is very friendly, and they're good neighbours, and they'll always help you out, but a lot of the atmosphere has gone, a lot of it is dog–eats–dog, which doesn't make for friendly relationships. They're moving a lot of immigrants into the Island, which, though I've got nothing against them, they're moving so many it's causing problems (Harriett Jones).

In these and many similar accounts we are presented with an image of an 'island paradise', a state of perfect self-contained social harmony which has been suddenly invaded and brutally destroyed by aliens. This island exists in people's minds as occupying a homogeneous time and space: it is a place where the population is supposed to reproduce itself identically from generation to generation, and where its cultures of kinship and community have somehow survived the closure of the docks:[32]

> Our family have been living around here since well before the war. We've seen a lot of changes, not all of them for the better, but we survived them. We've had our ups and downs like any family, the docks going, but we've pulled through. What has always kept us going is the desire to get the best for our kids, and to make sure as far as we can that this is a good area for them to grow up in (Paula Drake).

The family is central to this version of local history and geography – it binds the transmission of values and the patrimonies of place into a fixed sense of home.

An ex-docker remembers:

> Those members of my family who have moved away still come back as often as they can to re-establish their roots. Home is where the heart is, and my heart is here on the Island. If I could imagine myself at home anywhere I'd be sitting in an easy chair, writing or reading, doing some paper work, and I'd be gazing out over the river. I wouldn't live anywhere else. I'm happy here. This is where my home is. This is where all my activities are and I'll fight my corner here (John McVitie).

In so far as family provided a model and a metaphor for all other kinds of social relationships, it could be deployed to naturalise practices of exclusion which might otherwise look like all too familiar examples of discrimination.

> Every family has its black sheep, the odd ones out, who don't really belong; you don't get on with them, so, well, so you try to avoid, or keep them at arms length. Well it's like that with some of the ethnics – we don't tend to mix with them (Jane Dobey).

This notion of kinship, and of everyone sticking up for their own kind, allowed Islanders to both celebrate their own insularities and ignore their effect in freezing out 'the ethnics'. How is this for a version of the open society:

> In the old days, before the ethnics came, this used to be a really friendly place. People used to leave their doors open, anyone was welcome to drop in for a cup of tea and a chat, you wouldn't think twice about it. But since they came, with all the problems, vandalism, mugging, and all that they brought, people are afraid to go out and you certainly wouldn't leave your door open nowadays. It's a great shame (Mary Scott).

This open doors policy only applied to those who were regarded as indigenous, not to 'immigrants'. Open doors in this context is a misnomer, since it is based on a strategy of social closure within restricted networks of family and friends. In its racialised form, as here, it becomes a device for blaming the 'ethnics' for the very exclusions from which they suffer. More than that, they are accused of turning the Islanders 'natural open mindedness' into fearful prejudice.

The fact that the Island was regarded as a haven of 'old East End values' meant that any change tended to be seen as a catastrophic advent of the new. Ted Johns recalled:

> What really saddens me is the breakdown in warmth in the old social structure. The slums have gone and good riddance to them, but so has the positive sense of solidarity. In its place you've got racism. I don't go to Bow very much now, because the area is so changed. I'm a stranger in my own land in that sense.

The idea that immigrants are making the indigenous strangers, or second-class citizens, in their own land was another common refrain. There was a continual search for some little bit of the Island which had somehow remained pure and uncontaminated by the undesirable changes associated with the Bangladeshi presence. Mostly this fantasy was centred on Cubitt Town:

> I know the area and I've always lived round here. I used to know everybody on the Island when I was on a milk round during the war but it's altered tremendously. This part of the Island around Cubitt Town is the only part that's not really altered (George Docherty).

Historically, Cubitt Town was where the stevedores, the higher-paid skilled dock workers, and their families lived, most of them Irish Catholics. Millwall, in contrast, was more industrialised, more 'protestant' and regarded as an altogether rougher area:[33]

> The two sides of the island were quite different and where anyone talked about Cubitt Town to people living here in this part of the Island, they were as remote as talking about people in Hackney. The Cubitt Town people looked upon the people of Millwall as belonging to another world. We didn't know much about Cubitt Town ... (Joan Mackay).

That distinction was reworked so that Cubitt Town was now regarded as the core of the Islanders' community. The distinction, however, was no longer one of religion or socio-economic status but of race.[34] Cubitt Town is seen as a white area – an area which is safe for whites.

We asked our informants to mark the areas which they felt were safe or dangerous and to explain why. Cubitt Town was invariably marked safe by this group:

... it's safe because you've got the police station nearby, the docklands settlement which is always open, you've got George Green school, which has always got a caretaker that you can get to if you're in trouble – they'll always let you pop in and use the loo or whatever, it's a very well-lit area, you've got the takeaway shops which are always open, the area is used mainly by whites and yuppies. My aunt lives there too (Jean Laidlaw).

On many of the personal maps drawn by informants, the association between space and race is very close. In one interview one of our informants let this slip when she was asked how she felt about her immediate neighbourhood and she replied, 'it's all white, I mean it's all right, down our way'.

But why is the safety of Cubitt Town described in terms of a series of bolt holes? It seems that even 'down our way' has its hidden dangers, because this 'white space' is seen as being threatened internally by invasion from the 'ethnics', as in this account :

I always used to feel safe round here [Cubitt Town] but not any longer. There's a lot of racial nastiness about. I don't feel easy with my children walking down the street. Last year my youngest daughter (aged 17) was walking down the street by George Green and a lot of Asians spat at her. I mean luckily one of the boys in the group, she had this Asian boy friend for a time, he was there so she was safe. But it does make you wonder (Paula Smith).

It did not apparently make her wonder that maybe her daughter walking down the street with an Asian boy might be seen as a threat or a challenge to the authority of the Asian elders. But the story does allow her to portray her family as being entirely free of racism, whilst all the prejudice is on the side of the Asians.

The sense of creeping invasion was present in many accounts. Here is a typical example:

For as long as I can remember there have been certain places on the Island where the Bangladeshis predominate. As I've got older the amount of them seems to have grown. Perhaps it's just that I've become more aware of it. I mean when I went to Cubitt Town School, there was just a couple of Asian people and black people, but now when I walk down there there's big clusters of Asians (Mike Davis).

The construction of Cubitt Town as the core of the Isle of Dogs, which is itself imagined to contain the essence of the Old East End, and which also represents core British values, became central to the racialisation of space in this area. This was not just about the demarcation of territory; it served to articulate a particular autobiographical claim on the part of these self-styled Islanders to represent an authentically indigenous population. What distinguished this group from other residents, both white and Asian, was the sense that 'being born and bred' on the Island gave them special rights and privileges in relation to education, housing and local amenities, which other groups did not have.

Fight or flight? Imagining im/mobilities

So far the picture drawn has been confined to the Isle of Dogs itself. But even the most confirmed Islander was connected to a much wider and geographically dispersed network of family and friends. In fact the Cockney Diaspora has been going on for a very long time, and has sent people from the Isle of Dogs not only down river or out into rural or coastal Essex but also overseas – to Australia, Canada and many of the ex-colonies.[35]

Often these patterns of migration are seen as one-way, one-off moves, especially where ethnic minorities are concerned. But in the case of the Islanders, we discovered it was more often a case of a to-ing and fro-ing that was part of a family tradition and carried across several generations. The tradition started in the 1920s when Easter Enders took to the seaside in a big way, making day and weekend trips to Clacton or Southend, which of course quickly became the site of fond memories.[36] In the summer, journeys out to the hop-fields of Kent became a way of combining business with pleasure, having a holiday in the countryside that paid for itself and set you up for the winter.[37] In the second world war, moving out of town served a grimmer purpose, as thousands of East Enders fled the bombing and their wrecked homes and trekked out into the Essex countryside in search of sanctuary.[38] Some of them stayed and built their own homes, most famously the 'Plotlanders' of Canvey Island and Jaywick on the East Coast, who created a kind of rough and ready do-it yourself ex-urbanism.[39]

With the end of post-war austerity, the better off East Enders began to look to places they had visited on holiday as sites for their retirement homes. And where 'nan' went the rest of the extended family often followed.[40] Even if they didn't, family ties remained strong, and generated a lot of to-ing and fro-ing between the East End and rural Essex. Kinship networks may no longer have been matrilocal but they stayed matrifocal.[41] But by the 1990s Cockney evacuees from the 'blitzing' of the East End by wine bars and art galleries were discovering that the East Coast was no longer just the last port of call for retired criminals but a place where marinas and night clubs were a flourishing part of the 24/7 leisure and pleasure economy. How are we to understand this complex pattern of im/mobility? How far – and when – had it become racialised? How did it connect to the problematics of 'white flight' – the catchall explanation popularised in the media? What were the reasons for moving out which East Enders themselves gave?

When we asked our informants whether they intended to stay put or move we were in for another surprise. We expected the self-proclaimed Islanders to voice the fiercest pride of place, and to make the most vehement statements about staying put. We certainly did get this response from one 'rights for whites' campaigner:

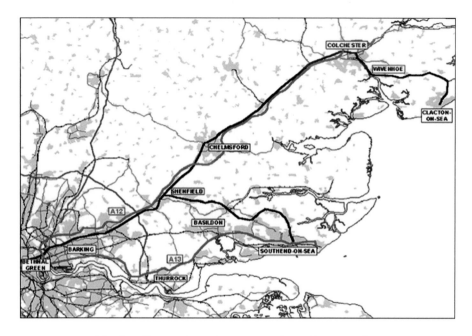

Moving East: migration routes from East London

Well there is a lot of people who would like us Islanders to just pick up and go, but we're not going to be run out of the area by a bunch of people who have no real roots here but are walking around as if they own it. No way, no chance. Hitler couldn't get us out and this lot aren't going to do it either (Joe Francis).

But this kind of Custer's last stand racism was actually a minority response. Amongst the older generation of Islanders there was a much more ambivalent and complicated attitude. Where people were able to run the whole gamut of place identifications associated with Island race-ism – Cubitt Towner-Islander-East-Ender-Cockney-English-British – and where this coincided with membership of an extended and geographically dispersed social network of family and friends, they were able to take a more relativistic and relaxed (but still racially tinged) view of demographic change on the Isle of Dogs. So we got statements like:

When I go and visit my sister in Shenfield and hear the way she goes on about the Asians there and what they are like, I come back here and think, well perhaps it's not so bad here, we've got problems but every place where you've got a mix you're bound to have some problems, there's good and bad in every community. And I think to myself, well if it got really bad here I could always move to my sister's, or even my Aunt's in Clacton, she's got a really nice place there but I am quite happy here really (Prue Green).

Because she felt could always move if she wanted to, Prue Green felt she didn't have to. And aspirations for a better life could quickly stir up anxieties about what might be lost as well as gained in the move. This might open up a space for the elaboration of racially coded rationales:

> Well we were thinking – may be when Sammy is a bit older – the schools round here, they are really are not up to much. You know they've really gone down hill a lot since I was a kid. And the local FE college, it's just for the ethnics, none of our young people will go to it. I sometimes think he'd have a better life somewhere where there's more room, where it's safe to play out, more fresh air, better schools, less crime. The only thing that is stopping us is Frank's job – he's well settled where he is, he doesn't really want to change. I guess he could commute in – everybody does these days, don't they? But it's not ideal. And then we would miss some of the people round here – they're really good neighbours some of them – not all, there are a few bad pennies, but if we went out to some small town out in the sticks it might not be so friendly (Charmaine Pearson).

But it could also open up a space for accommodating to change :

> At first people round here got the hump with the ethnics, but over time we've got to know them, and they've got to know us. We each have our own ways, which may seem peculiar to the others, but we're learning to rub along together. Of course you get the odd one that's aggressive, or up to no good but every community has its bad apples, doesn't it? And let's face it, like I say to my neighbour who's Asian, better the devil you know than the devil you don't. (Florence Harding)

There was a widespread sense amongst the Islanders that their children had no future in the area because the job opportunities generated by the new economy were beyond their reach.[42] This was often joined to the belief that the schools were favouring ethnic minority pupils by pursuing 'multicultural' policies. In Charmaine's case, however, this push factor was counterbalanced by the pull of local attachments. For others there was no problem:

> No, no, I was born here and I'll die here. People these days are always going on about the grass is greener on the other side of the street but – well, there might not be much grass round here, but it's where I was brought up. My brother and uncle still live round the corner. A lot of people think it's a rough old area, but there's always a lot going on here, why would I want to move? (Harry Belknap)

Where such impacted identifications combined with geographically dispersed social networks, people could avoid feeling trapped by exporting their model of insularity and connecting it to a wider racial geography. These 'island hoppers' as we came to call them, made frequent visits to friends, workmates and relatives, who also lived in what they regarded as white spaces in outer East London and Essex. In some cases this enabled them to hold on to an to an 'all white down our way' perspective – the wider society was still basically safe (because coded white) even though it was riddled with 'black spots' (like the Isle of Dogs). But in other cases their movement between the Isle of Dogs and Essex was precisely what tipped them over into a 'Custer's last stand' position, because they generalised their model of the Island: a dangerous black space with a few safe white bolt holes – to the region as whole.[43]

Finally, where the social networks were as insular as the pattern of identifications, we found the most overtly racialised version of white flight, from the succinct: 'the more they come in, the more we go out' – a classic piece of Chicago school ecology – to more elaborate ethno-demographic scenarios:

> The joke is these people from rural places all over the world want to come and live in Stepney, and us lot can't wait to get the hell out to the countryside. We are definitely going to move, if we possibly can. We are really fed up with the way things are round here. It's all right for the people who live in Canary Wharf, they move around all the time, they have security guards, they send their kids to private school, they are not stuck on these lousy estates having to put up with the noise, the spitting, the smell of the cooking, all day everyday. But what chance do we have of getting someone who has a nice place in the country wanting to swap flats with us round here? (Bert Sweedon)

The fact that positions of mobility and immobility are here posed in class as well as race terms seems to enable the speaker to get some argumentative purchase on the situation instead of being simply overwhelmed by it. Where this does not happen the space of flows takes on a more ominous and unconscious resonance, as in this story from a 16-year-old white boy:

> I had this funny dream about an enormous tidal surge that came up the river and just demolished everything, people, houses, just carried them away out to sea. And there was all these ethnics in boats and canoes, paddling around, they didn't seem bothered, we was all swimming about in the water, just trying to keep afloat, they smiled and waved at us but they didn't offer us to come on board (Johnny Smaldon).

One possible way of interpreting this dream, at least in the context of its retelling, is to see it as an oblique comment on the 'sink or swim' philosophy promoted by Thatcherism. The Bangladeshi community were widely regarded by the Islanders as keen supporters of enterprise culture, and indeed envied for their business ability.[44] In this nightmare scenario, it's the 'ethnics' who are making waves as they paddle their own canoes, while the whites are drowning in their own anger, resentment and envy.

Images of a world turned upside down and running out of control were a strong motif in many of the Islanders' stories. Sometimes this might be expressed in terms of physical geography:

When I was a kid I used to enjoy going to stay with my nan in Clacton. She moved there when her old man died, and we all used to go up there for the summer. We had a great time – it's like East End on Sea down there. But now my missus keeps going on about how we should move there for the kiddies' sake, but what the hell would I do there? Work on the pier? There's no jobs. As far as I'm concerned, it would be the end of the line.

The vision of a dead end future was strongest amongst this middle generation, who were in a sense stranded between the old and new East Ends, lacking the resources of their parents to hold on to a viable memoryscape, yet not able to make the transition into a post-industrial world. But how did the younger generation, who had grown up in the midst of these changes, make sense of them? Would they be able to reject the defensiveness of their parent culture and reach out to embrace a more inclusive sense of local identity? Would they be up for living the Olympic dream?

Growing up East Enders

What follows is a series of vignettes of particular moments of encounter with issues of class, 'race' and imagined community as these materialise in the context of my research with children and young people in Docklands.[45] These case studies raise many of the questions that are crucial to the long-term legacy of 2012. The first study is about what happens to young people when there is closure around a version of white ethnicity. The second is a little object lesson in the way multiculturalism engages with issues of difference and gets it wrong. The final story illustrates the process through which a more inclusive identity for the East Ender is being negotiated by children and young people themselves, and offers a more hopeful sign of the times.

The first transcript is from a discussion with a group of ten- and eleven-year-old white boys attending a primary school in Cubitt Town that had a predominantly white intake, drawn largely from ex-dockers' families. The school was deliberately trying to keep alive a sense of working-class community even as its real infrastructures were collapsing. Its curriculum and ethos were as deliberately old-fashioned as the building itself. Parents and grandparents who had gone to the same school could be sure that their children would be singing many of the same hymns, taking part in the same historical pageants, and learning the same English lessons as they had done. The rationale was that it was necessary to provide this sense of stability and historical roots for children who needed the sense of security that traditional forms of learning and discipline provided at a time when so many of the familiar landmarks of their childhood were being bulldozed around them.

Some of the children who attended the school had been actively involved in a series of attacks against black and Asian families who had been moved into one of the most run-down estates in the area. The head was concerned that something should be done. The school had a policy of disciplining any child found guilty of making racist remarks, and claimed to have silenced even the most vociferous offenders. At the same time he permitted the expression of racialist views in a mock election, since that was an education in the workings of democracy. Standing against its red (Labour), blue (Tory) and purple (Lib-Dem) rivals, the white (racialist) party won easily on a programme of voluntary repatriation for black immigrants. So at one level the local culture of racism was explicitly outlawed while at another level it was being given a legitimate space of representation.

Nevertheless the head thought that an outsider, a supposed expert in this kind of thing, might have a useful role to play. As he put it, it was a question of letting these kids get it off their chest. 'Lance the boil, Mr Cohen, lance the boil.' The medical metaphor should perhaps have warned me of what was to come when I took a group containing some of the hard-core racists out of school for a preliminary discussion, which, with their permission, I taped. It was clear that they had been waiting a long time for this opportunity to 'say what we really feel about blacks', as one of them put it. This is what they had to say:

PC Let's look at this thing about being British. Some of you, from what you've said, feel very proud to be British. It brings everyone together. Now what about black people who feel they're British? They're born here after all. They're also going to feel proud of being British aren't they?

Darren (in a small voice) Yes, that's right.

Mark (loudly) Oh come off it, Jesus Christ!

John I've got a Scandinavian name. God knows when, it must be one of my really early ancestors – so I feel I'm British because I go back all down the line.

PC That's an important point. People who feel they're British come from all different parts of the world, from Europe, from Africa, from India.

John I didn't originate from Scandinavia.

Darren One of my ancestors came from Denmark, but they went to South Africa so I'm South African.

John It's probably my great, great grandfather who got married to an English woman. Heysens is a strictly British name, yeah, cos I looked it up.

PC Well, what do you mean by British? British Welsh, British Asian, British English or what?

John It's English. I've got Saxon blood in me. I can't actually find out the meaning of the word [Heysens] but it's something to do with ley lines, power lines. I feel good to have a British name.

Mark But if their parents are born in Africa (no Darren I'm not saying against you) ...

Paul Or any country ...

John And they're born in this country, then to me they're not British. Different colours …

PC So it's not where you're born …

John Yes, it's where you're born *and* the colour.

PC Ah, that's different. They're two different things.

Mark No, No, No. They're mixed together.

PC Well, there may be a lot of people who are born here, whose mothers are British, who may also be black.

John Oh! That's an insult to me!

PC Why?

John You put me in the category of being black. If I were born in this country, black, and my parents weren't British, I know for a fact I'd have my brains – I was going to say something else – kicked out of me.

PC Why?

John Cos I'm black, which I'm not.

PC You're just imagining if you were, because you know black people have a hard time of it.

John Cos I know the resentment against blacks. It will always be there.

Mark (to PC) It's just stupid what you are saying. We are living in a white country. Can you imagine us having a black queen?

PC I'm not sure, but you obviously can.

ooooo

Alan (speaking for the first time) Say you had a sun tan, a white person might think you was black, and go up to you and stab you in the back.

Mark You can't say that cos John's got blond hair and black people have black hair.

John Hold on a moment (turning to PC, rather threatening) Are you against whites?

PC Why do white people want to get a suntan? They spend a lot of time and a lot of money going on expensive holidays abroad so as not to look white. What's all that about?

Alan Cos they think it looks nice.

Paul Like Peter Hills (a boy in the school). He acts all flash cos he's been to America and he's got all brown.

John That don't make him look black. Does it make him look like a toilet cleaner?

Alan If they had black hair and brown eyes and they was sunburnt, and say you thought it was a black person and you went up behind them and stabbed them …

John What, with blond hair?

Alan Black hair.

Mark When we played the black kids at Drakes (a local youth club), the folks were all cheering us on because they didn't like black people.

John Me and Paul play for Drakes. It's all white. Well there's one half caste – that Michael – he's a nigger – he's small for his age and fat.

Darren (in a small voice) Well I don't think there's much difference between a white and a half caste actually, because one of my best friends is a half caste.

John and Mark (mimicking Darren's stutter) Half a caste, half a caste. You mean half caste, stupid.

Mark Miss X is German and she's got blond hair and blue eyes.

Paul So has John.

Darren We've got a Chinese teacher.

John Yeah, and I hate her. She goes 'Ah so'.

Mark We've got two black teachers.

John I know and I hate them. They act all flash and walk around as if they own the place. But they are real divs. One of them can hardly speak English … just got off the banana boat, my dad says.

Mark I've met plenty of blacks and I've had some stabs in the back from them personally.

Paul Knives?

OOOOO

John Hold on, Darren wants to say something. We're treating Darren as one of us, even though he isn't British.

Darren Do you go down Deptford High Street often?

John I've heard that if any white person goes down there they get mugged. The niggers just hang about all day sunning themselves, which is a waste of time for them, but then some poor kid comes along on his way home from work and they nick all his money.

Paul My mum went over there [Deptford] once and she was nearly mugged. There's a video shop where they all hang out.

Mark Me and John are going to school in Deptford and that is a black area, you know. A blacks' paradise over there!

John Niggers galore!

Mark They all clan together don't they. They help each other out but they wouldn't lift a finger to help one of us.

John It was the same with the Jews. If they had a cousin they'd buy off their cousin, and that cousin would buy off another cousin who would buy off their dad and the dad would buy off the granddad.

PC Well it looks as if you're going to have to come to terms with black people if you're going to school in Deptford. You're going to have to learn to live with them and get on with them, whether you like it or not.

John No. If they call me anything I'm going to show them what I'm made of – all the business. I'm going to kick their heads in.

Darren Well I went down there with my friend and we didn't see anything like that. We just went shopping in the market.

Mark The other day we was down the market this side of the water and we saw this geezer come up out of a manhole and he was speaking some foreign language. I dunno what it was – Russian I think.

Paul Yeah probably was Russian, cos they had one of their warships out there in the river. I saw one too, come out of the ground. He didn't know where he was. He started talking to these black muggers and they showed him where to go. They're probably working together in the sewers you know. My dad says if Labour win (the election) the Russians are gonna take over the docks and maybe the whole of London.

PC I think the Russians probably have enough problems of their own at the moment. But how many of you think that if Labour gets in it will be bad for the area?

Chorus They're rubbish ... they're all pooftas, wankers ... Lib Dems for ever!

PC Well what do you think would be good for the area? What would you like to see happen here positively? And what are the bad things that you would like to see something done about?

At this point a flip chart was introduced and I wrote down the group's suggestions:

WHAT WE WANT ROUND HERE	WHAT WE DON'T WANT ROUND HERE
A swimming pool	Bulldozers
A cinema	Houses for rich people
More white people	More black people
More jobs	Gays, Snobs, Medallion Men
More space to play	Car parks

My Dad says ...

These are the views of children on the cusp of adolescence, for whom issues of identity and difference, power and relationship to the wider society are anyway of increasing concern. But these are also children who were growing up working-class at a time and in a place where the customary links between each of these terms have weakened or snapped. And this is especially the case for boys. The kind of male occupational succession which underpinned the culture of dock work is a thing of the past. For girls, in contrast, the matrilocal – or matrifocal – culture, with its inter-generational networks of support, remains more or less intact. The question then is what use do these boys make of whiteness to grapple with or evade this problem? How do categories of race, nation or ethnicity get mobilised to reinvent the culture of white labourism? How does it connect to their code of masculinity? Is this culture something to which these boys are still somehow being apprenticed, or can it only be imagined as a lost inheritance, part of a collective memory of a world that no longer exists?

I do not think it helps to understand what is going on in this discussion to hear it simply as a reiteration of received adult opinion. The notion of adult ventriloquism – of the adult speaking through the child – is a popular view amongst teachers, who often blame working-class children's bad attitudes and behaviour, including racism, on parental influence or failure. Although at several points in the discussion 'my dad says' is used to preface a racist remark, I think this must, in some cases, be understood as a ritual invocation used to authorise the statement, rather than as literal quotation. In a matrilocal culture where mum's word rather than dad's is law, and where sons no longer follow fathers into work, its citation here has a double compensatory function; it enables the boy to speak from the place of the father, and hence to assume in language a manhood that cannot be guaranteed through any other means;[46] and at the same time it lends an aura of legitimacy to racist statements of which the child is well aware most adults (including the interviewer, teachers and possibly parents) disapprove, and which they sometimes actively censor. But if my dad says – then it's OK.

It is significant that the first 'my dad says' is used to reverse the traditional imputations of ignorance, and attribute it to black teachers rather than white pupils. The scandal seems to be that the state has put a black in place of a white as a source of quasi-parental authority over the child – and all in the name of preserving 'traditional family values'.

In this discourse, the presence of a black, Chinese, or indeed any member of an ethnic minority, in a position of direct personal authority over whites is taken as a sign of their having 'taken over', not only the local power structure, but the government of the country. 'They' have become part of the ruling class. 'They' have not only taken our jobs and houses, but our exams. And now 'they' are running 'our' schools. Remember that in this case the school itself encouraged a proprietorial attitude on the part of white parents. This takeover is described through the idioms of territorialism – the teacher is 'acting flash', as if he owned the place. On the street and in the playground this might be countered by the usual formula of ritual insult leading to physical injury, as the gangs fight it out to see 'who rules round here'. But in the educational setting the issues cannot be settled in such a straightforward fashion.

The cited insult – div – was a popular term of abuse used by the children, associating stupidity with being a dummy and hence by extension a 'mummy's boy', or cry baby. It also, of course, evokes in a peer group idiom the teacherly sarcasm directed against less academic children, who often get their own back by using the term against the brighter, more middle-class pupils who supposedly are not streetwise. In this case, however, the child's word is put into the father's mouth, from whence it is directed as an insult against the teacher. In this game of trading places the black teacher has been put in the shoes of the working-class child, whose father has replaced him as the sole arbiter of knowledge. It's a double whammy.

In this discourse a black teacher is an oxymoron. The very idea that blacks could teach whites something is held up to ridicule. Sanctioned by 'my dad says', the school counterculture can safely deploy racist idioms not just against black pupils, but in a more general attack on the official middle-class values of the school. And if these values include multiculturalism or antiracism so much more grist to its mill.[47]

What's my line?

In the discussion about national, ethnic and racial identifications, these elements are strenuously juggled in order to avoid the possibility that black British, like black teacher, could be anything other than an absurd contradiction in terms. But in attempting to define who they are and where they are coming from in terms which make black and British mutually exclusive categories, these boys get themselves into a real twist.

John starts with a classic – we might say pre-modern – statement of racial lineage. In terms of nationality his ancient pedigree is evidently Scandinavian. Yet he feels he is British because he goes back 'all down the line'. At the moment he said it, I had an image of him as a Young Viking. Perhaps his family romance was a kind of Norse saga centred around an exotic parent who had carried him over the North Sea on one of their marauding expeditions! His actual account of his family history was rather vague. But if his great grandfather had actually married a local English girl, then it all made more sense.

The docks had done a lot of trade with the Baltic states. Many of the old houses had been built out of Scandinavian timber scavenged by dockworkers. There had been Finnish and Norwegian seamen's missions in the area right up until the docks closed. Many of the sailors must have jumped ship and settled down with local girls. This intermarriage with foreigners was not always popular with the local lads, but on the whole it was tolerated, even at times encouraged. Because, of course, it whitened the area, set it off as a cut above the rest of the waterfronts with their 'tiger bays', their dangerous and disreputable multiracial mix of lascars, Malays, Chinese and Africans. In terms of local labour history then 'Scandinavian' became interchangeable with 'British' as a synonym for white.

John does not know this history and indeed almost all its material traces have been effaced from the local landscape by the closure of the docks. And this leaves him with a puzzle about his patronym – Heysens. He cannot square the circle at this level; a baptismal name is not a self-signifying act of identification; it needs to be confirmed by family genealogy and community history to function properly as a myth of origin and destiny.[48]His assertion of the 'strictly British' nature of his obviously Scandinavian patronym indirectly points to what it has come to stand for and yet conceals the suppressed history of white labourism within – a whiteness that in this context 'dare not speak its name'.[49]

Cut off from pursuing that line of enquiry, his search for a stable identity leads him in another direction, to the English and to 'Saxon blood'. In other words to a myth of national origins which makes the Saxons and in particular King Alfred the founding fathers of ancient English liberties associated with the rights of the common people in their struggle against the Norman and other foreign Yokes.[50] John may well have learnt the details of this story at school, but he has put it here to quite particular use. It provides the missing link in a genealogy which has apparently been buried in the meaning of his name. The evocation of a Saxon blood line leads him straight into the druidic underworld – ley lines, invisible conduits of magnetic energy running under the earth, linking up centres of sacred power into a unified body/soul politic of Arthurian legend. And all this is suddenly in John's grasp by virtue of the magic contained in his name!

By his own account the construct made John feel he was part of something vastly bigger than himself but also immensely strong. Perhaps the device offered a feeling of self-sufficiency in which all the tensions generated by these disjunctive identities might dissolve. This young Viking with Saxon blood, bearing proudly a strictly British but all too foreign sounding name, whose Englishness depended on Celtic traditions, was certainly looking for some such escape route. But the more he tried to discover a purified sense of identity, the more hybrid he became. Thus encumbered John had to wrestle with the niceties of *jus sanguinis* and *jus soli*, the crux of British immigration policy since the war.[51] It was here that the impossibility of producing a watertight system of classification to ensure that if you were black you could not be British, and vice versa, struck home.

When I tried to distinguish between the two principles of nationality, Mark is in a sense right to correct me and say 'no they're mixed'. In fact these boys combine the two principles to produce an axiomatic definition which is certainly internally consistent, and corresponds to the commonsense racist view: the British are those born in this country whose parents are white. Yet, as the next section of the discussion, shows even this watertight definition cannot quite abolish the anxiety of influence created by growing up in a multiracial society.

White under the skin

No sooner does whiteness emerge as the kernel of these boys' identity than it becomes problematic as a source of lethal misrecognition. Reduced to a matter of skin pigmentation, colour is obviously a matter of relative rather than absolute difference.[52] Alan worries that a white boy with a dark suntan might be mistaken for black and become the victim of racist attack. But help is at hand. The repertoire of racial binarism is not restricted to skin alone. The presence or absence of all manner of somatic and behavioural features may be used for this purpose. In this case hair colour is tried as a new dividing line. Blacks can never be blondes and blondes can never be black! This may reinstate the blonde hair blue-eyed Scandinavian look as the ideal body type but it does not solve Alan's problem of what to do about all those sunburnt whites with black hair and brown eyes, whom racists will mistake for black. Skinocracy definitely did not rule OK.

This is an entirely fictional problem set up to think with as these boys worry at what meaning to assign to physical features as markers of 'race'. The exchange between Paul and John swiftly and brutally resumes the actual social semiology of colour. Bronzed bodies are a sign of affluence, expensive transatlantic holidays and residence in exotic climes; by extension brown is something even poor white boys can become by just sitting in the sun. But for John the important point is that in doing so they are still white under the skin. This metaphysical whiteness is difficult to articulate in the language of skin politics. What John does is define it by what it is not, reaching for an image of blackness which belongs to its symbolic function. The reference to blacks as toilet cleaners is not just about a menial job which no whites in their right mind would do. It is not even saying blacks are shit. They are associated with dirt, because dirt is matter out of place. And blacks in this scenario have no place in the sun.

The attempt to naturalise whiteness fails to resolve the worrying ambiguity introduced by changing pigmentation. John's attempt to give colour a fixed characterology still did not produce any positive depth to it. Whiteness is only given content when it is anchored by a narrative of real and/or imagined community.[53] Mark and John here introduce the story of a football match at the local youth centre, in which their all-white team is cheered on from the terraces because they are playing a black team and 'the folks don't like blacks'. This youth centre was in fact built as a last grand gesture by the area's 'Irish mafia', and is widely regarded as a living monument to white labourism. But even this homely picture of volkish racism lending its voice to a nationalism of the neighbourhood is marred by the presence of a 'half caste' who disturbs the symmetry of the scene.

The mapping of skin politics onto territorial rivalries invariably racialises space. Skin covers the whole body, to which it gives a single all-enveloping colour. The colour coding of the local body politic follows the same totalising logic; an area is imagined as all over black, or white, Bangladeshi or Jewish, irrespective of the actual demographics. This is a form of 'ethnic cleansing' which airbrushes quite large minorities out of the picture. One of the key issues in the local numbers game, in fact, was just how many immigrants it takes to effect a colour change. In this part of docklands at this time, even one black family seems to have been one too many and to threaten its white designation. Equally, for these boys even one mixed-race member of a football team is enough to disturb its whiteness. John insists that the 'half caste' is black, Darren that he is white. There seems to be no middle ground on which the meaning of these terms could be renegotiated. Or is there?

Tall stories

In many of the discussions I recorded with this group there was a continual refrain of grievance and complaint about the personal injustices they had suffered as whites. This often took the form of feeling that something was going on behind their backs which was doing them down.

I think we can get a glimpse of what is happening in the section where the boys attempt to put into words some of their anxieties. Much of this focuses on the theme of black street culture and crime, and undoubtedly draws on moral panics about mugging orchestrated by the mass media.[54] But threaded through this is another vision – of a black El Dorado, where the inhabitants sit around sunning themselves and living a life of ease on their ill-gotten gains. John's little vignette certainly seems to support the thesis, associated with the research of David Roediger in the USA, about white working-class racism being driven by envy and resentment of blacks' free and easy life style.[55] Black people are portrayed as criminally lazy and parasitic, enjoying themselves at the white workers'/taxpayers' expense, while rejoicing at being together, in their own self-sufficient community, having found a paradise they can call home. But I think this view is to underestimate the intensity of the ambivalence which such narratives generate.

What does it mean for these white boys that they cross the water and enter an alien world, which is also a paradise where they do not belong, and are robbed of what they have earned by their own labour, either by blacks possessed of legendary sexual powers, or by Jews with their mysterious gift for self-enrichment? The manic glee of John's 'Niggers Galore' and its link with his anti-semitic view of Jewish mutual aid seems to suggest an underlying phantasy about a closed community which regenerates itself through inbreeding: a mirror image of his own racial utopia.

His throwaway line about 'doing the business' gives us a clue as to his real enterprise. Under the auspices of his moral crusade for white rights John is planning to embark upon a criminal career. Not only in the literal sense that if the police practice what they preach about their commitment to prosecute racial violence John's activities will sooner or later land him in trouble with the law. But also in the symbolic sense that in making racism his business, his 'productivity' will be measured by the number of heads he kicks in.

Mark and Paul take another tack, one which is more likely to remain at the level of symbolisation rather than being acted out. In a little *folie à deux* they construct a conspiracy theory about Russian communists and black muggers joining forces to take control of docklands and the whole of London. Black and white underworlds meet in a single project of world – or at least metropolitan – domination. A version then of the popular belief that an unholy alliance of middle-class lefties and black community activists had taken over the local state and was secretly using its power to disadvantage the white working class.

The credibility of the tale is guaranteed by 'my dad says', and my dad says that Labour is to blame – the ultimate hidden hand which is out to stab the country and its erstwhile supporters in the back. Again I think this citation is primarily a strategy of authorisation for a very tall story. But it also does here contain an element of ventriloquism. We are hearing the father's talk through the child. Certainly the reference to the Labour Party provides a cue for the group to display their contempt. And when it comes to formulating their own demands we are given a perfect résumé of the double-facing agenda of white labourism: a series of impeccably communitarian demands for improving public amenity and resource combined with a policy of excluding everyone but themselves from enjoying them.

Nevertheless there is a moment when John fleetingly takes the role of the Other and puts himself in a black boy's shoes as the target of his own attacks, albeit only in the next instant to slip back into his accustomed place. Why else does he need to deny so quickly that any shift in position is possible – that racial hatred will 'always be there'. And a similar shift in sociological imagination occurs when Mark suddenly envisages Britain having a black queen.

There is only one dissenting voice in this discussion, apart from mine. Darren comes from South Africa and knows all about racial apartheid 'from the inside'. He is John's main, indeed only, adversary in the debate and he suffers the consequences. For he interrupts the flow of racist talk in more than one way. He has a stutter, which of course gets worse when he gets agitated. John and Mark cruelly seize on his speech impediment to wind him up and ridicule his defence of hybridity. Yet what their mimicry amplifies is not his despair but theirs. For they are not able to entirely wipe out from their minds what Darren is struggling so bravely to put into words: that it is not necessary to go on labouring under whiteness, there is another possible world in which racism has no sway.

Behind our blacks

There is one point in the discussion where John turns to me and asks rather aggressively whether I am against whites. It is only in this moment of confrontation that the word itself is used. For the rest of the time the references are coded and oblique. It did not seem at the time that the boys were much concerned about my own position. But I should have known better. If ideology always works behind the backs of its subjects, then it always strikes when and where and in ways you least expect it.

On our return to school after this session, John suddenly got very anxious about what would happen to the tape. He was worried that I might show it to the head or someone else in authority and get them all into trouble. I explained that it would be transcribed, and the names and other details would be changed so no-one could identify either the school or them. This seemed to reassure him and I thought no more about it. Next week when I went into the school the head called me into his office. He looked angry and upset. There had been a complaint from one of the children in the group that I had used bad language. This could not of course be tolerated. Teachers had to set a good example in terms of self-restraint. The boy's mother had been in to complain. If it happened again the project would be stopped. He did not seem particularly impressed by my denial of the charge. And indeed I did begin to feel as if I must have been guilty of some indiscretion – some of the things the boys had said had made me very angry. The only way to find out was to listen to the tape. At this suggestion the head got even more agitated. Where was the tape? It should not have been made. What was going to be done with it? It should be erased. Even though we had explained at the outset that we would be making tape recordings as part of the research and had given the usual guarantees of confidentiality, this did not satisfy him now. No more taping!

Now, what had happened here? Clearly my reassurances of the previous week had not been believed. John still thought that I would use the tape behind his back to expose his racist beliefs and activities and, as he admitted later, 'have him taken away and put in prison'. So rather than have his bad language – i.e. his racist discourse – taken down and used as evidence against him, he had gone behind my back to the head and accused me of bad language. Perhaps he also secretly hoped that I would be taken away and put somewhere where I would be incommunicado. He had thus neatly turned the tables on me, put me in his boots, in the attempt to get me to feel as paranoid as he was. I was being put in the position of a naughty boy, while he, using the head as a kind of ventriloquist's dummy, tried to shut me up.

It was not in fact difficult to feel that people in this school were ganging up and doing what they could to undermine the project. Support from other staff had been minimal. I got a sense of a closing of the ranks against an unwelcome intruder. My work threatened to undermine theirs. I was in effect a potential 'blackleg' who didn't belong in this community of practice. My position within it may have been peripheral, but its legitimacy was in question. In other words I was being given the same treatment as was being daily meted out to the Vietnamese and Bangladeshi communities, just as earlier it had been experienced by the Jews. As for the tape, this had ceased to be a medium of mechanical reproduction – it now directly stood for the racist discourse it had recorded. The racism was no longer in the school or in the community, or in even the children's acts or words, it was in the tape. And so it could be simply erased, the record wiped clean, by the press of a button.

Memory maps

The secondary school we chose for this project placed community issues, including race relations, very high on its educational agenda. It had an art department strongly committed to multicultural approaches. We devised a project around a memory mapping exercise that would enable pupils to anchor their own individual life histories in a wider cultural geography. They were given a small blank map of the world and asked to indicate the places where they had spent some time, either living there, or visiting. These small maps were then placed in the centre of a large sheet of paper, and lines drawn out from these points to mark off the different areas of the memory map. The young people were asked to think about these different places, and to note down any strong images which came to mind. This might be a physical landmark with strong associations for them, in terms of significant people; some situation or event they remembered taking place there; or, something different or special about the place which they liked or disliked. Our particular focus was on areas where the young people felt safe and at home, or saw as 'foreign', and the circumstances under which what was felt as unfamiliar or different might be perceived as exciting or threatening.

These were cartographies of the imagination, in which fantasy was as important as fact.[56] As one boy pointed out to me rather indignantly when I demurred at his placing Glasgow somewhere to the west of Leeds, they were after all supposed to be doing art not geography.

Those young people who had experienced long distance migration (e.g. from Bangladesh or Vietnam) understandably tended to stress the discontinuities between past and present, between the landscapes of their early childhood and living on the Isle of Dogs. How this was signified varied enormously. One Bangladeshi boy did a happy smiling self portrait next to his family home in Bangladesh, in contrast to his glum faced alter ego who was positioned by the side of an 'English' house which was connected to images of a pound note, a cricket bat and a camera. He commented that England was a rich country full of tall buildings (like Canary Wharf), while Bangladesh was poor, but more fun because all his cousins were there. But it was not just a simple split. The tensions of the diasporic experience are also present. A recent photograph of himself in school uniform, the image of the English schoolboy he was partly trying to become, was not located with the signifiers of Englishness but linked to a 'life line' that took him back to Bangladesh.

Jaswinder's memory map (detail)

The most complex and sophisticated memory map was produced by a Bangladeshi girl (see illustration). It was rooted in a specific historical moment in the struggle for national independence. Jaswinder described it as follows:

> It was a long time ago, in 1971, I think. Many Bengali students died fighting in front of the Medical College. They were fighting because of their language, Bengali. Bangladesh was called East Pakistan at the time and no-one could speak their own language. Because of that they fought and died. So they built a memorial to them which I show here, and every 21 February they go there with flowers. The soldier in the picture is to remind us of what the military did. They went to knock down the memorial again and again, and again and again we rebuilt it until they had to give up and we were free.

In amongst the wreaths, and the pictures of different scenes from the life of Bangladesh, she places a photograph of herself aged five, the age at which she left home. The inscriptions in Bengali refer us both to the actual events she describes and to the issues of language and representation which were their focus. These issues clearly do not just belong to the past or to the origins of Bangladesh as a nation. They are very much alive in her own personal struggle for independence as a Bengali girl growing up in the East End today. This dual meaning is also picked up on the other side of the picture where she explores signifiers of Englishness: the archaic English script, country houses, her school, a Christmas scene, a jar of coins, stamps, and various conventional symbols of modernity. The cross-referencing is deliberate – she compares Bengali and Christian rituals, and picks up the colour of the Christmas tree in the area around the Memorial. The two sides of the story are literally stitched together, with this suture placed along the exhaust trail left by the plane which has carried her from Bangladesh to England.

How then was the memory map read in the classroom context? The art teacher defined the project in terms of his own version of multiculturalism. For him this was to do with learning about other cultures, and dissolving stereotypes of prejudice. It is from this vantage point that he asked Jaswinder to explain to him the meaning of her memory map:

Teacher Tell me about this side of the picture, which is something you know about and I know absolutely nothing about. Where did you get the pictures from and what do they represent?

Jaswinder This cart is being driven by an ox, people travel round in them from one village to another. They carry their clothes and food in them.

Teacher What exactly is going on in this one, just tell me, it looks like some kind of agriculture but I can't work it out. Are they rice planting?

Jaswinder No, I dunno, they're digging the land with something.

Teacher It's very obviously irrigated because there is a helluva lot of water around. It's a very fertile looking area.

Jaswinder um

Teacher You're not clear on that one by the sound of things.

Jaswinder No.

Teacher What about that one?

Jaswinder It's a mosque. It's in the capital city and it's very famous. I think it's the largest one.

Teacher So it's a tourist attraction. What about this one, where did it come from?

Jaswinder It's from a booklet I found in a restaurant, about old calendars and cards.

Teacher Tell me about this, about the sea.

Jaswinder Every morning in the villages the women get up very early and take the jugs with them and go and fetch water from the river.

Teacher These national symbols (a flag and a Royal Bengal Tiger) are easier to understand than those scenes of everyday life. Could you tell me a bit about that one? It's a very peaceful scene, everyone looks very quiet and relaxed.

Jaswinder They are all washing clothes and there is a man over here, I think he's selling something.

Teacher Is this village typical of what you'd see or is it prettified?

Jaswinder That's quite typical. Most of the villagers are farmers and they have cows like the ones shown here. This is the picture of a big forest.

Teacher Would that be in Silhet in the north?

Jaswinder No, it's in the south.

Teacher So it's in the delta where there was that terrible flooding.

Jaswinder That one there is from Silhet where they have tea plantations. The women and children pick the leaves …

Teacher (interrupting) … which is back-breaking work I imagine. This looks like a special kind of tree.

Jaswinder It's a banana tree, which you get mostly in South East Asia.

Teacher Is it an export commodity, something Bangladesh sells to the rest of the world? Or is it mostly for home consumption?

Jaswinder I don't really know.

Teacher What about this lady, she's all dressed up looking very smart, what is she up to?

Jaswinder I dunno (giggles), but that's one of these carriages, driven by cows.

Teacher But she's not dressed for work, this woman is going somewhere special. Any ideas? She's rich by the look of things. I wondered whether she might be a bride going to a wedding, a princess even?

Jaswinder She could be. Maybe she's just going somewhere.

Teacher Now I've never seen that in my life before. Tell me about that.

Jaswinder There are festivals, and the women decorate their hands with jewellery or um …

Teacher (interrupting) … Henna? I've seen them draw the patterns. And what about the hands? Are they in prayer?

Jaswinder In India, it's a form of greeting

Teacher Yes that's right. That's lovely, it's like a greeting card. What festival might it be? Is it Diwali because of all the light?

Jaswinder Could be Diwali or it could be Eid

Teacher Ok. They are the only two I *do* know so it has to be one or the other! Now tell me about this one. This is a monument to Bangladesh. It's not the same as this other one though is it?

Jaswinder No that one was built earlier …

Teacher This is more famous, I've seen this one more.

Jaswinder Cos a lot of people fought to get rid of the dictators who didn't come from the country but took out all the riches

Teacher Sheikh Mujib was the leader of the Bangladeshi side, wasn't he? That was the period. So back to the village life, there is that cart again. Right this looks like a fortress. What the hell is it?

Jaswinder It's the parliament building.

Teacher Oh!

Jaswinder And there's a park round there. And there's a mosque nearby, there's a very famous poet buried there and there's an art college nearby. And this monument, the big one, is near the medical college. This is a peacock, it also symbolises the country, because there used to be a lot of those around.

Teacher You've taught me something there, because I knew about the tiger but I had no idea about the peacock. There is an awful lot of traditional stuff on this. Does this represent in your view a rather romanticised view of the country, rather a tourist view of the country?

Jaswinder Yes.

Teacher Yeah.

Jaswinder I used to go there every year with my grandparents and my cousin lives in a place like that with hills so um (sighs).

The teacher starts by making a profession of his ignorance. True to the formula, he is learning about other cultures. The roles and even the power relations are supposedly being reversed. For now the pupil is supposed to be the teacher, the teacher the one who learns. However in practice nothing of the kind takes place. The teacher reads the picture, continually offering interpretations which are signalled as displays of his intimate knowledge of Bangladeshi history and culture. The pupil is put in the position of simply confirming the teacher's superior power of understanding of her own culture. At several points she herself is made to profess ignorance. In many instances when she starts to offer her own reading the teacher interrupts to foreclose her interpretation with one his own. Despite all this she still manages at several points to assert the validity of her own local knowledge, which is based on visits to her family in Bangladesh. For the rest she can only resist teacherly imposition by keeping silent or playing dumb.

The whole thing reads like a parody of the colonial relationship between a European anthropologist and native informant, in which the latter produces the 'raw material' in the form of artefacts, in this case the memory map, which is then 'cooked' by the former into a finished product of knowledge in a way that has little or nothing to do with local understandings, and everything to do with a certain form of scientific rationality which is being imposed upon them as a condition of their legibility. The invisible pedagogy of this teacher silently communicates this message; even as it claims to be overturning colonial forms of knowledge/power, at another level it is reproducing them.[57] It is not that Jaswinder's cultural memoryscape is being directly invalidated, but that her power to interpret it, her status as its story teller, is being put under duress. What can happen when this grid of interpretation is removed was illustrated by another piece of work.

The making of the Indian cowgirl warrior

As part of this project we wanted to devise some co-operative activities which would encourage the children and young people to explore more directly those imaginings of self and other that could be used in constructing their own version of community.

What follows is an account of a group of seven- and eight-year-old girls who did just that. Amanda was Vietnamese Chinese, Sharon was from a local Irish family, Rachel's mother was local white working-class, and Yolande's family were from Kurdistan. We drew a large outline figure and invited the girls to work together to create a character by filling in the features as they wished (see illustration). What happened next was to be an object lesson in what can sometimes be released by such simple means.

There was very little preliminary discussion. Each of the girls took a different part of the body and started drawing with their coloured felt-tip pens. And as they drew they talked; this took the form of a running commentary on the whole character they imagined they were constructing from the part they were immediately working on, and these discussions in turn affected what they drew. Out of this dialogue what came to be known as the Indian Cowgirl Warrior gradually took shape (see illustration).

The Indian cowgirl warrior

As the children worked they wove an intricate web of associations around the figure they were assembling, yet in a way which integrated all its elements into a harmonious whole. This was no Frankenstein's monster, but a creature given life through a shared impulse to narrate, rather than dominate, the process of its creation. So where does 'it' come from? The figure bears some resemblance to the character in Chinese mythology described by Maxine Hong Kingston at the beginning of her autobiography.[58] This is not a case of direct cultural influence, I think, but because the 'warrior' plays a similar function in articulating these girls' dreams of a different, and non-traditional, feminine role. Nevertheless, as we will see, the way this role is envisaged and deliberated about contains its own highly specific set of histories.

The first problem in giving birth to this collective brain child was to give her a name, and after that to define her essential mission in life:

> She's called Sandy ... No Jo ... Sandy Jo ... she fights and bangs people's heads together but only the baddies ... she's a warrior ... she's a bad warrior ... no a good warrior ... cos if people beat up their best friends she helps them out ... sometimes she's mad ... she's mad about the baddies shooting people dead ... she chases after them and bangs their heads together, saying 'pack it in' ...

What could have triggered an argument between Rachel and Yolande is quickly resolved by the intervention of Sharon; she combines the two suggestions into a single composite name in which all the 'parents' can feel they have an equal stake. Such co-operative and compromise solutions characterised most of these discussions. This can be seen immediately in the way moral characteristics are debated. The girls want to portray female assertiveness in a positive light, but this causes some problems. Yolande felt it was always bad or mad to fight. But Rachel and Sharon argue that it's OK if you are on the side of the goodies, and do it to rescue people from trouble and help friends out! So the Superego Militant can take on a feminine form. But in the process the 'Warrior' is somewhat domesticated, cast in the role of a mother, or a teacher banging naughty children's heads together and telling them to 'pack it in'.

In the next sequence, the scene shifts and the 'Warrior' finds herself suddenly transported to the Wild West. But this relocation in turn sparks off a debate about her ontological status – is she real or imaginary?

> she's a cowgirl ... a cowgirl warrior ... I saw one in a film, she had boots on and these prickly things on behind [spurs] ... I like Supergirls ... so do I ... the cowgirl lives in heaven ... No Way ... No Way ... she lives in a desert. Every morning she gets up, she cleans everything up, and she goes to work ... she does something very important ... she's not real, is she, cos she's just in a film ... she cleans everything up then she goes to the man making the film and says 'can I have a cup of tea first cos I've come a long way to get here' ...

Again we see how quickly a new element is integrated into the story line, but this syncretic impulse also begins to undermine the realism of the whole enterprise, especially with the entry of 'Supergirl'. We are in the ethereal world of movie and TV heroines, where 'anything is possible', even heavenly choirs of cowgirls.

But Sharon will have none of this. She brings the discussion down to earth with a bump by grounding 'Supergirl' in the realities of women's work. Her cowgirl is a working-class girl who lives in a desert (it is certainly no heaven), who is involved in both domestic and waged labour, but is nevertheless positively valued: her work is very important to the community. At this point Yolande gets confused and more than a little anxious about the sudden switch from Hollywood to the kitchen sink. She can't handle the contradiction if it is real, though it wouldn't matter if it was 'just a movie'. But Sharon is more able to integrate aspects of reality and phantasy into a single construction, without confusing them. She does this by drawing a 'pen portrait' of someone who first cleans up the film set and then stars in the picture being made.

At one level this startling juxtaposition of charlady and film star represents an extreme, polarised, version of women's dual roles as drudge and idol; Sharon mimics the daydream of the housewife she might yet become: to escape the confining realities of the domestic round by having one's true talents 'discovered' at last.[59] But in daydreams the game of wish fulfilment is always one of loser wins. By definition it does not challenge reality principles, in this case belonging to the sexual double standard. But Sharon does not take this path. She is not writing a script for the Hollywood dream factory. Quite the reverse. She is trying to reconcile her positive sense of working-class identity with her wider social aspirations as a girl. And she does it precisely by debunking the mythology of instant 'stardom'. Her movie actress is a working cowgirl, someone who goes to the director and says 'can I have a cup of tea because I've come a long way to get here'. She wants her aspirations recognised in material as well as symbolic terms. It is the man's turn to make the tea, while she puts her feet up and has a well-earned rest!

The class status of the cowgirl warrior having been resolved, the debate now moves onto another terrain of confusion: her ethnicity. Rachel is doing her face and announces, 'I'm going to do the colour of the skin'. Thereupon Amanda speaks for the first time: 'do it yellow'. But Rachel refuses: 'No I'm going to do it brown ... I know, let's make her an Indian ... an Indian cowgirl'. And this suggestion is greeted with a chorus of 'Yeses' from Yolande and Sharon, but not from Amanda, who looks hurt. Yolande then turns to Amanda and says in a comforting tone of voice 'You're an Indian'. But this is immediately contradicted by Sharon – 'No's she's not' – at which Rachel and Sharon break out into giggles.

Care has to be taken in interpreting this exchange. The effect on Amanda is crushing, and echoes other contexts of social exclusion she experienced in the school. But there is also another, more complex, process of negotiation going on. Amanda makes a bold move to claim the cowgirl as her own. Rachel, however, knows that cowgirls are not usually Chinese, although warriors most definitely are. However at this point it is the cowgirl not the warrior who is uppermost in their minds. In saying she is 'going to do it brown', Rachel is denying Amanda exclusive ownership of the image by giving it a skin colour which belongs to *no-one* in the group. However this also means that the cowgirl is magically metamorphosed into an Indian. When Yolande turns to Amanda and offers her honorary membership of an Indian tribe, she seems to be denying her real ethnicity. But at another level she is expressing a shared kinship between a Turkish and a Chinese girl, as members of ethnic minorities who face discrimination. But that act of solidarity is immediately attacked by the two white girls, who must feel threatened; if they giggle it is partly perhaps out of the sense of dissonance aroused by the thought of a Chinese Indian; but it is also partly out of anxiety lest their own ethnic credentials should be put on the line. It is exactly at this point that colouring the face brown ceases to be an act of identification with black people, or a means of preventing the figure being monopolised by any one member of the group; it becomes instead part of a strategy to distinguish people on the basis of skin difference.

Yet this device did not, in fact, resolve the issue; it only compounded the confusion. For there is an ambiguity about the term 'Indian' in this context. Are they referring to Native Americans or the inhabitants of India? At this point I intervened for the first time to ask them what they knew about 'Indians':

where did they come from? Rachel suggested Africa; Yolande, loyal to Amanda, suggested Hong Kong, while Rachel said simply 'the desert'. Their answers revealed a personal geography of identification with the figure which may have had little or nothing to do with reality but also made their own creation belong in a wholly 'other' world. How could they then reclaim it as the product of a shared enterprise?

For this purpose it was necessary to construct a new myth of origins. And now it became clear to which country of the mind this 'Indian' belonged:

> first there were cowboys ... no the Indians ... then the cowboys came along ... they were looking for treasure ... a great big block of gold ... they fight a lot ... they fight about money ... and princesses ... the Indians come along ... they're warriors ... they bang the baddies' heads together and tell them to stop.

In this dialogue Amanda for the first time fully participated. She could bring her gift for story telling to bear in reclaiming the figure for everyone. Sharon starts by stating the traditional colonial mythology of the American frontier. But this is quickly contradicted by Rachel, who knows better – the Indians were there first. Amanda now suggests one of the real motives behind the settlement of the American West: they were looking for gold. This appeals to Sharon's material imagination: there were a lot of fights about money. But for Amanda gold and buried treasure clearly have a more mythological significance and she persists in adding a fairy tale theme about princesses. When the Indians make their entry it is implicitly to avenge this pillage and rape. Naturally they are warriors, and in a reprise of the opening motif, they are invested with a legislative and peacekeeping role. They bang the cowboys' heads together and tell them to stop.

But now it is clear just who or what these cowboys represent: they are the boys in the playground whose racist taunts are making their lives a misery. In lieu of any effective intervention by adults, these girls can only look to themselves, to their own power, here represented by the hybrid character they have jointly created, to step in, bang the boys' heads together and tell them to stop.

This vantage point is reached through their own internal negotiations, and it necessarily follows a tortuous path. For en route they have to grapple with a whole series of contradictions related to gender, ethnicity and class. Members of the group are continually shifting their positions vis à vis each other and the issues under debate. In the process they are setting their own agenda, and staking out areas for further work. And my job was to not intervene, through any irritable reaching after fact.

At the same time we should not forget that what held the group and their collective creation together was not just talk, but the act of drawing. In looking at the final picture it is hard to believe that it was made by so many hands. The process of figuring out always has to be iconic as well as discursive. It is about redrawing an inner landscape of thought and feeling around a significant image which represents that process mimetically whilst also making it narratable.[60] This is something that can never be forced upon children by prescriptive 'insights' and the rhetorics of 'positive imagery'; instead we are directed towards a more complex process in which a range of possible meanings are explored, definitions proposed and challenged, and through these shared deliberations a unique work of dialogic imagination emerges. It was because the Indian Cowgirl Warrior worked at this level that its making authorised Amanda to speak out and thus helped her to begin to find her own distinctive voice, as a Chinese girl, within the group. And in so doing she made space for other, more hopeful, stories to be told about what it means to grow up an East Ender today.

The construction of the Indian cowgirl warrior as a focus of dialogue about class, 'race' and imagined community illustrates some of the resources and strategies that can be mobilised against the closures around these issues which we saw in the talk of the white boys. It offers us a glimpse of a popular – rather than an elite – form of cosmopolitanism. It is not about 'celebrating difference' or asserting some kind of essential identity, but creating a possible world in which the toxicity is taken out of community relations and something like an un/common culture can be built.[61]

In these brief case studies we have traced a micro-politics of discourse and story-telling through which issues of power, identity and belonging are being negotiated by a generation of budding twenty-twelvers, their parents and grandparents, as they struggle to create a viable living space for themselves in a rapidly changing environment. Some of these little island stories provide the building blocks for grand narratives of Britishness that point in quite different directions and imply very different kinds of civil society, not all of which we might want to live in. But they also point beyond any simple fixed distinction between insider and outsider accounts, mono and multiculturalism, reactionary and progressive forms of community action. Even where positions seem most intransigent there is sometimes room for manoeuvre and potential shift. As discussed in the introduction, the imagination of community – whether anchored to 'race' or 'class' – is inherently unstable.

Looking at the material as a whole there is, however, a discernible pattern that emerges. Irrespective of age, gender or ethnicity, there were those whose sense of ontological security was directly and immediately bound up with their attachment to place. They were more dependent on site-specific amenities and social networks, more invested in insider stories, and felt more threatened by the changing social geography of their area. In contrast, there were those whose attachments were to non-place realms of identity, who were more conscious of how outsiders saw them, and more adventurous in their range of contacts and activities. These differences were not just indices of psychological disposition (i.e. signs of introversion/extroversion), but linked to the distribution of social and cultural capital. As a general rule the more of these networking resources an individual had, the more confident and resilient they were in dealing with change. The most defended subjects were those who had the least social and cultural capital, who needed to protect what they had by clinging tenaciously to its most locally embedded forms and as we will see in part two, these positions have a direct bearing on patterns of stake-holding in the Olympics.

It is tempting to extrapolate from what has been happening in London's docklands over the past decade to anticipate what is likely to occur in Stratford in the aftermath of the Olympics. But in order to get these wider co-ordinates of change in some kind of perspective we have first to take a step back and consider some of the structures that have governed the remaking of East London – and this will be attempted in the next chapter.

3. From Canary Wharf to Stratford via Thurrock and Southend:

London's eastwards turn and the making of Thames Gateway

Cities, like container ships, take a long time to change direction. In the twentieth century West London was where most of the new 'hi-tech' industry was concentrated, much of it in ribbon developments into the outer suburbs. In contrast, because of the ancient legal prohibition against dirty and dangerous manufacture being located within the City boundaries, London's smokestack industries, and the city's industrial working class, were concentrated in the East, well down river and downwind of the posh parts of town, around the docks and along the north bank of the river, all the way to Dagenham and beyond (*50, 62-4). Here gas works, sewage works, power stations, oil refineries, chemical plants and brick factories dominated the landscape they so richly polluted, while electricity pylons and railway marshalling yards stalked across what was left of the countryside.

Here is how one working-class boy growing up in Stratford before the second world war remembers the scene:

... Even the Yardley lavender factory in Carpenters Road could not disguise the vile and pestilent odours created by the chemical works of Boake Roberts and the singular aroma arising from British Feeding Meals, which converted domestic refuse into animal foods. Peculiar smells from a warren of manufacturers of fertilisers, vitriol, soaps, inks and varnishes, blended with the fetid nauseating stench of bone-boiling, glue making, pie making and numerous diverse odours from countless obnoxious industries gave that part of Stratford a unique atmosphere indeed. The sulphurous, putrid brew swirled upwards, clinging to the soot and smoke of the London and North Eastern Railway Company, to choke the lungs, blacken the washing and coat the houses with a sticky patina of permanent grime.[1]

John Claridge, View towards Stratford 1960

This was also where the capital dumped its rubbish. Outer East London was the capital's scrapyard, where landfill sites proliferated, and mountains of abandoned cars and fridges grew up alongside motorways. The Bata factory at Rainham and Cunard's Passenger terminal at Tilbury were notable exceptions to the rule that when it came to modern manufacture west was best.

Long before Stratford became known as 'Olympic City' it was famous for being a railway town and the hub of East London's industrial economy. The decline of this economic base in the 1980s, epitomised by the downsizing of Ford Motors in Dagenham, was mainly an effect of the broader competitive failure of British manufacturing in the post-war period, exacerbated by policies of deflation and high exchange rates in the Thatcher years, which led many industrial sectors to go to the wall. But it had a dramatic local effect. The shift to a post-fordist economy based on distributed networks of small, or downsized, enterprises, flexible specialisation and just-in-time production was accompanied by a massive loss of riverside jobs, the relocation of many of the food and produce markets, and widespread disappearance of manufacturing industry, all of which ensured that the East London 'horseshoe' which comprises the 'Olympic' boroughs of Hackney, Tower Hamlets and Newham remained amongst the most deprived in the country.[2] This occurred at the same time as a massive expansion of financial and business services and their relocation from the old historical centre of concentration in the City eastwards to Canary Wharf. As a result the lines of tension between West and East was dramatically re-aligned. The West End literally came and saw and conquered the East – not in the name of a civilising mission, not to get off with the rough trade, but in order to reconstitute itself as the hub of a global knowledge economy.[3]

In inner East London, in Spitalfields, Whitechapel, West India Docks and Hackney, the old industrial warehouses were rapidly converted into hives of creative industry; design studios, loft apartments, art galleries and wine bars provided the cultural quarters where a new bohemia of artists and writers mingled with business executives and media types to establish a critical urban mass quickly dubbed the 'new cosmopolitans'.[4] Brick Lane may have become the new front line of racial tension, but it also provided an important public stage for the multicultural middle class to strut its radical chic (*127-131).[5]

Gentrification also went ethnic in less fashionable parts of town, as newly affluent Asian professionals and business people moved with their families from Tower Hamlets to Essex hamlets in less than one generation; on the other side of the tracks the East End underworld relocated from the once mean, now gentrified streets of Bow to the 'leafy' lanes of Basildon and Billericay;[6] Clacton, once the last resort of East London's pensioners, began to take in younger refugees from Ford's Dagenham. If you believed what you read in the colour supplements during this period, East London's Cockneys fled en masse from the racially tense inner city neighbourhoods where they had grown up to places associated with 'England's green and pleasant land' – or at least to the mud flats and sandbanks of the Thames Estuary. Whereas the move out to Dagenham and Hornchurch in the 1930s and again in the 1950s was widely hailed as a step in the direction of modernisation, the more recent migration further downriver from Barking Reach to Brightlingsea has been seen to represent not just the end of the industrial economy but the end of the line for the English working class as a whole (*70). Living Labour was dead. It had deserted the labour movement, voted for Thatcherism, bought Mondeos and become completely absorbed in a culture of what Raymond Williams presciently called mobile privatism.[7]

As for those who stayed behind, because they were too young, too old, too socially immobilised or too poor to get even one foot on the first rung of the private housing ladder, many continued to live on and off East London's thriving hidden economy. Those who found themselves trapped in welfare poverty or backyards industry were, as we have seen in Chapter Two, often assimilated to an underclass, a new kind of 'residuum' carrying out low paid 'McJobs', and occupying what planners referred to as holes or tears in the urban fabric. Not surprisingly then, some of these groups came to be characterised and sometimes demonised as suffering from 'poor whites syndrome', even when they were Asian. Cockneys, having been comprehensively rehabilitated by their contribution to the myth of the blitz, now found themselves no longer the backbone of the post-nation but resuming their traditional pariah status as a race apart.[8] Sometimes they were glamorised as providing a little local colour, useful for the repackaging of the East End as an exotic venue for the cultural tourist industry: the custom of slumming dies hard. The 1990s saw erstwhile pearly queens camping it up for the passing trade, whilst young Asian comedians stepped into the shoes of Charlie Chester and stood up in 'authentic Cockney' pubs to tell anti-racist jokes that would have had the cheeky chappy doing a knees-up in his grave.

In fact commentators with their ears to the ground detected many new signs and sounds of the multicultural times emanating from the East End. In the 1980s Romford's Ian Dury's Blockheads blended ska and pub anthems with rock'n'roll to give a distinctive two-tone flavour to white men talking the blues. The bard of Barking, Billy Bragg, re-wrote the anthems of the free-born Englishman in the raw idioms of punk, and located them in a very precise memoryscape:

> For as long as I can remember, whenever my father and uncles spoke lovingly of their motorbikes, of speed and the wind in their hair, the road they spoke most of was the A127, the Southend Arterial, with its three-mile straights, out beyond Gallows Corner. It was where they could push their Nortons and Triumphs up to 100mph, 'doing the ton' down to the Halfway House roundabout and back. For their sons, the Boy Racers in their two-door Ford Capris and jacked-up Escort Mk1s, the road to ride was one of sharp bends and swift change-downs, of New Towns and land fills – the A13. This was the main drag out to the Promised Land of the Goldmine Discotheque on Canvey Island, caravan capital of the world. This was the route to the Kursaal at Southend and a plate of cockles or a cup of whelks. This was the road to the paradise of the Kiss-Me-Quick Never Never Land of the Essex Coast ... Me and my dad have joined the Saxons and the Peasants' Revolt in history, but the A13 is still there, rolling through a Springsteenesque landscape in which riverine Essex takes the place of the New Jersey shore, a tarmacadam trail to the Promised Land.[9]

In the 'noughties' Nitin Sawhney and Dizzee Rascal developed a musically sophisticated but still raw East End edge to the Cockney diasporic groove. Chas and Dave have been made to sound like the end of pier concert party they always were. Meanwhile on the streets, parks and playgrounds of East London, Cockney rhyming slang was being translated and made over into a black rap attack on Babylon by Smiley Culture. Elsewhere in Thatcherite-cum-Blairite Britain, Estuary English – that strangely frozen interlanguage where the cockney guttural softens to an Essex burr – came to epitomise the new cool melting pot that social mobility and the 'end of class' was meant to be creating.

It was no coincidence that the eastwards turn in London's growth should be accompanied by a cultural turn in policies of urban regeneration, and not just because the ex-docklands areas provided so much badly needed space for London's expanding creative industries. The definition of culture expanded too. Its terms of reference now included Zen cooking and Feng Shui, hip hop and pogo dancing, not to mention video gaming and wind surfing. In this more democratic form, the function of culture was to transform the 'regen' landscape into a fresh and excitingly exotic territory for the 'Wharfers' and the other newly arrivant East Enders to explore.[10]

What the new urban explorers in fact found on their doorsteps was a vast building site, and surrounding it a post-industrial wasteland comprised of heavily polluted brownfield sites, abandoned factories, boarded-up shops, derelict pubs, run-down estates, and scrapyard after scrapyard. The challenge then was to turn this scene of ruination – which was also the graveyard of so many working-class hopes and struggles to build the New Jerusalem in their own back gardens – into some approximation of a 'des res' area where single young upwardly mobile professionals would want to live.[11] And even, one day perhaps, bring up their children.

Canary Wharf had quickly established itself as an iconic landmark of the new economy, even if it also had to ensure that, despite its E14 snail mail address, its telephone code (0207) located it where it counted most, in the world of virtual communication, within the boundaries of the old City of London. Yet no amount of glossy property developers' brochures could disguise the fact that at the heart of this new metropolitan centre lay a profound inner emptiness and absence.

In her 'River History' Lavinia Greenlaw documents one way this vacuum was filled with an ersatz history:

> A film crew arrives, on a costly location shoot
> For *jack the ripper*. It's a crowded night.
> Intent on atmosphere, they've cluttered the alleyways
> with urchins, trollops and guttersnipes
> who drift to the waterfront when they are not working
> and gaze across at the biggest emptiest office block in Europe
> and its undefendable, passing light.

But apart from a film set, what was the identity of docklands without the docks? A playground for watersports enthusiasts? A site for post-industrial archaeologists to dig? A riverine prospect to gladden the eyes of tired advertising executives?

Over time as the economy picked up, a place identity of a kind did emerge, largely due to the status of the Wharf itself, and its dense concentration of workers: it was the City beyond the City walls.[12] But it was more difficult to establish a similar identity for that vast expanse of dereliction down wind, down market and downriver of the Wharf, formerly known as the Royal Docks. Not to mention the rest of the all-but-collapsed maritime economy and its hinterland stretching along both banks of the river from Dagenham through Rainham Marshes, Thurrock, Grays and Tilbury all the way to Southend. How to make this 'terra incognita' into marketable real estate? That was the challenge set for the creators of 'Thames Gateway' – the largest and most ambitious attempt to regenerate a de-industrialised area in Europe. But help was at hand.

These developments did not go unnoticed by artists and writers, many of whom were now living in the East End, and who indeed were often the advance guard of the new settlers; first by their presence and then through their work, they put the area on the cultural map and gave to what was otherwise widely regarded as a soulless 'Cockney Siberia', a colourful and more culturally inhabitable frontier image; it allowed those moving in to think that they were pioneers, living a little, but not too, dangerously at the rough edge of town.

The group – although it never was one, still less a 'school', comprised historians, novelists, poets, photographers, painters and performance artists; over the past twenty years they have produced a renaissance in the way the urban landscape is depicted.[13] Their work was influenced as much by each other as by what was happening in and to East London; they were acutely aware of the Blakean and gothic traditions discussed in Chapter One, as well as experiments in modernist art and literature and post-modern narrative. As a result there is a diversity of approaches. Patrick Wright's *Journey through the Ruins* provided a documentary account, written somewhat in the style of Orwell's *Road to Wigan Pier*, of the devastating effect that Thatcherite policies were having on the inner city – and in particular Hackney – during the 1980s. Patrick Keiller's films cover the same ground, but, like the scripted walks of Janet Cardiff, break with documentary realism and insert a fictional narrative between the city landscape and its navigation, to create a mysterious, multi-layered memoryscape out of sync with itself.[14] Peter Ackroyd's *Biography of London*, whilst also concerned to peel away hidden layers of meaning, remains more factually embedded and anchored in historical chronology. His historical novels set in eighteenth and nineteenth century London often explore the terrain mapped out by the gothic imagination, but again anchor the story in graphically realistic descriptions of its urban texture. In the apocalyptic science fictions of Michael Moorcock and J.G. Ballard, as we have seen, the gothic strikes back, after the manner of Arthur Machen and Richard Jeffries, to create a twenty-first century vision of Blake's London/Babylon.

In the paintings of Jock McFadyen there is an interesting convergence of influences.[15] His early work was informed by the gritty realism of Sickert and the Euston Road School, and by the industrial cityscapes of L.S. Lowry. But his move to East London, where he has lived and worked for the past thirty years, has stimulated his gothic imagination. He produced a powerful series of paintings of East London's 'lost' cinemas, some of them derelict, others turned into bingo halls or pubs, in which the buildings look all too haunted by their past. Graffiti is an ever present feature in his urban landscapes, and their palimpsest of inscriptions becomes a powerful visual metaphor of the 'writing on the walls', a graphic reminder that amidst the glittering edifices of hypermodernity – which he also paints – there is another kind of conversation going on.

In the 1990s, soundtracked by Billy Bragg's hymn to the A13 and Ian Dury's praise songs to the Essex badlands, he began to explore edge city, seeking out the badly stitched seams of East London's urban fabric: flyovers, railway lines, the interzones where city and country meet, and to populate these no man's lands with characters who might also prefer to remain incognito. McFadyen's figures have been compared to Francis Bacon's, and they certainly often look the worse for wear as they cling to one another, or sit, huddled in isolation in bus shelters or subway stations, trying to keep warm. These are narrative paintings in which the dreadful has already happened; the people in them certainly have a story to tell if only they could get the words out. In *Piggy Back* (see illustration) we can only guess at the

Jock McFadyen, Piggy Back

nature of the bond between this couple posed so dominantly yet so precariously against the backdrop of Canary Wharf. This poignant image of resolutely human frailty stranded in waste ground while the Wharf, downsized, looks almost fragile against the night sky, serves to underscore the transvaluation of values that McFadyen seems to be aiming at, not least in reversing the power of place and people in depicting this figure/ground relationship.

Iain Sinclair's work is perhaps the best-known, and is certainly the most controversial of the group.[16] A self-styled 'travelodge tramp' and literary mud lark, he has staked out his territory with a series of novels and commentaries which explore London's 'other scenes' in a way that embeds their occulted history and geography in a sharply material sense of the urban landscape and its changing forms. He is deeply influenced by the gothic tradition, but has no time for the moralising sentimentality of the romantic ruinologists or urban slummers. He is vehement in his opposition to the iron cage of rationality in which modernist planners have attempted to contain the lines of desire that Londoners have drawn across their city streets, but his writing owes most to the experimental techniques through which writers like Virginia Woolf (*Mrs Dalloway*), James Joyce (*Ulysses*) and John Dos Passos (*Manhattan Transfer*) have sought to transcribe the effervescent rhythms of modernity in London, Dublin and New York. As a result his novels read like stream of consciousness travelogues, chronicling the edginess of the metropolitan scene as it imprints itself on his characters' thoughts and lives, while his documented walks in and around London are essentially works of fiction aiming for an imaginative truth, rather than a purely factual one.

He has frequently been accused of vicarious flaneurism, and certainly he is no ethnographer; he is a scavenger of impressions, just passing through, not staying around long enough to observe closely, let alone participate in the scenes he describes. The subcultural geography he traces is produced as part of a narrative strategy that is geared up to register spaces teetering on the edge of becoming non places, their denizens non-persons; but he is not about to re-locate his human material in any more familiar kind of landscape that would restore their capacity to tell their own tales. His memoir cum anti-Olympic rant *Ghost Milk: calling time on the grand project* – the main title is a characteristic quote from Don De Lillo's novel *Underworld* – is something of an exception to this rule, since it includes an account of his adventures as a young man about Stratford Town, inter-spliced with scenes from his encounters with assorted unconventional characters from in and around the Olympic Park. Yet it is still a highly moralised landscape, which has a cautionary tale to tell about the destruction of urban wastelands by slash and burn re-development.

The East End is Sinclair's favourite haunt and he materialises its ghosts with a sharp eye for the surreal phenomenology created by its rapid regeneration, detailing with loving care the wreckage produced by the often violent collision of the area's past and future, almost as if it was being curated for an exhibition. Like McFadyen, his other preferred stamping ground is edge city, where the wilder forms of economic and social life can take root and flourish.[17] Where urban economists see signs of the city's endless capacity for self renewal, he detects a more hidden and possibly more productive attempt to resist the gravitational pull of the megalopolis.

His novel *Dining on Stones* is a good example of the Sinclair method and style. The book can best be read as a sequel to *Downriver*, the novel set in Docklands on the cusp of its transformation in the mid 1980s, which turned Sinclair from a cult literary figure into a public intellectual. *Dining* announces itself as a road novel, and the influence of Kerouac and Burroughs is evident throughout, as is the clipped forensic prose style of Dashiell Hammett. *Dining* is more downriver than *Downriver*, both in the literal sense that it is set further east, in the Thames Gateway, where London's badlands merge into those of Essex, and also in exploring the more extreme reaches of the gothic imagination. And the tone of the book is as edgy as the landscape it describes:

Effie wasn't part of the story. That much was clear. She introduced me to a location she had a thing about once; she'll return as a friend, a tripper.
'So the first time I ever came here', she said, 'it was by train, at night. I walked from the station to the main part of town. Everything was deserted. I couldn't believe my eyes. I kept walking, hardly anyone to be seen. The restaurants were getting ready for the night. But who were they preparing the tables for? The ghosts? The dead? At night everything is transformed.

Anything can happen. Nobody will blink, nobody will hear you'.

I was getting ready to audition. I could become one of those ghosts. I saw Effie to her train.

And I stayed put. The next morning I walked into an estate agent's office in the Old Town: the woman was preoccupied, servicing the thick tongue of a rubber plant with a Slavic thoroughness. You could hear the rubber squeak. The man, jacketless, tilted heavily on one elbow, was giving handshakes on the telephone. Amused eyes weighed me up: timewaster. They know I don't have the equity but they slide, without breaking away from plant or phone, through the motions.

'What are you looking for – exactly? Low forties? Sixty ceiling? We specialise in cheeky offers. You never know your luck.'

'A second chance', I wanted to reply. New birth certificate, clean passport. Less pressure around the skull, fewer bills. And I'd like to meet the woman described to me by another woman. A writer, artist of sorts, whose name is mentioned, with awe and affection, in an off-highway shack, a breakfast bar in West Thurrock. Red and green sign – THE LOG CABIN – reflected in rainwater on the indented lid of a blue tin drum. Oily beads plopping from hanging basket: rusticated Americana. Estuary ambiguous: the flavour of the times.[18]

The extract begins by laying out a topography of the urban uncanny: a ghost town, a restaurant feeding a city of the dead, night time where everything familiar is transformed and anything can happen. Then the action switches to an apparently more mundane scene, a visit to the estate agent, except that there is something decidedly odd and unsettling about the way the woman is treating that rubber plant ... Then we are back on the road again, with Kerouac and the beats, and a literary encounter in an 'off highway shack'. The A13 has been metamorphosed into Route 66, the Log Cabin with its neon sign and 'rusticated Americana' might be straight out of a painting by Edward Hopper, or Jock McFadyen, but its edge-of-town seediness is given a precise location: a breakfast bar in West Thurrock. The short staccato sentences that at first sounded so hard-bitten Brooklyn now take on a more local Essex boy twang. We are somewhere in mid Atlantic, but this too is given a local habitation and a name – estuary ambiguous – and suddenly the Thames Gateway in its very dislocatedness has become flavour of the month.

Sinclair's methodology, especially in other hands, can produce mixed results. His technique is basically cinematic, creating a collage of images which riff off each other, at times reading like a literary equivalent of a musical mash up and giving an aesthetic gloss to the scene. Here for example is his description of a visit to the Olympic Park during an early phase of its construction:

Visit here as early as you like and there will be no unsightly tags, no slogans; a viscous slither of blue. Like disinfectant running down the slopes of a urinal trough. Circumambulation by the fence painters is endless, day after day, around the entire circuit; repairing damage, covering up protests. Sticky trails drip into grass verges, painterly signatures. Plywood surfaces never quite dry. Subtle differences of shade and texture darken into free-floating Franz Kline blocks.[19]

At its most superficial this method yields a simple inventory of the esoteric and bizarre, an eccentric, off-the-wall guide to aspects of the urban landscape overlooked in the tourist literature. And a knee-jerk reaction against any form of modernism. At its most strategic we are offered a way of exploring the city's development that brings to light its underlying fault-lines, the cracks in the edifice of modernity and the symptomatic states of mind of those who have got stuck there.

The trajectory of London's eastward's redevelopment that I have briefly sketched is erratic. It hops, skips and jumps about, leapfrogging over places that badly need regenerating, like Canning Town and Purfleet, concentrating instead on a few premium investment sites. It follows the Dockland Light Railway from Canary Wharf to Stratford but then it suddenly stops.[20] The result is an urban fabric with lots of new holes in it, providing niches for the popular gothic imagination, which all too rapidly populates them with bogeymen; this is also what attracts writers and artists in search of raw material, only too pleased to refurbish these interstitial spaces as ideal homes for creative experimentation. The flaneur, the lyric urban poet, the post-modern ethnographer, make the running as interlocutors of this edge city; all of them feel most at home where cultural and social mixes are at their most flamboyant. Their political and aesthetic challenge is to find hints of otherness in less promising milieu, to become connoisseurs of suburban streets and run-down public housing estates, parking lots and out-of-town shopping malls.[21]

Through the work of these intermediaries a new kind of orientalism has emerged, in which affluent East Enders discover the inscrutable face of poverty living on the edge of their gated communities, just out of reach of their charitable assumptions and providing a persistent point of disorientation. For in this version of 'splintering urbanism' you get on the train at Canary Wharf expecting to arrive in Stratford, but fall asleep and find yourself in Thurrock instead. All the shops and even the internet cafés are shut. And it has started to rain.

A space of flows?

The Thames Gateway Plan for Sustainable Communities, to give it its official title, was a major attempt to tackle the structural effects of de-industrialisation in London. The largest regeneration project in Europe, its purview stretched from East of Tower Bridge on both sides of the river down to the mouth of the estuary, taking in twenty mostly discontinuous development zones on the way, including inland Billericay and seaside resort Southend (see map). The plan was conceived in a period when much of government thinking about regeneration was focused on creating new platforms for regional development.[22] Up until the 1980s the aim of regional policy had been to serve as a mechanism for the central state to tackle socio-economic inequalities through redistributive

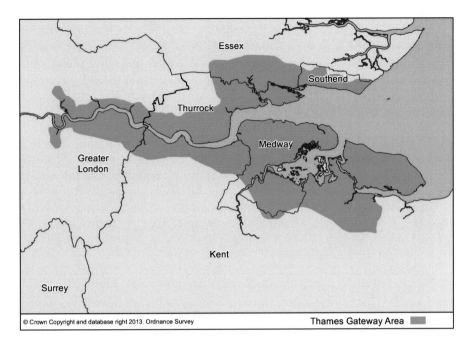

Map of Thames Gateway

forms of public investment, for example by channelling resources from the relatively well-off South East to the North of England. With the shift to a market-oriented, deregulated model of regeneration, the aim became to enhance an area's competitive advantage in the global economy by building upon existing assets, whether material, cultural or social.[23] For this purpose new forms of partnership had to be created, operating at a supra-local but sub-regional level.

As an instance of this new kind of administrative space, the Thames Gateway was designed to provide an elastic framework for economic activity linking downriver London to Continental Europe. Given its scope and scale, cutting across the existing planning jurisdictions of both central government and the local state – whose stakes nevertheless had to be represented – the Gateway evolved a delivery apparatus of quite bewildering complexity, completely lacking in any mechanism whereby the populations in the different areas could come together and make their collective voice heard. The plan still appealed rhetorically to a redistributive strategy, and gained support from hard-pressed local authorities, but its main thrust was towards the big players in the global economy.

One key task for this new structure of governance was to stitch together a Thames Gateway story to fill the vacuum created by the collapse of the old river and port economy. Partly this had to be woven out of the unravelled storylines associated with the maritime and industrial trades which for over three centuries had materially connected communities living on the North and

South banks of the Thames; these narrative threads now had to be woven into a post-imperial and post-industrial landscape – one based not only on the flow of capital goods but of information and cultural goods. The prime mover in the unfolding story of regeneration was no longer the river itself – now relegated to a supporting role as a purveyor of carefully edited picturesque waterfront views – but the road, rail and air transport links which were to connect the area to Europe, and transform it into a 'space of flows'.[24]

Much thinking on London's transport development was influenced by Paris, whose Regional Express Railway network (the RER) had sought to improve the economic integration of the greater Paris region. The RER provides a high speed link between destinations located in all quadrants of the city, passing through its centre and producing a lattice-like network to complement the familiar radial hub-spoke pattern of the earlier rail system. In London, Crossrail and Thameslink have constituted a slowly developing orbital railway system in which Stratford has once again become a major hub, only this time of a post-industrial economy.

Unfortunately, one of the concomitants of such a globalised urban landscape is a new kind of 'terminal architecture':[25] giant shed-like structures housing logistic centres and transport hubs, sport stadia, shopping and entertainment complexes, often existing alongside featureless dormitory-type conurbations populated by commuters still trapped in the gravitational pull of the metropolitan economy (*155-8). In the case of Thames Gateway, such an outcome may be one of its regeneration logics, but it is also strongly contra-indicated: nothing is more calculated to put off the international companies seeking to relocate their HQs in high quality environments than proximity to such non-places where people are just 'passing through'.[26]

The main attempt to mitigate this effect has been centred on imaginative re-descriptions – or re-brandings – of place. Thames Gateway was to be a 'sustainable community', to hold out the promise of new and more environmentally friendly forms of civic amenity, held together by a shared sense of belonging and place identity. So just at the point when regionalism goes global in a material sense, it also goes local in purely symbolic terms.[27]

The Gateway became the focus for the project of a new localism which tried to insert a 'bottom up' approach to regeneration, based on the principle of double devolution (from central to local government, and from government to communities), into what was all too palpably a massively top-down operation. But because the Gateway is made up of so many disparate and disconnected communities who do not feel they are part of a common enterprise, the proposal to decentralise its delivery also conjured up the prospect of 'Balkanising' its governance, and perhaps for that reason it never got off the drawing board. Instead, architects and planners started talking about the Gateway as a new kind of 'linear city', an 'inbetween city', or even as forming part of a polycentric megalopolis, in the hope that this would somehow give narrative coherence to the enterprise.[28]

Thames Gateway superimposed its own confused spatiality on what was already a fractured geography. The volume of social interaction between West and East End had the effect of intensifying the North/South cleavage created by the Thames, which became much more of a physical barrier now that it was no longer a major artery of trade. Riverine communities that had hitherto been linked through a network of economic and social relationships turned their back on the river and each other. In fact East London has never included the South bank in its orbit. Thamesmead, opposite Barking, is South London not East. Meanwhile on the North bank, the now radial, now orbital, transport network triangulated Stratford, Canary Wharf and the Royal Docks into a new metropolitan configuration, as each of these emergent centres of economic activity began to exert their own gravitational pull on London's traffic with the world.

New things happen

Perhaps the most extraordinary aspect of the Thames Gateway story was how little of it leaked out to the people actually living in the designated zones of change. A survey showed that only 43 per cent of those interviewed had ever heard of it, and of these only a third knew that it was something to do with regeneration. Eleven per cent thought it was the name of a supermarket chain, and only 2 per cent had ever attended any consultation event associated with it. On this evidence the Gateway was one of the best-kept secrets in modern planning history, confined to those directly involved, professionally or politically, in its implementation. Partly this can be put down to a general withdrawal from civic involvement of any kind, but some at least of the blame must be laid at the door of the government departments and quangos that had administrative responsibility for delivery. Their chronic failure to embed the project in local communities, despite sometimes elaborate consultation exercises, is down to the fact that they produced lots of glossy documentation but refused to consider ways in which the process of public deliberation could actually be facilitated. At the very minimum this meant building informal networks between communities across the Gateway and creating new platforms of civic engagement.[29]

It was out of some recognition of this failure that Yvette Cooper, the then communities minister responsible for the plan, in conjunction with the Thames Gateway Strategic Partnership, commissioned a report from the Commission for Architecture and the Built Environment (CABE) in 2006.[30] The project set out to map the social, cultural and environmental character of the Gateway, with the aim of 'informing the strategic development of its unique identity'. The report claims that it is based on listening to what people in the Gateway have to say. A number of workshops were held, although it seems that most of the people who attended were the usual suspects – professionals of one sort or another already concerned with TG. Sir Peter Hall, the plan's original architect, and Sir Terry Farrell, both have major talk-on parts. It is this rather narrow range of quotation and comment which is used to give the text evidential credibility. In contrast, the report by the IPPR, *Gateway People*, for all that it is based on only four focus groups, gives a very different and much more negative picture of popular perceptions.[31]

The CABE report is entitled 'New things happen', and it is divided into three main sections: *Where it's at*, which talks about the economic role of place making; *New things happen*, which sets out the Gateway's Unique Selling Points; and *Exploring the Vision*, which deals in turn with *Redefining Work*, *Reconnecting with Nature*, *Reasserting Individualism* and *Reinventing our identity*, the core values the report espouses. The tone throughout is jaunty and upbeat, and is set in the preface by John Sorrell, CABE's chair. He calls the report a 'visionary guide to TG's future', and claims that what has come through in this study is a pioneering culture. 'Perhaps this comes from living at the turning of the tide. It makes the Gateway feel less like a place and more like a journey.'

Two points are perhaps worth making here: to re-describe what purports to be a report of a piece of research in these terms effectively blurs the distinction between an evidence-based policy document and promotional literature, a move that is typical of the narrative turn in urban planning.[32] Secondly, the image of pioneers living adventurously at the edge of tidal change is a central trope of the whole document. A narrative landscape is mapped out, peopled by rugged individualists, whose spirit of innovation and enterprise is located both geographically as a special character of estuary dwellers (courtesy of Joseph Conrad) and historically as the special patrimony of an island race (courtesy of Winston Churchill). All kinds of stories are recruited for this purpose. The Plotlanders of Canvey Island, who built their own homes in defiance of the law and all known planning regulations, are welcomed on board, as are the decidedly dodgy dystopic denizens of Iain Sinclair's post-industrial wastelands; Billy Bragg's travelling story of the A13 and Ken Worpole's survey of Essex's radical hinterlands also make guest appearances. All these once discordant voices are made to sing in tune, their descant seamlessly blended into a harmonised discourse of neoliberal modernity. So this is how the Wild East came to be civilised and settled by a new class of ex urban gentrifiers – by turning its erstwhile economic and social marginality into a unique selling point.

The report's green credentials are impeccable – and undoubtedly the sections dealing with environmental issues are the strongest, or at least the most persuasive. Yet the report also dodges the Number One issue – the building of so much new housing on a flood plain at a time when some scenarios of global warming predict tidal surges well beyond the capacity of existing barrier defence systems to contain. The Canvey Island floods of 1953 are conspicuous by their absence from a document concerned to establish its roots in local history. Missing too is any mention of recent experiments in designing hydraulic cities to combat flood risk. Presumably in both cases such references might have conjured up less than positive images of the area's past and future. Against this background, all the talk about promoting a new environmental aesthetic 'capable of inspiring innovation in architecture and landscape design' begins to sound like eco-elitism – greening the Gateway to enhance its desirability as a place to live and work for those whose incomes give them a wide range of choice and who can afford to pay more for a better quality environment.

The final section on 'reinventing identity' draws extensively on Billy Bragg – with a sideways nod at Simon Schama's *Landscapes of Memory*, to claim that the Thames Gateway Estuary is the first port of call for every new influence, and as such distils much that is common to a more general national identity. What this wider identity consists of, apparently, is the resilience required to mix local cultures with a continuous influx of new populations and ideas. This robust cosmopolitan character, with its 'spirited pioneering identity', is contrasted with 'soulless suburban sprawl' – which along with industrialism is the real villain of the CABE regeneration story. The fact that local prides of place can sometimes turn nasty and be less than welcoming to newcomers, especially if their faces or cultures are visibly different, is not mentioned. Presumably it is not something about which the audience for the report – described as clients and investors in both the public and private sectors – want to hear. Yet on the last page there is a strangely ambivalent image/text statement, which manages to both indirectly recognise and disavow the issue.

Am I that name? Lollipop lady reinvents the Gateway

On the left-hand side of the page there is an unattributed quote:

Local people want to ensure their presence is recognised by continuity. This can come down to such simple [author comment: and inexpensive] things as naming streets after local characters.

In its patronising crassness this has surely to win some kind of prize for dropped brick of the year.

On the right-hand side of the page is a photograph of (according to the caption) Lollipop lady Mrs Sutton watching over the morning school run at Southend on Sea (see illustration).The lady in question is shown holding a stop sign, whilst on both sides of the crossing are large billboards advertising luxury apartment interiors, presumably aimed at Southend's new creative class. So just what kind of traffic is she trying to stop? We are left to guess. Mrs Sutton's own views on Thames Gateway or the regeneration of Southend are not available. Perhaps one place to start a different kind of narrative is just there.

In the narrative landscape which we *have* been offered, the key drivers of the story are formulaic ideas – sustainable community, pioneering spirit – which are variously embodied and articulated by specially designated place holders. The formal elements of this grand narrative are all present: the initial moment of disequilibrium represented by the TG plan itself – breaking with old ways of thinking about work, planning and the environment associated with the era of industrialism and suburbanism; the provocation, which the report by its very publication is supposed to elicit; the actions which are to flow from it – making new things happen; the sanctions, which are hinted at in passing if challenges are not met and opportunities missed; and finally re-equilibrium – the seamless blending of past, present and future in a new compact between nature and culture, symbolised by the creation of an all-embracing estuarial identity and economy. For this purpose the story-line makes continual use of flashbacks and flash forwards. It is nothing if not proleptic: from section to section the argument is advanced in such a fashion as to forestall all possible objections, even though exactly what these might be is never stated! Although much play is made with the notion of the open, dialogical nature of the exercise, the wide consultation, etc, this discourse is as monologic as the most prescriptive kinds of policy statement issuing from a government department.

There are, however, traces of other narrative genres. The mytho-logics of regeneration are present in the epic battle struck between the forces of Enlightenment and Progress – represented by the Knowledge Economy, Green Politics, the New Individualism and Localism – versus the forces of Darkness and Reaction – represented by Industrialism, Suburban Sprawl and the insular solidarities of Old Labour. There are also hints of a hidden hermeneutics centred on the issue of civic disengagement and the democratic deficit, because amidst all the upbeat aspirationalism there is an anxious reiteration of the need to establish a higher common principle to do with a sense of shared belonging or collective identity. There has to be more to place building than cultivating your own selfish prospects, claiming more room and a better view, or cultivating your garden as a refuge from the storms of history.

Finally, buried in amongst all this are some rational propositions about the need to consider new ways of designing and delivering the built environment; in particular there is a useful focus on the need to encourage construction companies to experiment with new ecological building forms which challenge the cultural conservatism of home buyers.

The writers of the report were undoubtedly faced with a difficult – indeed impossible – task. Civic Imagineering – the marketing of a place to potential visitors or residents – is easiest when the place itself has easily recognisable and well established assets.[33] The Lake District and the Yorkshire Dales practically sell themselves. But while the Thames Gateway estuary does have a desolate beauty, and in places a 'wasteland' aspect which appeals to some painters and photographers, it entirely lacks the picturesque charm of the Thames Valley, or the coastal sublime associated with mountainous seas breaking against rugged cliffs to be found in parts of Cornwall. Promoting the Gateway as an adventure story, a new frontier waiting to be colonised by pioneering spirits, is a good marketing strategy aimed at young professionals, but is contra-indicated for almost everyone else, especially low-income families and senior citizens.

Moreover, identities cannot simply be imposed on places. Places take a long time to develop an identity that means something on the ground, and this is invariably produced by communities themselves, and culturally embedded as a narrative distillation of shared experience. Tyneside and Merseyside have strong regional identities of this kind, rooted in their industrial pasts as ports and shipbuilding centres, but reinforced by their distinctive contribution to contemporary culture, including of course football and popular music. In contrast it is hard to imagine anyone, when asked where they live, ever replying that they 'come from the Gateway' with the same conviction and pride that people say they come from the East End. So perhaps, rather than inventing estuarial traditions to establish a tenuous link between so many disparate places, it would be better to recognise Thames Gateway for what it is: a planning-cum-scripting device applied to a multiplicity of discrete regeneration projects branded under this name. In describing it as a journey rather than a place, CABE's director hints at the problem, but it is not adequately addressed in the report itself.

What it points to, though, is another strategy, one that ditches the attempt to construct a grand unifying narrative and instead allows more locally situated stories to gain a foothold. For the fact is that the Thames Gateway sits awkwardly in a geographical imagination of the nation. There are no white cliffs to suggest a rugged island fortress, no mountains to offer sublime prospects, no picturesque pastoral, only miles of desolate mudflats and sandbanks, shifting treacherously with the tides, merging sea and landscape under enormous skies. As we have seen it is this very amorphousness that makes the area so attractive a subject for writers and artists. For here the political challenge posed by the porous nature of the nation's boundaries is doubled over in the aesthetic challenge of giving them a precise compositional form.

That the challenge can be met was demonstrated by a collaboration between Ken Worpole, a cultural historian-cum-environmentalist concerned to explore a grassroots version of 'going with the flow', and Jason Orton, a photographer working on a project to document the Gateway's regeneration. Their *350 miles* is unusual in at least two ways.[34] Worpole mixes the genres of personal memoir, tour guide and political commentary to great effect, combining natural and cultural history to provide a seamless web of associations linking the people and places he talks about. He is especially good on the nonconformist individuals and groups who have been such a feature of Essex life, but he does not recruit them for an ideological message. Given that his family were part of the Cockney Diaspora, moving from the East End to Essex in the 1950s, he is keen to show that this was *not* about 'white flight' but prompted by a kind of popular environmentalism. He succeeds in demonstrating that there is more to Basildon than Essex Man (or Essex Girl), and that Jaywick Sands is not populated by dodgy characters out of an Iain Sinclair novel. In fact his whole strategy represents an implicit critique of Sinclair's gothic pedestrianism; rather than searching for bizarre discords in the figure/ground relations thrown up by post-industrialism, he is concerned to explore the historical byways that lead to the present unstable configurations of the area's identity.

Jason Orton's camera is also alert to shifting contours, as represented by the tideline, that liminal space between land and sea that Rachel Carson has so brilliantly described and which has long served as a natural symbol of change.[35] But he rescues the tide from historical cliché. For there is another sense in which his photographs explore edginess. In stark contrast to Worpole's dense human portraiture, there are no people in his pictures. The land and sea scapes are empty of all but birds. This radical de-population is not about an empirical fact – for, though few people nowadays work the wetlands or the sea, that scape has now become busy with recreationalists of every kind. Their absence from the picture and the intense stillness that pervades these scenes speaks of something else, something we might describe as a coastal uncanny.

The picture of the derelict Bata factory (see illustration), shot from a vantage point looking across what is now a brown-field site, shows the modernist ruin looking almost immaculate, until on closer inspection you notice the broken windows and peeling paint. Other buildings in this series – the Minewatching Tower at Dengie, the now decommissioned nuclear power station at Bradwell, Nissan Huts overgrown by brambles, broken bits of pill boxes piled up on a beach – all these images refer us back to the pictorial conventions of romantic ruin sentiment in both its picturesque and sublime registers.[36] But if the shades of Constable and Turner are sometimes evoked, it is only to put these pictorial conventions in question. Military and industrial architecture, like modernism itself, was built to weather the storms of history. But these buildings, made redundant by the onward march of globalisation, remain strangely untouched by time. Wind and water scoured, sun bleached, yet essentially intact – the final triumph of form over function. Orton's eye captures the irony brilliantly as his camera poses these monoliths against sky and field, silently commanding the prospect of their obsolescence.

Jason Orton, Bata factory East Tilbury

A new spirit of capitalism – or business as usual?

The broader question raised by Thames Gateway and the eastwards turn in London's regeneration is whether this is business as usual, or whether we are seeing the emergence of a qualitatively different kind of urban process. Regeneration is often held to exemplify the destructive creativity of modern capitalism. But the cultural turn now seems to promise to effectively mitigate if not entirely remove the destructive impact of large-scale urban development and to promote an entirely creative process of environmental and social renewal in which – to anticipate the 2012 Olympic slogan – 'everyone is a winner'.

The release of this creative energy is only possible because capital has already first destroyed the material and social basis of its own earlier industrial formation, and hence cleared the way for the emergence of a 'creative class', people who are employed in a wide range of local/global cultural services, including design, marketing and communications. As we have seen, this is the key target population for Thames Gateway, and they are indeed a relatively new phenomenon.[37] They are part of an enterprise-cum-management culture that seeks to deliver the goods precisely by *not* talking about profit maximisation; growing the business is now about achieving harmony, balance and, of course, sustainability. Norms of efficiency and instrumental rationality are out; constructing the beautifully crafted business plan is in. Courtesy of

129

post-modern management theory, the new age business person and the evangelical bureaucrat reinvent themselves as artisans of the avant garde. The hip estate agent now joins the poet in asserting that 'people live not in places, but in the description of places'. The narrative turn in planning discourse fuses language which deletes human agency and causality with its opposite – an idiom of hyper-individualism which proclaims the expressive *jouissance* of 'living the good life'. Obsessive self-referentiality has become a necessary counterpoint to a world in which 'stuff just happens'.

Luc Boltanski and Eve Chiapello have discerned here a new spirit of capitalism in which art has replaced religion (more specifically Protestantism), absorbing the aesthetic critique of industrialism into its post-industrial work ethic. Here is how one of its gurus describes the phenomenon:

> The manager knows that the contemporary business world is chaotic and unpredictable, where rules of logic and rationality, let alone morality do not prevail. So he sets out to achieve some kind of aesthetic order and ethical meaning, by providing a quality product and service, and educating the client or consumer to appreciate it.[38]

Once the irrationality of market forces is fully recognised, the way to go is to go with the global flow and learn to ride the increasingly unpredictable waves of capitalist renewal rather than attempt to bend these forces to the corporate will. What that means in practice is protecting your own niche market by establishing a distinctive and innovative business profile. Just as the launch of a new policy document becomes an end in itself, in terms of the publicity it creates for the 'Thames Gateway brand', so the performativity of the business plan lies in the artfulness or moral persuasiveness with which its mission is communicated to potential clients, not in any evaluation of objective measures of failure or success.

The relationship between the cultural turn in regeneration and this aesthetic/ethical make-over of its business conduct was brought home to me in the offices of one of the UK's largest civil engineers, responsible for major development projects in Thames Gateway. The office space was open plan but subdivided by a series of floor to ceiling glass walls. Engraved on each 'wall' was a series of words derived from the company's mission statement viz:

INNOVATION–INTEGRATION–COMMUNICATION–MUTUALITY–
PARTNERSHIP–TEAMWORK–INTERACTIVE–FUN–LIVING–
OUTPERFORM–VALUE–COMMITMENT–SMOOTH–SUSTAINABLE–
IDEAS–FINANCE–INTELLIGENCE–FINANCE–TRAVELLING–
COMMUNITIES...

The apparent transparency of the inscriptions – it is possible to see through each word as the eye alights on first one, then another – belies the total opacity of the concepts to which they refer. It is literally impossible to extract any connective tissue of meaning from this array of buzzwords, but the palimpsest effect impresses the viewer by its sheer scope and scale.

The narrative turn in Thames Gateway planning certainly makes for a conversational space in which civil engineers and social engineers can once again talk to one another, if only about branding strategies; but it also offers a point of purchase for members of the professional service and creative class who are its preferred workers and residents: it is a story which they can literally buy into.

Back to the future

The CABE report was in many ways prophetic. One of its key messages, that individual enterprise can foster community spirit, anticipated a central theme in the new social agenda that the Tory Party launched in the run-up to the election of 2010 under the banner of 'the Big Society'. The Tory strategy was to identify New Labour with state interventionism, and to portray themselves as the true heirs to the tradition of social solidarity, self-help and mutual aid espoused by R.H. Tawney and the Guild Socialists, and practised in the past by working-class communities themselves before they became dependent on state benefits. It was an audacious ideological move, and, if nothing else, it shifted the debate onto a terrain where the Tories held the initiative.

Seen in the light of this argument, the Thames Gateway Plan, with its raft of quangos, was a soft target. The plan could easily be portrayed as a typical example of New Labour's dirigisme, an unwieldy bureaucratic machinery, unaccountable to local electorates, spending large amounts of public money to little effect. The Tories proposed to eliminate a whole tier of regional and sub-regional governance, and devolve the quango's planning powers to local councils, or in the case of major infrastructural projects to central government. For example, consortia of local councils would bid for inward investment, and local partnerships would directly manage development projects in partnership with private companies. At the same time, voluntary organisations, co-operatives and social enterprises – the so called third sector – were to be encouraged to expand to fill the gaps in provision opened up as the frontiers of the state rolled back, and in this way build the 'Big Society'.[39] As a strategy of urbanism, the Tories' localist agenda implied renewed emphasis on conservation, heritage and traditional styles of architecture, as well as a small-scale, piecemeal 'bottom-up' approach to regeneration.

The 'Big Society' came to be widely seen as a cynical ploy to put a positive spin on the draconian cuts to public services needed to tackle the huge deficit created by bailing out the banks during the fiscal crisis of 2008-9. Nevertheless it has changed the political environment in which urban planning takes place. It is still too early to assess the wider and longer lasting effect of its implementation, but the immediate impact on the Thames Gateway project has been all too predictable. The development corporations have been abolished and the Government Office for London closed. The Greater London Authority has taken over most of the functions, and some of the staff from the old quangos. The plan itself has survived – there is too much at stake in it to simply abolish it – but it is now very low in the present Tory-led administration's list of priorities. What was once New Labour's flagship regeneration project has been relegated to a sideshow. It will be up to local authorities to sustain the initiative, with 'light-touch' support from the Department of Communities and Local Government. What this means in practice is that major infrastructure projects, such as Crossrail and the Shell Haven container port, are completed, and premium sites, such as Ebbsfleet, with its fast transport links into central London and the continent, or Bluewater Shopping City, continue to attract major new residential and commercial developments. But many smaller projects have been scrapped or put on hold until such time as the economy picks up. In the Royal Docks, for example, both the Biota, a mega-aquarium to be run by the London Zoological Society, and an extreme sports centre have been scrapped, along with the proposed Thames Gateway Bridge linking south and north Woolwich. If the recession deepens, the Gateway's counterfactual history – the story of all the projects that did *not* happen – is set to become its major legacy (*152-4). Left purely to market forces, Thames Gateway is likely to become a prime example of splintering urbanism.[40]

Some ambitious schemes, consistent with the CABE vision, remain on the stocks. There is an imaginative proposal to build a major new offshore airport on a floating platform at the mouth of the estuary, to relieve pressure on Heathrow and Stanstead, and for a system of cable cars to link the north and south banks of the river near the Medway towns. Terry Farrell's proposal for a National Wetlands Park still has major institutional supporters, including Boris Johnson and the GLA. But perhaps the most significant long-term development in 'greening the Gateway' is likely to come from the attempt to rebalance the economy by expanding the manufacturing sector. For this will involve creating new green-collar jobs in energy, transport, construction and aggregates, and the Thames Gateway is an obvious site for their location. Finally, the success of London's bid for the 2012 Olympics inevitably concentrated public attention – and more importantly both public and private sector investment – on Stratford; and for a considerable period of time to come the games legacy will continue to siphon off resources that might have otherwise been deployed further downriver in the Gateway.

As the Olympics demonstrate, the advent of the recession has not spelt the end of culture-led regeneration. It has merely given an even harder edge to what is demanded of the cultural economy: to provide a platform for creative enterprise, to generate jobs and make a profit. And although the post-modern idiom is now quite out of fashion – its concerns with aestheticising business culture seeming merely frivolous in these more precarious times – the recombinant forms of urbanism or 'junkspace' to which it gave an ideological gloss continue to flourish, as do concerns with public place making and the urban realm.[41] As we will see, the Olympic Park is a spectacular case in point. As for the narrative turn in planning, spinning stories about places in order to sell them to potential investors or residents has never been more à la mode. The Olympics, with its re-branding of East London, is a prime example of this process.

At a political level the challenge remains of how to combine effective public accountability and local democratic control with the efficient administration of large-scale public investment.[42] Everyone agrees that something had to be done to simplify the Gateway's Byzantine structure of funding and management, but no-one quite knows how to go about doing it. In that sense Thames Gateway is a good test bed for the new thinking about the relationship between state and civil society that the Labour Party has to do while in opposition. So too is the Olympic legacy.

Much of the debate now centres on rethinking the politics of representation, and in particular claims of the local vis à vis the regional and the national.[43] There is a growing awareness within the political class that the existing co-ordinates of governance do not map easily onto the space of flows; part of the democratic deficit has to do with a failure to create new and more flexible forms of public participation in the decision-making process that take account of the fact many people are on the move or have only a transitory engagement with their locality. Again this is an issue raised with particular urgency by the building of a whole new area of London in and around Olympic Park, to be known as East 20.

The fight for a just city, in which all citizens have equal access to its amenities and opportunities, and which supports innovative forms of public culture and civic participation to that end, has always been an important aspect of municipal socialism in its more radical and imaginative moments.[44] That is another issue that connects the fate of Thames Gateway to that of the Olympic Park, as does the question of whether regeneration is just another, politer, name for gentrification. The future of the two projects is thus intimately linked, politically, economically and ideologically, and it is the terms and conditions of that connection that will be explored in the second half of the book.

PART II

The 2012 Olympics:
between the artificial paradise and the beautifying lie

'What *is* a Caucus-race?' said Alice; not that she wanted much to know, but the Dodo had paused as if it thought that *somebody* ought to speak, and no one else seemed inclined to say anything.

'Why,' said the Dodo, 'the best way to explain it is to do it.' (And, as you might like to try the thing yourself, some winter day, I will tell you how the Dodo managed it.)

First it marked out a race-course, in a sort of circle ('the exact shape doesn't matter,' it said), and then all the party were placed along the course, here and there. There was no 'One, two, three, and away,' but they began running when they liked, and left off when they liked, so that it was not easy to know when the race was over. However, when they had been running half an hour or so, and were quite dry again, the Dodo suddenly called out 'The race is over!' and they all crowded round it, panting, and asking, 'But who has won?'

This question the Dodo could not answer without a great deal of thought, and it sat for a long time with one finger pressed upon its forehead (the position in which you usually see Shakespeare, in the pictures of him), while the rest waited in silence. At last the Dodo said, '*everybody* has won, and all must have prizes'.

Lewis Carroll, *Alice in Wonderland*

The important thing is not winning or taking part. There is no merit in an easy victory. There is no virtue in having taken part if you have given less than your best. The Olympic ideal is false. If it were not false, there would be no prizes. There would not even be any races, because to be in a race is in itself a prize. It was not the Greeks who formulated this so-called ideal; it was a rich French nobleman whose whims are now indulged at the expense of the young … The Olympic Games are a magnificent event, the very pinnacle of sport and physical endeavour, but the so-called ideals behind them are a hypocrisy.

Brian Glanville, *The Olympian*

There may be some sports are painful, and their labour
Delight in them sets off.

William Shakespeare, *The Tempest*

Ian F. Rogers, Boundary fence, Olympic Park 2010

4. London calling 2012:
Notes on the haunting of
an Olympic story

Narrating London

> Girl with ridiculous earrings   why do you bother
> To slap the boy   we all assume is your boyfriend
> And is lolling over   that bus seat   shouting
>
> *It's a London thing* He is obviously a knob
> but a happy one   and that   it seems to me
> is the important   though not localisable   thing
> Ahren Warner Dionysus

London is always calling from somewhere just beyond the horizon

Ford Maddox Brown, London's Soul

L ondon's power of attraction, its capacity to act at a distance, both on the imagination of its own inhabitants and on those it draws in as immigrants or visitors, took on a special significance with the advent of the Olympics. The theme of London as 'the world in a city' was central to the successful 2012 bid.[1] The capital was defined for this purpose as a unique amalgam of ethnic diversity, enterprise culture, and civic pride, epitomised by East London, the bid's main focus. For so long the city's poor relation, but now the prime location of Olympic hopes, East Enders discovered to their surprise that their cultures, previously regarded as bearing all the hallmarks of multiple deprivation, disadvantage and difference, were now a unique selling point as symbols of community cohesion and platforms of aspiration for hosting the games. The folk devils of many a moral panic about the urban underclass were now suddenly folk heroes of an 'urban renaissance'.

Despite this focus, in choosing a theme for the Opening Ceremony, London was replaced by an updated, multiculturalised version of Britain's island story.[2] Perhaps the decision had something to do with the disastrous version of the host city story shown in Beijing, featuring a double-decker London bus, a bizarre assortment of 'Londoners' and, for its climax, the spectacle of David Beckham kicking a football into the crowd. Partly this squeamishness had to do with the desire not to over-emphasise London's dominance over the rest of the country, though it would have been perfectly possible to decentralise the proceedings, with parts of the opening and closing ceremonies coming from other towns and cities. But I think it also had something to do with the peculiar position that London and Londoners occupy within the body politic and how this affected the way that the city became 'Olympified' in the course of the bid campaign.

In its lead-in to the games, the BBC portrayed London as a city in waiting, 'ready with one heart and one voice to throw open its doors in welcome to the world'. A brief sequence showed the Blitz and the devastation caused by the 7/7 bomb attacks, with images of Londoners in 1940 and 2005 resolutely carrying on with business as usual amidst the ruins. The voice-over commentary told us that the people of London were resilient, used to triumphing over adversity, and thus especially fitted to demonstrate the true Olympic Spirit. The Myths of the Blitz and Olympism coalesced to form a new, hyper-mythological, narrative of the capital city, in which its power and identity were derived from the mysterious capacity of its inhabitants to be at their best in the worst of circumstances.

In fact being a Londoner has for much of the city's history been a very nebulous affair and only occasionally has taken on clear definition. As Ahren Warner's poem reminds us, the 'London thing', although pervasive, is not easily localisable. London as it is recorded musically is a case in point. During the Blitz, Noel Coward's song 'London Pride', about a flower that flourished amidst the bombsites, helped to make it into a symbol of the capital and the nation's resistance, but it did not say anything about what the city meant to those who lived there. In the immediate aftermath of war, Flanagan and Allan's 'Maybe it's because I'm a Londoner' became almost a national anthem without ever becoming specific about just what it was about London that was so lovable, or what was so unique about being an inhabitant of the metropolis. It was enough to evoke a shared sense that the city had somehow survived a battering and Londoners still had something to sing about. Perhaps, for some Londoners of that generation, the song might have continuing relevance in describing the city's experience of the games.

Love affairs with cities are notoriously difficult to articulate. Cities are so large, complicated and internally diverse that it is impossible to sum up their character or identity in a few lines; indeed the fact that they necessarily remain mysterious and in some sense 'terra incognita' is one of their attractions. Most musical attempts to capture the city's essence name particular features that have strong positive associations: public landmarks or events, personal haunts or encounters, out of which a musical memoryscape can be constructed.[3] Gershwin's 'A foggy day in London Town' described how a sense of desolation is dispelled by a romantic encounter, and in similar vein Ray Davies's 'Waterloo Sunset' offers a tower block prospect on a city that celebrates its anonymity (people so busy/makes me feel dizzy) as an opportunity for young lovers to meet. London's musical landscape contains a number of hotspots which have attracted more than their fair share of attention. Soho predictably tops the list with over twenty songs, although only Bert Jansch and John Renbourn's soulful rendering of its bohemian underlife is likely to become a permanent musical landmark. There are distinct genres. There is the song which describes the sense of bewilderment experienced by a stranger to the big city.[4] There are upbeat songs, like Saint Etienne's dreamy acid-house celebration of London park life, but just as many exploring the discordant or dystopian aspects of London Babylon. The Pet Shop Boys' 'East End Boys and West End Girls' offers a sardonic take on the social polarisation of the Thatcher years, while Nick Drake discovered the strange as well as the familiar in his *Mayfair*. East London has its anthems too, from Dave the Drummer's spaced out *Night in Hackney*, to Ian Dury's *Plaistow Patricia* and the *Ballad of Barking Creek*. The immigrant experience has been well documented, from Lord Kitchener's optimistic calypso *London belongs to me* to Sonny Boy Williamson trying, not very successfully, but very bluesily, to make London his home.

Soundtracking London's identity for the Olympics was thus never going to be an easy option for the Ceremonies team. Sampling the musical and cultural diversity of the cosmopolis is complicated by the fact that the mash-up constitutes its own idiom, the musical correlate of the city's own hectic multi-accentuated rhythm; the rush and rich mix of musical idioms is not just about living life in the fast lane, but a mesmerising measure of just how decentred the cultural trajectory of London's growth has now become.

In the 1950s Londoners could tune in to the Home Service and listen to 'In Town Tonight', introduced by Eric Coates's 'Knightsbridge' signature tune followed by a cacophony of car horns until a voice shouted 'stop!' and the announcer's mellifluous and impeccably Oxbridge accent intervened reassuringly to tell us 'Once more we stop the mighty roar of London's traffic, to bring you ...'. But today the mighty polysemic roar of London's cultural traffic with the world cannot be halted, and nor can it easily be re-assembled into a cosy supper time news story.

The metropolitan ethnoscape: insular and inclusive

London may be 'the world in a city', but its cosmopolitan culture has, for most of its history, been articulated through – and, many would claim, submerged under – a quite insular narrative of the nation. 'London calling' – but only as the official voice of a United Kingdom. As Lord Coe put it in his closing words in the Olympic stadium 'London 2012 was Made in Britain'. What might otherwise find expression in a sense of popular municipal pride is thus redirected into a patriotic duty to represent the nation to itself and to the wider world. In principle this narrative is inclusive, but in practice it has tended to reduce what is capital about the city to the story of Capital itself, the city as the City; or else it turns London into a stage for the management of national events of commemoration, celebration or mourning. This is not an identity that many Londoners may want to own, especially as it makes them an object of envy to the rest of the country. The very fact that London bid for 2012, ahead of the strong claims of Manchester, Glasgow and Liverpool, stirred up regional and national as well as civic jealousies.[5]

So we have a peculiar situation: London as an object of popular sentiment is a floating signifier, and 'Londoner' is an empty box waiting to be ticked by anyone and everyone who lives there, its inclusivity carrying no substantive identity tag and requiring no commitment. In contrast, London as a capital city, front office of Great Britain plc, is a fixed asset, strongly anchored to an imagined community of the nation, and forced to carry a burden of representation which many feel is a liability. As a result of this double dispensation, the 'Londoner' remains a somewhat haphazard figure, being composed of whoever turns up on the day to make up a crowd scene for ceremonial occasions, waving flags and singing the national anthem. The Olympics, following hard on the Queen's Jubilee celebrations, provided a perfect setting for such a display of popular loyalty.

Attempts have been made to give some substance and credibility to a distinctive metropolitan identity by inventing various 'London traditions', usually associated with the figure of the Cockney.[6] There is an interesting history to this. In the early Victorian period, Cockneys (aka white working-class East Enders usually employed in street trades) were variously described as being of 'low intelligence', suffering from physical deformities, workshy, untrustworthy and 'talking in a rough incomprehensible tongue' – definitely fully paid-up members of the urban underclass, a race apart. However from the 1870s onwards, when Cockney comedians started to appear regularly on the music hall and subsequently the Variety stage, a change in public estimation took place; now the Cockney was a 'cheerful chappie', sharp-witted and even sharper-tongued, whose social pretentions, like those of 'Burlington Bertie from Bow' might be laughable, but whose loyalty was never in doubt. By the time of the blitz in 1940, when the resilience and fortitude of London's East Enders was held up as exemplary of Britain's stand-alone spirit of defiance, the rehabilitation was complete: the Cockney had been transformed into the backbone of the nation, and as such into 'a true Londoner'. As Noel Coward, hardly a man of the people, put it: 'Cockney feet/mark the beat of history'. Nowadays, though, the figure of the Cockney has become something of a caricature and a period piece, as for example in the 'schlockney' purveyed by Chas and Dave. Only as featured on TV's *EastEnders* do Cockneys have any street cred. Moreover, as a municipal patriot the figure of the Cockney can sometimes strike a rather nasty xenophobic pose. For all these reasons 'Knees up Mother Brown' and 'Gertcha' were not on the play list for 2012, despite strong local credentials and a walk-on part for Pearly Kings and Queens in the People's Parade in the opening ceremony. Nevertheless, as discussed in the first part of this book, 'Cockney' could become an honorific title applied by Bengali and black youth in East London to themselves; even if it did little to endear them to white East Enders who thought they had a monopoly on its use, it gave them another point of purchase on the cultural scene.[7] Smiley Culture's 'Cockney Translation' did the business, while Wiley's version of 'Bow E3' showed that those now born within the sound of its bells were creating a new East End vernacular, talking black.

So there was somewhere for 'Londoners' to go if they did not want to elide their identity with that of the nation, or leave it as a purely formal property devoid of any real substance. The template for such adhesion had been established long before 'multiculturalism' became a buzz word. Not long after 'Maybe it's because I'm a Londoner' became a hit, an Ealing comedy film came out that offered a rather different vision of the city. *Passport to Pimlico* told the story of an area of London that decided to declare independence from the rest of the city and the country, and go it alone. The film pokes gentle fun at British, or rather English, insularities at a time when the country was ready to move on from the 'island story' that had sustained it during the war.[8] But one reason for its success was that it portrayed a nationalism of the neighbourhood that had strong roots, and not just in urban villages like Pimlico but also in council housing estates and deprived inner-city areas up and down the country.

Here prides of place are exercised in the form of territorial loyalties – and rivalries – centred on strong, highly-localised networks of affiliation which still give these communities some claim on the city's resources and identity. Such little niches in the urban fabric offer a safe refuge to those who see the wider environment as dangerous or hostile, while for others, more outward-looking, it provides a vantage point from which to explore what the city has to offer in the way of excitement and economic opportunity.[9]

From the 1950s and 1960s onwards, London's arrivant communities from the New Commonwealth and elsewhere adopted the same strategy, as they settled in and effectively colonised different parts of the city, often initially encountering strong resistance from longer established and strongly entrenched inhabitants who objected to the way these 'outsiders' were imposing their presence and way of life on its landscape.[10] As discussed in previous chapters, in the inner East End of London, the demographic transformation was relatively rapid, although in areas like the Isle of Dogs, it was marked by considerable tension and conflict.[11] The fact that being a Londoner was such a nebulous, open-ended affair, meant that the term could be appropriated by any number of immigrant and diasporic communities, and invested with some sense of allegiance without compromising their core identity, or even requiring them to mix much with anybody else.

An alternative vision of the Londoner could thus be grounded in the city's ethnoscape, and draw upon these local histories of interaction to construct an image of popular cosmopolitanism.[12] This was its attraction as a template for London's host city narrative. But this also runs the risk of opening up a potential space of representation for community relations that are often less than harmonious; as every group clamours to have its individual contribution to London's story recognised, old wounds may all too easily open up. As soon as some substance is given to the notion of the Londoner, and the identity tag has resource implications, it becomes contested. And that is perhaps why it proved safer to relocate the main 2012 Olympic story away from one about a city with such a complex local history, to focus on an enchanted 'isle of wonders' where all such insularities can be magically dissolved in the simplified idioms of a now globalised multi-culture. But was such a move really necessary?

The interplay between all the dimensions of London/er identity – local and global, national and ethnic, metropolitan and cosmopolitan, popular and corporate, diasporic and indigenous, cultural and political – all pulling in different directions, inevitably results in a confused pattern of affiliation, by turns centripetal and centrifugal. All things being equal, the Olympics tend to strengthen centripetal tendencies. They pull people out of their neighbourhood redoubts and provide a platform for a wider sense of affinity with the city, even though it is as well to remember that when the party is over, civic prides can sometimes turn parochial again.[13] At the same time the realpolitik of the Olympic bidding process ensures that although the games are awarded to individual cities, the outcome is decided by a lobbying process which puts a premium on the level of governmental support. So, too, in the coalitions that form the boards of the bid planning and delivery bodies, where municipal authorities find themselves very much junior partners in relation to corporate and government interests.[14] The only exception to this, as in much else, was the Barcelona Olympics.[15]

The attempt to construct a credible London story-line for the Olympics came up against a contradiction at the heart of the city's representation: the capital possesses a corporate identity and brand image of immense power, which, aided by the gravitational pull of its economy, draws in people and investment from the rest of the UK and the world. Even in these hard times, London continues to call from over the horizon. This would not be possible if it had not, once upon a time, been the hub of an Empire, and was not, today, one of the centres of global finance.[16] But while this has concentrated great wealth in the city, it has also helped create great social inequality. It has made a few people very rich and kept a lot of people relatively poor.[17] Those who can access opportunity structures plugged into the global knowledge economy and people trapped within highly localised, sometimes hidden, economies may be next-door neighbours but they live in quite different worlds.[18] As we saw in part one, these fault lines run quite visibly through the urban fabric in East London, as gated communities of affluent professionals spring up amidst often run-down public housing estates.

It is not surprising, then, that London lacked a strong unifying narrative that was convincing to most of its actual inhabitants. In the Panglossian 'can do' vocabulary of the Olygarchs, however, this was not so much a problem as a solution waiting to happen. 2012 was not only about making over 'a pretty terrible part of town', but a chance in a lifetime to invent a completely new identity for Londoners, one that everyone could own. But just what does such an 'Olympic' identity consist of?

The Olympic movement has its own story to tell through the games, its own specific message that the host city is supposed to relay along with the Olympic torch. It is a message that has both mythological and ideological dimensions and in the official grand narrative, as presented on the International Olympic Committee's website they are closely worked together.[19] The record of sporting actions that forms the backbone of the story, its folk tale, consists of a selective sampling of exploits used to illustrate the Olympic values of noble and peaceful competition: the athlete who overcame serious injury to win his event against all the odds; the black and white African sprinters who join hands in a victory lap to symbolise the overcoming of apartheid; the youngest ever swimmer to win gold; the first Pakistani to compete in the pentathlon and so on. The Olympic narrative is structured around these sublime and aleatory moments in which its values are enacted.

In adding its own instalment to the Olympic story, each host city and nation is supposed to give new substance to this formulaic mission statement, or at least to interpret its own view of the world in conformity with the Olympic ideals. In this context some commentators have recently talked about the 'end of ideology' and a 'historical compromise' between the values of commerce and community. By no coincidence this has happened alongside the emergence of cultural festivals and sporting events which have become major sites of profitable investment and entrepreneurial activity. Carnival Capitalism featured strongly in the London Olympics and will be discussed in depth in Chapter Seven.

For the moment it is enough to note that to 'Olympify' London's story for the purposes of the bid campaign involved inventing an imaginary city, a city at one with itself and the nation, in which 'everyone could be a winner' and live the 2012 dream. Everything that was problematic about the city's past, present and future was airbrushed out of the picture of a vibrant, entrepreneurial, ever-expanding city. This promotional strategy was not unique to the Olympics, however. It is part of a general trend in urban imagineering that emphasises the role of the city as a pleasure ground and is linked to capitalism's cultural – or rather multi-cultural – turn.[20]

The bid posters portrayed an aspirational world in which obstacles were there just to be overcome (^174/5/7/8). If you can hurdle over Tower Bridge, or dive off the Thames Flood Barrier, then the sky's the limit. Yet the project remained haunted by the negativity it disavowed. To organise such a glittering and costly display in a period of austerity inevitably invited the thought that there might be a certain 'return of the repressed'. The spectators of the Opening Ceremony were urged to 'be not afeard' though 'the isle is full of noises', but the fear was that some of the noises might come from people who did not feel they were part of its vision and whose disaffection might well be a matter of concern.[21] For there was another story about London waiting, unbidden, in the wings and it too had an anthem.

Antinomies

London calling ... the zombies of death
Quit holding out – and draw another breath

The ice age is coming, the sun is zooming in
Meltdown expected, and the wheat is growing thin,

The Clash, *London Calling*

The Clash's 'London Calling', briefly sampled during the Opening Ceremony, conveys an apocalyptic vision of London under siege from global warming and its own inner demons. The song belongs to a tradition of writing about the city going back to William Blake, who talks about its 'furnaces of afflicion' and 'stupendous ruins', and draws a picture of the capital as 'Babylon', devouring the hopes and dreams of its inhabitants through its monstrous appetite for growth. As we saw in Chapter One, the gothic imagination has played an important role in populating the city's cultural landscape with spectral presences.

Although its influence remains largely confined to literature and the arts, London Gothic has sustained a vigorous counter narrative to the official guides to the capital's heritage and the ever onwards march of its modernities.[22] The Olympics provided this otherwise dispersed set of attitudes with a rallying point. The ruinologists mobilised en masse against the Olympic Park because its construction demolished a whole landscape of urban dereliction that had fed their fertile imaginations. Here is a typical lament, voiced by a keen angler on the River Lea:

> There is talk of regeneration, the promise of the Olympic clean up which may turn out to be nothing more than a cosmetic act and one which is already ridding the river and its plain of any last vestiges of a twentieth century life. Portakabins, caffs, allotments, scrap-metal merchants, caravan sites, container yards, tyre and brake centres, amateur football pitches, pylon parks, abandoned railway lines, derelict factory units, thunderstruck oaks, graffiti tagged bridges, stolen car and shopping trolley graves, a thousand single shoes and half a dozen Georgian pocket watches once swallowed by pike and lying under a foot of black silt, all will be cleared, erased, or purchased compulsorily and built over.[23]

Meanwhile Iain Sinclair and the psycho-geographers are patiently waiting for the cracks to appear in the Olympic Park paving stones, and for its structures to fall into disrepair or disrepute so that they can be reclaimed as the ruins in reverse they were always meant to be. Sinclair, on a tour of inspection of the park during the early 'Dig, design, demolish' phase immediately slips his prose into apocalyptic gear:

> The Olympic Park was a newsreel of the fall of Berlin run backwards, from present boasts about urban renewal to the bombed and blasted killing fields ... What remains in these ravished topographies is a category of war zone architecture: concrete bunkers, electrified fences, unexplained posts, burned out warehouses, stripped woodland, fouled water. Grand Project development is accidental archaeology. A séance with future ruins.[24]

To put down Sinclair's *Ghost Milk* and pick up the latest instalment of LOCOG's *London 2012* report is to wake up out of a dystopian nightmare into a world full of happy smiling faces, where the sun is shining whatever the weather and there is always vitamin-enhanced, sugar-free honey for tea. Once the shift in viewpoint has been made, it is not difficult to construct a good news story about 2012. Even if the hoped-for bonanza for London's tourism,

Jason Orton, Olympic Park under construction 2010

hospitality and cultural industries largely failed to materialise, the upbeat ceremonies and sporting triumphalism associated with medal successes of Team GB in both the Olympics and Paralympics gave a boost to the nation's *amour propre* and turned the whole event into a character-building exercise; for many young East Enders, for the 2012 volunteers and for the athletes and spectators these few weeks may have amounted to the most memorable and exciting time of their lives. Yet the after-effect of the games and its long-term reputational status depend not only on these immediate experiences, important though they are, but on a wider narrative framework through which the event is evaluated.

Writing the Olympics

In the closing ceremony of the 2012 games Lord Coe basked in official approval: it was a job well done. But that is only the beginning of the story. After every Olympics there is a public reckoning, or rather multiple reckonings, as the various stakeholders, the International Olympics Committee, the local organising committee, government departments, municipal authorities and a host of smaller fry undertake detailed audits. Some of these address immediate worries: did the games live up to expectations? Were the athletes and visitors satisfied with all the arrangements? Were the various projects delivered on budget and on time? Did the Games make a profit or loss? Were the targets for job creation and skills training met and did young people benefit from these and from the opportunities to take part in sport? Other accounts attempt a more long term and comparative evaluation.

One of the things that makes the Games unique and different from other mega sporting events is the scale of the infrastructure they create, and the great importance now attached to its role in establishing an enduring civic legacy. The Olympic story is now pre-eminently a regeneration story, and each chapter of it is, in large measure, about the city that hosts it. It is what is left behind as a material resource, what is transformed in the socio-economic environment and what is constituted as a lasting cultural heritage that counts and each aspect of legacy has developed its own specialised narrative.

There is now a large literature devoted to the anticipation, recollection and evaluation of the Olympics, forming a globalised space of information flow connecting Games past, present and future, and mainly generated by the Olympic movement itself.[25] Much of this material consists of official documentation produced by the IOC and the various local organising committees and stakeholders. The information contained in these reports is mostly technical, although some attempt is usually made to characterise the unique qualities of the event and convey a sense of its occasion.

The festive spirit of Olympic 'communitas' is not, however, likely to be captured within an iron cage of bureaucratic rationality. More of a 'human interest' angle is provided by memoirs, biographies and newspaper articles written by key players, including athletes and sports administrators. Sometimes these narratives take us behind the scenes, but these are usually carefully selected glimpses of the Olympics in action, designed to convey an impression of how difficulties were overcome through personal dedication and teamwork so that a successful outcome – a gold medal, or a beneficial legacy – was delivered. Triumph over adversity is the leitmotif of these auto-mytho-graphic accounts, which rarely stray off the beaten track.[26] Olympic guides and souvenir books take the same official line, lavishly illustrating the host-city story, with pictures of the Olympic site, the opening and closing ceremonies and highlights of the sporting action, while slavishly following the triumph over adversity story line. And this too is the favoured format of heritage videos. Potted histories of the Olympics, illustrating its key moments, also form part of this large and largely ephemeral literature.

But public curiosity is inevitably focused on what happens behind the scenes, especially when things go wrong, and this has resulted in an investigative literature largely written by journalists and commentators with an axe to grind. This muckraking 'sociology' is also dominated by mythological or ideological themes.[27] It provides an *unhappy* ever after story which specialises in finding skeletons in the cupboards of key Olympic players, dramas of political intrigue, bribery and corruption, doping scandals, and innuendo about the private, especially sexual, lives of the athletes – in a word, everything that is anathema to the Olympic and city authorities but which is food and drink to the anti-Olympics movement. These behind the scene accounts and the occasional confessional tell-all memoir in turn fuel a public debate conducted in the media, and increasingly online, in which Olympophiles and Olympophobes lock horns.

Finally there is a literature that aims to constitute a meta-narrative organised around the quest for forms of knowledge that will locate the event's ultimate meaning, and worth. In pursuit of this 'gnoseological' goal a whole research industry is now assembled around the Olympics, using a wide variety of methods and approaches to investigate every aspect of the Games, from the architecture of its stadia, to the zeitgeist expressed in the uniforms designed for the national teams. What is significant about this literature, from the present point of view, is the way it creates a global interpretive community, an academic subculture centred around interrogating the Olympic heritage and investigating the legacy of particular Games. Through conferences, journals, and online forums the significance of each Olympiad is continuously analysed and debated. And as each Games adds its own chapter to the story, and deposits its archive in a new study centre, the scope and scale of the research endeavour continually expands. Much of this activity is about making comparisons: host cities are made to compete against each other, retrospectively, for the accolade of 'best ever', and a kind of informal league table established along these lines. This mirrors and amplifies the fact that sport has become a 'pan agonistic' phenomenon. The athletes in the ancient games simply competed for the immediate prize and fame, and no records were kept. Now comparative statistics of the performance of athletes, teams and host cities are kept globally, across space and time.[28]

An Olympic story thus has a very long tail to it, and one that is increasingly wagging the dog in so far as host city bids are judged as much by their largely incalculable long-term benefits as by what they will immediately deliver. The final, evaluative, part of the story, in which its meaning and worth is spelt out, has become split off and spun out so that it now forms a quite separate field of discourse, a sequel to which the Games themselves are merely a prequel. And around this a whole consultancy culture has become established. We will look at legacy and evaluation narratives in more detail shortly, but immediately it is worth noting the importance of Olympic research in creating – and sometimes changing – the reputational status of host cities after the event, while also establishing bench marks for future games.

For example Barcelona, has, for the past decade, remained top of the Olympic legacy league because it is widely regarded as having the best ever regeneration story; as a result it has become a ritual site of pilgrimage for any budding host-city planning team anxious to discover the secret of its success. In fact the city's achievement had to do with a unique and unrepeatable combination of factors in its favour.[29] The creation of Barcelona as an Olympic success story is in some part a retrospective illusion, which glosses over some rather unpleasant facts, for example that new house prices in the city increased by some 250 per cent between 1986 and 1992 when the Games took place, that prostitutes and the homeless were rounded up and driven out of town for the duration of the Games, and that the host city set a new world record for going over budget while the Port area did in fact eventually become gentrified.

The Barcelona story suggests that what makes an Olympics memorable or not, especially to its host communities, is the conjuncture in which it takes place and which its advent comes to symbolise. Thus the 1948 London Olympiad, which came to be known as the 'austerity games', seems to have scarcely registered in the collective memory of Londoners or the country at large; people were still war weary, still dealing with the aftermath of family separations and losses, and still living under a regime of privation, including food rationing.[30] Mass Observation's correspondents were singularly unexcited by the event itself and mainly concerned about the British athletes' diet and whether they had enough of the right food to eat.[31]

London 2012 was not a remake of the austerity games: too much money was spent on it for that. But nor was 2012 ever going to be associated with an economic miracle. The bubble of prosperity created in and around Stratford may not burst, but its effect is unlikely to extend much beyond its newly gentrified hinterland. London 2012 wants to be known as the legacy Games, but it seems unlikely that the regeneration story it will have to tell, at least in purely economic terms, will justify that title.[32]

Perhaps then the London Olympiad might be remembered for bad news rather than good? That, understandably enough, was the Great Fear of the Olygarchs and the rank and file twenty-twelvers. The possibility that the Games might yet make history by its bad side, that Hegel's old mole might blindly surface where least expected and wanted, was a nightmare from which the organisers found it difficult at times to awaken.

Ground control

The spectre of financial malpractice or terrorist attack haunted the official imagination of 2012, despite the stringent measures of internal audit and site security put in place. One of the paradoxes of such measures, however, is that far from increasing the sense of public security they actually produce greater alarm and despondency. The location of ground-to-air missiles on the roof of high-rise flats in Bow and overlooking the Olympic Park created an atmosphere that one of the residents described as a cross between a North Korean Party congress and a minor war. The grim requirement to secure the zone against attack resulted in lockdown measures costing over a billion pounds and was hardly a good advertisement for 'living the dream'. But the deployment of such an extreme, militarised, form of ground control, while it was obviously in response to 7/7, was also intrinsic to the Olympification process. The creation of a *cordon sanitaire* around the Olympic site gave spatial expression to the purified view of the metropolis as a harmonious organic totality that informed the urbanistic vision of the 2012 project from the very outset.[33] So too was the high security transport network (ORN) established for ferrying athletes, officials, media, sponsors and VIPs to and from the venues which, in effect, created a reticular exclusion zone across the city. Many Londoners grumbled about the disruption and the fact that the city was being made to dance to the tune of 'get me to the track on time' just to ensure that athletes arrived in peak condition. But this spatial logic was anticipated in the bid campaign itself with its dramatic imagery of athletes bestriding the city, hurdling over Tower Bridge or using the Thames Barrier as a diving platform. What was 'Olympian' about

London, the posters implied, was the capacity of its urban fabric, as represented by these iconic landmarks, to support exploitation by an elite in order to enhance competitive advantage, something of an old fashioned story as far as its citizenry was concerned. The same principle was on display in the closing ceremony when Tower Bridge, the Gherkin, and the London Eye were used to provide a backdrop to the party scene but never actively featured in the narrative. Meanwhile all around Stratford familiar buildings disappeared behind giant wraps advertising Olympic sponsor's products, as the whole area became 'Olympified'.

The best East London can get? Stratford 2012

There was more to the security measures than risk managerialism run riot. In 2012 the very real questions raised by the anti-terrorist security measures were camouflaged by a symbolic law and order issue related to the youth riots of the previous year (*177). This was a move on the part of a government which could not or would not engage with the social consequences of the economic recession and its cuts to public services. It was much easier to mobilise public support for a crack down on looters, alias King Mob, than to deal with the intractable question of how neo- liberal states are to protect their citizens from terrorist attack without abrogating the civil liberties that represent their main claim to legitimacy.

There was a direct connection between the strategies developed by the police to deal with the 2011 riots and the methods of lockdown and crowd control used for the Olympics.[34] There were a number of different perspectives on understanding the urban crowd and its behaviour in operation here. From the standpoint of the Games organisers the preferred image was of a festive crowd, celebrating physical closeness and conviviality.[35] Yet there was also the fear that such crowds might become intoxicated with their own power and/or become subject to panic attacks. So they also justified measures of precautionary containment in case the festivities got out of hand and people started to enjoy themselves too much (>129/30).[36]

This brings into focus the second standpoint which fixes on the lonely crowd. There is a whole discourse of urban regulation that features the 'invisible' metropolitan mass, perpetually on the verge of coalescing into a riotous mob under the command of a charismatic leader who knows how to manipulate its atavistic drives; this crowd calls for pre-emptive action in the form of special measures to keep it on the move. This is complimented by the notion of a somnambulistic crowd hypnotised by its own capacity for auto-suggestion and prey to sudden flights of fancy or frenzied crazes, a delirious crowd which therefore has to be immobilised and dispersed.[37]

In the contemporary street theatre of urban politics there are two key crowd formations. There is the 'mosh pit' formed in raves, more or less violently creating an 'eye' in the crowd in which dancers can barge into one another in time to the beat. And there is the 'kettle' in which police split up and surround demonstrators to prevent them from forming into a large mass. Both were in evidence in 2012. The organisers of the opening ceremony provided designated spaces in the arena where carefully vetted members of the local community were invited to demonstrate their enthusiasm for the proceedings. And the police ruthlessly harassed and corralled the cyclists of Critical Mass as they tried to create another kind of urban space whose lines of desire conformed neither to the circulation of commodities or the concentration of power.

A crowd of sports spectators is neither a mob nor an atomised mass, although it has the potential to become both. Nor is it merely festive; its attention is concentrated not dispersed. It occupies an ambiguous position in the scopic regime of surveillance, in that it involves a multitude of people watching what a very small number of other people are up to on the field of play, and, in so far as its behaviour is constantly monitored by CCTV cameras, it also entails a very great number of people being closely observed by very few.[38] The volatility of the spectating crowd – which way will it turn – makes it in principle the very stuff Olympic dreams-turned-nightmares are made on. The lockdown strategy for 2012 involved both keeping crowds on the move and immobilising protesters to prevent them getting anywhere near the site.

In fact the 2012 crowds behaved with considerable decorum, in combining conviviality with partisanship. Their demographic was overwhelmingly affluent and middle-class. They knew how they were expected to behave. And by and large they did. If spectators booed George Osborne, the Tory Chancellor of the Exchequer who had been responsible for cutting benefits to the disabled when he came to hand out Paralympic medals, it was because his presence affronted their sense of propriety. Whether it was question of the economy or sport, he was simply the wrong man in the wrong place doing the wrong job.

Mood music

Sport is all about rapid mood swings, and, like any mega event, the Olympics intensifies both the manic and the depressive phase. After all the build-up and hype, there was always the danger that the event itself would prove something of an anti-climax, unless something really awful happened. There is, in any event, an inevitable come-down once the party is over. In the case of 2012, however, this bi-polar structure of feeling was embedded from the outset, with the agony of 7/7 following on from the previous day's ecstasy at the bid's success and then given added emphasis by the sudden change in the economic fortunes of both London and the country.

The original bid was put together in a spirit of high optimism – year on year growth, we were told by Gordon Brown in 2005, was assured, the boom would go on for ever. This confidence, as well as the civic boosterism inevitably associated with any Olympic bid, gave some credibility to the upbeat message. When a year later the fiscal crisis struck it was too late to change the story – the strap-lines were already in place – even if the claim that 'everyone is a winner' now had a somewhat hollow ring. Having raised public expectations so high, the Olygarchs were hoist by their own petard, and could not devise a strategy to downsize the project and ground it in more realistic goals. Instead the aspirational 'can-do' message was refocused to convey a determination to overcome present difficulties by an act of will. Resilience – that *mot d'ordre* which unites the Olympic spirit with the spirit of the Blitz – was once more mobilised. Yet the fact is that the young people to whom the message was primarily addressed were also the most vulnerable to unemployment, and no amount of resilience, or skills training, was going to conjure up new jobs.[39]

As a result the legacy optimists are haunted by the spectre of an embittered 'lost' generation of young twenty-twelvers, inspired by all those back-the-bid campaign posters only to find their rising hopes melting into the thin air of austerity, as the promised opportunity structures fail to materialise and they are left to sit around in disgruntled reminiscence groups, lamenting the passing of the good old days when, for a few weeks in their lives, everything seemed possible. The scenario evokes an altogether different after image of London and 2012: the Olympics seductively calling to young Londoners from just beyond the horizon of their actual possibilities, and then abandoning them to their own devices, turning streets that should have been paved with silver or bronze if not gold into desolation row. London Babylon strikes back.

Grand narratives

Disaster scenarios belong to what is sometimes called a 'grand narrative'. The term implies that the story has a grandiose aspect to it or at least fits the particularities of everyday experience into some bigger picture which gives it a moral resonance and/or some explanatory power. Values only come into focus when the actions through which they are enacted are placed in some wider context and have to be justified.[40] It is a characteristic of grand narratives that their chief protagonists have a privileged or prophetic role to play in their unfolding, and while they may be revised as a result of internal debates within their interpretive communities, they are as immune from external critiques as they are to the impact of external events.

There are a number of possible grand narratives within which the Olympics might be evaluated, each of which inscribes the project in a very different value nexus. In the first case the Olympics are read as symptomatic of larger forces at work in the society, in particular, nowadays, those related to globalisation. This is not just down to fact that the games are a unique mega event, a sporting equivalent of the United Nations Assembly, but that hosting them is the material sign of world city status.[41] Their delivery presupposes a critical mass of facilities, including a networked infrastructure of transport and communications, that is integral to the global economy; a scale of procurement that only the largest companies with global resourcing and supply chains can provide and a level of national affluence sufficient to sustain such a large investment in public resource. Capitalism, according to this view, is the only game in town and globalisation is its middle name.[42]

This may be good news for the corporate sector, the construction, tourism and hospitality industries, property developers, and all those who for one reason or another are 'going with the flow'; but the benefits of globalisation do not, in the usual course of events, trickle down as far as the poorest sections of the host society. London's pitch for the 2012 Games, with its priority promise to deliver jobs and prosperity to the East End, staked a claim to be the exception to this rule, and to be judged within that economy of worth.

Globalisation and its local dis/contents were very much at the heart of the 2012 pre-Olympics debate.[43] There was considerable overlap between anti-globalisation rhetoric and the arguments deployed against the Olympics. The nay-sayers pointed to the threat of gentrification and the pricing of local working class people out of the area as a subtle form of social, if not ethnic, cleansing ; the new shopping city at Stratford, dominated by global brands, taking trade away from the local street market and local suppliers; small businesses being unable to compete with the big boys for the lucrative Olympic contracts; the level of corporate sponsorship required to make the games commercially viable destroying any claim to ethical business practice; and finally the dislocation or erasure of existing cultures and communities, and the creation of a sanitised and heavily regulated piece of city.[44] Capitalism is here very much the villain of the piece: first it spoils our fun by importing the spirit of unhealthy competition and the protestant work ethic into sport, destroying its ludic joys and then it ruins our health courtesy of MacDonald's and Coca Cola. Finally, to add insult to injury it uses tax-payers' money to subsidise an event that yields mega profits to disreputable private conglomerates, the likes of BP, Rio Tinto, Adidas, Arcelor-Mittal and Dow.[45] Against these worst case scenarios the Olygarchs and Olygopolists point to Barcelona (yet again) as proof positive that it is possible for a city to stage an economically profitable games whilst still delivering substantial benefits to its least well off citizens. London 2012 would show that the spirit of Capitalism and Carnival were alive and well and joint partners in the Olympic enterprise.

Whether mobilised for or against the Olympics, the globalisation thesis dissolves their specificity; it treats them as an epiphenomenon or at best as just another mega event. In contrast the second interpretive frame places the Games centre stage. The Olympic movement has its own organic intellectuals, its researchers who belong to the 'Olympic family' and who treat each Games as a distinct moment in an ongoing history.[46] In these sui generis accounts, each Olympiad is assessed in comparison with previous ones in terms of what it adds – or sometimes subtracts – vis à vis the movement's and the host city's reputation. The actions of the local organising committees, and how they respond to particular challenges are closely observed, and using a raft of performance indicators (120 at the latest count) the IOC delivers its verdict: best Games ever or not quite up to the mark set by its predecessors.

The third grand narrative belongs to those who claim to speak for the nation.[47] Thus 2012 was treated by the government as an opportunity to show off the 'best of British' to the world and the outcome judged by what the event contributed to the country's morale and sense of well being, as well as its economic recovery. Social enterprises, community organisations and the so called third sector may have played only a marginal role in the actual delivery of the Games, but rhetorically, they were very much where the action was.

The final narrative concerns those Olympic goals which transcend the Games and the host city /nation interest and constitute what I have called a para-Olympic perspective. The story concerns the local progress made in the world-wide struggle for human and democratic rights, gender and racial equality, social and economic justice and a sustainable planet. The issue is how far any Olympiad advances or frustrates these political causes. Although elements of this narrative play an important part of the rhetorics of the Olympic charter, the economy of worth it implies has never played a central operational role in any Olympic compact. It has, nevertheless, played an important critical and oppositional role.

Games Time or Olympics terminable and interminable

When, in the closing ceremony, the Olympic cauldron was extinguished and the flag ritually handed to Rio for 2016, it announced not the ending of the London Olympics but of a particular, liminal, phase of its existence. The Games themselves may be allowed their moment of glory, filled by the legendary exploits of sporting heroes, but as far as the Olygarchs are concerned they are only a blip on the screen. For their sights are set on higher, or rather, more down to earth goals.

The notion that an Olympiad will be more remembered for what happened afterwards than anything that actually took place, is of very recent origin: it dates from Barcelona 1992. Before then it was enough that the Games passed off without incident, athletic performances improved, everyone had a good time and then went home to get on with the rest of their lives. But one of the games people now play with an Olympiad, now that regeneration is the main item on the agenda, is to stretch its temporal horizon almost to vanishing point. 2020 used to be the time frame for completing the project but policy documents emanating from the Department of Culture, Media and Sport now blithely talk of 'decades' before the full legacy impact is known and one recent presentation of the Olympic Park legacy put it at 100 years plus.[48] At this point 'legacy' becomes coextensive with the life span of the Park itself and becomes quite meaningless as the basis for calculating costs and benefits. Could we measure Queen Victoria's 'legacy' by estimating the revenue generated by the Albert Hall since it was built? And even if we could it would tell us nothing about what she has come to represent or the impact her reign has had on our culture and society over the past century. Contrary to what bankers and property developers think, a price cannot be put on posterity.

When Fidel Castro was asked what he thought the legacy of the French Revolution was, he famously replied that it was still too soon to tell. In his equally famous defence of his espousal of revolutionary violence Castro also claimed 'History will absolve me'. Those for whom history is a tribunal that delivers a verdict – having replaced God as the final arbiter of human affairs – are likely to consider it a matter of long duration, if only to postpone the day of judgement for as long as possible. But can such a principle be applied to the Olympics?

One of the better accounts of an Olympiad, the XVII in Rome, is subtitled 'the Games that changed the world'. But did they? The Olympics may be a global media event, but that is not the same thing as occupying the world historical stage. They have their own internal memory politics, local, national and international, but these remain molecular in their impact and largely confined within the world of sport. The Rome Games are remembered, if at all, for the doping scandals, and putting the whole issue of shamateurism on the front pages, but they only changed public perceptions of Olympic sport, not the subsequent course of Italian, let alone world, politics. Even where macro-political events directly impinge: Berlin 1936, Munich 1972, Moscow 1980, they do no more than dramatise a particular conjuncture in international relations with which they happen to coincide. This may well define how an Olympics is remembered: Jesse Owen winning the sprint in Berlin; the Black September massacre of Israeli athletes, these are defining moments in Olympic history. But if Owens had lost to his German rival, the second world war would not have been averted. To claim an Olympiad has an epochal significance whose impact can only be judged over a very long duration it would be necessary to demonstrate that had it not happened, the course of world history would have been different. Such counterfactual claims are difficult to sustain. Tommie Smith and John Carlos' famous black power salute in the 1968 Mexico City Games is part of an enduring legacy of African-American struggle and has also entered Olympic folklore.[49] But whatever momentum it added to the civil rights movement at the time, their action did not fundamentally affect the outcome, in the way that the campaigns to desegregate schooling, the march on Washington, the assassination of Martin Luther King, or the Detroit riots did. Equally the Beijing Olympics symbolised China's 'opening to the West', and the award of the Games was a mark of recognition that the country was now a major player on the world political and economic stage; but however significant a moment it was for the Chinese people the Olympiad was no turning point in their world affairs. It came after the event, and was the culmination of a process that began three decades earlier with Nixon's visit and the inauguration of ping-pong diplomacy.[50] If the Beijing games had never happened China's strategic position in the world economy and its diplomatic power would not have been significantly altered. So although symbolic actions play a vital part in the battle for hearts and minds, and the Olympics can provide them with a transient world stage, they should not be burdened with the task of substituting themselves for political and economic struggles. World events can certainly affect the Olympics – most notably in the case of the two world wars leading to their cancellation. But no Olympic Games ever changed the world.

In what sense then can an Olympiad be said to 'make history'? As we have seen the Olympic movement is strongly committed to a Whig interpretation of its own history. Each Games is supposed to go one better than the next in setting new benchmarks of athletic performance and in the standard of amenities. Olympic history is here driven by the aims, objectives and ideals of the movement itself or by the intervention of extrinsic forces which frustrate or modify them. A 'record' within this teleological frame is one that marks progress. On the athletics field it may be experienced as a one-off never-to-be-repeated event, a singular achievement surpassing everything that has gone before, but this does not necessarily obliterate the memory of what has spurred it on. Rather the record holder enters the Olympic hall of fame to take his or her place amongst a long line of ancestors, conserved for all time as part of the movement's heritage, even though the record itself is probably destined to be 'smashed' or 'broken' before too long, the violence of the language bearing the trace of the 'oedipal' rivalry which it sublimates. The Olympic memoryscape is littered with cracked records that are condemned to endlessly repeat their moment of glory, unless and until they are synthesised with one another to play another, although no less monotonously triumphal, tune.

This version of 'making history' is modelled on the logic of generations. Each up and coming generation strives to define itself by its unique moment of advent to History; in claiming to embody the zeitgeist, the young pretenders seek to emulate and surpass the old guard, often by violently rejecting their accomplishments, only to find that they are in turn surpassed by their successors whilst their record of achievement is conserved, possibly to be rescued from oblivion by generations still to come. This dynamic is certainly present in the rivalry between athletes, and also between host cities; it accounts for much of the gossip that passes for cultural commentary about Olympic trends. Attempts to mitigate its worst effects are made by appealing to a common heritage. The 2012 headliner 'inspire a generation' posited an unproblematic process of inter-generational transmission without a hint of oedipal ambivalence. Nevertheless legacy under the sign of modernity is never not a matter of 'the old' versus 'the new'. In the *Grundrisse* Marx put it like this:

History is nothing but the succession of the separate generations, each of which exploits the materials, the capital funds, the productive forces handed down to it by all the proceeding generations. And this, on the one hand, continues the traditional activity in completely changed circumstances, and on the other modifies the old circumstances with completely changed activity.[51]

What for Marx was a dialectic, becomes in other hands a purely linear narrative in which one event generates or 'begets' another, leading to a common sense historicism based on dangerously fallacious 'post hoc, propter hoc' arguments of the type : first the immigrants came, then unemployment rose, therefore they are taking our jobs; or first London got the Olympics, then we came out of recession, therefore 2012 produced an economic miracle.

For those who like their history to be a clear cut story of heroes and villains, winners and losers, the Olympics are clearly a gift, but in a society where profound social amnesia accompanies the obsessional remembrance of trivia such morality tales do not necessarily help create the conditions for a better or deeper understanding of the past. 'Olympic history' is brilliantly packaged for the instant nostalgia market, but it rarely illuminates either history or the Olympics.

This difficulty in establishing historical credentials underscores the fact that 'games time' is peculiar. We are dealing with a moveable feast of athletics that takes place somewhere different every four years but always aims to reproduce identical sporting conditions; participation is both site specific and discontinuous, each event being produced at the intersection of a unique geo-political conjuncture, even though the principle of periodicity is cyclical and the narrative legacy is cumulative, as chapter after chapter is added to this story without an end.[52] The Olympic ideal itself is timeless, or mytho-poeic, in the sense that it represents another possible world in which peace, equality and justice (or respect, friendship and excellence) prevail; however its realisation takes place within a delivery framework that is rigidly linear, organized as it is around a succession of 'milestones' yielding a very concrete and short term sense of duration. The diachronics of the Olympiads imposes a principle of global synchronisation on other mega sporting events, like the World Athletic Championships or the World Soccer Cup, to ensure they do not clash; at the same time the four year cycle disrupts the dominant principle of periodicity which organises public history into decades or eras. Evaluation of legacy, in 'rerunning' Games against one another introduces a principle of reversibility into the time frame, while heritage as an inter-generational thing involves an all too elastic sense of duration going forward'. Finally the enactment of the Olympic motto evokes a notion of 'making history' as an iterative process of record breaking, while memoryscapes are organised around a cluster of discrete moments that define the historical individuality of each games.

So 'games time' involves the convergence of a bewildering multiplicity of different temporalities, what might be termed a 'hetero-chronology', whose scale oscillates between milliseconds and decades.[53] Games time has also become compressed, as a proliferation of events are squeezed into ever tighter media schedules. In his novel *Gold*, Chris Cleave describes a situation where the rules of entry into the cycling competitions had to be changed to reduce the number of competitors, because the advertisers in regional media markets are demanding fewer heats and more finals in prime time TV. He comments on the process of acceleration:

> this was what had become of the world that children used to ride their slow bicycles through in endless arcs. Time had been restructured like a bad debt. The long languid hour had been atomized. Manifestos were shrunk to memes and speeches were pressed into soundbites and heats were truncated into finals ...[54]

In 2012 the restructuring of debt involved not just time but space. The Marathon was scheduled to be run through the streets of East London, finishing in the Olympic Stadium and enabling the local populace to get a grandstand view of this highlight of the Games. It was a way of publicly recognising the nation's obligation to the immediate host community. However it was not to be. In the event, other, more pressing, debts were called in. The route was at the last minute relocated from East End to West End, to comprise three loops, starting and finishing in the Mall and passing by Admiralty Arch, Trafalgar Square, the Tower of London, the Houses of Parliament and other well known landmarks. Various excuses were given for the change of plans. One was logistical. If the East End route had been chosen, Tower Bridge would have had to be closed and this might have resulted in traffic jams. Security was another get out clause. The narrow streets around Stratford would pose a risk and the police insisted on a lockdown. This would mean that East Londoners would not have been able to see the finish in any event, so they might as well not have any opportunity at all to watch it. The East London boroughs were furious at this reneging on a long standing promise and pointed out that there must be something seriously wrong with LOCOG's risk management strategy if these issues had not been foreseen. The real reason for the volte face, however, had nothing to do with these issues; it was about the logistics of staging the marathon as a global media event. Sky TV and other corporate media insisted that it take place in an iconic environment instantly recognisable by viewers around the world. So forget about London being the world in a city, what the world needed to see on its screens was the familiar face of the City as the once upon a time heart of Empire, now historic hub of a global economy.

It is difficult, then, not to conclude that when push came to shove in 2012, the shots were called by a political economy in which civic claims were brushed aside in favour of a media marketing agenda, by a culture of hospitality in which the priorities of security trumped those of conviviality, and by a moral economy organised on a 'rob Peter to pay Paul' principle to justify a payback which defaulted on a debt of honour to East Londoners.

End games

Games time may be differential, but its advent also marks a specific and indeed unique conjuncture and this 'plenary time' imposes a certain time signature on the event itself.[55] Lord Coe drew on the full range of Olympic chronicities when, in his address to the Opening Olympic ceremony he claimed in almost the same breath that 2012 was about living for the moment *and* making an indelible mark on history, that London was a city which never stands still *and* that everything in its past had prepared it for this Olympic culmination, and finally that Londoners would be able to tell their grandchildren that 'this was our time and we got it right'.

The 'longitudinalising' of the 2012 Games may thus well be a stab at posterity but cynics have suggested that it is just as much based on the hope or expectation that sometime between now and whenever the economy must pick up and so enable 2012 to at last deliver the material goods. Certainly the state of the national economy remains the white elephant in the room. The Olygarchs don't talk about it much. However there is a very material aspect to the desire to stretch the time frame: it is based on a calculation of how long it will take to recover the public debts incurred in staging the Olympics by realising – and that means selling off – the Olympic Park's assets to private companies. Economic forecasters have suggested that three decades at least will be required for this purpose. Pay back time in the 2012 never never land, like old Father Thames itself, just keeps on rolling on and requires that the legacy of debt be somehow presented as a gift worth having.

A project that takes six years to plan and deliver, two weeks to happen and possibly several decades to recover from (or, if you prefer, to realise its full regeneration potential) clearly makes special demands on its imagination. The legacy narrative has been compared to a catalytic converter in that it reduces noxious policy emissions to tolerable levels but only by branding everything that happens in East London over the next quarter of a century with the 2012 logo. But perhaps a better analogy would be to the soap opera. The legacy story could be read as a series of subplots, with different agendas (economic, environmental, health, etc) each having their own story line, as key players come and go, and first one and then another theme holds centre stage. Each new episode starts by recapitulating the story so far and ends with a tantalising 'to be continued'; while the setting – Olympic Park and its environs – provides the unities of time and place to hold the drama together. And like the TV version of *EastEnders*, this is a story that will run and run. Will Stratford become a fully fledged town centre, a new hub for outer East London, just as Canary Wharf is for the inner East End? Will the momentum of London's eastwards turn be halted at Stratford, or continue on downriver into the Thames Gateway? Will the Lower Lea valley, the Olympic Park's immediate hinterland, be given a new lease of life, and the Park itself blend into the urban landscape, or will regeneration falter, and the sports facilities remain underused? To find out tune in next year, or the year after, or the year after that …

Yet there is also a sense in which, from beginning to end, London 2012 is likely remain the same old regeneration story, because, across its successive iterations, the underlying script remains unchanged. The scope and scale of the project have not been downsized, and in the credibility gap between its optimistic rhetorics formed in better times and the gloomy prognostications of future circumstance, the ghosts of Olympics past assemble, some encouraging or consoling, others threatening or mocking as they tell their various cautionary tales.

I have suggested that the Olympic story necessarily has a mythopoeic dimension – it is about a once upon a time when everyone lived happily – or unhappily – ever after, as well as a 'gnoseological' one – examining the reasons why the project succeeded or failed, and 'what dunnit'. The problem is that these two aspects have become so entangled that it is all but impossible to reach a rational judgement about outcomes through any process of consensual validation.

The burden of my argument in this chapter is that this confusion is epitomised by the time frame that has been wrapped around the Games. The strictly delimited time span of the payback legacy has been transformed into the much more elastic time scale of *heritage*.[56] In the more conventional terms of legacy politics a framing that essentially belongs to what is normally referred to as 'soft legacy' has been applied to the evaluation of hard legacy. It is a rich source of confusion, whose only plus is that it is no longer possible to pretend that there is some final objective day of reckoning.

Whatever principle of accountancy or accountability is applied to the Olympics it is always too early or too late. In the build up to the Games and during the event itself, when public and media interest is at its height, it is impossible to have sufficient evidence to reach reliable judgements. There is the ever present risk of exaggerating the costs or the benefits to come, or worse, confusing them. Then, after the event, the prospective illusion gives way to a retrospective one. It is always easier to be wise after the event, to say 'I told you so', or fall back on speculations of 'what might have been, if only'. But by this time no-one much is listening. Public interest has been exhausted by the saturation coverage, the Olympic bandwagon and the media circus have moved on, leaving behind only the professional interest groups, the Olygarchs and Olympophobes, to settle old scores, while the academics move in to clear up the conceptual mess, sift through the mountain of information left behind for clues to their particular research questions and argue amongst themselves about what it all adds up to.

London 2012 – a Games of more than two halves?

In a city where some people are conspicuously much more winners than others there were bound to be those who felt they were losing out in the Olympic stakes and had nothing to lose if the project were to fail. For the nay-sayers, the dreadful already happened with London winning the bid and things only went on getting worse. Amongst Londoners who had a positive stake in the Olympics – the twenty-twelvers – those who had otherwise the least going for them nevertheless seemed grimly determined to have a good Olympics, in much the same spirit as their grandparents used to talk about having a good war: surviving what might potentially have been a disaster, with memories of shared predicament, conviviality and windfall opportunity. Yet as we will see in Chapter Ten their sense of legacy ownership remains provisional and not to be taken for granted.

What all this points to is 2012 becoming not just a tale of two cities, but also of two, or more than two Olympics. In the officially accredited version, the Olympic motto 'faster, higher, stronger' perfectly describes the youthful energy and ambition that animates the vital thrusting growth of the city in its eastwards turn as well as the medal successes of team GB. The alternative version tells the downside of the story, recalling everything that is tragic and scandalous about a capital whose passion for growth has resulted in policies and processes which distribute its benefits to a few and its costs to many. Its motto might be 'slower, lower, stronger', projecting a downsized vision of 2012 and its legacy in which public expectations are reduced, the city's rate of growth adapted to what is sustainable and the power of local communities to withstand the pressures of global capitalism increased.[57] There are also two legacies, a debt legacy, which involves selling off as much as possible of the assets of Olympic Park to the private sector to pay back what is owed to the public purse and a gift legacy in which the assets are handed over in the form of an endowment to community organisations as repayment of a symbolic debt owed by the nation for the way the people of East London played host to the Games.[58] There is no easy point of reconciliation between these different perspectives; political economists, market economists and moral economists don't talk to each other much, although their joint participation in the post-Olympic debate will hopefully help to bring them into some kind of dialogue.

London is a palimpsest of many histories; it has outlived feudalism and industrialism, seen the rise and fall of Empires, including its own, survived wars, both civil and global. Its third time lucky Olympics will deposit its own layer of narrative but is unlikely to fundamentally disturb this more deeply sedimented memoryscape. For the metropolis will always call the world from just beyond the horizon of its possibilities to satisfy their hopes and claims, and, as we will see in the following chapters, this is no less true of the Olympics.

5. In the Zone:
labourhoods and bodyscapes
@ the Games

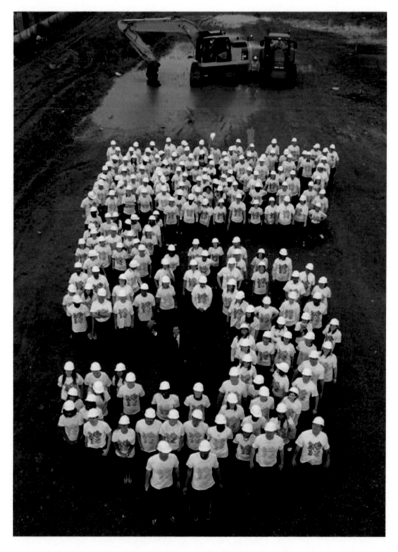

One of the number? Lord Coe with the Olympic site workforce,
Carpenters Road 2007

Photo essay: The Groundbreakers

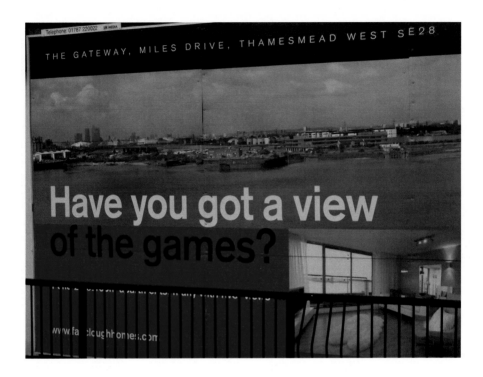

Entrance to Olympic Site 2006

Site Archaeology

Entrance to the Main Stadium

Pat Loughrane

Excavation

Sonia breaks through

Tunnel vision

Data miner

Machine Vision

Landscape with cable drums

Going Home

Bank Statement (Marshgate Lane)

The contempt in which the mechanical arts are held seems to have affected to some degree even their inventors. The names of these benefactors of humankind are almost all unknown, whereas the history of its destroyers, that is to say, of the conquerors, is known to everyone. Why are not those to whom we owe the fusee, the escapement, the repeating-works of watches equally esteemed with those who have worked successively to perfect algebra? Moreover, if I may believe a few philosophers who have not been deterred from studying the arts by the prevailing contempt for them, there are certain machines that are so complicated, and whose parts are all so dependent on one another, that their invention must almost of necessity be due to a single man. Is not that man of genius, whose name is shrouded in oblivion, well worthy of being placed beside the small number of creative minds who have opened new routes for us in the sciences?

Denis Diderot, *Preface to Encyclopedia*

The means of vision – matter is transformed and reborn by Imagination. The means of production – matter is transformed and reborn by Labour. At a certain period of human development the means of vision and the means of production were intimately connected ... But this relationship was violently and fundamentally altered by the accumulation of capital, the freedom of trade, the invention of machines, the philosophy of materialism, the discoveries of science ... The relationship of production to the means of vision – the emotional side of our nature – has been mankind's greatest problem.

Humphrey Jennings *Pandaemonium*

OOOOO

I grew up in Barrow on Furness, at a time when shipbuilding was still going strong, and I became fascinated by what people can make with their hands and with technologies. But then the shipyards closed and when I left school I decided to go to mining college instead. I'd always been interested in geology, so this seemed like a good move. But then the pits started to close so I moved sideways into tunnelling. It's an interesting industry because very little of it can be formally taught. The learning process involves gaining an understanding and respect for the ground. We are groundbreakers, we have to negotiate with the ground and reach agreement with the forces of nature. Steering a full-faced tunnel boring machine is like steering a submarine blind underground. You have to have a feel for the earth, as well as all the technical information you need to keep it on course.

Kevin McManus (chief engineer)

There's a lot of contaminated ground on the Olympics site, and we have to find out what's there so when the boring machine goes through they know what it is going to hit. Otherwise they are drilling blind. We hit gases twice which knocked us out ... now we all have gas alarms and special protective clothing. You find a lot of nasties, oil, contaminants, some interesting stuff too. We have found dolls, shoes, nice bottles, some real antiques – still waiting for the unexploded bomb.

Sean McKusker (rigger)

When you go down there, in the tunnel, you lose all sense of whether it's day or night. In the summer it's not so bad, but in the winter it's a bit funny, because you go down when it's dark and you come up when it's dark. You begin to wonder whether you are ever going to see the sunlight again. It's like being a mole. But you get used to it. It may not suit everyone, but the job has its bright side, the lads are good crack and the money is not bad

Alan Peake (concrete finisher)

We work 12-hour shifts. We have half an hour break at 11 in the morning and 5 in the evening, for our sandwiches. We don't come up. I don't mind the shifts. I have always done shift work. Nights and days. But it is hard sometimes. Sometimes at night my wife says to me 'what is wrong with you?' and I say 'I am tired from working hard'.

Sami Bici (loco driver)

I used to work down the pits and when they closed I moved into tunnelling. My job is to maintain the TBMs, and make sure they are up to scratch. And then when that's finished with I work as a fabricator, designing and making up special things that are needed on the site but you can't get off the shelf. Getting a job in this game is all word of mouth. It's who you know, not just what you know, that counts. It's a very close-knit community. We all keep in touch with one another, and we know what's going on around the country, what money's being paid, what conditions on the job are like. It's how we manage to get by, especially when times are hard.

Bob Sheldon (tunneller and fabricator)

Tunnelling is a special kind of job. It's in your blood. We look after one another, it's like a family in a way. If someone is off sick, or has an accident, we have a whip-round to make sure his family is all right. You don't get that same spirit in most other jobs, it's usually everyone out for themselves. It's something to do with the danger. Your life depends on the people you're working with. I like a challenge. I drove lorries in Iraq for the Americans after the fall of Baghdad. It was dodgy, some people got blown up, but the money was good. I came back because I was missing my family and the sense of community in work and I heard about this job.

Colin Laughton (miner)

I was working as a traffic marshal to make some extra cash while I was at college studying science and computers, and I met this guy who said why don't you go for training as a banksman. I thought he meant working in a bank, but then he explained it was a bit like what I was doing already only more skilled and more money, plus it was for the Olympics. So I went for my ticket and I got it. The banksman is responsible for the slinging and securing of loads that go into and out of the pit shaft. The crane man is blind, he can't see over the edge into the pit bottom, so you have to be his eyes, and produce signals that tell him exactly what to do. If the load isn't strapped right and properly balanced, if it goes down wrong and slips, then people could get hurt. It's a team effort. We have a solid gang – the craneman, the banksmen on the surface, the pit boss below. On the site health and safety is very strict because of the Olympics. It's quite different from India, where there are lots of accidents in construction. Still there they have eight-hour days, five days a week, whereas here it is twelve-hour shifts and you could be working seven nights in a row. That is bound to affect your concentration and can lead to accidents. When the tunnelling is over I want to stay on site and get a job in construction, because I live nearby in Newham. I feel that the Olympics is a big chance for us in Newham and also for my community, and we have a responsibility to make the most of it.

Rohan Mistry (banksman and Newham resident)

You don't get Irish lads over any more. It's been prosperous there until recently so they don't have to go abroad looking for work. A lot of them are going to college now and getting an education and they don't want to get their hands dirty. So that generation is going and now we are looking to the East Europeans. This town won't function without the East Europeans and all the other immigrants. They are hard workers. That's the way it is, that's the way it should be and that's the way it's always been in East London. It's great. We are all immigrants here. I'm an immigrant. The East End is where people come to get a start in life.

Pat Loughrane (crane driver)

This new shift system we've got, seven days on, four off, it really ruins your social life. Because one week you may get only two day's work and the next you'll be on nine shifts. It varies from month to month. It means you can't plan much ahead. And it could cause problems with budgeting. One week you may have a lot coming in and the next hardly anything. It's good for the lads from Manchester or Ireland, it means they can go home and see their families, but it's ruined my social life. I don't really have one at the moment. I think the only reason they brought it in is so they get more flexible working arrangements and save money. But there's no union, so there's not much we can do about it.

Les Mawson (grouter)

None of the sites I've worked on have been unionised. Some of them are very dodgy as regards health and safety and they have very poor facilities. Like you need to be able to go and wash to get contaminants off your hands. But if you ask for toilets or washing facilities they regard you as a troublemaker and you don't get asked back. But on this site, because it's the Olympics, they are running a tight ship. I remember the UCATT strikes. I went to one of the meetings and asked them what was it about and they said, never mind, just put up your hand to vote for the strike. I thought I can't be doing with this. As a driller you're your own boss. There's no-one on your back, and as long as you give them what they want they leave you alone. If you don't like the conditions on a job, you just move on to another site, not go whingeing to a shop steward. We're not usually on a site for more than a fortnight anyway. This Olympics job, eighteen months, is very unusual. Mind you when there's a recession, we're the first to get hit. No one is going to employ you.

John Wild (Rigger)

I got the job through my dad. He's a loco driver and one day the pit boss was asking around if anyone knew someone looking for a job so my dad put me forward and here I am. The first day I was here it was a bit weird. There was an accident and someone got crushed when a load fell off the train. My job is to load up the train that goes to the face: the skips, the grout cart, the bogies that carry the concrete rings for the tunnel. I work with this other lad. We're skivvies really, we fetch and carry a lot of stuff for the pit boss. I was worried I'd get a lot of funny stuff from the men, stitching the new boy up, what with being the youngest there, but perhaps 'cos my dad was around, and there wasn't time, they left me alone. I enjoy the banter, but you have to be careful who you try it on with, because some of the men think it's disrespectful coming from a young kid. It's an old fashioned kind of job.

Mark Pollard (pit boy)

It's like being the conscience of both management and workforce. On one side you have the managers saying 'we need this job done'. On the other the workers saying 'no way, it's too risky'. You're in the middle, and you have to do a balancing act. You have to put systems in place to reduce the risk to a level acceptable to the workforce, and you have to ensure that the job gets done on time and the firm's profits don't suffer. I see my job as keeping the workers out of hospital and the management out of court. You have to look at the Olympic site as a disaster waiting to happen, and everyone on it as potentially acting with suicidal stupidity. The site itself is marshland, it's heavily contaminated, and because of the war it's a potential bomb site. If you don't get it right you could end with a dead body. My job is a bit like a goalkeeper's. If I keep a clean sheet, no-one notices I'm there. If I make a few spectacular saves, I get noticed and congratulated, but if I let in too many goals I lose my place in the team.

Bill Chappell (health and safety engineer)

Office workers look at us and just think hard hats, navvies…yeah they lump us all together but each one of us is different… you get all sorts down here, jokers, professors who think they know it all, piss artists, people who know how to handle a guitar as well as shovel… we look after each other and each one of us counts.

Martin McDonagh (miner)

I live in Stratford, but I don't think the Olympics is going to benefit ordinary working-class people. It's more likely to price us out of the area. I know this old woman, she lives in one of the council tower blocks overlooking the Olympic site and they're going to knock it down to ten storeys. She lives on the twelfth floor, so they moved her out, but they didn't find her anywhere local, they moved her to Mile End where she doesn't know anyone. All because of the Olympics. And if you walk round this site now and ask how many people come from round here you'll be lucky to find a handful.

Peter Campbell (steel fixer and local resident)

I've lived here all my life. My parents had this pub before me, and now with the Olympics we've got a real chance to make this area into something special. But we've got to give the locals a chance with the jobs. You're going to have people coming from all over the country to work on the site – we've already got the East Europeans – but you don't give local people a chance. It's so wrong. They're building a whole new city and we've got an ideal opportunity to train a whole generation in construction skills and they fluffed it.

Janet Dooner (local hotelier and community forum member)

What's different about this being the Olympics site? Well, there is a lot of suits running around the site looking important, and getting under your feet. But it's mainly the media – you get all these people filming you and asking stupid questions – like do you enjoy working here? Then there are the talking heads. They pose them up against the site, they yak away about the Olympics and all it's going to do for the area, and then they go away and you never see them again. One day all the workforce was made to line up so we made a big number five – five years to go – and there was Lord Coe standing in the middle in his hard hat as if he was one of us. It took about an hour just standing there so they could get the picture they wanted, and that meant an hour lost which we had to make up when we got back to work.

To me the Olympics are nothing. It's just another job, only the money's better, and you're on site a lot longer than other jobs. But once I'm out of here, that's it. The Olympics is just about a lot of people making money and a name for themselves. So what else is new?

Mike Forester (scaffolder)

I feel proud to have worked on the Olympics. In 2012 I'll be able to say to my kids I helped build that. The eyes of the world are on us down here and we are going to show the world that we can build the best Olympics ever.

Paul Andrews (site engineer)

Site works

The Powerlines project was part of the first phase of the Olympic Park construction which started in 2006.[1] It involved digging two large tunnels across the whole site, extending for several miles between West Ham and Hackney, in order to reroute underground the power cables from the electricity pylons that dominated the site, and which were due to be demolished. At the same time the site was being cleared and prepared for the actual construction phase, and this involved demolishing many buildings, and treating heavily polluted soil.

My research in the site took place between September 2006 and April 2007 during the last phase of the project when the tunnels were nearing completion. I interviewed surface and underground workers as well as managers on site, and also conducted site observations. The interviews focused on the workers' backgrounds – how they had come to be in this line of work – their experiences of working on the site, and their views on the Olympics. Some members of the local community were also interviewed.

The materiality of building work and its technologies appears to offer consoling evidence that things really are what they seem to be, because they can be shown, demonstrably, to be happening. What you see is what you get. Yet this very transparency hides the density and complexity of the fabrication process. The nature of that complexity is described in the term itself.[2] 'Fabric' means both a manufactured material and a frame, structure, or texture. The term thus refers us to a form of worked-on matter that has something irreducibly symbolic about it; fabrication – making things up – has the connotation of artifice or even dissimulation. Yet this aspect is often ignored. For architects, a fabricator is the company that makes the materials out of which their design is built. On a building site, a fabricator is someone who designs and makes up new components that cannot be purchased off the shelf. But in the artists' impressions and models that architects use for rhetorical purposes – to persuade clients or communities that their scheme is the best thing ever – the other sense of fabrication, a story made up to conceal the real, comes into play. When planners talk of urban fabric (and of holes in it), they are always referring to facts of social and cultural geography, not just to the physical environment.[3] For example, in the case of the Olympic Park, the designers referred to the site as a 'scar' or 'tear' in the urban fabric that needed to be 'stitched together' or 'zipped up', while some in the local community accused them of 'sticking their knife in the wound' or 'peeling the gash': this language not only draws on a familiar image repertoire that represents the city as a body, with a head, heart, lungs and circulatory system, but also refers to a whole phenomenology of urban dislocation that is associated with regeneration projects.[4]

This bears on the whole question of how the construction and regeneration story of 2012 is to be visually represented.[5] The ODA's approach was to document the physical transformation of the Olympic site through the use of time-lapse photography that showed each stage of its development, and then to lay on top of this a commentary about incremental progress, driven by a resolute determination to meet targets and overcome all obstacles. If the resulting narrative lacks a properly epic dimension, it is because the material scale of the project has taken precedence over any more social and imaginative approach: what is missing from such an account is any sense of what the site means to those who worked on it, even though for many it became an important *lieu de mémoire*, a source of shared stories and, in some cases, of a richly imagined world.

I have coined the term *labourhood* to connote the symbolic role that workplaces play in the lives of their communities, and to highlight the fact that the narrative threads spinning out from such sites get tangled up in all manner of extraneous discourses.[6] The material process of production creates a special kind of yarn in which manifold actions at a distance shuttle to and fro between a multiplicity of groundworks, supplying a chain of messages – instructions, reports, diagrams, inventories – through which the site is conveyanced from virtual to physical reality and back again. In this space, between map and territory, plan view and site circuitry, tunnellers, bricklayers and crane operators go about their business alongside architects, engineers and security guards, each, without quite recognising the fact, relaying their separate impressions on tablets no longer set in stone, but in a virtual design process whose full import is only registered after the event. It is these hidden and largely unconscious lines of assembly which have to be captured as well as the more deliberative practices of decision-making.

From this point of view, a building site can be made to speak many languages, both human and non-human. The repetitive nature of much construction work means that what is memorable about it, and considered worthy of narration, are the incidents which interrupt its routines – the risks, the accidents, the emergencies, the disputes, the craic. In one experiment a bricklayer under hypnosis could remember the distinguishing features of every brick he had laid over the past month, and an office worker every email, but when interviewed about their jobs they talked about working conditions in terms of boredom and monotony and how it was combated; they highlighted incidents of conflict and comradeship. The memory politics of work narratives require that both sides of the story – the routine and the interruptive – be given equal weight, if only to counterbalance the tendency of the managerial version to smooth over the difficulties and the worker's counter narrative to sometimes over-emphasise them.

Yet a building site is no Tower of Babel. There is a common language of labour in the terminologies applied to materiel, equipment and customary work practice that cuts across social divisions. Restoring narrativity to things as well as people requires a standpoint which stays close to the ground, following the manoeuvres, the little moves that push things on, without reducing them to a simple unfolding of some grand narrative or master plan. For example, in the construction of the Olympic Velodrome a crucial aspect of its acoustic and visual aesthetic was the wooden walls. The workmen noticed that when they used a nail gun to fix the slats into place, shards from the nail became embedded in the wood, and these in time would rust and stain because of the high temperature maintained inside the building. The only way to avoid this discolouration was to revert to the old fashioned hammer. A small enough detail, but one which has made a big difference to the outcome as well as making considerable savings on maintenance costs. The intervention of craftsmanship here left both the architectural vision and the public purse intact.

The workforce belonged to two very different occupational cultures, experienced very different working conditions and inhabited social worlds that rarely met or impinged on one another on site. The tunnellers worked twelve-hour shifts, from 7 to 7, with alternating weeks of night and day shifts. They took their meals and rest breaks underground and only came to the surface in an emergency. The surface workers, including the office staff, worked normal 9 to 5 hours, went shopping in their lunch breaks and ate in the staff canteen. The tunnellers were almost all from other parts of the country and lived locally in digs, while the surface workers were Londoners.

Tunnelling is difficult, dangerous and dirty work, although also a very technologically sophisticated process. It borrows much of its terminology and culture from coal mining, and many of the tunnellers came from ex-coal mining communities, but it involves a quite different labour process. The tunnel boring machine (TBM) is the main protagonist in the story. The TBM has a cutting face with scythes embedded in it which mine the earth, rather like a corkscrew; it is steered along a predetermined route, using lasers to keep it on track. Even so it is possible to hit obstacles that had not been anticipated. Near what used to be Bromley-by-Bow gasworks, one of the TBMs hit an underground storage dump full of dangerous contaminants that had not been picked up on any of the surveys and the tunnel had to be evacuated while the problem was fixed, causing a delay of several days.

The TBM is accompanied by a team of miners and engineers who fix concrete rings in place to secure the tunnel, remove the excavated soil and service the machine. Much of the time they are working in mud and water up to their knees. The pit boss is in charge of the pit shaft and the transport of men, machines and materials between the surface and the tunnel face; he is the human link between the crane operators and banksmen above and the loco drivers and miners below. Mobile phones have now made communications much easier and it is possible for the miners to be in constant contact with the site engineers on the surface.

The TBM plays a key part in shaping the interaction of materiel, equipment and workers, and a central role in the industry's folklore.[7] Each TBM is given a women's name and invested with certain 'feminine' characteristics. In the case of the Olympic site 'Sonia' was regarded as capricious, needing careful handling and liable to break down if not treated properly, while 'Helen' and 'Lucille' behaved themselves and were altogether more docile and reliable. Giving machines women's names is a tradition as old as industrial capitalism and almost as old as patriarchy, but in a culture of 'elemental' labour based on the aggressive domination of nature and often heavily sexist banter, the feminising of its key technology may just imply a subliminal recognition that it is not after all wholly a man's world, despite the fact that it is still so difficult for women to make headway in the manual trades.

There were other traditional features to the culture. There was the primacy given to hands-on experience – learning by watching and doing, rather than through formal training; of recruitment being largely through informal word-of mouth-contact; and also cases of sons not only following in their father's footsteps but working alongside them. For some boys, growing up working-class can still entail an apprenticeship to a patrimony of skill and know-how transmitted through the family.[8]

Tunnelling is highly specialised, and its workforce moves from site to site around the country, often in groups. The nomadic aspect of construction has traditionally made it very difficult to give priority to employing local workforces, and has hampered union demands to employ direct labour. Many of the men I interviewed had worked together on Heathrow Terminal 5, and quite a few had been on the Channel Tunnel project. A lot of the tunnellers were from Tyneside, Yorkshire and Kent – all ex-mining areas. A few of them had worked down the pits before they were closed by Margaret Thatcher. Their working conditions and often unsocial hours meant that they had little time or energy to do more than eat and sleep when not on the job; they often shared digs, and a few had been taken in as lodgers by local people. Some drank in local pubs, and most reported that they had no trouble with the locals, although they didn't mix with them much. There were some exceptions to this rule; there were some fights with local youth, and, perhaps not unconnectedly, some fraternisation with women from the neighbourhood. And there were some very old-fashioned attitudes to 'immigrants' amongst a few of the younger white workers, although in general 'race relations' on and off site were good.

The shift system was seven days on, four off, which made it possible for people to travel back to spend time with their families, but because the amount of work – and hence money – varied from week to week it was difficult to budget and plan ahead (see Les Mawson's comment). On an hourly pro rata basis, the tunnellers were the highest paid workers on the site, though by the time they had paid for their digs, sent money home and saved up for much needed holidays they had very little disposable income left at the end of the week.

Relationships amongst the workforce were generally reported by them to be good. Despite occasional communication problems, the Irish and East Europeans got on well together, and the quality of the 'crack' was much commented on. Joking relationships always were a good solvent of social tensions. Both workers and management stressed the importance of teamwork. The site management structure was of bewildering complexity, principally because there were two main tunnel contractors, each with their own internal communications network and chain of command. Add to that an elaborate system of subcontracting, and another layer of bureaucracy in the form of the Olympic Delivery Authority, and the result was predictably Byzantine.

Relations between management and workforce were also reported on both sides to be generally good, although the site was not initially unionised, and there were unresolved issues to do with shift and payment systems, speed-up and safety that a union official would normally have taken up. In later phases of the construction, when a union agreement was in place, and convenors were on hand to deal with issues as they arose, industrial relations were not always smooth. Many of the smaller subcontractors found ways to get round the regulations, and the targets for widening access to training and apprenticeships were not met.[9] However, as noted, there was a strong health and safety ethos across the site, and this, alongside a number of other factors, militated against the formation of an anti-management 'shop floor' culture.

Some of the workers, like the riggers, were independent artisans in that they owned their own equipment and exercised considerable control over their conditions of work. They were not technically self-employed but were very much their own bosses. But perhaps the major reason why there was so little conflict is that both management and workforce tended to close ranks against the Olympic Delivery Authority who, on both sides, were seen to be interfering busybodies who knew little about construction and just got in the way. The constant media visits and the large numbers of ODA officials running around with clipboards made the site managers nervous and the workforce impatient: they just wanted to be left alone to get on with the job. They were under great pressure to meet deadlines and could not afford delays, but were also aware that health and safety issues were paramount. If there was a serious accident it would hit the headlines and inevitable comparisons would be made with the Athens Olympics and its appalling safety record; yet the additional precautionary measures demanded by the ODA also slowed the work process down.

All this made the Health and Safety engineer's job even more than usually fraught. As far as he was concerned the Olympic site was a potential death trap, a disaster movie waiting to happen (see quote from Bill Chappell). Chappell was a keen devotee of the genre, and as he gave me a guided tour, pointing out potential hazards, he quoted incidents from different films to illustrate his points. His imaginative remake of the landscape included a running commentary on Hollywood's lack of site-specific awareness and a lecture on why the *Towering Inferno* need never have happened.

The fact that the site was continually being photographed, filmed and visited meant that the workforce, especially those employed on surface jobs, quickly became conscious that they were expected to play a role in the unfolding media story about 2012. The labour process itself became part of the Olympic Spectacle, as banksmen and crane drivers, brickies and welders, performed their tasks for the benefit of the cameras. Only the tunnellers were spared because it was too dangerous to allow site visitors to go underground to see the TBMs in action – even though their conditions of work better equipped them to represent the heroic, 'Promethean' aspects of manual labour.

Another issue that management and workforce agreed on, but which caused the ODA great anxiety, was the workplace demographic. The difficulty of recruiting suitably qualified local people and attracting young people to enter the industry was the subject of much head-shaking and shoulder-shrugging. Now that the supply of young Irishmen had dried up, for the reasons Pat Loughrane explains, it was only the advent of the Poles, Albanians and other East Europeans that plugged the gap. The site managers continually complained that they could not find suitably qualified local workers, and that young people were not coming forward in sufficient numbers. The reluctance of young East Enders, especially from the Asian community, to work in the construction industry can partly be put down to the cultural marginalisation of manual labour, and the low status that these jobs now have in their communities; and partly it is due to the rhetorics of aspiration that were promoted so vigorously by the Olympics. 'Living the Olympic Dream' was about jumping over Tower Bridge, not standing knee-high in muck stuffing grout into a seam of concrete tunnelling. The Olygarchs hoped that the allure of 'working for the Olympics' would draw young people in, but they miscalculated the effect of their own propaganda. Nevertheless, as the experience of Rohan Mistry shows, local training initiatives and word-of-mouth contacts on the ground could make a difference, even though the latter might also support forms of social closure in occupational cultures from which minority ethnic communities are excluded. An on site Olympic skills academy might perhaps have gone some way to overcoming the resistance of young East Enders to entering the manual trades, although the recession was always going to be a disincentive.

2012 was supposed to be all about delivering jobs and skills training to East London, not providing more opportunities for migrant workers from the EU (see Janet Dooner's comment). Just how much of a political hot potato this was I discovered when the ODA asked me for some 'exemplary' quotes from the interviews for a small exhibition they were mounting for visiting International Olympic Committee monitors. One of the quotes I selected was from Pat Loughrane (see above), who commented favourably on the considerable number of East Europeans working on site and how well they had integrated with the rest of the workforce – thereby wholeheartedly endorsing the official 2012 story line about London as a 'world in a city', with a vibrant multicultural presence.[10] Despite this, and the fact that the demographic of the workforce was hardly classified information, it was all too much for the ODA. Gordon Brown had gone on record as saying that the Olympics would provide 'British jobs for British workers', and the influx of migrant workers from Eastern Europe had become a source of moral panic in the popular press, as well as some local communities. The ODA press officer was alarmed that somehow the media would get hold of the 'story' and the IOC would start asking questions. Rather than having to face down any xenophobic reactions it was better not to raise the subject at all! What was essentially a good news story for the IOC was seen as a potential public relations disaster – and spiked.

When East meets West

I have suggested that there is more to the fabrication process than meets the eye of the casual observer or is captured in official records. What is missing from most accounts is well illustrated by an interview with Gary Carpenter then aged 18, who described the people he met and the things that happened while he was working with his dad on the Olympic site.[11] Their job, as riggers, was to bore holes into the ground to collect soil samples for laboratory analysis, so that the precise geology of the site could be established prior to its decontamination and the undergrounding of the power cables. Gary's father Mark was very knowledgeable about the subject – in effect a geologist – and he was also something of an amateur archaeologist since his hobby was collecting objects he unearthed around the site. He had found Roman coins and pottery fragments and many other things, each of which had a story attached to them.

When I interviewed them I was struck by the closeness of their relationship, and by the fact that this father and son team represented a very 'old-fashioned' aspect of working-class culture. Gary had started working with his dad as soon as he left school, and in effect became his apprentice. They both took great pride in the job, and also from the fact that to a large extent they were their own bosses. They were taken on as a team and moved from site to site, deciding when and where they would work. At 18 Gary was earning very good money, and drove a Lamborghini to prove it.

In the course of the interviews they both mentioned a game that Mark had devised for Gary as an eighteenth birthday present. 'It's full of little private jokes' Gary told me, while for Mark it was a 'good bit of memorabilia for us'. It consisted of a customised Monopoly Board entitled 'Gary's Olympic Site', with all the locations renamed after people they had met, particular incidents or events that had occurred, and other site-specific associations. Gary gave me a guided tour of the board one weekend, in the course of which he told me 27 short anecdotes, each one linked to a place name.[12]

The telling of these stories did not follow a strictly temporal sequencing, and nor was the board organised wholly topographically: the placing of one story next to another was not determined simply by where or when it happened in real space and time. The old format was tweaked in a number of ways, as West End locales were replaced by East End. To those familiar with London's social geography, locating the following story about Mark's brother on what was once 'Whitehall' makes its own kind of point. The Whitehall square was renamed *The Lying Tongue*:

> This is about my Uncle Paul. When I first started drilling with my dad, he worked with us. But when I started getting more comfortable around my dad, and we'd do a lot of horseplay, he didn't like it. Perhaps he felt left out … He realised that my dad had ideas for me getting into drilling and being part of the business. Then one day he rang up and said he was quitting, 'cos I was taking the piss out of him all the time. My dad told him I was no threat, but he said he was going back to lorry driving. But then we found out that he had gone and got himself a job with another drilling company, so he had lied to us. He'd got a long tongue but he lied with it, even though my dad had taken him in when he needed help.

Under the general name of 'crack', banter, joke and story-telling play an important role in this occupational culture, in affirming its solidarities as well as its boundaries and easing internal tensions. This was evident in many of Gary's anecdotes. The management, and unpopular workmates, were often the butt of these tales, as in *The Gaping Mouth* (formerly Fleet Street):

> There was a bloke on site called Paul Mann. He was an ex-traffic warden but decided to become an engineer. And there was this other guy, Jordan, he was an Australian. We used to do a lot of Jamaican talk – like 'Yeah, man' and 'How y'a doing bro', and all that – and one day when we were with Paul, Jordan come up and asked him what his name was and he went 'Paul Mann'. So of course Jordan just thinks he is trying to be cool, saying 'man', and we all fell about. Paul used to just stand there all day with his mouth open, doing nothing. He was the laziest man on the site. He was always stuffing his mouth, and if you threw anything in his direction it was bound to go in. He was just a very annoying kind of bloke.

The caveat 'only joking' enabled otherwise taboo topics and attitudes, linked to social anxieties about issues of sex or race, to be publicly voiced. One example was on display in the square *Is My Turban Dirty Road* (formerly Northumberland Avenue):

> This is just a joke, it started at home when a mate of mine rang up the Indian takeaway and ordered some stuff that his brother would come in to collect. And when the bloke in the restaurant asked for his name he spelt it out letter by letter I-S-M-Y-T-U-R-B-A-N-D-I-R-T-Y. And the bloke goes 'Is my turban dirty?' It was just a laugh. I didn't mean anything bad. I think a person with a turban would find it funny.

When the joking stops, a seriously disturbing picture emerges as in the *Dog House Alley* square (formerly Pentonville Road):

> There was this scrapyard merchant down the road and he had a Rottweiler. I knew he was mistreating it. He didn't feed it properly, just left it out in the damp and cold. He was due to move out so I said to him 'I'll buy it off you and give it a good home. How much do you want for it?' And he goes 'five hundred quid'. Well there was no way I could afford that, so I rang the RSPCA and told them about it and they come down and took the dog away. I said I'd like to have him but they rang me the next day and said that he had to be put down 'cos he was suffering from hip dysplasia and cataracts – he just hadn't been looked after. But I have a heart, you know what I mean, I could never mistreat an animal.

The ostensible referent of this story – finding a stray dog – may not be a reliable indicator of where it is heading, and in this case the ill treatment of a pet is used to symbolise the 'barbarism' of a whole community; and this in turn prompts a highly racialised reference to the presence of 'immigrants':

> The people round here don't care about nothing. They don't look after their pets, they don't look after each other, they're worse than animals. They're ruthless ... The East End is a shit hole, it's a dirty area. It's gun crime, it's stabbings, it's lawless. A friend of mine found a dead body in a dyke, just down from here. It's not a nice place. I've had a few run-ins with the locals, nothing serious. There's a lot of immigrants round here – you don't see a lot of white people. Why is it so coloured?

A story about a 'posh' workmate is given an appropriately high status site: Pall Mall, here renamed *Hawkins Wine bar*:

> This is about a bloke called Hawkins, he was very dedicated to his work. He never left the yard till about eight o'clock at night. He was very friendly but quite posh. He'd say 'I'm quite partial to a thimble full of wine'. He never actually drank very much. Anyway we liked him, so we gave him a wine bar, because we could.

In contrast, *Hotel California* (formerly the Piccadilly square) links the reputation of West End Piccadilly as a red light district with a local strip club:

> It's a strip bar in Stratford. There was a bloke called Dave who worked for the bomb disposal squad. He was always going on about this place. He loved it in there and spent most of his free time there. Quite a few of the lads used to drink in there, but I never went there myself.

The two premium sites were reserved for Aidan Thornton, a man for whom they had the highest regard on account of his military background and the dangerous job he was doing. Park Lane was renamed *General Thornton* and Mayfair became *Aidan's Army Surplus Store*:

> [Aidan] was a bomb detector and a very good mate of ours. He was ex-army, he'd been a sergeant major. He was a very military bloke – the way he walked, swinging his arms. And he talked kind of strange. He'd use these big words, which you didn't know what they meant until he explained. But he wasn't at all stuck up. He also had a moustache. I asked him once if he'd seen any fighting but he didn't like talking about the army. He used to bring in his old army stuff, trousers, jackets, waterproofs, all nice stuff. We always used to ask him to check out bore holes for bombs because we knew he was reliable. They found lots of munitions on the Olympics site, hundreds of shells.
>
> We got a spray can what they used to mark the ground and sprayed 'General Thornton was Here' everywhere. We had a lot of good times with him. No-one thinks of people like Aidan. But if he hadn't been there we might have had a bomb go off and there would be no more Olympics.
>
> Everyone on the site did something towards the Olympics and they should get recognised. I met so many characters on the Olympics, but now everyone has gone away ... I'll never see them again but we'll all remember each other. When I come back to it in the future I can think 'yeah that's what happened, that was really good'.

The capacity to name places is a fundamental aspect of power. The narrative landscape created by the Carpenters features people who never get their names on any official map, and whose presence is normally only registered in statistics. Gary's Game is unlikely to appear in any official record of the 30th Olympiad of Modern Times, but it does indicate the gap or tension that exists between the planner's vision as exemplified in artists' impressions and the territories of meaning carved out of everyday circumstances by ordinary people who live and work in these areas.

An interesting illustration of this point was provided by another version of Monopoly that was recently created by a group of young Bengali East Enders.[13] Their board is re-mapped in terms of their own locally situated geography (*117); the market values they attribute to the variously chosen locations reflect their reputational status and identity within working class, and especially Bengali, youth culture. Street markets, parks and other public spaces, such as Sheesha Bars, feature prominently on this game board because they are popular teenage haunts, and many are given by their local vernacular names. So, for example, Stepney Park becomes Spider Park, Mile End Park is Teletubby Land – so called because it resembled the rolling grass hills of the TV characters, and hence evoked happy childhood memories; Watney Market is located in the poorest part of town because it is a well known youth hang out, notorious for its drug scene; while The Great Wall of Cannon Street, another hangout, is given a slightly higher evaluation. The measures of worth given to each site were not purely reflections of their market value, as they were on the original Monopoly board, but bound up with personal associations and/or assessment of their cultural status within the Bengali community. So, for example, some sites are important landmarks in local community history: Altab Ali Park is where a Bengali man was murdered in a racist attack, which, as the group put it, 'caused the Bengali community to rise up'. York Hall (a famous venue for boxing), Brick Lane and Maas Bazaar have all been moved slightly up market, while equal prominence is given to the East London Mosque, Tower Hamlets Further Education College, Green Street Market, Tobacco Dock and the ExCel Exhibition Centre. These are all, in their different ways, sites of social and cultural aspiration, symbolic assets as well as material amenities; some are part of the indigenous Bengali ethno-scape; others (like Tobacco Dock) belong to the gentrification process. The premium sites (Mayfair, Park Lane, etc) are faithfully allotted according to the priorities of the new economy: Stratford's Westfield Shopping City, Canary Wharf, and Riverside (Thames Gateway's star brownfield development) are all places which these young 'Bangla-cockneys' now feel is on their map if not yet part of their manor. Westfield has certainly been taken to their hearts, but Riverside is there because of its iconic status in the *EastEnders* title sequence. Like Canary Wharf or the Isle of Dogs, it is somewhere they might drive through or briefly visit but not hang out. Interestingly the Olympic site itself is conspicuous by its absence from the board, reflecting the fact that it remains a virtual no-go area for many young East Enders. Nor is Upton Park included, perhaps because these young Bengalis do not on the whole support a football club that is still clearly identified in their minds with the white working class and the 'old' East End.

The topography of the working-class city as shaped by these young Bengalis does not so much challenge the dominant economy of worth as stake a claim for their community's assets and amenities to be fully recognised as part of it. The fact that the traditional Monopoly Board is in many ways out of date – the Old Kent Road, for example, is now one of London's property hot spots, rather than a low-value stronghold of Cockney 'lowlife' – underlines the *lack* of correspondence between map and territory as an intrinsic feature of the capitalist city. It is this which opens up a space in which an alternative cartography, a different politics of representation, becomes possible.

Fabrications of masculinity: the physical cultures of manual labour and sport

There are other kinds of incongruity at work in the way the Olympics were fabricated. There is a curious double standard in the way contemporary physical culture is regarded. Those who continue to perform 'elemental' forms of manual labour, like the Olympic Park groundbreakers, are sentimentalised, or regarded as muscle bound dinosaurs, while athletic performance is hypervalorised because it offers a compensatory ideal – an image of fitness, health and wellbeing linked to skilful techniques acquired through persistent and often painful effort. The holding of manual work so low in public estimation while such a high value is placed on athletic endeavour is all the more strange because there is such a strong connection between the two kinds of activity – in terms of their physical techniques, the measures that have been developed to monitor their performance and the role that sport has played as a focus of aspiration within manual working-class and especially immigrant communities.[14] How are we to understand these links?

Historically, growing up working-class for boys has been an apprenticeship to an inheritance entailed in one of two bodies – either the artisan's or the labourer's.[15] Artisans are identified with and by the tools of their various manual trades, which are often thought of as a prosthetic extension of bodily skill moulded by customary usages of handicraft. For the early labour aristocracy, skill, as a function of this specialised manual dexterity, was a form of cultural and social capital, transmitted from generation to generation, from master to apprentice, or from father to son. This patrimony was thus not only in your hands, but in your blood and bones. It conferred a special pedigree that could be transmuted into an almost mystical sense of ownership: the job itself being held in trust for the generation to come. In terms of wider aspiration, this community of labour saw itself as the backbone of the nation, jealous guardian of a precious heritage of democratic freedoms.

In contrast, those who labour with their whole bodies, with shoulders, backs, thighs or feet playing a major role, have been treated as an inferior and generic type of worker; they were called 'hands' precisely because they lacked any specialised application of manual skill. Here the musculature of the labouring body is transvalued primarily through its masculinisation; only as a vehicle for the assertion of forms of physical strength and endurance associated with masculinity could these otherwise abject forms of work be invested with a sense of prowess and pride. The effect was most pronounced amongst workers whose conditions were especially severe and involved great physical hardship and danger. These workers often spoke of having 'coal in their blood', 'iron in their veins' or 'seafaring legs'. It was as if the legacy of labour entailed a principle of consanguinity, derived by some strange alchemy from the very nature of the material they handled. In grim fact, they often had coal dust in their lungs or iron filings under their skin, and could not swim to save their lives. But in possessing and 'transmitting' this phantom body from generation to generation it was possible to imagine that it not only survived but triumphed over physical adversity, including the final adversity of death. In this way, workers who were widely regarded as forming a 'race apart' from the rest of society gave that position a positive, rather than negative, meaning. They too might form the backbone of the nation. In the cultures of both artisanal and elemental labour, the working body was thus rendered into a fit object of masculine identification, albeit in quite distinct ways, linked to two different ideologies of labourism.

This distinction was carried over into sporting cultures, for example in the opposition between the 'boxer', who displays ring craft and the subtler skills of the noble art, and the 'fighter', who just slugs it out; or between athletic performances that are primarily displays of technique and tactics, and those which are feats of stamina and endurance. We are dealing here with what might be called *bodyscapes*, distinctive configurations of embodied practice, each with its specialised zones of application, its own ergonomic norms and pathologies. For example, many of the workers employed on the Powerlines project suffered from 'white finger', a motor disorder caused by the vibrations of pneumatic drills and TBMs, and some had early-onset deafness due to the noise of the machinery. The office workers and site managers also had problems with their hands, due to their intensive use of digital technologies, especially laptop keyboards. Athletic disciplines also have distinctive injury profiles: swimmers are prone to suffer from asthma due to prolonged exposure to chlorinated water, hurdlers from heel and ankle problems – and so on, depending on which organ or body part is subject to stress within each sport. The discourses of industrial and sports medicine, despite their obviously different terms of reference, create bodyscapes based on rigorous zoning principles, linked to norms of productivity and efficiency rather than forms of excitation and pleasure.[16]

It was the freedom of the athlete's body from the disciplinary regimes of labour which made it such an object of aesthetic admiration and scientific curiosity at the end of the nineteenth century.[17] The birth of modern Olympism contributed to this in connecting the Hellenic code of homo-social masculinity to Muscular Christianity as institutionalised in the educational system developed in Europe by political and cultural elites.[18] Athletes were put on a pedestal, from whence their 'classical' virtues could be held up as an aristocratic ideal; an invidious comparison could be then made with the physical and moral condition of the masses resulting from the impact of modern industrial 'civilisation'. Yet important though this was in creating a culture of appreciation for popular sport amongst the upper classes, the main focus of interest was on the instrumental rather than expressive aspects of athleticism.[19]

The fact that athletes were concerned to push the boundaries of physical effort beyond existing norms and to overcome fatigue was of great interest to industrialists anxious that the hands they employed should perform their actions with the utmost efficiency and attentiveness. Economy of effort was the watchword and technology came to their aid. The development of chrono-photography by Edward Muybridge and Edgar Marey, with its freeze-frame depiction of the athletic body in motion, created the possibility of Frederick Taylor's 'time and motion' studies which were used to monitor and improve the productivity of manual workers in the factory. It is no coincidence that Laban's method of movement analysis, now best known for its association with dance, and with kinesiology in sports medicine, began life as a way of notating the gestures of operatives in the Fordist factory (>76-93). The notion of the manual worker as a human dynamo and of the athlete as a piece of physical engineering draw on the same bio-energetic model. In his autobiography, Lord Coe, who was coached by his engineer father, quotes with approval Buckminster Fuller's definition of man as machine:

> Man is a self balancing, 28 jointed, adapter-based bi-ped and electro-chemical reduction plant, integral with the segregated stowages of special

energy extracts in storage batteries for subsequent activation of thousands of hydraulic and pneumatic pumps with motors attached ...[20]

The story comes full circle with the development of scientific sports training methods that are inspired by ergonomics and industrial psychology as much as by bio-mechanics, and are designed to maximise athletic efficiency through a careful monitoring of anaerobic levels and the application of 'positive thinking'.[21] This is matched by the ever-increasing public scrutiny and commentary on the anatomy of sporting performance, from the close observation of body language on the field of play to the statistical analysis of work rates – by the athletes themselves, by coaches, trainers, referees and journalists, and, of course, by fans. One response by athletes to this increased surveillance has been to adopt grandstanding tactics, drawing on marketing strategy to project a distinctive body image via the use of personalised gestures, clothes, hair styles or catch-phrases. Steve Ovett started the trend with his victory wave back in the 1960s, and today Usain Bolt has carried the art of 'body marketing' to a new level of theatrical hype.

There is an equally convoluted history to the link between manual work and athleticism as sites of popular masculine aspiration.[22] Bodies hardened by the performance of heroic forms of labour and by the physically punishing disciplines of sport have long been closely associated as masculine ideals. The more athletic kinds of manual work, involving agility, dexterity, stamina and courage, have an elective affinity with sports that require these same dispositions, and this undoubtedly facilitated their implantation in working-class cultures. While navvies, miners, dockers and other workers in heavy industry were often regarded as a 'race apart', their prowess as boxers, footballers, swimmers or cricketers transformed them into the backbone of the nation (>18-55).[23] Sport was not only a pathway out of the working class for those whose aspirations were blocked by discrimination, it was also a means through which the labouring body could be transvalued and thereby triumph over its degrading conditions of employment and deskilling under industrial capitalism.

On the dance floor and in the more strenuous regimes of male athleticism, techniques of the body linked to manual labour became dissociated from the abjections of toil. Submission to physical self-discipline became the male body's own labour of love, a source of self-appreciation and pride as well as aesthetic admiration by others. Under the banner of 'economy of effort', physical cultures learnt to mimic the human dynamo of the workplace in their own forward march of productivity. 'No gain without pain' aptly sums up the way in which the protestant work ethic became libidinally charged as medium of sporting endeavour (>114/5).

Meanwile, the advent of the knowledge economy has meant that mental labour lost its special aura of intellectuality and its association with an independent intelligentsia. The office workers and technical staff who currently design, operate and maintain the worldwide digital information flow are engaged in a mode of production that has become both dematerialised and disembodied. The culture of manual labourism, and in particular its modes of masculine physicality, have been officially declared redundant.[24] Yet they continue to lead a vigorous after-life, if only as a focus of nostalgic regard, social protest or homo-erotic desire. Pumping iron in the gym rather than sweating it out in an iron foundry is what is now supposed to turn working-class boys into 'real men'. Extreme sport, like extreme work, attracts those who like to imagine themselves living dangerously, while their actual everyday lives are increasingly devoid of physical challenge. It is an arena of highly individualistic embodied practice in which tough masculinities – and, increasingly, tough femininities – can strut their competitive stuff (>105-112).[25] But this shift has to understood in its historical context.

The traditional apprenticeships of masculinity and manual labour saw the young lad placed in a subordinate position in relation to the 'master' and the men, made to sweep up, run errands, make the tea and generally perform domestic tasks in the workplace associated with women's work in the home. Practical joking, sexual teasing and bullying was also a feature in many workplace cultures, all designed to force the boy to dissociate himself from the despised, quasi-feminine position into which he had been put by apprenticing himself to a form of tough masculinity, mastering its techniques at the same time as the skills of his manual trade.

The shift from manual to mental labour skills associated with the feminisation of work, the growth of 'emotional labour', and the related emergence of gender bending, unisex fashions and androgynous body ideals, may not have dismantled the sexual divisions in social production, but it has challenged patriarchal attitudes and opened up a space for the performance of masculinity as masquerade.[26]

Sport, because it is a mimetic discipline – you learn how to do it by closely observing, copying and modelling yourself on what other, more skilled and experienced practitioners do – has remained embedded in a strong form of masculine identity. Moreover many coaches are ex-athletes, so that the tutelary frame is very much that of master or mentor and apprentice, and as such highly congruent with traditional ways of learning to labour within the manual working class.[27] All of this has made life very difficult for gay athletes, even though increasing numbers have come out. Yet the times may be changing. Today sports science has become a specialised multi-disciplinary profession so that the figure of a charismatic coach inspiring exceptional effort from his protégé by dint of the close, quasi-parental bond between them is in danger of becoming as redundant as the form of masculinity it reproduces. The culture of male athleticism has responded by transforming the 'tough love' of male bonding into a form of emotional labour that opens up a space for the expression of tender masculinities, for example in the acceptance of physical vulnerability, and in the shared agonistics of coming to terms with injury, loss of form and competitive defeat. The culture of compulsive hetero-sexism may be far from finished, but there are some encouraging signs that its hold over the younger generation of athletes is weakening.

Race-ing the games

The history of physical culture in the twentieth century may have been about breaking the link between social and sporting elites and problematising the dominant codes of masculinity, but in terms of 'race' it has been a different story. The Olympic movement remains haunted by the spectacle of Jesse Owens winning the 100 metres in the Berlin games, at a stroke destroying the myth of Aryan superiority only to reinforce another equally racist one, of the black athlete as a noble savage, whose 'innate' physical prowess was the flip side of congenital mental inferiority.[28] Jewish athletes, like Harold Abrahams, had to contend with the complementary myth – namely that Jews were rootless cosmopolitan intellectuals, too clever for their own or anyone else's good, whose unhealthy misshapen bodies, characterised by bent backs and noses, and large grasping hands, unsuited them for any kind of work other than making money through various kind of double dealing. Under this sign, a Jewish athlete was a contradiction in terms.[29] In this way the division between mental and manual labour became highly racialised and located black and Jewish athletes on different sides of its great divide.

These myths that millions lived and died by are now largely discredited.[30] But there are still areas of debate that are haunted by notions of biology as destiny and this perhaps accounts for contemporary resistance, particularly within the left, to the idea that genetics can play any role in shaping the vicissitudes of human existence.[31]

However, the Human Genome Project has begun to show that some functional characteristics do differentiate population clusters – most clearly in the predisposition to certain diseases and in types of physical ability; and it does appear that athletes from certain populations do better on average than others at certain sports. For example East Africans – most notably Kenyans, Somalians and Ethiopians – have famously dominated marathon and long distance track events in recent years. This cannot be explained by reductive arguments based on genetic or environmental determinism. It is down to a subtle dialectic of natural and cultural selection. Physical and material cultures have an elective affinity for certain sports and this will tend to select young people who possess the dispositions required to succeed. Their success will in turn enhance the national prestige of their sports and encourage more young people of similar physical ability and background to participate, especially where other pathways to advancement are limited.

For example, in the East End of London, a succession of immigrant communities have thrown up boxing champions over the past century: Ted 'Kid' Lewis and Jack Berg from the Whitechapel 'shtetl', Billy Graydon, John H. Stracey, Terry Spinks from the Irish/Cockney presence, the Italian Tony Magri, and James Cook, Nigel Benn, Audley Harrison and Lennox Lewis from the black community. Amateur boxing clubs like Repton and Eton Manor, as well as training gyms and fight venues, have been a prominent feature in the area's cultural landscape, and many boxing promoters and trainers have been drawn from similar working-class and immigrant backgrounds (*125).[32]

So what accounts for the fact that these populations, exhibiting such a wide range of phenotypical variation, are all equally over-represented in the recreational and elite echelons of this sport? Certainly not genetics! Clearly one common denominator is the fact that boys and young men from these communities were growing up in environments where being handy with your fists and knowing how to stand up for yourself in a fight with your peers had definite survival value. Street gangs were the first training grounds of many a people's champion. The transition from street fighter to boxer, and from amateur to professional were so many steps forward for young men, whether white or black, Jewish or Muslim, who had little else going for them, and their reputations in turn encouraged the younger generation from their communities to follow in their footsteps.

As a general rule a sport becomes racialised whenever it becomes a vehicle for contesting discrimination on the part of minority ethnic communities, and is de-racialised when these institutional obstacles are removed, even though popular prejudice may continue. Still there are always exceptions. The case of Becky Brunning offers a cautionary note. Brunning is a comedian whose great grandfather, a Welsh coal merchant, won a silver medal in gymnastics in the 1912 Stockholm Olympics. Her avowed ambition was to follow in his footsteps, and partly as a publicity stunt, partly as a way of telling her family history, and perhaps half seriously, she put together a performance and campaigning website in which she proclaimed that she was carrying, not the Olympic torch but the Olympic Gene. What she had not reckoned with was the existence of a group of extreme Welsh nationalists who believe in the special athletic genius of the Celtic 'race', and took her at her word. They must have been mortified to learn that Brunning, whose knowledge of the pummel horse was limited to riding childhood ponies, was not considered a serious contender for Team GB – a fact that they no doubt put down to prejudice against her Welsh ancestry.

So while possessing a physique with the ability to fire muscle fibre more efficiently than your competitors might help you inch ahead, everything that got you into that position is down to training and mental effort, including that last lunge at the tape. The danger of any type of argument from biology is that it gets pushed into a form of genetic determinism: if genes appear to give some competitors an unfair advantage (like performance enhancing drugs), then some people are beginning to argue that, since, unlike drugs, they can hardly be banned, those athletes whose DNA contains what is now being called the 'Olympic gene' should be handicapped. So Usain Bolt should start three metres back from the rest of the field to give them a chance? Moreover the argument cuts both ways: Eurasians who have, on average, more natural upper-body strength, dominate weightlifting, wrestling and field events. Should they also be handicapped so that these events become a level playing field for Asian and African athletes? As soon as we go down this road, we find we are on a slippery slope that leads us straight to an Olympic dystopia where the 'race' that counts always belongs innately to the swiftest, strongest and tallest.

The changing codes of male athleticism

I have suggested that, historically, there has been a close fit between *labourhood* – the culture of masculinity and manual work – and *bodyscape* – the formations of embodied practice through which physical skills and disciplines are transmitted and/or represented. Thus in sporting practice the male athlete was treated as an apprentice, who learnt his trade from a coach who was a master at the craft. As the boy grew in skill and confidence, so he took a more prominent role within the community of athletic practice, until eventually he could become a mentor or coach in his turn and pass on his expertise to a new generation of beginners.

This model of apprenticeship is often linked to one of inheritance, though there is tension between the two notions as well as affinity. In the inheritance model athletes are born, not made; their predispositions are considered to be innate, and transmitted either genetically or through some kind of cultural osmosis from kith and kin. Boys are chips off the old family block, and life is about fulfilling a more or less congenital destiny, following in the footsteps of your father. Still, even athletes who see themselves as 'naturals' or as having sport 'in their blood' need to have their raw talent trained – which is why, within this traditional framework, coaches so often function in loco parentis, or indeed may actually be parents, as in the case of Seb Coe. In any case the key relationship is always with the coach, and is often about living or failing to live up to his expectations, rather than rivalry with peers.

The rise of the professions to cultural and demographic prominence has introduced two new models of the life course – vocation and career – which have complicated and to some extent displaced the older ones.[33]

The notion of vocation – of life unfolding as a quest for an authentic selfhood or 'calling' was initially confined to marginal groups (bohemians, artists, mystics) but by the 1970s it had spread to the business and professional world. The subsequent rapid development of the personal growth movement and life-style counselling saw the emergence of a new genre of coaching books, and many of these focused on physical activity; there were titles like *The Inner Golfer* and *How Jogging Can Change Your Life* and even *Zen and the Art of Tennis*. At the same time the ethical and aesthetic value of recreational sport was given a new lease of life as a form of do-it-yourself therapy. For example running or walking turned out be a better – and cheaper – treatment for depression than any amount of pills. The explosion of private gyms and personal fitness centres testifies to the extent to which this culture has now become implanted within the middle class. Within the world of professional sport the psychological dimensions of athletic performance have been given ever greater emphasis; the sports psychologist has become as important as the physiotherapist in every athletic back-up team. Success in sport, it turns out, is as much in the mind as the body. Within the Olympic movement there has been a call to return to the classical values of aretism – the pursuit of sporting excellence for its own sake rather than for extrinsic rewards. Gracefulness in execution, rather than competitive spirit, was to be encouraged as a way of reviving amateur values.

Contrastingly, career as the dominant paradigm of sporting life has been associated with its professionalisation. What had begun life as a model of middle-class mobility had by the 1970s become a generic definition of social aspiration for all social groups. The career athlete was the product of the new sporting academy system which creamed off the most promising talents, gave them intensive training, and fast tracked them into elite teams and high profile competitions. Athletic careerism privileges the agonistic aspect of sport; everything is dedicated to gaining competitive advantage over rivals. Every performance is a test, an examination that has to be passed to qualify for the next step on the ladder of success, a trajectory indexed to increments in professional status, media fame and financial reward. It's a world where winner takes all; there are no prizes for the also-rans and the taint of 'loser' becomes the worst of taunts. A mirror image, then, of corporate business culture and the way the Spectacle of Fame has become subject to bureaucratic protocols of evaluation.

It is interesting to read sporting memoirs in terms of which of these autobiographical models dominates the account, and to see how images and metaphors from a number of different paradigms may be used to characterise different aspects or phases of the athlete's life course. Seb Coe's autobiography *Running my Life* opens with a chapter about his family history and early years in which he stresses his strong sense of kinship with his father. This is followed by a chapter entitled 'Apprenticeship' that details his early running experiences with a local athletic club, and in the next chapter we learn how his relationship with his father metamorphosed into that of athlete/coach. Later, the book settles into its stride as an account of the ups and downs of the journey to 2012; and what is significant here is Coe's ever larger and more grandiose sense of personal mission, as if he had been destined for this role, and in it had found the fulfilment of ambitions that even his successful international athletic career had left untouched. But the title of the book itself gives a clue as to its dominant paradigm: life as a career plan requiring professional managerial skills to ensure its goals are reached.

In contrast Bradley Wiggin's memoir, *My Time*, is perhaps an all too predictable road movie, a close-up warts-and-all account of life in the saddle. Central to this story is the fact that Wiggins senior, a well known cyclist in his day, jumped ship when Bradley was nine, so that his grandfather became the key male figure in his growing up. It was Granddad who persuaded young Bradley to take up the sport, but he died before he could see his protégé's final Olympic success. From a teenager Bradley cocoons himself in the cycling world, in an apprenticeship which transforms a problematic inheritance into another, more viable patrimony, bound up with mastery over the mechanics of his trade. As he puts it:

I've always loved cycling because it's you against the machine. You apply yourself to something in your life, and then it's all about numbers, pace judgement, putting the ride together, having it all go to plan. You do the training, you get this power; it's very quantifiable. I love the sense of accomplishment.[35]

At the end of the book he restates his street credentials as a working-class hero, a stroppy kid who grew up on the wrong side of the tracks in Kilburn and was too cool for school, but ponders whether he should accept a knighthood if offered. What if he turned it down? His mum reassures him: his granddad would never speak to him again if he did.

The contemporary culture of elite sport represents a hybrid corpus of knowledge and know-how, a creative synthesis of mental, physical and emotional labour that cuts across the social distinctions between them. No matter that in reality the elite male athlete is the living antithesis of the all-rounder, having been selected and trained from an early age in a specialised discipline and usually possessing a one-track mind to go with it, or that, far from embodying healthy living, the professional sports person is dogged by physical injury: all that merely adds to the glamour and prestige of the athletic vocation.

The realisation that games are won or lost in the mind as much as the body offers a permanent rebuke to a society and a schooling system that still ruthlessly distributes 'brain' and ' brawn' – those who are regarded as 'academic' and those who are not – to different and unequal social destinies. Symbolically, sport bridges the widening gap in moral and social status between manual and intellectual work, providing the semblance of a common culture as well as a space of dialogue between tough and tender masculinities. It is this which gives sport its historically progressive character, despite all the reactionary values and practices with which it is enmeshed. It is also what gives the Olympics its elective affinity with youth.

Sporting chances? the athletic body and the youth question

When Lord Coe took a posse of young East Enders with him to Singapore to help clinch London's bid in 2006, he knew what he was doing in exploiting their street cred for his purposes. But it was not a flash in the pan. The bid campaign was strongly youth oriented, and much of the sports and cultural activity that took place in the run-up to the games was youth focused. Young East Enders found themselves 'fitted up' almost overnight as a heroic 'Generation X' of twenty-twelvers, standard bearers of a vibrant and enterprising urban multiculture, brimming with healthy aspirations to better themselves and their community. However the recession's drastic curtailing of opportunities for young people subsequently placed a large question mark over the official assumption that the youth would be up for living the Olympic Dream.

'Inspire a generation', the 2012 buzz word, thus took on a special weight as a moral exhortation. And it was ritually enacted in the opening ceremony as an older generation of Olympians literally handed the torch to a group of young aspiring athletes to light the Olympic cauldron. The Who's anthem to youth culture 'Talking bout my generation' soundtracked the closing moments of the games. But this was no mere tactical opportunism, borne of political desperation; it was part of a long standing Olympic script.

Youth is at the heart of the Olympic message. The appeal to the idealism of young people, the belief that youth embodies a principle of hope, energy and enthusiasm for a better future is one of the most cherished and enduring of the Olympic movement's invented Hellenic traditions.[35] The image of bronzed young men wrestling in the Athenian Gymnasium before a crowd of male admirers remains an iconic statement of traditional Olympism, onto which Coubertin piggy-backed a mission to create a new world of international solidarity through sport.[36] His vision was not just influenced by the classical education of the English public school, with its ethos of aristocratic amateurism, homo-social team spirit and 'fair play'; he was also deeply impressed by the popular youth movements that grew out of the first world war in many western countries.

Coubertin saw in the Wandervogel, and in the scouts and guides, mass organisations dedicated to the proposition that through the fraternisation of youth the divisions of the old world and the wounds of war could be healed. Sport and the Great Outdoors were to play a key role in this new civilising process, drawing on the culture of rational recreation that had emerged amongst the working classes as a response to the degradations imposed by the early period of industrialism. In reality some youth movements, like the scouts or boys' brigades, were patriotic or religious in orientation; others, like the Woodcraft Folk or the Wandervogel, were environmentalist, while still others were linked directly to political parties of the far left and right. But they had one thing in common: a belief that the devil, in whatever guise, makes work for idle hands, and that young people's libidinal energy needed to be channelled in some appropriate social and ideological form, whether through physical drills, organised sports and gymnastics, hiking or marching in step to an anthem or exposure to the rigours of direct encounter with the forces of nature.[37] Character building might involve tests of endurance or courage, with or without association to pseudo-tribal rites of initiation; it might require displays of moral commitment to a political or religious faith; but it always involved armouring the adolescent body against its more unruly desires through some form of emotional identification with a collective ideal.

It is interesting that no new youth movements arose out of the second world war, perhaps because of their tarnished pre-war reputation; indeed it was the Olympic movement that carried the torch for the 'youth international' throughout the cold war years. The West now saw the rise of 'the teenager' and the advent of Youth Culture.[38] During the heady 1960s and 1970s, commercial youth culture, with its triple manifesto of sex, drugs and rock'n'roll, was anathema to the Olympic movement – as it was to the official guardians of youthful idealism, East and West. You couldn't imagine Bob Dylan or Alice Cooper getting into training for track and field – even if it transpired that Mick Jagger was a keen cricketer, Bob Marley played football and many a rock star was a dedicated follower of their local team as well as the latest fashion in designer drugs.

Youth subcultures may not have been sporty but they had their elective affinities for sport. Rockers, Greasers or 'bikers' were keen followers and sometimes participants in speedway, and every English and Scottish football club had its skinhead crew. Hippies were into mountain bikes and skates long before they became fashion accessories for the metrosexual young man about town. Thanks to its mainstreaming, youth culture made 'youth' less a description of age or status, more a statement of aspiration shared by everyone from nine to ninety, a cosmetic commodity purveyed by the life-style industries, promising to postpone the debilitations of age almost indefinitely. Moreover, the new millennium signalled the end of fin de siècle decadence – exit the New Romantics – and gave young people who were into sport a place on the catwalk; sports clothes, so long the preserve of black youth, went viral and became a global lingua franca of popular fashion, providing a unisex and trans-generational outfit for anyone after the casual look.

The implied equation between athletic and youthful bodies may have been a purely aesthetic one, but it certainly helped push sport up the political agenda.[39] It was left to the 'hoodies' and Chavs to claw back some vestigial 'bad boy' resonance, and get the gear branded as the uniform of a new demonised underclass: baseball hat worn the wrong way round, expensive brand trainers but with the laces undone, a football shirt or T-shirt sporting a logo or image of some athletic star and, of course, a tracksuit with a hood – all this added up to 'attitude'.

Already in the early 1960s Alan Sillitoe's short story *The Loneliness of the Long Distance Runner* had mapped out the territory. His young working class anti-hero, Colin, is sent to Borstal where he is 'volunteered' to take part in a cross country race against boys from a neighbouring public school. His plan is to seize the opportunity to go on training runs in the surrounding countryside, but to shatter the staff's illusion that he has been reformed by sport by demonstrating that he can outrun the field and then throwing the race so as to deny them victory:

> I won't get them that cup even though the stupid tash twitching bastard[of a governor] has all his hopes on me. Because what does his barmy hope mean? I ask myself. Trot-trot-trot, slap-slap-slap, over the stream and into the wood where it's almost dark and frosty-dew twigs sting my legs. It don't mean a bloody thing to me, only to him, and it means as much to him as it would mean to me if I picked up a paper and put a bet on a hoss I didn't know...[40]

We will never know what happens to Colin when he was released, whether he becomes an old lag or a self made businessman, because Sillitoe never wrote a sequel. But we do know that his successors in 2012 were still getting into trouble, still sticking two fingers up at authority, and still making the most of the opportunities presented by the Olympics to do what they enjoy most: running wild through back streets with the wind in their hair and using the opportunity to think up a scam or two. Sillitoe's short story attempts to demolish two cherished myths at one go: that participation in sport is necessarily a civilising process, and that it offers disadvantaged youth either a leg up or a form of escape from the oppressive circumstances of their everyday lives.[41] Instead it suggests that the freedoms carved out of their constraining circumstances are not amenable to recuperation. But that is perhaps Sillitoe's romantic anarchism coming out. For the subsequent history of working-class youth cultures and sport suggest that recuperation may indeed be the name of many of the games they play.

Disciplining the bodies of working-class young men has a long history. The panic about the physical capacity of an ill-nourished working class to fight during the first world war drew on a well-established discourse of Victorian medicine and social reform which made an intimate connection between physical appetite and moral hygiene; drunkenness, gluttony and other unsublimated lusts for life were regarded as social vices, not only because they destabilised the family but because they undermined the capacity for work and public service and sapped the vital energies of youth.[42] The emergent health insurance industry added its weight to the clamour for a more preventive and interventionist strategy, in which citizens were urged to adopt a daily regime of fitness exercise as a means of prolonging an active and productive life style. And all too often the distinction between those with healthy minds in healthy bodies, and those whose physical abjection was regarded as a sign of moral depravity became racialised.[43]

In the last decade the biopolitics of sport have increasingly been focused by public concern about the growing extent of obesity and its impact on both quality and length of life. It seemed that a nation of shopkeepers and shopfloor workers had become a nation of fast-foodies, shopaholics and couch potatoes; in particular the working classes, no longer employed in heavy industry or heavy duty manual jobs, but still addicted to a diet suitable for those who spend their days expending a large amount of energy humping stuff about, were in the front line of the moral panic about health. The old poster image of bloated capitalist and emaciated worker was replaced by another – the tanned and toned gym-fit business executive, and his overweight janitor stuffing his face with crisps while watching a TV monitor. The link between eating bad food and having the wrong ideas about self and society was thus no longer the preserve of cranky vegetarians; and nor was weight-watching and jogging a hobby to be enjoyed exclusively by people of a certain age and class. In societies where work had become increasingly sedentary and emotionally stressful, and leisure pursuits reduced to 'chilling out' (i.e. doing nothing), the spread of 'affluenza' became a major focus of government concern and intervention.[44] Young people were the main target of new programmes of health education, which stressed the need for regular exercise and a 'five a day' diet regime as a form of preventative medicine in order to forestall premature illness and death and the attendant drain on public resources.

Sport was recruited as major element in this new homiletic addressed to the young. Indeed it has been seized upon as something of a panacea. According to its zealots, doing sport is a cure for juvenile delinquency, social alienation, obesity, substance abuse and all manner of other social ills. And it still forms 'character'. This evangelical view of sport provided an important additional rationale for Britain's Olympic bid, and for the large amount of public money subsequently devoted to community sports programmes. Inspirational news stories of young people whose lives have been turned around through their involvement in the Olympics were an important part of the media build up to the 2012 Games.

The evidence from other Olympiads suggests that the health dividend is small and short-lived amongst young people, not so much because of the 'Sillitoe factor' but because the gap between recreational sport and elite professional performance is so great.[45] The Olympification of any sport only widens that gap – so that, while national success may increase public interest and enthusiasm and widen the demographic of participation, the attrition rate remains correspondingly high. But this is only the flipside of an inspirational rhetoric that fetishes the elite athlete as a role model but signally fails to embed itself in the everyday lives of working-class young people.

The problem is that today the role model is simply a figure of transient adolescent identification; it is no longer part of an actual community of practice, a mentor or guide offering a substantive form of apprenticeship to the budding young pretender. Last year's track hero may thus all too easily become this year's has-been crush. You may admire Usain Bolt and have his pin-up picture on your wall, but that does not mean you will be inspired to spend large amounts of free time in training to become the local champion sprinter. Far easier to buy the branded tracksuit and take the dog for a walk around Olympic Park. The long distance dog walker is never lonely.

Despite this caveat, the public health agenda has enabled the Olympic movement to update its historic message and appeal to youth. But this is not the only string to its bow. 2012 articulated its rhetoric of youth empowerment not just through the language of sport, but by talking about 'community' and 'regeneration'. Regeneration here means tapping intrinsic sources of social renewal that have been damned up, and which it is the task of Youth as the standard bearer of the future to release. This bio-energetic model of urban renaissance has become increasingly 'greened' and linked to the theme of environmental sustainability: the planetary resource that one generation must hold in trust for its successor. 'Youth' and 'community', both conceived as unitary and unifying categories, were thus interpellated as joint stock holders in the 2012 Olympic Dream factory. Meanwhile the factory's real owners, Coca Cola and Adidas, seized the time to promote Youth Culture – and their products – as forging an organic link between music and sport. Coca Cola turned a local warehouse into a giant advertising hoarding in the form of a mural depicting Usain Bolt and other Olympians moving to the Cola beat, while their 'beat box' on Olympic Park allowed young visitors to create their own soundscape by mixing the grunts and groans of athletes with 'Anywhere in the World', the company sing-along song for the Olympics. Buy Coke, the bio-energetic drink ...

To pin the hopes of a generation of East Londoners to the Olympic dream could be variously seen as an exercise in wishful thinking, a cynical form of brand marketing or a species of pseudo-communitarian politics. A realistic strategy for enabling disadvantaged young people to overcome the difficulties they face at a time of recession, it was not. And even if the project is undertaken in good faith, it begs the central question of what athletics, and youth itself, is for.

Unlaborious effort

Male athletes and many young people exist within a regime of envisagement in which it is still better to be seen than heard, and where the ability to 'just do it' counts for more, in terms of both statistics and status, than any amount of talk. The spectacularisation of sport puts athletes on a pedestal, admired both because their lifestyle requires the highest degree of career planning (re-described as vocational 'dedication') *and* because their performance represents the highest form of drama. Nor surprisingly the dual obligations of the managerial and thespian roles, the personal tensions this creates, and the function of coaches in mediating them, form the core plot of many novels and memoirs of the sporting life.[46] For the athlete's body may be disciplined, but it is rarely docile. It is driven by the desire to be 'in the zone' of peak performance, to be fully present to itself, and yet it remains dependant on a whole apparatus of regulation that is outside its control and can frustrate even the most imperious of its ambitions.

The attempt to integrate labourhood and bodyscape within a single space of representation, to unite workmanlike attitudes with the aesthetics and biomechanics of sport, is what being in the zone is all about.[47] Ruskin anticipated much recent discussion on the relationship between art, work and sport when he wrote: 'The most beautiful actions of the human body, and the highest results of the human intelligence, are conditions, or achievements, of quite unlaborious, nay of re-creative effort'.[48]

Many accounts by athletes of being in the zone approximate closely to 'unlaborious effort'. Pablo Morales, a triple Olympic gold medallist in swimming at the Los Angeles and Barcelona Games, once described the feeling as 'being lost in focused intensity'; Roger Bannister described his experience of running the first four-minute mile thus: 'the earth seemed to move with me. I found a new source of power and beauty, a source I never knew existed'.[49] And sprinter Kris Akabusi talks in similar vein: 'It was so simple and easy. It was like jogging. I could see everything before I did it. I felt so powerful, so in tune, in balance. It was a perfect melody, a rhythm. I was flowing'. This is very close to the state of open, free-floating attentiveness described by artists and writers when they are at work, and which can also be summoned up when reading poetry or listening to music. But in the case of sport, ecstasy is always attended by agony. The zone is bordered by a threshold of pain and anxiety. Bannister writes: 'I leapt at the tape like a man taking his last spring from the chasm that is engulfing him'. In *The Tempest* Shakespeare brings the two sides of the story together when he talks about some sports which are painful but 'their labour/ Delight in them sets off'. This is, we might say, the special calling of the athlete, to embody the duality of this structure of feeling – often, for all that, without being able to represent it fully in words. That is a task for poets.

In his book *In Praise of Athletic Beauty*, Hans Gumbrecht makes a cogent plea for recognising sport, both in its performance and spectatorship, in these terms, as a primarily aesthetic experience.[50] He chides academics for feeling obliged to interpret sports culture as symptomatic of wider – and usually negative – social forces, rather than understanding it for the forms of excitement, pleasure, and entertainment it yields. Ruskin is also on hand to remind us that dis-alienated manual work has a strongly aesthetic dimension. However the fact is that the aesthetics of sport and work are continually being subsumed and exploited by more profane motives. Here is an example from a lifestyle counselling service of how the experience of being in the zone is rephrased in the aspirational business idioms of contemporary self-improvement and career guidance: 'To get into the zone and stay there, the aim must be in alignment with your life purpose. Roger Bannister's target to run a mile in under four minutes is an example of a *smart* goal: Specific, Measurable, Attainable, Realistic, and Timely. If you want to succeed in your life plan then you must learn to limit yourself to what is smart for you'.[51]

When Denis Diderot embarked on the grand project of his *Encyclopedie* in 1750 his ambition was to bring the artist, the scientist, the architect and the artisan together to map out the whole corpus of human knowledge. He wrote in the preface:

> This is a work that cannot be completed except by a society of men of letters and skilled workmen, each working separately on his own part, but all bound together solely by their zeal for the best interests of the human race and a feeling of mutual good will.[52]

For Diderot the division of mental and manual labour was not so much a social barrier as a principle of active collaboration. For John Ruskin and William Morris the revolutionary role of the artist and the artisan was to supersede this division altogether.[53] They both resolutely opposed the creation of an aesthetic regime in which art was freed from any connection with labour, and from the ethical obligation to represent or engage with the external social world. If Diderot had been around today, the encyclopaedist would no doubt have seized the opportunity of the building of Olympic Park to create a new inventory of the arts and sciences deployed in its construction. It would be truly inspiring to visitors to Olympic Park to be able to listen to such an account in the words of the workforce itself.

As it is we will have to be content with using the occasion to reflect on the missed possibilities of such a project, recognising that what remains most relevant about the original Hellenic culture that inspired Coubertin was precisely a world in which Pythagoras, Plato and Pindar, the mathematician, the philosopher and the poet, were united in their admiration of athletes. The corrosion of pride in workmanship, the encouragement of exhibitionistic styles of performance in sport and art, the worship of Nike goddess of Victory, rather than Hephaestus, the god of Artisans, the sublimation of the desire to excel in the drive for competitive advantage at any cost, are the same false coin circulated by the contemporary culture of capitalism – and one which has strong currency amongst young people.[54] These values need to be refuted in principle and refused in practice. In the following chapters we will consider how far they are challenged or endorsed by the Olympics, in the economic compact struck with host societies, in the machinations of the sporting spectacle and in the cultural politics that informed the 2012 ceremonies.

"And they said the legacy would fade..."

6. Thanks but no thanks: gift and debt in the Olympic compact

Shortly after the announcement of London's successful bid, the organisers made an announcement saying 'THANK YOU LONDON'. They did not thank the IOC for awarding them the prize, they thanked the inhabitants of the host city, whose support for the project they had spent so much time, money and advertising effort in enlisting. In the first flush of self congratulation, so brutally foreclosed by the bomb attacks the following day, the first thought of the bid campaigners was to express a debt of gratitude to the people who had, seemingly, gifted them this opportunity.

The announcement was in response to the fact that one of the key tests for the legitimacy of a city's candidature is the level of support for the bid amongst the citizenry as measured by focus groups, polls and press coverage. This is the one brief semi-plebiscitary moment in what is otherwise a massively top-down command and control operation. But who had really passed the test and needed to be thanked? Clearly it was the PR people who successfully massaged public opinion and sold the Olympics to Londoners. But thanking the People has a special payoff in so far as it carries the implication that there is some kind of compact with them based on a relation of mutual indebtedness, and that this principle of balanced reciprocity is a pact sealed by the Olympics. This is clearly what the 2012 Olygarchy wanted to believe to be the case, even though it does not remotely correspond to the actual state of affairs. For in reality LOCOG and the ODA were the dispenser of funds through which they procured the services and allegiances of businesses, community organisations and others who stood in a more or less clientelist relation to them. Against this background the hoped for benefit in thanking Londoners for backing the bid was not only the enrolment of their further support for the project but their commitment to believe that they were equal partners in a shared enterprise going forward to 2012, even when they clearly were not. But was there more to this than a populist gesture?

I think we are dealing here with an elementary structure of sociality and the way it is politically exploited. If someone, a complete stranger, say, with whom you happen to be sharing a table at a lunch counter, thanks you for passing the salt, it is customary to reply something like 'you're welcome', or 'it's nothing' or 'don't mention it'. But though the courtesy may be slight it touches on something profound. As David Graeber has reminded us, to thank someone suggests that he or she might have acted otherwise and that therefore their choice to act this way, a decision which, as we say is 'in their gift', creates an obligation, a sense of debt in the beneficiary.[1] Some Londoners, after all, did refuse the offer of LOCOG's thanks and opposed the Olympic bid.

Yet if you were to ignore or refuse the request for the salt, you would be breaking a fundamental rule of commensality and this would leave a very bad taste in the mouth. There is, for instance, a rule in many traditional kinship societies to the effect that once you have broken bread or shared salt with someone, you can never be their enemy. So when you do pass the salt to your fellow diner, and they thank you and you reply 'don't mention it' or 'it's my pleasure', you are reassuring them that you are not actually inscribing a debit in your imaginary moral account book. Instead you imply that they did *you* a favour because in asking you to pass the condiment they gave you the opportunity to do something you found pleasurable and rewarding in itself, that is, sharing a table and a meal, or the chance to display what good table manners you have. And as they say, one favour deserves another. When you actually did that favour it is unlikely that you thought 'well, OK, I'll pass the bastard the salt because that means there will be a payback time and he will have to pass me the sugar which is on his side of the table, later on when I need it'. In other words your 'gift' of the salt was not conditional on a reciprocal gift of the sugar. You assume that your partner in the meal is bound by the same unwritten law of commensality, civility or good manners as yourself, and would pass you the sugar in any case, though perhaps a bit grumpily if you had been rude enough to refuse his prior request for help in seasoning his meal. However this symmetry of shared hospitality has its limits. Neither party expects whatever gratitude they feel to extend to offering to pay the other's bill.

Now suppose one of the diners is a hard case, who never does anything for nothing, who never makes a move without calculating its personal costs and benefits, and who always makes rational choices on the basis of self interest. In other words he behaves as capitalist enterprises behave and how some economists suppose we all behave in conformity with their model of 'homo economicus'. Only pass the salt if you know you are going to want the sugar and are sure that this is the quickest and cheapest way of ensuring you get it given you. From this standpoint what initially appeared to be a freely given favour turns out to have all kinds of hidden strings attached to it and enmeshes the participants in a tacit calculus of reciprocal debt. I owe you one, no you don't owe me anything, actually it's me who owes you etc. Tit for tat. Give as good as you get. Gift and counter gift. You scratch my back and I'll scratch yours.

So there are two quite different possible logics here, one belonging to what Marcel Mauss, the great anthropologist of gift economies called 'individual communism', the everyday, intimate, forms of mutuality that enable people to rub along together, to collaborate on joint projects, to behave with an open ended generosity without feeling indebted to one another;[2] favours are done for others simply for the fun of it, or because it makes the donor feel good and it is the giver who should be grateful. Then there is reciprocal giving between equals which creates mutual indebtedness and cements social relations of friendship or alliance. Within this kind of moral economy one favour always deserves another. There are also more competitive strategies of prestation in which donations are a form of one upmanship or where the aim is to induce a debt or obligation that enables the donor to exercise power over the recipient. This kind of moral economy transacts and legitimates relations of social inequality based on differential wealth or prestige.

When the bid campaigners said 'Thank you London', which logic was at work? Were they saying to Londoners, in effect 'we will remember what you did for us in helping us win the Games and we will repay your loyalty by ensuring that we deliver on our promise to bring real benefits to the city'? Or were they tacitly drawing on an entirely different etiquette according to which Londoners are supposed to reply, 'No, please, it is us who should be thanking *you*, we owe you for bringing this wonderful gift of the Olympics to our great city, which will make us all healthy, wealthy and wise and we will repay this debt by continuing to enthusiastically support everything you do in the future'.

If it is not easy to decide the issue, it is because both logics may, in fact, be in use. This, however, is not the end of the story. For every thank you there is a please. As children, when we are taught 'manners', we are told to say 'please' as a way of commuting what otherwise might be construed as an order – 'pass the salt' – into a request. Subordinates, like children, are not supposed to issue orders to superiors, like adults. Conventionally, workers are not supposed to tell their employers how to run their businesses or even how their own work process had best be organised. But a request, which might be translated into 'I humbly beg or beseech you', or 'I would be much obliged' is a suitably deferential statement which puts the speaker into a position of indebtedness and may elicit a desired response from authority. We learn very early on that prefacing a demand for a mars bar by saying in effect 'it would please me greatly if you would grant my request', rather than saying 'gimme' is more likely to bring the desired result. For who could resist giving pleasure to a child, or a needy adult, especially if the request has given you the pleasure of being able to display your largesse, and of perhaps being praised for your generosity or charity at the same time?[3]

Despite the fact that Cadbury's were a 2012 Games sponsor not everyone thinks mars bars or the Olympics are good for you. A large amount of money has to be spent in persuading people that this is indeed the case. In the age of 'communicative planning', where public consultation is the order of the day whenever grand projects are launched, there are lots of pleases and thank-yous flying around. The property developers and planning authorities humbly beseech the communities they are seeking to regenerate to consider that the plans proposed are in their best interests, have only been formulated after extensive consultation and will bring them great benefits. Of course their approval is not strictly necessary, so the developers are really doing the community a great favour in going to all this trouble, and they should be grateful enough to return it by signing up to the plan. It does not then matter if it is the planners who will decide the outcome rather than the people's elected representatives, and that, if there are major objections, it is the state which will ultimately adjudicate.[4] The consultation process is intended to forestall public enquiries by creating a compact based on an exchange of favours which creates the conditions for a consensual validation of the plan and makes any real negotiation and hence any substantial compromise unnecessary.[5]

There are other more brutal but possibly less mystifying ways to go about the business. When Lord Coe tried to explain to a Chinese official all the consultative hoops he had to jump through to get planning permission for the Olympic Park, the latter was horrified. What happens when you cannot get agreement to demolish a building, he asked. Coe explained about compulsory purchase orders. 'Oh, in China we don't need a CPO, or to waste time going around consulting people', the bureaucrat replied, 'we have bulldozers'.[6] One thing communist parties have never understood and done their best to suppress is collective action arising out of a culture of mutual aid, what David Graeber rather mischievously calls actually existing communism.

These examples show that gifts often come with hidden strings attached, and they get so tangled up because there is more than one economy and ideology at work. As an example of this, consider volunteering, which is the very embodiment of the Olympic spirit and one of the great success stories of 2012. Voluntarism is a public form of private philanthropy, and like philanthropy combines elements of genuine generosity and competitive gift exchange. At one level, charity, or caritas as defined in Christian theology, is an act of selfless – and preferably anonymous – giving, a form of mutualism modelled on the reciprocal devotion of God for Man and Man for God which takes the practical compassionate form of doing good works in the community. But if virtue is supposed to be its own reward, for the religious it also brings salvation. Philanthropy, like religion, is a way of storing up goods in the next world, putting God in your debt and ensuring that she returns the favour by admitting you to heaven. It can become quite competitive, philanthropists vying with each other to see who can outdo the other in good works, and in the splendour of the monuments they build to their own generosity. Private philanthropy is also a way of legitimating the accumulation of great wealth by redistributing a small amount of it as handouts to the poor whose exploitation has produced both the donor's wealth and the recipient's dependency on it in the first place. Moreover the poor are expected to be grateful for the charity, and only those who are, are deemed worthy of it. The undeserving poor, who have not learnt to say please and thank you, get nothing. So here giving not only requires and reinforces ritual displays of deference, but enforces a logic of symbolic debt which even further impoverishes the recipient of the gift.

Voluntarism is a form of public charitable action and it too is Janus faced. As a genuine expression of the culture of mutual aid, it draws on the volunteer's longing for a relationship to political economy that is not based on exploitation or the cash nexus. Volunteers, by definition, derive no material benefit from their efforts, although others may do so, which does not mean they do not get other, symbolic, rewards. Their efforts earn and clearly deserve public gratitude. Yet this is only one side of the story. Being a 2012 games-maker not only makes you feel good, it may earn you a special status amongst your peers. Being chosen is itself a kind of prize, a mark of being a good and loyal citizen and it enhances your public reputation. It also looks good on your CV. If you are unemployed it may help you sell yourself to an employer and get a job, and so there may be some hope or expectation of a pay back in time to come; cashing in on caritas may have to be the name of the volunteering game in a time of economic recession. Just look at the competition for internships in which young people work for nothing, sometimes for years, in exchange for the work experience and good references, in the hope of getting their feet on the first rung of an occupational ladder.

In 2012 Olympic voluntarism could not escape becoming implicated in various ideological manoeuvres. Games-makers found themselves tacitly enrolled in the popular patriotism promoted by LOCOG, who pitched volunteering as a return to the ethos of post-war national service. You owe it to your country. The London Olympics Needs You. In 2012, as in 1940, never have so many owed so much to so few. The volunteers also found themselves willy-nilly recruited for David Cameron's vision of the Big Society, as an example of what ordinary citizens could achieve once the frontiers of the crypto-socialist, nanny-welfare state were rolled back.[7] It was quite a burden of representation to place on such young shoulders by an administration whose idea of give and take is to exhort the citizenry to donate large amounts of time, money and energy to restoring the fabric of civil society which its own austerity policies have badly damaged. Yet in my view the standing ovation given to the volunteers at the closing ceremonies was not a vote of confidence in Tory paternalism. Rather, it was eloquent testimony to the fact that the games-makers came to signify a spirit of public service that was not going to be destroyed by the cuts or be used as their alibi.

As a final example of the subtle dialectics and crude thoughts of gift and debt let us take a counter factual. What if the London bid had failed? Would the bid campaigners have then issued a statement saying 'Sorry London, we got it wrong, we let you down, but we hope you will forgive if not forget us'. Such apologetics are an attempt to cancel the debt that has been created by the gift and terminate the cycle of prestations or favours while at the same time legitimating the compact despite the fact that one of the parties has defaulted on the deal. It is a form of plea bargaining in which those in positions of power say, in effect, to their subjects – please don't judge us too harshly, see how we are humbling ourselves before you, thank you for your forbearance, and we beseech you, don't abandon faith in us – we will do better next time'.[8]

Of course it is always better to exchange words rather than blows, to return favours and to give as good as you get, as long as you do not end up taking an eye for an eye. In any case there are always party poopers, people who have not learnt good manners and who upset the balance of the reciprocity. For example the nay-sayers refused to 'buy' the Olympics and when invited to participate in the Olympic compact instantly replied 'thanks but no thanks'; in effect they were saying to the Olympic authorities 'you want us to carry the torch for you but our only use for it would be to set light to the stadium and make a bonfire of your vanities'. Or to revert to our diner example, 'you have passed us the menu but there is only one set meal consisting of fried mars bars which is not our idea of a healthy diet. And then you expect us to foot the bill even though you promised a free lunch'.

There are gifts, in other words, which incur debts that turn out to be bad news, either because their reciprocation would spell disaster or because what is supposed to be an asset turns out to be a liability: the proverbial poisoned chalice. For example, the anonymous donation of blood may be a pure act of selfless giving, or a commercial transaction but in either case, if the blood is infected so is the act of giving it, especially from the point of view of its recipient.[9] It matters little in this context if the contaminated blood was sold by a junkie who needed the money, innocently volunteered by a gay man unaware of his HIV status, or maliciously gifted by someone who wanted to spread the virus so that others might share his fate. What is lethal is precisely the hidden essence of the gift. In such cases it is not the motivation of the donor, or their relationship to the recipient, but the intrinsic nature of the gift itself which is paramount.

The most famous example of this kind of prestation is the story of the Trojan horse.[10] This cautionary tale about legacy has bequeathed to us the most famous line of Vergil's Aeneid from which schoolboys of my generation were introduced to the fiendish intricacies of Latin verse: Timeo Danaos et dona ferentes – I fear the Greeks and the gifts they bring – and it probably sums up the way some feel about the Games: they are indeed a Trojan horse, thinly disguised as a mars bar, which unsuspecting city fathers have let within the city walls.

In the history of colonialism there are many examples of gifts which entail acts of theft or piracy and rationalise oppression under the guise of a free and equal exchange. The Inuit proverb 'by gifts one makes slaves and by whips one makes dogs' seems an apt description of this 'civilising mission'. There is the famous complaint of the African chiefs vis à vis their dealings with the first European missionaries: 'Before you came, we had the land and you had the bibles, now we have your bibles and you have our land'. This in turn inspired the tit for tat exchange when the Empire struck back, 'we are here because you were there'. Then there is the exchange of reciprocal lacks. When Zionists drove the Palestinians from their promised land, they did so under the slogan 'A people without land for a land without a people'. The symmetry of the equation, guaranteed by the moral economy of diaspora and the right of return, at a stroke erases the Palestinian presence, and denies them the right to exist as a nation or a people. A somewhat similar equation has underwritten London's Olympic bid, albeit with less drastic consequences.

There is a view amongst some anti-Olympic zealots that East London's soul has been sold for the proverbial mess of potage and that a sizeable chunk of what was once a rich ecological wasteland-cum-ruin has been turned into a modernist wilderness. But the actual terms of the compact offered were different. The London Olympics team needed the East End to justify their bid. The multiple deprivations of the area gave them a rationale they otherwise lacked. If they had sited the main venue in a leafy middle class suburb like

Blackheath the bid would not have made it to Singapore. But in the bid document the terms of dependency were reversed: East London was supposed to need the Olympics to regenerate and lift itself out of poverty. So once again what is tacitly being affirmed is a relationship of mutual obligation and debt between a quasi governmental agency and a section of the citizenry. As if they were equal partners in a common enterprise. However this also holds the rather interesting implication that some East Londoners might actually act on the compact and begin to demand a substantial stake and say in the Olympic project. As we will see in Chapter Ten this has led to considerable frustration and disillusionment.

It is interesting that in describing these transactions, which are supposed to be all about gifts and bounties and civilities and to draw on the language of mutualism, prestation and hospitality for this purpose, instead we find ourselves talking about debts, the risks of not paying them, and the payoffs for doing so, and whether we can afford to be generous; in other words we are using terms which describe individuals when they seek to maximise benefits and minimise costs, the language of rational calculation, of economic rather than moral obligation and entitlement. This code switch applies especially to negative reciprocities. We talk about paying someone back when we exact revenge, of someone paying their dues when we criminalise, imprison or otherwise punish them, and in the free-for-all that is consumer society there is the implied coercion in making clients or customers 'an offer they cannot refuse', a term which is also, by no coincidence, applied to the threat of violence, often in the context of that system of enforced debt known as a protection racket.

What we are concerned with here are two very different economies of worth. At one level we are dealing with a *moral* economy, a set of normative attitudes and customary practices concerning the social relations and behaviours that surround a local economy and which have traditionally regulated the availability of food, the prices of subsistence commodities, the proper administration of taxation, and the operation of charity. In times and places where the church has played a role in these mundane matters, the notion of a 'just price' has often prevailed. This is sometimes referred to as a subsistence ethic: the idea that local social arrangements should be organised in such a way as to respect the needs of the poor. A high value is placed on mutual aid, for example helping neighbours get in the harvest, build or repair homes, or to recover from setbacks, illness or bereavement. In this culture individual and collective action are legitimated by appeal to tradition or customary rights or common law and there is no need to keep a precise record of the transactions, because their meaning consists in the memories they evoke, not their itemisation in a balance sheet. Within this framework debts are moral obligations, not legally enforceable contracts. We rightly call them debts of honour because they depend on the performative power of language embedded in relations of trust: my word is my bond. Moral economies can be communitarian and egalitarian, but they can also be hierarchical, and support systems of patronage, as is the case in strongly patriarchal societies. As a general rule, gifts or debts exchanged between unequals, while they may transform negative into positive reciprocity, reinforce existing power relations, especially if these are dissimulated as relations of equality. Giving becomes either an act of condescension or deference.[11]

Although moral economy flourished in pre-capitalist societies, it has not withered away under capitalism but, on the contrary, constitutes both a support and a source of opposition to the market economy; in the first case this means introducing certain regulatory principles which mitigate the socially destabilising effects of 'savage' capitalism; in the second it provides a site of popular resistance to neoliberalism and its globalising impact on local communities, their ways of life and livelihood.

To recap the argument so far, there are two kinds of gift giving, one that operates according to the rules of a moral economy and another that becomes enmeshed in the market. In the first case gift giving is primarily for the sake of human solidarity; it is a form of limited or conditional altruism, whose motto might be 'from each according to his ability, to each according to his need'. There may be strings attached to these gifts, but if they are reciprocated it is a bonus, not a payback. The proverbial wisdom of this practice is summed up in the saying 'don't look a gift horse in the mouth', i.e. don't check the animal's teeth to see how old it is, just be grateful that you have been given the pleasure of having a horse to ride, even if it is an old nag. And, as we also say when someone has given us a particularly inappropriate present, 'it's the thought that counts'. Thanking is etymologically linked to thinking, so it means: every time I wear this awful pink tie with blue spots, I will be thinking fondly of the colour-blind friend who gave it me'. The value of the gift within moral economies is thus primarily symbolic, and lies in what it represents about the relationship between donor and recipient, not in the thing itself. The gift is a token of the type of relationship it enacts and there are often quite elaborate, context specific, conventions about what it is appropriate to give to whom under what circumstances. This kind of gift exchange is the bedrock of mutual aid and everyday, actually existing, communism.

Gift giving for the sake of competitive advantage is quite a different proposition. It should actually be called debt giving, since the effect, if not always the conscious intention, is to place the recipient in a one-down position of owing the donor something. As long as the transaction remains confined within moral economy it merely endorses social hierarachy. But once it becomes caught up in capitalist relations of exchange, once the gift also functions as a commodity, a quite new set of negotiations becomes possible: the more you give to charity, the more you are entitled to make on the stock exchange. Under the sign of capital the primary meaning and worth of a gift resides not in the thing itself and what it signifies about its donor or recipient but in its market value. Yet a gift has also to convey a message beyond the cash nexus, for instance about the relative socio-economic status or public esteem of the parties to the transaction. So the moral economy, in which the type of gift serves as a token of the exchange in which it is embedded, has to be reactivated. Question: What do you give a billionaire who has everything? Answer: A tax break. In other words the gift is transformed from being a mere commodity into *an incentive*. Examples of this kind of prestation are: aid and trade policies towards developing countries, the practice of giving backhanders, 'sweeteners' and other kind of bribes to secure contracts or jobs, bonus schemes to encourage greater productivity and speed up from workers (often by relinquishing hard won workplace rights). These gift/bribes are the please-and-thank-you niceties of the moral economy transposed into the idiom of commodity relations. Which is why they flourish in the interface between Western business culture and the Asian Tiger economies, where traditional social morality retains a strong normative presence in the midst of rampant capitalist entrepreneurialism. These are by definition gifts with strings attached, and their proverbial motto is 'you scratch my back and I'll scratch yours'. Such actions are justified through appeal to the laws of supply and demand and they need to be closely monitored so that accounts can be kept and payback time notices issued. This is baseline 'pull yourself up by your own bootstraps' capitalism gifted with a human face.

In the history of the Olympics there are many examples of such transactions. As the leader of the team for the successful Sydney bid once famously admitted, referring to the lavish hospitality meted out to IOC delegates prior to the voting, 'they have to have a sense of obligation to you when they go into that room'. Accusations of palm greasing, extravagant gifts and general bribery and corruption in the IOC's dealings with candidate countries abound, and are gleefully seized on by Olympophobes, but they are best understood as the normal way business is done where market and moral economies intersect under capitalism.

Moral and market economies exist in various kinds of relationship, and in weak or strong combination. They may come into direct conflict. The term was initially coined by E.P Thompson in his study of collective bargaining by riot in eighteenth-century England, but it could equally apply to the Poll Tax riots, the Brixton police riots or the street riots in British cities in 2011. Thompson commented on the bread riots of the 1840s: 'This was rarely a mere uproar which culminated in the breaking open of barns or the looting of shops. It was legitimised by the assumptions of an older moral economy, which taught the immorality of any unfair method of forcing up the price of provisions by profiteering upon the necessities of the people'.[12] Similarly the young rioters of 2011 were not just looting shops to get their hands on goodies they could cash in to help pay the rent, or else enjoy for a street party, they were implicitly protesting against a double bind in which they were both demonised and praised within the dominant moral economy for their forms of mutual aid *and* marginalised within a market economy that denied them job opportunities while celebrating their potency as consumers.

The two economies may come into more peaceful competition and co-exist in different spheres. We can behave like capitalists at work and communists at home or play. Ideologically, the moral economy furnishes a humanism which compliments economism in proposing a panglossian world in everything is for the best and class struggle has been definitively transcended by the sovereignty of the individual.[13] It can also furnish a strategy of accommodation to the market; it constitutes a baseline of human solidarity in many workplace cultures, comprising numerous small ways through which the job is made easier, less alienating and more controllable through co-operative practices, but which also enable workers to collude in their own exploitation. It also operates in a more individualistic mode within middle class occupation cultures in the demand for job satisfaction.[14]

In so far as the two economies become part of the fabric of everyday life their interaction generates many of its more common existential dilemmas. For example, let's imagine that on the last day of the Olympics we go out with some friends to a quite expensive restaurant to celebrate that it is all over and exchange experiences. Everyone is in a good mood, the food and service are excellent and then comes the bill which is only affordable because there is a discount for parties. But what to do about the 'gratuity'? To tip or not to tip, that is the question. Service has not been added automatically to the tab and as the term implies we are free to decide whether to give one or not. It is 'in our gift'. So do we just add the customary ten per cent? Unfortunately we happen to know that the waiters in this restaurant are very poorly paid and rely more than most on tips to make up a living wage. Yet if we increase the tip are we merely colluding with this exploitation and increasing the worker's dependency on our charity? There is also the suspicion that the waiter's deferential attitude as he served us was expressly designed to make us feel more than usually indebted. The tip is pay back time. Worse still, having read Sartre on waiters we are all too aware of the 'bad faith' that might be involved here.[15] Is our tip merely condemning both of us to lead an inauthentic existence, playing a role that neither of us believes in, but pretending it is who we essentially are? But if we don't tip at all then the waiter will suffer materially. Why should he be penalised merely to salve our philosophical conscience? But if we don't tip, in a context where it is customary to do so, then we have broken a social compact; furthermore, if we want to go back to this restaurant, it behoves us to be generous to ensure of getting a warm welcome and a good table next time.

Even suppose we manage to resolve the issue amicably it might not be the end of the story. On the way home I am accosted by a rather dishevelled young man who demands I give him some money so he can get a bed for the night in a hostel for the homeless. No 'pleases' from *this* young beggar, just 'gimme'. Within the framework of moral economy, there is no problem: giving alms to mendicants is a social and religious duty. As the Koran puts it, 'the only giving is to the poor, the rest is exchange'. But I am an atheist as well as a socialist who believes that private charity is no solution to problems that need to be dealt with structurally through public policy making. Then again the Thatcherite in me thinks 'he is probably a junkie, if I give him some cash he will only spend it on drugs and I will be reinforcing the culture of dependency by giving him a handout'. Furthermore, if I do give him some money to get rid of him now, it means that if I bump into him again later he will only ask me for more, since he will remember me not with gratitude, as someone he owes to leave alone but as a soft touch. Still this sturdy beggar is staring at me rather aggressively. Perhaps he's going to mug me? So I'd better cough up! Better a gift than a theft and a bloody nose. But, hang on, that's giving in to a bully and, moreover this guy is demanding money with menaces, and possibly false pretences, so maybe I should call the law and get him put away. Then at least he will get some treatment. Now I really have joined the class enemy. Perhaps after all I am just a mean bastard who is willing to give money to a fawning waiter because he makes me feel like a VIP, but refuses to help out a young man who is clearly down on his luck.

This constant to-ing and fro-ing between contrary positions of identification associated with the exercise of jurisdictional power or judgemental authority, and positions of moral abjection or social deference is, I suggest, how most of us live the intersection of the two economies of worth. This process of trading places is not just a game going on in people's heads; it is institutionalised in the rhetorical practices of 'empowerment' that are currently on offer in many areas of social policy and which simulate the giving away of power while dissimulating its actual concentration. The forms of community consultation that took place in East London in relation to the construction of the Olympic Park were a classic example of this process.[16]

Where the market becomes disembedded from these moral and social relations, and serves as the sole measure of value, we arrive at neoliberal economism. Mrs Thatcher thought there was no such thing as society, but her attempt to return to what she thought was Victorian morality, involved pursuing a monetarist policy for deregulating markets that removed any point of moral engagement with its consequences; commodity relations in the form of an 'enterprise culture' became a self validating system, with the consequences we now know. Yet the re-embedding of the economic in a structure of social and moral obligation can be equally problematic. Nudge economics which is currently flavour of the month with policy wonks in the Cameron administration is a case in point.

Behavioural economics, to give its proper name – it does indeed represent a fusion of behaviouristic psychology with neoliberalism – looks for cheap, cost effective wheezes to incentivise citizens and consumers to make rational and moral choices in both their own and the public interest by using carefully chosen triggers designed to activate and reward socially responsible behaviour.[17] So if you want to stop people dumping their old cookers and prams on a piece of waste ground, offer them a randomised reward, say vouchers to be spent in a local supermarket, if they sign up to a scheme to have these items collected from a municipal dustbin area and paint green feet on the pavements leading to it, to show them the way. Or, to take another common example, send people a letter telling them that their neighbours have increased the value of their property by installing solar panels, and more people will follow their example, if only because they want to keep up with them in the social rat race. Nudge economics rarely attempts to appeal to people's generosity; it is most successful when it mobilises competitive self interest. If it works it is only as a self fulfilling prophecy of how rational choice operates in a market economy when it is tweaked and the carrot, not the stick, drives the donkey.

Nudge economics is central to the 2012 health, environmental and community legacy agendas. The aim is to link the aspirational with the inspirational and exploit feel good factors associated with the Games to encourage greater participation in social programmes. Partly, of course, this is to persuade people to adopt a healthier lifestyle by doing more sport and physical exercise, and partly to get disadvantaged communities, especially the young, to adopt a 'can do' attitude to their lives and make the most of their opportunities. According to this scenario, cycling to work is not only healthier and reduces your carbon footprint as well as your waistband, it allows you to imagine you are Bradley Wiggins and even if you have grown up on the wrong side of the track, you can still get on your bike and get a job, if not a medal. That is the nudge factor in theory. In practice it is a different story. I recently interviewed a group of unemployed school leavers in East London who had taken part in a pre-Olympic community sports programme; they told me they thought Bradley was great but a bit of an anorak and cycling was uncool, their idea of wheels was a motorbike or old banger they could soup up; they didn't see how doing more exercise in the gym would help them get jobs, when there weren't any to be had, nor would it make them feel better about being unemployed.

Embedding is thus not an ideologically neutral process, though it is often presented as if it were.[18] It involves a process of subsumption, either formal or real, of one set of economic values and practices by another and what appears to be a merger is in fact a takeover bid. Where subsumption is formal it involves using the images and discourse of the moral economy to justify, promote and sometimes conceal the process of marketisation.[19] David Cameron's opportunistic borrowing of the language of mutualism and Guild Socialism to promulgate his vision of the Big Society is a good example of this: the moral economy of gift exchange and really existing communism mobilised to rescue really existing capitalism and its debt crisis. So too is the 2012 slogan 'everyone's a winner' which was issued by Newham Council in response to London – or was it Newham? – winning the bid, and which borrows the motto of co-operative gift exchange to 'overlook' the fact that the Olympic bidding process, like the free market, is a competitive zero sum game, in which winner takes all and there are no consolation prizes for the also-rans.

Real subsumption occurs when certain features of the market economy are subject to forms of regulation which derive their rationale from the moral economy and this modifies the actual behaviour of capitalist enterprises, albeit without transforming the basic structures of capital accumulation and profit. The greening of capitalism, the development of an ethical business culture, the social responsibility agendas of some corporations, welfare economics are all examples of this trend. As we will see in a moment the dual economy of the Olympics provides many examples of both formal and real subsumption.

Under this dispensation, then, commodities are treated as if they were gifts, and vice versa. Or to put it more structurally, the operation of the moral economy is simulated in order to dissimulate the workings of the market economy. The protestant work ethic is a classic example of this inversion of the real in and by the imaginary. In contemporary consumer culture we can see it happening in the now all pervasive 'buy one, get one free' offer. The very notion of a 'free gift' implies that there is a category of 'unfree gifts', gifts with strings of hidden debt attached, for as the saying goes 'there is no such thing as a free lunch'. An amusing illustration of this involution is Tony Hancock's famous sketch 'The Blood Donor', whose cautionary moral is that no gift is so rarefied that it cannot be commodified, and no action is so disinterested that it cannot be subsumed under a different system of accountancy based on the calculation of costs and benefits rather than abilities and needs.[20] Which brings us to the Olympic legacy.

The four avatars of Olympic legacy

Discursively, a legacy takes the form of a declarative statement, a written will or public document, which is performative or legally binding or both, and which conveys a set of instructions for disposing of post-mortem assets which it is mandatory for the legatees to carry out. But what this actually means in practice and effect depends on the social, economic and moral framework in which the instrument is embedded. And in order to understand what is at stake in the current Olympic legacy debate we have to fill in some of the back story.

In the kinds of patriarchal and pre-capitalist society where moral economics ruled OK, legacies were part of a system of customary arrangements for transferring land, property, and other assets, primarily from fathers to sons. Sometimes inheritance was partible – it might be shared between all the members of the family, although entailment sometimes limited the beneficiaries to a favoured few; but amongst the propertied classes the law of primogeniture prevailed, and younger sons and daughters had to seek their fortunes through marriage or emigration. Family legacies were in the gift of the head of household, and assets, both material and symbolic were regarded as *heirlooms* to be held in trust by one generation for the next. What was inherited was not just wealth, or poverty, but standing in the community, the family name and reputation. Legacy as *heritage*, a grid of inheritance thrown over the life cycle, certainly created tensions within families;[21] the plot of many a Victorian novel pivots on the drama of disinheritance, as errant sons are dispatched ignominiously to seek adventure and their fortunes abroad; the scene in which the family assemble to listen to the deceased's will being read and all the long-buried animosities are revealed was a central device to accomplish the denouement of these family romances gone wrong. Legitimacy – and hence illegitimacy – defined in terms of blood relationship is a crucial trope in this narrative; as Dickens brilliantly explores in *Great Expectations*, the dream of inheritance, as well as the actual disposition of the legacy, is a way of ensuring that the issue of ancestry and descent continues to cast a long shadow over the lives of both heirs apparent and the young pretenders to their 'throne'. For all the conflicts it engenders, this moral economy also ensures continuity of cultural heritage between the generations. Whatever the legacy materially consisted in, and for the poor it might be little enough, it represented an emotional bond of kinship between donor and recipient, a permanent reminder of the life they had shared together.

Legacy was thus about the commemoration and conservation of the past.

Many things were accumulated solely in order to be passed on, it was their symbolic or legacy value, not their use or exchange value that counted. We might call this a principle of *gift legacy* in that the act of leaving something of oneself behind involved no obligation to directly reciprocate but it did entail a principle of strategic generosity which the heir, in the role of trustee, would feel under some pressure to continue in order to preserve the patrimony for successor generations. Legacies were thus gifts with definite strings attached, explicitly so in the case of entailments, but these bonds were those of consanguinity – blood is thicker than water was another key motto – and attachments, both social and sentimental, to community were paramount. It also follows that the owning or disowning of an inheritance involved intensive emotional labour on the part of potential beneficiaries.

This moral economy had a horror of debt and usury. 'Neither a lender or a borrower be' was its favourite motto, emblazoned on many a family escutcheon. To be in debt, or worse, pass debt on to one's children was only less reprehensible than to profit from others' debts, and both cases jeopardised one's standing in the community. Amongst the landed gentry and the well-to-do personal worth might be expressed in money terms; how much annual income derived from their estates, and how much the daughter's dowry was a key factor in the marriage market so that legacies became the fulcrum of dynastic alliances and power struggles, as well as sibling rivalry.

All this was anathema to capitalism which is primarily concerned with the liquidity and marketability of assets. It is a mode of production and consumption of wealth whose circulation and distribution is primarily through the market rather than inheritance. In fact inherited wealth and position come to be regarded with as much suspicion as poverty. Hierarchy and deference give way to meritocracy, gift exchange becomes part of the struggle for competitive advantage, and the bonds of community and kith and kin are replaced by impersonal contractual relations. Legacy is no longer an ancestral heritage from the past but from the donor's standpoint an *investment in the future,* and from the recipients a *dividend*, its worth measured by the financial benefit it promises to bring.

Capitalist economies can only grow and thrive if they continually produce new commodities, reach new markets, and if most of what is produced is entirely consumed. Cultural goods are now acquired not for their legacy value but as a means to reproduce and enlarge existing moral, social and intellectual capital, which ultimately can be realised within a cash nexus. Knowledge, trust, reputation and aesthetic pleasure are thus not valued for themselves or as part of patrimony to be bequeathed to another generation but for their income generating potential. The profit to be gained from collecting books or works of art is not the pleasure or instruction they afford, but the contribution they make to an investment portfolio. The hero of liberal capitalism is the self made man, not the connoisseur or the curator of ancestral dreams. In this scenario the heir apparent and the young pretender are replaced by the stake holder and the business partner as key dramatis personae in stories of entitlement and disavowal, just as they feature in the stage management of real struggles over the ownership, control and transfer of resources and assets. The legacy is now a site of rational calculation not of sentimental attachment between benefactor and beneficiary. We might call this a *payback legacy*, since it is about settling accounts, and sometimes, old scores.

Yet I have suggested moral economies do not simply wither away. They are subsumed under the new dispensation, sometimes become marketised and sometimes provide legitimations for capitalism that capitalism cannot give itself. For example wealthy entrepreneurs and industrial magnates like Lakshmi Mittal, frequently erect monuments to their wealth *and* generosity by financing iconic buildings or establishing charitable foundations, just as they buy art both as an investment *and* as a sign of their superior cultural taste. They want to be remembered for these public endowments and not for less creditable legacies – the shady business deals they may have done or the people whose lives they may have embittered in the course of building their empires. At the same time the concept of *endowment*, taken back into the moral economy from which it derives, offers an alternative form of payback legacy, and this, as we will see in the final chapter, has important implications for the future of the Olympic Park.

A final example of balanced reciprocity or trade off between the two economies can be drawn from contemporary consumer culture. In a throwaway society, fuelled by the planned obsolescence of consumer goods, collecting crazes abound, and they are no longer confined to the wealthy.[22] These collections of books, stamps, coins, photographs, beer mats, badges and all manner of ephemera are not only exchanged and traded, they become precious heirlooms to be handed down to children and grandchildren. The notion of an asset as an heirloom also has important implications for the future conveyancing of Olympic Park.

Unfortunately the interaction of the two economies is often much more destructive. For example firms may spend a lot of time building up 'good will' – relations of trust with clients, contractor and customers, with lots of pleases and thank-yous and sometimes gifts, accompanying these exchanges. This added value, the special legacy of trade, is seldom recognised by asset strippers when they take over a firm that is undervalued on the stock exchange or on the brink of bankruptcy. They save the business by destroying anything that does not directly contribute to the process of liquidating its visible assets, equipment, property and land, which often means that invisible assets like 'good will' are ignored. In the case of public companies that go into receivership the assets are sold off to the private sector, often leaving the liabilities and the debts to the state.

Moral economy under capitalism retains the horror of personal financial indebtedness. It may be OK to owe the bank, although the stigma of bankruptcy remains in middle class society. Solvency is still the straight and righteously narrow path to salvation. Hell is not oneself but other people you owe money to. We may no longer have debtors' jails, but the spectre of creditors and bailiffs at the door still evokes fear and loathing in the suburbs. In public culture, the threat of such negative reciprocities has led to risk-averse prudentialism and the precautionary principle. But there is a double standard in operation here. It is fine to cancel symbolic debts, the only price paid being a bad conscience, but material debts must be honoured at all costs, even if it means closing down hospitals and schools.

The paradox, of course is that lending and borrowing is the life blood of financial capitalism. Since the 1980s, living on the never-never has been encouraged not only by banks but by both Labour and Tory governments, for whom consumer credit was the easiest way to stimulate economic growth. Moral and social status, the issue of legitimacy and illegitimacy, become reduced to credit worthiness.[23]

When speculation in what turned out to be bad debts resulted in banks, and nearly the whole, seemingly solid, apparatus of financial capitalism going into meltdown, requiring a State bailout on an unprecedented scale, capitalism's own credit rating fell to almost zero. A generation to come will still be living with this legacy of debt, a payback which has involved the time honoured practice, derived from the (im)moral economy, of robbing Peter to pay Paul. It is the spectre of public debt that hangs over every Olympics, including 2012. £600 million is owed to the National Lottery, £675 million to the London Development Agency (alias the Greater London Authority) and, as we will see, this is an over-determining factor in London's legacy politics.

All this makes it imperative to keep precise records and accounts; this is possible because, in contrast to legacy-as-gift, legacy-as-payback generates transactions that are time delimited and indexed to the transfer of specified material assets. This is linked to the growth of an audit culture whose mode of operation in the Olympics we will be discussing shortly. But it is now possible to see that in this context we are dealing with not one legacy but two, one based on gift exchange and its moral economy and the other on debt servicing in the market economy. Each has its avatars in the hurly burly of Olympic legacy politics.

In the first case we are dealing with the narrative legacy of the games, which is generated through the free circulation and exchange of information, the swapping of stories, to create a shared memoryscape around each Olympiad, comprising a cultural heritage transmitted from generation to generation. It is a process which strengthens solidarities within and rivalries between the Olympic movement's various interpretive communities, and these exchanges are not, by definition, time delimited; they focus on symbolic or invisible assets and liabilities, and the act of owning or disowning the Olympic heritage. It involves a system of open-ended reciprocities in which no debt or obligation is being incurred.

Yet, of course, this narrative legacy, which is in its own right an invisible asset, may become marketised, commodified in the form of memorabilia produced by the Olympics heritage industry, exploited by civic imagineers to promote sports tourism and the hospitality industries, and be generally used to confer competitive advantage to the host city in the global cultural economy.

The payback legacy concerns the concrete plans for what is to happen after the Games, and concentrates on the disposal of material assets and liabilities – to whom are they to be bequeathed or sold off and under what conditions – and how debts of various kinds are to be negotiated within a time delimited frame. It constitutes the basic plot of the 2012 legacy narrative.

Both types of legacy are necessary to the framing of the Olympic compact. I have already hinted that one of the ideological sleights of hand performed by the compact is to pass off debts as gifts and re-describe what should be gifts as commodities whose exchange generates debt. In what follows we shall look in more detail at this interaction, to understand how the hidden or deep legacy of 2012 has come to be constructed. But first, to summarise the argument so far, below is an inventory of the distinctive features that characterise the dual economy of worth.

Table 1 Moral and market economies

Moral economy	Market economy
Heritage	Payback
Heirloom	Dividend
Gift reciprocity	Debt servicing
Name and reputation	Credit rating
Blood relations	Impersonal legal contract
Emotional labour of dis/ownership	Cultural/social/intellectual capital
Heir/pretender	Stakeholder/partner
Hierarchy/deference	Meritocracy
Mutual aid	Competitive advantage
Baseline communism	Baseline capitalism
Memoryscape	Audit
Legacy value	Use/exchange value
Symbolic assets/availabilities	Material assets/liabilities
Endowment	Asset stripping
Elastic timeframe	Delimited timeframe

Olympic economies of worth: the triangulation of values

When athletes are interviewed after some success on the field of play, after the ritual congratulations have been conveyed on behalf of grateful fans or the nation, it is customary for them to reply by, in turn, expressing their thanks – to parents and coaches, fellow athletes, sponsors and supporters without whom all their efforts would have apparently been in vain. They do not, on the whole, use the opportunity to praise themselves or big up their own achievements, perhaps in the confident knowledge that they can leave that to others. Athletes who do not observe this code of modesty are regarded as arrogant and tend to be shunned, or find themselves in for a 'pride before a fall' media scenario should their onwards and upwards progress ever falter.

In winning prizes, athletes thus imagine themselves to be paying back a debt they owe to all those who have helped them develop the special gifts or talents with which they have been endowed, whether by nature, nurture or God. It follows that if they lose, they are deemed to have failed to honour this debt, as we say they 'have let the side down', and can only redeem their position by redoubling their efforts to succeed. Part of their script, written for them by the moral economy of sport, is to affirm pride in representing the team or the nation, literally embodying their hopes, and to act as ambassadors for their sport. So letting the side down often carries an added burden of debt and guilt.

Of course sporting success also brings fame and fortune, it turns athletes, sometimes almost overnight, into celebrities; they find themselves in the media spotlight, courted by all and sundry and offered lucrative sponsorship deals by multi-national companies and advertisers. The market value of their reputational status can be accurately logged on their bank accounts. The impact on their lives can be traumatic and many sporting memoirs focus on the difficulty of managing the conflicting demands of public persona and private life. But these individual biographical dilemmas also speak to a structural issue.

The Olympics are a values tournament because they are produced at the intersection of rival economies of worth.[24] I have referred so far to this phenomenon as a 'dual economy' but I think a 'mediatised' economy' is perhaps a better term, because it suggests that its hybrid character does not just emerge spontaneously through some internal process of syncretism, but is produced through the intervention of a third force which plays an active role in giving the transactions a distinctive character. That key role today is indeed often played by the mass media in re-constructing the Games as a global sporting spectacle and by groups and organisations who have been called 'moral entrepreneurs' in that they create and enforce social norms by lobbying and campaigning around moral issues, usually to do with perceived threats to public and social order.[25] Most of the discussion of this phenomenon has focussed on the creation of moral panics, but it is just as much in evidence in the positive enhancement of social, moral and economic values. Mary Whitehouse's campaign in the 1960s against what she saw as the sexual immorality promoted by the 'permissive society' was, after all, called the Festival of Light, and was supposed to be a re-affirmation of Christian values, not just an exercise in scandal mongering. The moral entrepreneurs of the Olympic movement are the architects of the host city bids, the Olympophiles and, in so far as London is concerned, the twenty-twelvers, who all stress the gift legacy. It is left to the Olympophobes in unholy alliance with the free marketeers to organise moral panics around payback issues.

The other intervening variable between moral and market economies is supplied by *political economy*. This term refers to the governance of the body politic by the State through its ideological, legislative and coercive apparatus and its modes of intervention into economic life. In the present context I am going to use it to refer to the various governing bodies of sport and the Olympics, their relationships to both State and market, to the key players in the regeneration process, and to political lobbyists who become active around particular sport and regeneration agendas. It is at this level that the underlying tensions within the Olympic compact that are voiced in a somewhat indirect and displaced fashion by the moral entrepreneurs, take on a more concentrated and condensed form and become subject to specific strategies of mitigation.

The Olympic compact is always forged through a coalition of interests triangulated in this way and this, in turn, leads to the formation of a number of distinct cultures operating along different local/global axes:

(1) *Olympic enterprise culture*: promoting the Games as a political and

economic project. The legacy issue for this culture is how the various forms of capital generated by the Games are to be realised and distributed to meet different kinds of debt, whether in the form of dividends (viz, health dividends) or as paybacks for public and private investment.

(2) *Olympic endowment culture* concerns the gift legacy and how the assets of a Games are managed within a particular structure of conveyancing. How far is it possible to maintain a balance between the rival heirloom claims of local community stakeholders and the dividend claims of those whose political stake is institutional?

(3) *Olympic hospitality culture*: each host city develops a visitor economy around the Games, and has to manage the conflicting demands of commerce and communitas, for example to balance conflicting priorities of security and conviviality. Here the tensions between gift and debt legacies come most visibly to the surface, viz in the use of hospitality as a form of bribery.

The deep structure of the Olympic compact could thus be schematised as in the figure below.

Figure 1 The Olympic Compact

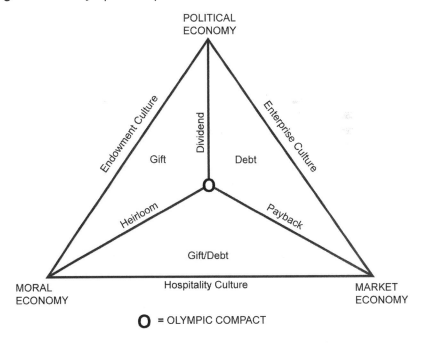

Market ideology

Today, the Olympic movement's determinant, but not always visible, economy of worth is provided by the worlds of commerce, industry and the marketplace.

It is not just that professional sport is big business and dominated by global interests and mega events, but that a 'winner takes all' market ideology has become the referential model for the norms and values of competitive achievement promoted through sport. This same ideology also provides a model of regeneration that emphasises 'gold plated' urban development and investment in premium sites with the effect of gentrifying the Olympic zone and its immediate hinterland. Finally, under the rubrics of this grammar, a Games's governance is judged in terms of efficiency of delivery, cost effectiveness, and the competitive advantage it confers on the host city or nation in the global marketplace. Whatever the balance of public/private investment in a particular Games, economistic criteria remain the preferred measures for evaluating and comparing outcomes.

The 1996 Games staged in downtown Atlanta, in the heart of the black ghetto, are usually told as a cautionary tale about what happens when market ideology prevails, and the private sector runs the show, riding roughshod over the needs of deprived host communities.[26] Certainly, measured as a return on capital investment the Atlanta Games could be counted as a profitable success, but despite some local environmental gain in the legacy Park, the regeneration benefits were minimal. In London 2012 market ideology was carefully sublimated in a rhetoric of aspirationalism, but it was nevertheless the major driving force in the delivery strategy of the ODA. Whether it will be subsumed or displaced by other economies of worth in post-games legacy policies remains to be seen, although as discussed in the final chapter, the signs are not propitious.

Moral economies

In an Olympic context, moral economies come in two flavours. There is the justification which insists on the unique character of the games as an inspirational project centred on an international community of elite athletes who are supposed to embody the Olympic values of excellence, resilience, collaboration and integrity. An Olympiad, from this standpoint, is a moveable feast of sublime athleticism, providing a hall of fame which drives athletes on to enter their personal zone of peak performance, and as members of the Olympic family serve as charismatic role models for the youth of the world, encouraging them to get fit and play fair. This economy of worth draws on familial – and indeed still largely patriarchal - norms and places a high value on inter-generational solidarity. Sport here is treated as having a purely intrinsic value, as having no purpose other than to be fully itself in embodying these values. In term of regeneration, host cities are regarded as heritage sites and the legacy of each Games a contribution to an ongoing epic narrative. I propose to call the moral entrepreneurs who carry this flag 'Olympo-patriarchs' to indicate their loyalty to the ideals of the founding father of the games. Many of them are certainly to be found within the ranks of the Olygarchy, but they also typically oppose the 'modernising' of the Games, which they regard as a betrayal of the gift to the world handed down by the good Baron. In the recent history of the Games, the Athens Olympiad judged itself a success in these terms under the rubric of the games returning to their ancient site of inspiration, although on other grounds (e.g. regeneration and governance), it is widely regarded as a failure, if not a fiasco. In London 2012 there were a few ritual nods in the direction of Olympic traditionalism, for example in Lord Coe's speech at the torch ceremony at Mount Olympus, but otherwise it was conspicuous by its absence.

Secondly, there is what might be called a Para-Olympic economy of worth, and which is indeed best exemplified by the Paralympic Games. Here neither fame, fortune or national pride is the key driver, but rather the desire to participate in an event that represents a community of athletic practice to itself. The value added is simply the strengthening of the bonds between athletes and with the spectators and the creation of an inclusive and convivial culture of hospitality. Sport is again valued for its intrinsic properties, which are here associated with a culture of *virtuosity* combining technical accomplishment with the aesthetic appreciation of grace, beauty and sublime performance, the instrumental and expressive aspects of sport being considered equivalent forms of the pursuit of moral excellence.[27] For Para-Olympians the regeneration value of a Games is twofold. The Games are judged by the quality they add to the urban environment, the architectural value of the infrastructure, and the role of the Cultural Olympiad in promoting greater appreciation of both art and sport. The material assets are considered as heirlooms to be handed over to the host community or its political representatives in the form of an endowment to be held in trust for future generations. The central task of governance is to facilitate this process and also create a framework for convivial exchanges between visitors and residents of the host city. In no Olympics has this grammar of worth been the dominant organising force, although it has sometimes articulated aspirations. In London 2012 it inspired some oppositional groups and was present in some media presentations of the Paralympics, including the opening ceremony on the theme of Enlightenment.[28]

Olympo-Patriarchs and Para-Olympians find themselves on opposite sides in most debates, the former suspecting the latter, not without reason, of radically egalitarian sympathies, while they in turn are viewed, again with some justification, as the conservative defenders of an outdated aristocratic ideal. Nevertheless the two camps are united in their contempt for the free marketeers, in their espousal of the amateur tradition in sport and in appreciation for the extra-economic, aesthetic, aspects of regeneration. There is thus something of a love/hate relationship between the two sets of moral entrepreneurs. The Olympic nay-sayers are often portrayed as curmudgeonly misanthropes and lumped together with the Olympophobes, but their objections are based on rational argument not irrational knee-jerk prejudice against sport in all its forms; the vehemence of their protests is grounded in their strong identification with the more idealistic elements in the Olympic Charter (^50-62). So the conservative defenders of Coubertinism sometimes have a sneaking sympathy for these protesters even if their actions are abhorrent. In London 2012 they joined the nay-sayers in denouncing the lockdown measures, albeit for very different reasons: what for one was proof positive that Britain had become a police state, was for the other an assault on the festive spirit of Olympic communitas.

Mediatised economies

Many accounts of Olympic legacy politics tend to stop at this point and focus only on the direct triangulation of the compact. But there have been very few Olympiads in which conflict between moral and market economies is directly registered at a political level in a crisis of governance. One exception was Rome in 1956 where doping and the whole issue of professionalism in sport came to the fore; the moral economists closed ranks and mobilised against the corruption of sport by big money and the collusion of the IOC in the process. More usually Olympic compacts are heavily mediated, opening up a complex field of alliances, conflict and compromise in which both moral entrepreneurship and political lobbying play a key role in establishing the different measures of value assigned to sport, to regeneration and to the governance of the Games. The legacy compact comprises a complex structure whose synergies are always partly conditioned by the forms of subsumption it entails.[29]

There are six intermediate regimes of value whose grammars have variously played a part in the setting of Olympic agendas and I will discuss each briefly in turn.

(1) Media spectacle

Today the corporate media provide a stage on which the values of Olympic sport are enacted in a special dramaturgy of fame. It is the sports journalists who stand in judgement over the performance of the athletes, the gossip columnists who write the stories that secure or demolish individual reputations, the editorialists who deliver the final verdict on the Games. The value of sporting achievement is here defined and measured solely in terms of the fame that accrues. This puts a premium on public impression management and techniques of self promotion; although it is never explicitly registered in a host city bid, it also informs much of the marketing and lobbying strategy associated with it, notably in the imagineering of the host city and nation, and the sports tourism which organises the pilgrim routes to the Olympic venues. As will be discussed in the next chapter, the close integration of hospitality and enterprise culture has given the media a key role in the political economy of the Spectacle and in marketising the Olympics. But, at the same time, the growth of social media has pulled on aspects of the moral economy, embedding sport and popular festivity in new circuits of evaluative response outside the control of the corporate media.[30]

The Los Angeles Games are generally credited with inaugurating the Olympics as a global media spectacle, not only in the opening ceremony but in the impresario style of management adopted by the Games organisers and the way Reagonomics was used to re-imagineer the Olympics. For the moral entrepreneurs of these Games the synergy between the values of media and market as evidenced by Hollywood, and also in a 'sim city' style of urbanism, perfectly matched the subsumption of civic enterprise under the national-popular ideology of the American Dream.[31]

In London 2012 the iconic stories, the ones that may define what the London Games comes to mean to posterity, were inevitably focused on the sensational issues that made good – or bad – news headlines: the scandals and panics about site security, the absurdity of the branding restrictions, the London cabbies protest against the Olympic road network, and the classic moral panic about an epidemic in street crime associated with an influx of professional gangs from Romania, Lithuania and South America. Yet 2012 was also the social media games. In the age of the blogosphere the conduits of gossip and rumour were no longer confined to the Olympic village or regulated by the official mediascape; athletes were busy tweeting and twittering to their fan bases who could tweet and twitter back while visitors were able to instantly record and relay their reports via smartphones to friends and relatives back home. Breaking news was thus no longer the monopoly of the accredited press in the international broadcasting centre and any analysis of the media coverage of 2012 has to include a sampling of this unofficial journalism which co-constructs its own version of events.[3]

(2) Bio-political

The bio-political economy of worth is centred on the athleticised body whose internal organs and external performance are constantly monitored as measures of its health or efficiency. This is a model body which has become increasingly marketised with the growth of whole medical, cosmetic, prosthetic and 'keep fit' industry organised around its maintenance and regeneration. But it also remains firmly embedded in a moral economy where it supports various pedagogies and therapies of self-improvement and, by this bias, connects to the aesthetic, ethical and emancipatory aspect of the Para-Olympian programme. In contrast, subsumed within a patriarchal frame, biopolitical regimes promote sport as a 'civilising process' for the dangerous and delinquent classes with the aim of installing deferential and decent minds in docile bodies. Articulated to national/popular ideologies, bio-politics construct an image of an organic polity purged of its 'pathological' elements. This has provided a strategy for choreographing mass support for totalitarian regimes through the media of sport and spectacular political rallies, as, for example, in the Spartakiads of the Stalinist era and the contemporary North Korean 'Arirang'.[33]

The 1936 Berlin Games, designed as a propaganda platform for National Socialism, racialised patriarchal Olympic values by subsuming the agonistics of athletic competition under the fascist vision of 'ubermensch' and the triumph of the will, while the ceremonies and stadium architecture gave an Aryan gloss to Coubertin's invented Hellenic traditions.[34]

In London 2012 the keynote message 'Inspire a Generation' – an exhortation addressed primarily to Olympic athletes as embodiments of athletic excellence – gave a traditional Olympic inflection to bio-political values of organic solidarity, but at the same time the rhetorical appeal to uniting people across gender, age, race and class articulated elements of the national-popular.[35]

(3) National-popular

The national-popular is a strategy for organising social identifications into an alliance of subaltern groups against the dominant power bloc by drawing on progressive elements of popular culture and 'nationalising' them.[36] Sport in general and the Olympics in particular have been an important platform on which this is stage managed. The aim is to encourage mass participation in sport as a way of combating disenchantment and withdrawal from the public realm and regenerating the body politic. The strategy is inherently unstable, and may be pulled in either a populist or nationalistic direction, in the first case being subsumed under a civic agenda, in the second under a bio-political regime.

In London 2012 the national-popular was directly articulated to market ideology in the headliner 'everyone's a winner', which was given a strong multicultural inflection in the ceremonies and the Cultural Olympiad, as well as a civic emphasis in the imagineers' portrayal of London as a host city embodying the British virtues of resilience, fortitude and a readiness to welcome strangers.

(4) Civic

The Olympics are increasingly judged as a civic enterprise and for what they contribute to public utility and the common good. Under this rubric, sport has a purely extrinsic value and is judged by what it delivers in terms of promoting forms of rational recreation associated with community cohesion and civic pride. The governance value is defined and measured in terms of bureaucratic indicators of public well being. All host city bids now pay lip service to this criterion but the extent to which it is actually applied depends on the degree to which municipal authorities can exercise democratic control over outcomes as against the power of the central State.

There is an inbuilt tension between the notion of well being as an index of community cohesion and its appropriation by the state as a platform for promoting its own version of national/popular unity. In the case of Beijing local power was minimal as the inhabitants of the 'hutong' immigrant quarter, demolished to make way for the 'Birds Nest' arena, discovered to their cost. The priority for the Chinese authorities was to use the Olympic facilities to demonstrate the country's advent to full modernity, not preserve the city's urban fabric or heritage and they did not mind jeopardising their carefully contrived media image in the process.[37] In the case of Barcelona, in contrast, it was the city which called the shots, and controlled the regeneration process so that its local working class as far as possible remained in place, while the rhetoric of Catalan nationalism gave the governance of the Games a populist emphasis that effectively neutralised opposition.[38]

In London 2012 the civic agenda pushed by the five Olympic boroughs predictably sought to maximise local benefits while minimising costs, and emphasised legacy as dividend, a material payback for the symbolic debt owed by the nation to East London for hosting the Games.

(5) Multicultural

The promotion of equal opportunities in and through sport, and the combating of all forms of prejudice and discrimination are now central planks in the Olympic Charter, and hence have to be built in to any compact with the host communities. The Olympic movement is formally committed to create a level playing field for all nations to compete in the Games. In practice the language of multiculturalism is used to promote and legitimate a number of quite different agendas : national-popular, civic and market ideologies are all now strongly multiculturalised and tend to decentre issues of 'race' equality in favour of integrationist and pluralist scenarios. Multicultural capitalism, the niche marketing of ethno-commodities, is a key aspect of how globalisation subsumes and exploits the local enterprise culture, and the Olympic hospitality and heritage industries have played an important role in that process. Multiculturalism within a patriarchal frame produces an elite cosmopolitanism, but when given a Para-Olympian twist becomes grounded in a popular communism of everyday life in which hybridity rules OK.

In London 2012 the multicultural agenda was headlined in the image struck of 'the world in a city' and the theme of cultural diversity was marketed as a unique selling point of the bid. A direct link was made between the city's economic dynamism and its demographic, implying that the wealth created in the City, the West End, and Canary Wharf, where the financial services, creative industries and other branches of the knowledge economy are concentrated, and where minority ethnic communities are still greatly under-represented in the professional workforce, was somehow derivable from the rich mix of poor people in London's East End.

(6) Environmental

Since the millennium, the environmental agenda has steadily gained in importance within the Olympic movement and now every host city bid claims to be putting on a greener Games than ever before. As a measure of sporting value, the green agenda supports physical activities that bring participants into a harmonious relationship with the natural environment and the Great Outdoors – running, swimming, sailing, climbing, cycling etc – and advocates measures to reduce the carbon footprint of sports stadia and other facilities. But its main impact, inevitably, has been on regeneration and governance. Sustainability is now supposed to permeate every aspect of delivery and legacy, and, in so far as it does so, it cuts across and to some extent unsettles the historical compromises that have been reached between the other economies of worth.[39] The green economy of worth is highly moralised – the very notion of sustainability involves ensuring that a generation leaves no bad debt in terms of pollution and depletion of resources behind and holds the planet earth in trust for its successors. It can also have a strong civic emphasis, in local programmes to reduce carbon emissions, promote alternative sources of renewable energy etc *and* become marketised through the development of green industry and social enterprise.

Environmental agendas can thus mediate between the rival claims of moral and market economies, but they can also become highly politicised in their own right. In the Sydney Games, Aboriginal demands for civil rights, including land rights, also articulated wider public concerns about the city's carbon footprint;

Table 2 Legacy values

	Sport value	Regeneration value	Governance value
Market	'Winner takes all'	Gold plated developments	Max benefits/ min costs
MORAL			
Olympo Patriarchal	Olympic family	Heritage heirloom sites	Inter-generational alliance
Para- Olympian	Virtuosity	Endowment site	Culture of hospitality
MIXED			
Spectacle	Celebrity	Urban imagineering	Host city brand
Biopolitical	Healthy mind/body	Evolutionary growth	Organic polity
National- popular	Mass participation	'Everyone's a winner'	Class alliance
Civic	Rational recreation	Community cohesion	Bureaucratic accountability
Multicultural	Equal Opportunity	Cosmopolitan urban fabric	'Order in variety'
Environmental	Great Outdoors	Eco-industry	Sustainable community

in this case the close imbrication of national-popular and multicultural themes in the Olympic compact effectively subsumed environmental concerns within a civic agenda which stressed the local benefits of the Games in promoting Sydney as a world city and left the Native Australian community once more out on a limb. Their bush cultures might be lauded for their sustainability, but their claims on the political economy were regarded as lacking in 'street cred'.[40]

London 2012 claimed that it was the first truly sustainable games, and a great deal of effort was expended in using recycled and low carbon construction material, solar energy and rainwater runaways, and in transforming the Olympic Park. However the fact remains that mega events by definition generate a visitor economy that leaves a large carbon footprint. In ecological terms the legacy of London hosting the Olympics and Paralympics is equivalent to adding a city the size of Cardiff to the UK.

The key issue for judging the outcome of London 2012 is whether market ideology has been subsumed under civic enterprise, and if so is this merely a discursive manoeuvre or has it produced substantive effects on both delivery and legacy, as well as on the measures of value assigned to sport, regeneration and governance? Alternatively, was the civic project of East London's regeneration merely a cover story for the marketisation of its assets? It is already clear that the synergy between the national-popular and multicultural agendas achieved through the media spectacle created a rhetorical platform on which biopolitical and environmental themes could be segued into a seamless web of assertion about the primacy of legacy values; however, the actual connections being made on the ground between the sports venues, the regeneration of Stratford and its hinterland and the post-Games governance of the Olympic Park seem to indicate that the core values of the 2012 Olympic compact are still being driven by the market. Table 2 maps the key features of the Olympic economies of worth in terms of their legacy values. The way in which these elements are articulated into specific compacts is schematised in Figure 2.

Figure 2 Olympiad profiles 1936-2012

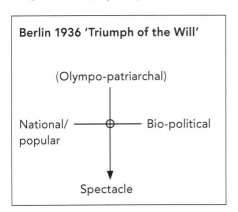

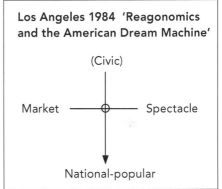

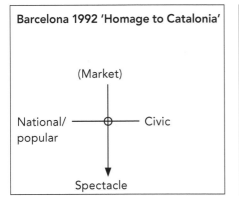

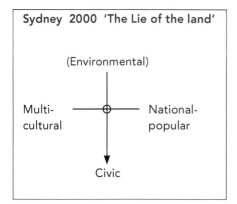

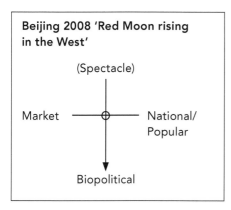

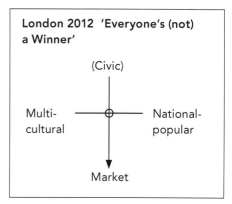

Key ⟶ Axis of subsumption (subsumed)

_____ Axis of synergy

O = Olympic Compact

Legacy politics and the pragmatics of classification

It should be evident by now that there are significant areas of potential conflict as well as coalition between different versions of what the Olympics are about and how they are to be judged. A moral economy that judges an Olympiad by its capacity to promote international understanding through sport is not going to have much in common with a political economy based on the cash nexus which claims that even the most imponderable aspects of the event can be subject to rigorous calculations of profit and loss. The profane values associated with the commodification of physical culture, the tourist exploitation of host city assets or the promotion of sporting fame are not easily made commensurable with the newly sacred values of multiculturalism, inclusive urbanism, sustainability and civic wellbeing. Much of the strenuous impression management undertaken by the Olygarchy involved persuading themselves and the rest of the world that there is no contradiction between these different criteria.

It is not surprising then that in the 2012 legacy narrative we see a whole lot of competing aims and conflictual objectives lumped together as institutional stakeholders (government departments, host boroughs, regeneration agencies and the GLA) fight to get items from their own agendas included. In one such list for East London there were eighteen legacy aims, ranging from 'improving place image and perception' to encouraging greater physical mobility and reducing carbon emissions. It is through this agenda setting process that conflicts of interest and priority are negotiated.

The brief of government departments is to stage manage a consensual definition of legacy issues while imposing parameters on their mapping that ensure the wishes of their political masters, preoccupied with market led economic growth, prevail. The Tory administration of the GLA, under the Mayor of London, Boris Johnson, has played a key role in cementing the Olympic partnerships between local and central government around a shared ideology of localism: the bonds of civil society are to be strengthened through a mixture of public and private philanthropy and the resulting community cohesion is supposed to mitigate the atomising impact of unemployment, welfare dependency, and the marketisation of the moral economy which the government itself is actively promoting. The political payoff of 2012 was supposed to be the validation of this project and hence this has provided the subtext of governmental evaluation.

Whatever the ultimate outcome of these internal power struggles, the immediate result is a proliferation of different evaluation schemes. In addition to the evaluation instituted by the IOC, each institutional stakeholder or political caucus cuts up the legacy cake in a slightly different way, often starting and finishing at a different point and there is also considerable duplication of effort. Lewis Carroll would have been delighted by this 'Legacy in Wonderland', but the Olympic authorities are not so pleased. In a desperate effort to impose some principles of commensurability on what might otherwise be an inchoate mass of incompatible data sets, the Department of Culture, Media and Sport produced a framework for meta-evaluation which, however, re-iterates the same methodology.[41] Unfortunately the problem is not just about the pragmatics of co-ordinating disparate research efforts, it is conceptual.

In most of the policy literature, a distinction is made between 'hard' legacy, by which is meant the Olympic facilities and the post-Games uses to which they are put – this being something urban planners and policy makers think they can fix – and the 'soft' legacy, which is everything else which they know they cannot: job creation, health dividends, sports participation or the 'rebranding' of East London.[42] This latter is often confused with what Jonathan Raban has called the 'soft city' – the city as lived and narrated by its inhabitants; but, as earlier discussion of the urban fabric suggested, the symbolic is itself part of the site construction process, and its material aspects are a reference point for what it is made to mean.[43] The hard/soft distinction is unsatisfactory for a number of reasons.[44] It brackets off decisions about real estate from wider social and cultural considerations, which may please the hard hats, but can have disastrous consequences; and it muddles up the categories and criteria that should be used to evaluate different kinds of asset. Conceptually a more useful distinction would be between those regeneration projects which are genuinely 'auto-poetic', that is which produce internally self generated effects that can be measured and communicated by quantifiable indicators built into their delivery, and those 'allopoetic' projects whose evaluation requires them to be embedded in an interpretive discourse other than their own.[45] So, for example, it is possible to evaluate a construction skills training programme solely in terms of the numbers of the target population reached and the level of skill attained and to compare these results with those of similar schemes. But a display of poems sited in the Olympic Park cannot be judged either by purely aesthetic standards (i.e. how good they are as poems) or by counting the numbers of people who stop to read them, only by interviewing a representative sample of visitors for their responses and canvassing the opinions of the wider creative community so that a variety of extra-poetic criteria (viz contextual relevance, site specificity) are added to their evaluation.

Allo-poetic projects can only be properly evaluated through qualitative research, based on ethnographic observation, depth interviews and focus groups, methods that place a premium on locally situated knowledge and explore the significations, values and stories that different groups attach to specific aspects, phases or projects of regeneration.[46] This approach does not treat 'community' as a homogeneous presence and in principle creates a platform for ongoing public deliberation and dialogue about what the Games come, retrospectively, to mean. As such it should be the preferred methodology for evaluating mediatised economies of worth. It contributes substantively to the narrative legacy of each Olympiad, even as it evaluates its legacy narrative. However the very embeddedness of these accounts militates against their commensurability, so that what they gain in concrete human interest they tend to lose in political clout.

Cutting across this distinction there is another one which is less discussed but just as important: that between visible and intangible assets or liabilities. This contrasts changes to the urban fabric – for example improvements to the transport system or housing stock, or the re-distribution of populations and resources due to gentrification – with a deeper and more hidden impact, affecting the social, economic and cultural life of the city, bearing on its patterns of ownership and control. So, for example, while the Olympics immediate impact on London's visitor economy can be measured in terms of hotel occupancy rates, or turnover in the hospitality, tourist and heritage industries, we also need to know how it has affected its *deep* economy, the *forms* of economic activity, the distribution of economic opportunities and how these in turn impact on the environment and on the health and well-being of its citizens. And this also means considering issues of sustainability and not just those of economic growth. Similarly we might want to investigate the impact which visible demographic changes have on place image and perception, but we might also want to know how far a new Londoner identity associated with the advent of the Games survives in a post-Olympic world. The conceptual distinction to be struck is between the phenomenal forms of urban life, what is readily observable and recordable about the city's traffic with the world, and the factors and forces that produce, organise and commodify its spatial structures.

As an example of how these two dimensions interact we might consider how the Olympic Park might be analysed in terms of the distinctions now proposed between different types of regeneration project and their legacies:

	Auto-poetic	Allo-poetic
Surface	Regeneration impact on local demographics	The Park as public amenity
Hidden	Regeneration impact on local land values	The Park as memoryscape

Reclassifying legacy in this way is not just an academic exercise, although it does add a properly conceptual dimension to its evaluation. Grouping together all the auto-poetic aspects of regeneration forces us to think more connectedly about the relations between different policy areas: economic, environmental, cultural and social. Similarly the redefinition of the soft city legacy consolidates a dimension that policy wonks tend to ignore or reduce to quantifiable indices of social participation; it offers scope for the development of an alternative framework of evaluation in which the voices and values of local communities can gain in epistemic authority and be better represented. Similarly the distinction between surface and deep or hidden legacies means that we can more easily distinguish between purely cosmetic design solutions to problems in the urban fabric and those which address its underlying social fault lines. In these two ways the evaluation of the legacy narrative – how far are its promises kept? – can become more closely integrated into the narrative legacy of each Games, as a precise element in its historical record.

Impacted truths: a note on the Olympic audit culture

One consequence of the emphasis on 2012 as the 'legacy Games' is that a large apparatus of evaluation has been built around assessing its immediate and long term impact on East London and the wider metropolitan and national society. Since it is such an important and costly enterprise, it may be worth taking a moment to consider how this audit culture works.[47]

If you ask a professional story teller what it means to give an account of an action she will say that it is to give a report about something that has happened principally in order to attribute responsibility for it; in other words it is a form of narrative explanation centred on human agency. If you ask your bank manager what an account is she will probably reply that it is a record or statement of your financial affairs, of how much you are currently worth, and yours is overdrawn. The merger – which is really a takeover bid – of these two principles of accountancy is part of a historic shift away from the notion of a final audit, the day of judgement where a person is called to account by a higher moral authority, and towards the notion of audit as a process of continuous self assessment where you monitor and evaluate your own behaviour in the light of some internalised principle or norm of social accountability. This frequently takes the form of applying a system of double entry book keeping to judging one's actions in terms of personal cost or benefit, profit or loss, thus creating a kind of audit trail of the inner working of the psyche considered as an agency of self interest and rational choice. It is a key way in which market ideology penetrates and re-organises the moral economy of the self.[48]

This is an essentially private process – and one therefore subject to all the ruses of self deception, so how can it be made available to public scrutiny? The answer lies in the notion of performance.[49] In the second half of the twentieth century the original meaning of the term as 'a dramatic presentation or display especially of conspicuous or irritating behaviour' (OED), increasingly gave way to its opposite usage, as a 'measure of efficiency in the way somebody carries out a routine or prescribed task'. The social sciences have played a vital part in engineering this discursive shift, in so far as they make use of dramaturgical metaphors for representing patterns of social interaction as 'role playing' but also furnish instruments for measuring social attitudes and behaviour in terms of their conformity or deviance in respect of statistical norms.

Bio-metrics, anthropo-metrics, psycho-metrics, socio-metrics, geo-metrics, chrono-metrics … it is no coincidence that these systems of metrication should have been developed in application to bodies regarded as requiring disciplined or co-ordinated effort: labouring bodies, military bodies, civic bodies, children's bodies and above all, athletes' bodies.[50] The various techniques evolved to capture the behaviour of these differently embodied subjects under conditions specified by each discipline have one thing in common: they create a grid of standardised measurement codified into common, quantifiable indices of 'performance'. It is this principle of performativity created by the machinery of metrication itself which enables these bodies to be tested, compared and judged, and differential values assigned to them in terms of their efficiency and/or effectiveness.[51] Metrication became an integral part of a panoptic system of governance, furnishing a new regime of mass observation in which the theatrical and the bureaucratic orders were merged: performance as dramatic display/visual exhibition and as measurable productivity/outcome become integrated into a single apparatus of control.[52]

This new system of evaluation enabled ever more precise benchmarks of success and failure to be constructed – the tiniest difference in performance being sufficient to draw the line between success and failure. It also enabled a whole array of disparate practices to be tested and treated as commensurable objects of calculation, even as it foreclosed value judgements about their ultimate worth. Instead what comes to be valued is the test itself for what it discloses about those subjected to it. As Marilyn Strathern puts it, 'the report on the output is predicated on the form of evaluation which it itself produces'.[53] She defines this as an instance of auto-poesis – it is about how a closed system generates its own self enabling rationality. The evaluation process thus sets its own endogenous norms of attainment. Audits evaluate the auditees' capacity to be put to the test of the audit.

We can see this process at work very clearly in the official framework of evaluation that has been put in place for the 2012 Olympics. The concept of a 'logic chain' is central to the methodological protocols which the framework is concerned to establish:

> Every evaluation must show through a customised logic chain how the project's delivery is expected to proceed from initial objectives to final outcomes. Some of these outcomes will relate to pre-determined project objectives set out in the project plan, while others will be outcomes that would be logically expected even if they are not included in or even aligned with the project objectives ... Logic chains need to be developed in the early stages of the evaluation based on expectations given the activities proposed and experience of similar projects. As the evaluation progresses, the logic chains should be refined, populated with evidence and, where needed, amended to better match the observed interactions. A final logic chain should be produced at the end of the evaluation reflecting the evidence and understanding gained in the evaluation process (source: DCMS 2007).

What is being evaluated, then, is a developmental logic intrinsic to the way an Olympic project is delivered, a sequential chain comprising 'objectives, inputs, outputs and outcomes', which precisely describes the trajectory of the audit itself and its particular form of narrative explanation. Auditability is thus built into the way a project is conceived, planned, and executed from the outset and what is being measured is just that. Then when it comes to assessing the value added by an initiative, its 'additionality', the principle of evaluation turns itself inside out; the value ascribed to a project by those whom it is intended to benefit – its internal economy of worth – is largely ignored and instead an external principle of counterfactuality is introduced, to guesstimate what the state of affairs might have been had the project never happened. This is not however a genuine exercise in the sociological imagination – these studies are not going to tell us what Stratford might have been like had London failed to win the Olympics – but rather a way of bracketing a project's effects off from the influence of externalities over which it has no control, and whose impact cannot be easily quantified. Paradoxically, focusing on what did not happen becomes a way of ignoring the wider implications of what did.

The Olympic audit is organised around the notion of impact. Who is impacted? Where is the impact felt? When is the impact felt? This is the holy trinity of research questions around which the evaluation of 2012 revolves. Impact studies operate with a unilinear model of causality: they are supposed to measure the effect of agency interventions on target populations and rarely take into account the reciprocal action of these populations on the agency itself. In an Olympic context they underwrite the notion that the essential story is about how the Games have changed the host community, rather than how that community itself has changed the Games. In modelling the purely immanent self referential dynamic of the agency, the impact study reduces the human actors to mere puppets and the communities who are supposed to be the beneficiaries into either passive supports or obstacles to the realisation of governmental aims and objectives, without any autonomous agency of their own.

Impact-driven auditry is a hard data discourse which carries most weight with 'hard nosed' politicians, policy makers and sports administrators on account of its replicable and largely statistical procedures; it gives the appearance of an objective and reliable narrative.[54] It also enables one Games to be compared to another in terms of a set of common performance indicators, so enabling a panoptic survey of past Olympiads to be conducted from a properly 'Olympian' i.e. global, perspective.[55] It is here that a forensic science dedicated to the continuous monitoring of programmes of social intervention designed to regulate and modify public behaviour establishes its pre-eminence in the art of how to manage knowledge as a process of public impression making.[56]

Yet in fact there is a ghost in the machinery of audit culture which continually undermines its credibility: its meaning. For as soon as the audit has to stake its evidential/knowledge claims in the public arena, it becomes enmeshed in narratives which articulate some higher order principle of interpretation: it becomes a story about aspiration or achievement, justification or blame, praise or disappointment. It is to this wider narrative framing we must now turn.

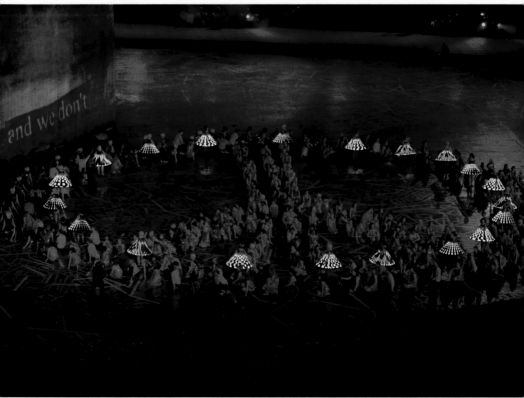

The politics of kitsch

7. 'No shit please we're British': kitsch, 'high' culture and carnival capitalism in the making of the Olympic spectacle

The Olympic ceremonies are meant to transport us into another world where the ideals of Olympism take on a local habitation and a name.[1] The Games promise to provide a brief interlude of enchantment, where the poetry of athleticism and the spectacle of contest can prevail over what is otherwise an all too mundane project of urban regeneration dominated by protocols of public accountancy.[2] The choice of the island as a vehicle for the 2012 host nation story was thus singularly apt. Islands are purpose-built for the imagining and designing of other possible worlds.[3] But if they are the very stuff that dreams are made on, they also serve to express the deeper, more unconscious aspects of the collective psyche.[4] As *The Tempest* reminds us, islands are there to be colonised. From the *Navigatio* of St Brendan to *Gulliver's Travels*, the quest for a lost island paradise, for an Isle of the Blessed, has linked the spiritual journeys of Western Christianity to the founding myths of nations and the profane motivations of maritime conquistadores. St Brendan was the patron saint of the Hanseatic League, after all.[5] Today, small and no longer remote offshore islands have been transformed into tax havens for the super rich whilst continuing to be marketed as the 'other Eden'.

Some people's dreams can become other people's nightmares, and islands have also been the location for some of the most terrible things that have happened to humankind. They are places of abandonment, exile and confinement as well as adventure. George Perec's dystopian fable about the Olympics as a struggle for the survival of the fittest, *W, or the Memory of Childhood*, is set on an island off the coast of Tierra del Fuego. Here, in a society dedicated to the pursuit of the Olympic ideal, where every aspect of life is dictated by the Games, the victors are feted and grow rich and strong, while the losers are fed on a starvation diet, lose the will to compete and die.[6] This is a land where sport is King, life is lived for the greater glory of the body, and the athletic vocation shapes the life of the state as well as ruling every aspect of civil society. Public morality is sports morality – everything that leads to victory in the sporting competitions is good, and everything that leads to defeat is bad.

Perec's thesis, that there is an intimate 'bio-political' link between modern totalitarianism and the regimes of training and performance associated with success at the Olympics, is not as far-fetched as it may seem. Others have made the connection between the homo-erotic ideals of male bonding favoured by the social organisation of Ancient Greece and celebrated in the original Olympics, and the militarised corps d'esprit adopted as the civil foundation of Fascism's (and some would argue Communism's) corporate state in the twentieth century. Certainly Communism's Promethean ideal of the proletarian body, freed from the toils of oppression through the conjoint disciplines of organised labour and mass gymnastics, has played a role in shaping the spectacle of the modern Olympiads, not least in the choreography of its opening ceremonies; and Leni Riefenstahl's mesmerising documentary of the 1936 Berlin games, with its hymn to the Aryan body beautiful and vision of athletics as a 'triumph of the will', continues to haunt the imagination of those whose brief it is to either stage or film the event.

In creating its spectacle of enchantment, the Olympic ceremonies had, of necessity, to exclude all such negative dialectics: the scandalous aspects of Britain's island story – its colonial conquests, its class antagonisms, its racialism – just could not be told. In so far as the darker, more tragic moments of this history were recognised – the dead of two world wars, the victims of 7/7 – they were contextualised as examples of national resilience in the face of adversity. These were feel-good ceremonies made for feel-bad times – and if they were, for a few brief moments, allowed to sing a sad song, it was one which in the singing only made it better and better. The basic message was summed up by Eric Idle in the closing ceremony:

> If life seems jolly rotten
> There's something you've forgotten
> And that's to laugh and smile and dance and sing.
> When you're feeling in the dumps
> Don't be silly chumps
> Just purse your lips and whistle – that's the thing.
>
> And ... always look on the bright side of life.

There was lots of smiling, dancing and singing in the opening 'Isle of Wonders' ceremony, and whistling in the light was a recurrent leitmotif in its soundscape. In the history of art and literature, this aesthetic strategy has a name. It is called kitsch.

Kitsch rules

The advent of Olympic kitsch is usually associated with the glitzy presentation at the opening of the 1984 Los Angeles Games, with its eighty-four white pianos played by Liberace lookalikes, not to mention 'Rocket Man'; all of which led commentators to talk of the 'disneyfication' of the Olympics, by which they meant not only that certain Disney characters appeared in it, or that the special effects were straight out of *Star Wars*, but that its storyline and presentation had a certain quality of arch sentimentality or schmaltz.[7]

This development is usually analysed as symptomatic of the way the Olympics have become a global media spectacle and, from the purist's point of view, desecrated by commercial values and media hype.[8] What has been less remarked upon is how the aesthetics of the ceremony have been transformed by cognate developments within the arts themselves, and the advent of post-modern notions of narrative and performance, which were so much in evidence in the 'Isle of Wonders' and the other 2012 ceremonies.[9]

As originally defined by Clement Greenberg, kitsch refers to the degradation of avant garde art by the advent of the ersatz or 'synthetic pleasures' of popular culture. In the 1930s the exponents of 'kulturkritik' saw kitsch as a vehicle for an anti-modernist aesthetics and reactionary politics. For Herman Broch it was 'the absolute negative pole of every value', while for Adorno it represented a travesty of art, associated with the rise of 'culture industry'. The concept has, for much of its history, been little more than a term of abuse, synonymous with poor taste or commercial values in the eyes of conservative defenders of elite culture, while for left-wing critics it is regarded as symptomatic of false consciousness and the commodification of art.

A less value-loaded way of defining kitsch would be to see it as involving a specific ritualisation of aesthetic practice on the part of both its producers and consumers.[10] The making of a kitsch object draws on a limited lexicon of ready-made features, and re-assembles them within a prescribed format. Unlike the artwork proper, the object lacks signature – the trace of the passage from artistic intention to accomplished expression is missing. Instead there is just a certain, often bizarre, logic of design. The collector or connoisseur of kitsch assimilates the objects to a pre-interpreted framework so that there is no 'shock of the new', only a reaffirmation of what is instantly recognisable, already liked and known, albeit in a shape or texture that often renders the familiar into something exciting or exotic. As an art form it is both reassuringly predictable and unnervingly strange.[11]

A new cutting edge was given to the term by Milan Kundera in the 1970s. In *The Unbearable Lightness of Being* he defines kitsch as 'whatever denies or excludes the negative aspects of life and satisfies the need to gaze into the mirror of the beautifying lie and be moved to tears of gratification at one's own reflection'.

Kitsch causes two tears to flow in quick succession. The first tear says: *How nice to see children running on the grass!* The second tear says: *How nice to be moved, together with all mankind, by children running on the grass!* It is the second tear that makes *kitsch* kitsch.[12]

For Kundera kitsch involves an act of *complicity* between its producers and consumers. He was thinking about the way totalitarian societies promote official 'regimes of happiness', but the concept could apply just as easily to the more individualistic forms of self regard promoted by the culture of consumerism, and to the positive images of cities and nations promoted by tourist industries or Olympic bidders.[13] One of its most pernicious effects is to corrupt nostalgia, to deprive it of its authentic melancholic properties, by converting the painful sense of loss or dislocation into a yearning for a cosy form of homeliness. Parting is always a sentimental occasion, but it is sentimentality with depth, or, as Ernst Bloch describes it, 'a tremolo hovering indistinguishably between surface and depth'.[14] Under the sign of Kitsch, however, nostalgia is no longer a way of recognising what we hold dear, or what is still familiar in the foreign country that our past has become; it is the return of memory to the superficial detail of an imaginary past in order to hold at bay the fears and anxieties of the present or to sustain the fantasy of what might have been. It is déjà vu without the Uncanny.[15] The tourist souvenir, which is the prime medium of kitsch, bears eloquent witness to this surrogate memory politics.

Since the 1980s, within the art world, kitsch has been rehabilitated and given a positive make-over, especially by post-modernists keen to relate to the aesthetics of everyday life.[16] The very fact that it exemplified bad taste or philistinism and was integral to popular culture was part of its attraction. It was a way of attacking or overturning the dominant canons of bourgeois cultural refinement and epistemic hubris.[17] In the work of the pop art movement (especially Andy Warhol), as well as in more recent work by Jeff Koons, Claes Oldenberg, Matthew Barney and Paul McCarthy, we see kitsch invested with artistic signature, albeit one which rejects canons of good taste and authenticity through the use of cheap synthetic materials, garish colours or special technological effects, to emphasise the unsettling or surreal aspects of kitsch. In fact surrealism itself went kitsch in the work of Salvador Dali, with his famous lobster telephone while in Paul McCarthy's work kitsch shows its seamier side. From the 1960s onwards kitsch joined the youth revolution; it went psychedelic, with florid, acid-inspired designs for clothes and wall paper; then gothic with the advent of heavy metal music, the fashion for lurid tattoos and dressing up for Halloween, finally gravitating into black street culture via hip hop and bling. Kitsch has increasingly been written directly on the body – tattoos being one of its major idioms; in fulfilment of Kundera's prophecy, it has also choreographed the body corporate in spectacles of mass allegiance to various regimes of happiness, most notably in China and North Korea.[18] Moreover in some Olympic disciplines, such as rhythmic gymnastics and synchronised swimming, where points are awarded as much for artistic presentation as technical skill, kitsch idioms of performance have increasingly become the norm.[19]

At the same time kitsch art has penetrated the higher echelons of the art market, with Damien Hirst's diamond studded skull entitled 'For the love of God', known in the trade as 'Vanitas goes Bling'; and it has moved down market in the massively reproduced work of Thomas Kinkade, whose hyper-picturesque landscapes provide a popular pastiche of every visual cliché of the American dream. Joan Didion described a Kinkade painting as 'typically rendered in slightly surreal pastels ... feature[ing] a cottage or a house of such insistent cosiness as to seem actually sinister, suggestive of a trap designed to attract Hansel and Gretel. Every window is lit to lurid effect, as if the interior of the structure might be on fire'.[20]

Meanwhile Odd Nerdrum and his Scandinavian school have developed a full-blown philosophical and artistic movement around a revisionist concept of kitsch that takes itself very seriously indeed.[21] The aim is to construct an aesthetic that breaks with the Kantian tradition of associating beauty with truth. For Nordrum:

> Kitsch is passion's form of expression at all levels, and not the servant of truth. On the contrary, it takes its distance from religion and truth. A well painted Madonna therefore transcends its holiness. As for truth, Kitsch leaves that to Art. In Kitsch, skill is a decisive criteria of quality.[22]

Nerdrum's paintings are certainly very skilful re-descriptions of the old masters – he is the first post-modern Pre-Raphaelite – but unlike the narrative paintings of Holman Hunt, George Watts and Burne Jones, to which his work bears a superficial resemblance, there is nothing nostalgic about the oneiric scenes he depicts – indeed he has re-invested kitsch with a sense of the melancholic and even the uncanny.[23]

Kitsch has also been appropriated by a gay aesthetic and worked up into an idiom of high camp, as in Matthew Bourne's all-male version of Swan Lake. Susan Sontag's influential essay defined camp as 'a distinctive sensibility emphasising texture, sensuous surface and style at the expense of content, adopting a studied attitude of parodic imitation towards the serious, whether in art or politics, while having a taste for the androgynous, the extravagant and the outrageous'. In many of the examples she gives – a lamp with a snake coiled around its base, a women wearing a dress made out of three million feathers, camp and kitsch have become almost synonymous.[24]

Thanks to the post-modernists, kitsch has now become cool and chic, providing a gloss on its own sources in popular culture. As one of its chief architectural exponents, Frank Gehry, put it, 'Disneyworld changed architecture for ever and for the better'. We might call this 'neo-kitsch', to indicate its evolution into a sophisticated medium invested with aesthetic value, which puts a stamp of cultural approval on idioms that are otherwise regarded as downright tacky.

It is the versatility of kitsch, the fact that it can traverse and cross-fertilise so many different media, crossing over between body art and physical culture, popular taste and elite sensibility, that accounts for its continued power as an aesthetic resource. It is a medium of bricolage and calculated artifice, and whether through its 'in your face' garishness, its mawkish sentimentality or its visual hyperbole, it demands to be seen and heard.

High days and low lights

Kitsch would not have gained its purchase on contemporary culture if it had not resonated with deeper trends in social consciousness. During the long boom years there was a pervasive shift in cultural politics, away from engagement with the often intransigent and tragic complexities of the real and towards a facile optimism, and a fascination with the consumer spectacle.

The boom years helped create a dream world where things went on getting higher, faster, and stronger all the time, while public hysteria and its crisis management increasingly become the order of the day. Symptomatic of this trend was the growth of a vast apparatus of popular celebration – London, for example, had more than one cultural festival for every week of the year. The emergence of carnival capitalism involved more than the commodification of popular pleasures, and the forging of a new alliance between creative industries and enterprise culture. It was part of a phantasmagoric economy in which house prices were supposed to go on getting higher and higher, everyone would enjoy a higher and higher standard of living, and all this would go on for ever and ever – until of course it all came tumbling down.

We might call this a 'high' culture because its undeclared aim was to prolong euphoria indefinitely, so there is *never* any coming down. It is no coincidence that this period saw the emergence of rave culture, or that taking Ecstasy and binge drinking should have reached unprecedented levels, and not only amongst young people. 'High' culture, or GrossKultur as it is sometimes called, is centred on practices designed to produce oceanic feelings of well-being and oneness with the world, with or without the use of drugs; it promotes a hypomanic, high-energy, can-do ethos, which fetishises the tactile, the incidental, the visceral and the expendable; in this intoxicated state of mind distinctions are either hypervalorised or 'mashed up' so that they auto-destruct. High emotionalism goes hand in handkerchief with the compressed codifications of the emotikon while pathos collapses into bathos. Where it runs up against complexity and contradiction 'High' culture circumvents the issue with a grandiose display of extravagant gesture or exhibitionistic performance.

GrossKultur endlessly recycles itself in an attempt to keep itself high; it mostly iterates on one note, but it can also innovate through the medium of kitsch. Kitsch offers both a point of anchorage in this unstable world – it enables us to know what we like because we like what we know – and also defends us against its implosion, because it shuffles the elements into an ever richer mix. Kitsch in this register not only de-sublimates, but *banalises* the sublime: it has helped make 'awesome' the adjective of choice for almost every occasion. As discussed in the introduction, Anish Kapoor's description of his orbital tower as 'going up and up and in on oneself' perfectly describes the psycho-geographical trajectory of this never-never land. Yet underneath all the giddy energy there is high anxiety, a sense that everything is hopeless, things are going from bad to worse, problems are spiralling out of control. No-one can stay high for ever. High culture underwrites a bipolar public culture which continually oscillates between prophecies of doom and the new dawn, boom and bust, cenotaph and jubilee, without ever finding a point of equilibrium between these extremes.[25]

All this is in contrast with what we might call Low Culture, a culture that grounds enjoyment and celebration in an awareness of their transience and fragility, in the bitter sweet recognition that what we are most attached to we must one day lose, transitional objects are indeed transitory, much is contingent, and we cast our bread on always troubled waters.[26] Out of this is fashioned a sense of life that is both tragic and richly comic. Grounded culture contains many shades of meaning and feeling, and develops aesthetic idioms for their modulation. It is slow culture, rooted in a gradual unfolding of the plot. It is exploratory, and delights in making the strange familiar and the familiar strange. It is at home in the Uncanny. This corresponds to what psychoanalysis calls the 'depressive position' in the sense that it is about integrating different aspects of the psyche, not splitting them off, but it is *not* all doom and gloom.[27] It is present as much through lyric poetry as in opera or dramatic tragedy. It deals with shit but does not become mired in it. It provides the low lights that set the excitements of high days and holidays in some kind of relief.

Kitsch left to its own devices can give an added aesthetic gloss to GrossKultur, but it is often better modulated through the idioms of camp or cool. Camp is High Culture looking in the mirror and laughing at itself until it cries the second tear of kitsch. Cool, as a style of studied indifference or moral insensibility, is a way of avoiding coming down without suffering the exhausting consequences of trying to stay high all the time; you stay with the hyper vibe but you are also laid back enough to stay in control.[28] You stop being quite so manic without becoming depressed. This is a highly unstable equilibrium because beneath its surface appearance of self regulation, it ramps up the fear of 'losing one's cool', so that when the narcissistic pose is challenged all the latent aggression is suddenly released and is expressed with even greater force. In the idiom of rave culture, what begins with a mash-up ends in the mosh pit.

This kind of sentimental education has wider ramifications than youth culture, however. There is a growing discrepancy between the high emotionality of much contemporary political language – not only in the touchy-feely idioms of caring communitarian capitalism but in the hysterical materialism which underpins it – and the *lack* of emotional response which it elicits as its target audience withdraws into a kind of numbed cynicism, but that gap is no longer even registered on the cultural radar.

It is not the case that what I am calling 'high' culture is always or necessarily confined to what in a more conventional frame of reference is called low-brow or popular culture. Or that 'low culture' is necessarily 'highbrow'. The Last Night of the Proms, with its patriotic anthems, is as much an example of GrossKultur as the most mindless kind of gangsta rap, the only difference being that it is masquerading as 'serious music'. But equally jazz'n'dub performer Soweto Kinch can live with lyric poets like John Burnside or Derek Walcott when it comes to expressing the tone and texture of emotional ambivalence. Eric Coates's frothy overture 'London calling' is categorised as 'light classical', whereas the Clash's version is grounded in a much darker view of the city's mode of address to the world. Punch and Judy belong to low culture, and so do much of children's literature and science fiction, industrial ballads and the Blues. Gothic novels like Mary Shelley's *Frankenstein* belong to low culture, but the kitschified idiom of 'Goth' is at the 'high' end of the spectrum. And it *is* a spectrum, rather than a system of fixed distinctions. Some genres and idioms are firmly lodged at the high or low end, others migrate between them.

Blues will always be at the low end, Acid House and techno-trance will always be 'high'. Within the world of classical music, romantics like Tchaikovsky and Wagner, whom Hermann Broch regarded as the geniuses of kitsch, have been popularised as GrossKultur, whereas Sibelius and Nielsen remain intransigently a minority taste. Carnival began life as low culture, exploring themes of life and death through the popular arts of parody and grotesque, and has only recently gone 'high' as it has become absorbed into the global media spectacle and become more than somewhat kitschified (^22).

Under the impact of carnival capitalism, the 'national-popular' has shifted its centre of gravity from 'low' to 'high', and in some cases this has had the effect of redistributing the markers of social status associated with certain genres and oeuvres. For example Shakespeare, whom Gramsci saw as epitomising the national-popular in so far as the playwright shared the same language and world view as his plebeian audience, has now become the preserve of an educated elite, and is definitely 'not for the likes of *Sun* readers'. Poetry, which used to be part of a popular oral tradition, has become a minority culture confined to literati, although its 'high end' – performance poetry – has re-engaged with the boys and girls from the hood. Meanwhile jazz, which used to be embedded in black vernacular street culture, has been ousted by the high-fiving jive-talking idiom of rap and now survives as minority taste – a musical subculture priding itself on its distance from the mainstream.

Cultures of celebration: a short history

It is tempting to understand these developments as a unilinear and irreversible process of decline from the good old days of robust plebeian culture to the hollowed out spectacle of self congratulatory pseudocelebrity represented by the Brit awards. Roger Caillois, the most eloquent exponent of this view, talks of:

> our impoverished festivals which stand out in so little relief from the monotony of modern life, and appear to be broken up and absorbed by it – even though there remain a few pitiful vestiges of the collective outburst which were the chief reason for the existence of the original festivities.[29]

Yet even he concludes with a nostalgic backward glance: 'there is no festival, even most dreary, which does not at least have its beginning in excess and revelry'. Inspired by Mikhail Bakhtin's vision of Carnival as the heteroglossic expression of popular revolt against the monotonous discourse of power, the Cultural Left sometimes hankers after a return to the prolefests of yesteryear: the Durham Miners' Gala and the Mayday parades; or else it continues to see Carnival as a world of social hierarchy turned upside down rather than what it has become: 'high' culture conducting its business as usual.[30] Yet this transition is no overnight sensation. It has a history of quite long duration.

The distinctively modern vision of festivity was first spelt out by Saint-

Simon in his *Proposal to end the revolution* (1817), in which he advocated the establishment of Festivals of Hope – ceremonies 'celebrating the glory of investments, the power of industry and the joys of commerce, stimulating citizens to work with passion by making them feel how much better their lot would be after they have brought these projects to completion'. These festivals were to be organised and scripted by what he called 'positive intellectuals', artists and thinkers inspired by his techno-meritocratic vision, whom he contrasted with the jurists and scholars who merely stood on the sidelines and carped. Hmm, sounds familiar … Saint-Simon's rationale for a socialist Utopia based on industry was nothing if not economistic in its values, and might well serve as a manifesto for today's Olygopolists: 'Money is to the body politic what blood is to the human body … thus the law of finance is the general law, the law from which all others derive or ought to derive'.[31]

The real question posed by Saint-Simon is how the vampiric power of capital – the fact that it reproduces and enlarges itself by devouring the very productivities it creates – is to be represented in a culture of celebration. Marx suggests an answer: through the power of the commodity to conform its consumption as well as production to its own idiom, its possession comes to be valued for what it celebrates about the owner, for the permanent enhancement of status it affords, rather than for the immediate and transient enjoyment of its use. Yet festivity is all about such immediate and transient pleasure, and as such points to potential forms of resistance to the commodification process as well as to its incorporation. It is where moral and market economies meet on grounds of neither's choosing.

Since the mid-eighteenth century, those who have had little or no stake in commodity production, either because they were excluded from it, exploited by it or simply opposed to it on ethical or political grounds, have nevertheless created their own forms of celebration, largely through the medium of riots, strikes, looting and symbolic actions, which often offered a mirror image of capitalism's own destructive creativity.[32] In these forms of popular protest we see elements of masquerade, pantomime, the making and burning of effigies, rituals of excess and misrule, all legitimated by appeals to a culture of mutuality and common justice threatened by the invasion of capitalist forms of exchange.[33] These practices often draw on pre-industrial forms of celebration linked to the seasonal rhythms of peasant economies, with their alternating phases of dearth and plenitude, barren times and harvest times. No wonder Marx called them the carnivals of the oppressed. Meanwhile Carnival as it developed in the context of new world colonialism became a platform for the popular contestation of the dominant white culture, a medium for asserting creolised idioms of identity and belonging that did indeed turn the coloniser's world upside down.[34]

So we have here two distinct models of festivity: one in which Capital or Industry figures as a dynamic force of human progress, enlightenment and emancipation, and the second where the underside of the story surfaces and living labour, resurrected from the dead, dances on its own erstwhile grave, as it celebrates a magical moment of plenty amidst the long drear winter of want. And so the contrast comes to be struck between the highly organised, rationalised and audited aspects of the mega event and the spontaneous, subversive, and anti-hierarchical character of popular festivity. It was these latter which Marcel Mauss had in mind when in his essay on the gift he talks about 'the joy of giving in public, the delight in generous artistic expenditure, the pleasure of hospitality in the public and private feast'.[35]

However, under the aegis of Carnival Capitalism these two utopias, one based on celebrating the protestant-cum-socialist work ethic and the other its determined negation, have become amalgamated into a single apparatus of celebration. A marriage has been arranged between communitas and commerce, gift and commodity; and it is not so much a case of a shrinking bride being overpowered by the seductions of a wealthy suitor, but more a *folie à deux*. In this world turned upside down the moral economy capsizes into the market economy, and the irrepressible desire to revel in oneself and the world is turned into a travesty of itself.

Under the track, the spectacle

This development was brilliantly anticipated by Guy Debord in his book *The Society of the Spectacle*. Debord defined the Spectacle as a generic form of alienation in advanced capitalist societies:

> Considered in its own terms, the spectacle is an *affirmation* of appearances and an identification of all human social life with those appearances. But a critique that grasps the spectacle's essential character reveals it to be a visible *negation* of life – a negation of life that has taken on a *visible form* ... The spectacle presents itself as a vast inaccessible reality that can never be questioned. Its sole message is: 'What appears is good; what is good appears'. The passive acceptance of its demands is already effectively imposed by its monopoly of appearances.[36]

If you replace 'spectacle' with 'Olympics' you will instantly get what Debord is driving at: the negation of the lived experience of sport (or art), whether as participant or observer (an experience grounded in what I have characterised as 'low culture'), through the interposition of forms of representation which merely simulate its effects while fetishising their positivity ('high' culture). Just think what is unconsciously implied when spectators say a sporting or artistic performance is 'phenomenal'.

Debord's analysis, first published in 1967, still provides one of the best critiques of this process; but however prophetic, Debord could not envisage the development of GrossKultur as a widespread phenomenon; or that capitalism would stage-manage the carnivals of the oppressed rather more efficiently than the state could suppress them; or that by the bias of multiculturalism the ritual idioms of popular mimicry, masquerade and misrule would fuel the manufacture of carefully branded and themed ethno-commodities. In their quest for authentically oppositional cultural practices the French situationists thought that graffiti would continue to articulate the true voice of those for whom there was no turning back. However Debord, as a connoisseur of what he called 'recuperation', would not have been unduly surprised to discover that this rebel art form would one day be recruited to furnish the official typography and logo for an Olympic Games.

Although *The Society of the Spectacle* emphasises the link between technologies of surveillance and social atomisation, it does not quite anticipate how far and how seductively the repressive 'planification' of everyday life would penetrate the private sphere and become internalised as a psychic norm through the intervention of therapies and pedagogies dedicated to 'self realisation'.[37] This more subjective dimension of the situationist critique of the Spectacle was developed by Raoul Vaneigem in his book *The Revolution of Everyday Life*, in which he traces the evolution of what he calls 'survival sickness', the application of a new kind of micro moral economics to the interstices of inter-personal relationships.[38] He writes:

> In our universe of expanding technology and modern conveniences, we see people turning in on themselves, shrivelling up, living trivial lives and dying for details. It is a nightmare where we are promised absolute freedom but granted a miserable square inch of individual autonomy – a square inch moreover that is strictly policed by our neighbours, a space-time of mean spiritedness ...[39]

The Olympics are a dramatic instance of how the trivial (does it *really* matter how many medals are won by Team GB?) becomes an issue of national importance, while mean-spiritedness become institutionalised in government policies. In our earlier discussion of the Olympic audit culture we noted how the metamorphosis of values into facts or norms occurred in the public sphere through the process of metrication. But what we are dealing with in the contemporary Spectacle is a whole *regime of envisagement*, in which the functions of performance, observation, recording, accounting and evaluating are not only individualised but collapsed or subsumed under a single forensic principle of governance, while simultaneously becoming de-materialised.[40] We no longer have to hear a bank teller count out our money aloud and hand it to us over the counter – we can remote-control all our financial affairs impersonally via ATMs and online. Yet this replacement of concrete by abstract labour also sets in motion a compensatory movement to re-materialise and re-socialise the process of regulation. For example, the more CCTV cameras are installed, the more neighbourhood watch schemes are needed, not only to supplement technical surveillance, but to mobilise locally situated intelligence to fill the social vacuum created by the withdrawal of the bobby on the beat. In this way the state forces civil society to police itself according to legal norms which it no longer has to impose but which are voluntarily adopted as a condition of social survival.

This surrogate activity often takes the form of fetishising the immaterial as a way of gaining a more or less magical purchase on the real. We learn to envisage the future – how will our projects turn out? – not by speculating about possible alternative outcomes and their implications, but by extrapolating from what immediately fascinates us about the present to a future that is predictable only as its facsimile. It was just this myopic concentration on the Spectacle of wealth creation and its immaterial mechanisms which led bankers who were playing the futures markets with their sophisticated econometric systems to over-reach themselves and bring the whole pack of cards tumbling down about our ears. In this world turned upside down, what is material, what really counts, is reduced to a matter of calculable profit and loss, and everything that is not so calculable is disregarded as 'immaterial'. This is precisely what the Olympic audit does. It involves a *bureaucratisation* of the Spectacle.

The operatic and the bureaucratic

The contemporary Spectacle has two aspects to it – the operatic and the bureaucratic. The operatic dimension involves a whole sensuous technology of seduction designed to excite interest, to distract and delight, to dramatise the incidental and simulate the carnivalesque. The model for this is provided by Wagner's attempt to create a total spectacle, which he termed a 'theatron', in which the distance between the spectator and the mise en scene is collapsed; the aim is to fix attention on the sublime work of art and induce a state of collective hypnosis by removing any source of distraction from the phantasmagoric spectacle.[41] Exhibitionism and voyeurism, the desire to show off and to secretly observe, are here situated – and sublimated – within a communitarian impulse, with or without the intervention of the state. Wagnerian opera is high kitsch, and it is this, rather than the fact that it provided a template for the Nuremberg rallies, which should inform our view of its influence on subsequent attempts to choreograph the body politic.

The theatron is already a step towards the second, bureaucratic, aspect of Spectacle – the capacity to co-ordinate and regulate perception, to impose bureaucratic norms of accountability and control on every aspect of public and private performance. The panopticon and the panorama are the model for this technology of disciplinary surveillance.[42] What it induces and exploits is the great fear of 'making a spectacle of oneself', of standing out from the crowd, or deviating from the norm, in a word engaging in the *vita activa* of political performance.[43] The spectacle of poverty, marginality and monstrosity that is produced by the interventions of social policy and measured by the forensic sciences owes its intimidating power to just this moral economy. Yet this is not merely punitive or self-punitive activity; it involves a process of active conformity which yields forms of pleasurable participation that are more than just a reduction of anxiety; participants are motivated by their desire to belong to civil society and enjoy the protection of the state.

We can see then how these two functions of the Spectacle can complement one another – but also in some circumstances, how they can enter into conflict. Sport is a premium site in which the operatic and bureaucratic orders of performance merge, where they become operationalised and concentrated in histrionic forms of public display whose effects can be precisely measured and rendered subject to rational calculation and comparison. Art is another. As Debord pointed out in his agitprop film *Critique of Separation*:

> the things that really concern us and solicit our involvement are those that deserve no more than to have us as distant spectators, bored and indifferent. Situations seen through the lens of some artistic transformation are often, on the contrary, the ones that attract us, that would justify us becoming actors, participants.[44]

In aesthetic terms the contemporary Spectacle has developed a distinctive form of audio-visual semiology, a digital 'son et lumière', that draws on idioms from the performing arts, circus, theatre and dance, and often incorporates elements of textuality, but which fuses all these elements within a multi-media mash-up that owes nothing to literature or drama and everything to cinematic syntax. In the scale of its orchestration it is perhaps closest to Grand Opera, but an opera filmed in cinemascope in which the processional has become a tracking shot, the choreography a way of composing patterns of movement that can be best appreciated in long shot, and the ritual interaction of performers a means of freeze-framing the narrative in close up. As we will see in Chapter Nine, all these features were on conspicuous display in the 2012 ceremonies.

In blurring the distinction between live performance and screen event, virtual and social interface, the contemporary Spectacle privileges the iconographic over the discursive, the logic of design over the aura of signature. For the situationists, though, the impact is not just aesthetic but political. What is being inaugurated through this regime of envisagement is a new dispensation of knowledge/power, an epistemic standpoint which perpetually oscillates between the telescopic and periscopic, the totalising gaze and the circumvention, suppression or recuperation of anything that obstructs its monopoly of appearances.[45]

There is no better illustration of this process than the jurisdiction which the International Olympic Committee exercises over the use of its symbols. The IOC is a curiously hybrid organisation. At one moment it behaves like a non-governmental organisation whose mission is to use sport as a vehicle for peace and national reconciliation; at the next it is a multi-national corporation jealously guarding its franchise and seeking to maximise its market share in the global sports economy. Finally it turns into a version of the Papacy, supreme authority of a world religion, whose dogmatic pronouncements have the stamp of infallibility for congregations of the faithful and whose internal processes of governance are a byword for secrecy, corruption and intrigue. All three are in evidence in the way the Olympic logo is used.

The image of the five rings is meant to represent the coming together of the five continents of the world in common ownership of the games; but the image is the exclusive property of the IOC, safeguarded by copyright law and special legislation; it has become a device for controlling the whole marketing and branding operation now associated with the promotion of the Games (^35).

The protected marks for 2012 included not only the Olympic and Paralympic symbols, but the mascots, the word 'London 2012', the words 'Olympic', 'Olympiad', 'Olympian' (and their plurals and words very similar to them – e.g. 'Olympix'), the Olympic Motto ('Citius Altius Fortius'/'Faster Higher Stronger') and the Paralympic Motto ('Spirit in Motion'). Although the main concern was to prevent ambush marketing – businesses using these marks to promote their products without paying a sponsorship fee – it has also extended to a diverse range of media both on and off line. A whole apparatus of surveillance has had to be set up to scan the global information flow for possible infringements. According to the LOCOG guidelines, it is all right to display the Olympic rings in the form of flower displays, or on home-made bunting, but not to put it on a T-shirt, a poster or book cover.[46] Spontaneous displays of patriotism were encouraged, but if you got carried away and draped yourself in an Olympic flag it could be regarded as an item of clothing and therefore forbidden.

Much of the rationale for 'defending the brand' is about preventing its use, or misuse, in such a way as to bring the Olympics into disrepute. Applied in a certain way this might amount to a double standard, in so far as publications which are at all critical of the IOC are refused permission to reproduce its symbols, whereas those which are more sympathetic are given the go-ahead. It is however possible for the images to be used for the purposes of editorial comment, so the ruling is inconsistent. The assumption behind these regulations is that the meaning of an image is entirely reducible to its commercial exploitation, and that its use signifies ideological endorsement. The power of the image is hyper-inflated; for LOCOG it is 'how we identify the Games, how we communicate our ambition and drive excitement and enthusiasm'; at the same time the image is deprived of its capacity to stir the imagination by drastically limiting the scope of its signification. It can only mean what the IOC determines, and is a little case study in how the Spectacle works as a bureaucratic apparatus, underscoring its basic message: 'What appears is good; what is good appears'.

Making bread out of circuses

If the state has succeeded in capturing the spirit of carnival, and enclosing it in an iron cage of rationality, it is because the 'spirit of carnival' has been actively appropriated, routinised and commodified as a means to regenerate capitalism itself. Today's mega-festivals, of which the Olympics are a prime example, are platforms for the dissemination of an ideology to end all ideologies. They offer a mystique of civic participation through the observation of communitarian rituals, while continuing to monopolise the means of cultural production. They answer to the need for periodic state-regulated expressions of public hysteria and excess by providing variously commodified media of multi-cultural consumption that operate on a global scale, giving a local habitation and name to privatised daydreams of a better world. Capitalism does not perform miracles – it cannot turn water into wine. But it has learnt how to make bread out of circuses.

At the same time these festivities have introduced a new principle of mediation between the old seasonal opposition between dearth and plenty and the less predictable modern cycles of boom and bust; gift and commodity are continually reversed into one another by investing the exchange process with a bio-political function, oscillating between the conservation of energy and its sacrificial expenditure. This model of balanced reciprocity was first derived from the science of thermodynamics at the end of the nineteenth century but subsequently diffused into many other arenas of public life.[47] For example it provided sports coaches and physical educationalists with the rationale for interval training, with its pattern of tension, release and recovery; more importantly it served as a powerful metaphor for the alternating rituals of asceticism and excess through which the protestant work ethic became libidinally charged. Pressed into service as a paradigm for the way the body politic itself should behave, it results in risk-averse prudentialism, accompanied by profligate demands on the public purse, and can thus become a major destabilising factor in the delivery of any mega event. Fortunately Olympomania 2012 avoided this trap. It not only offered momentary relief from the enforced asceticism of austerity, it also provided a platform for profitable investment in kitsch and 'high' culture, whether cool or camp, popular or artistic, a vast incitement for these idioms to do their aesthetic thing in style.

Carrying the torch: the rites of Olympic performance

The Olympic Spectacle is a complex phenomenon, a structure in dominance.[48] I have stressed, following Debord and Vaneigem, that it is not just a collection of images, but also concerns the power relationships that those images both mediate and make possible. To understand its power of attraction, and its elective affinity with kitsch, we have to take into account all the elements from which it is assembled, and how they interact. Let's briefly look at one of the central and seemingly simplest of all Olympic symbolisms – the torch relay.[49]

The idea for the torch relay is officially credited to Coubertin. The lighting of the torch from the sun's rays on Mount Olympus was meant to symbolise the link between the ancient and modern Games, and also to represent the 'spirit of purity' embodied in the Olympic ideal, while the relay itself, passing the torch from country to country, was to promote and directly enact international friendship between the youth of the world. In fact the torch relay was initiated by the organising committee of the Berlin 1936 games, who saw 'Aryan culture' as a direct inheritor of Hellenic values, and for whom torch ceremonies, as exemplified in the Nuremburg Rally, were an integral part of the national socialist ideology of 'volkgeist' (^144/5).

This back story was presumably lost on Lord Coe when, early in 2012, he stood at the foot of Mount Olympus before an assembled crowd of dignitaries, officials and actors dressed as heralds and priestesses of the Ancient Muse, who had just performed the ritual; he reminded them of 'the timeless Olympic values that transcend history and geography; values which, I believe, in these challenging times are more relevant than at any time before and particularly to young people the world over'. The president of the IOC, not to be outdone in dumb generalities, spoke of 'the torchbearers who carry this flame to London, spreading the message of sport's capacity to promote peace and to make our world a better place'.

The designers of the 2012 torch had a rather different and somewhat more specific brief. The torch was perforated with 8000 holes, representing the number of people from all walks of life who carried it around Britain, and who were chosen, at least in principle, on the basis of their voluntary service to local communities (^147). So it was meant to represent national unity and by implication the Tory vision of the Big Society. The torch was three-sided because, again according to the designers, it represents the triple aim of education, culture and sport and the tripartite Olympic motto. It was also made of recyclable aluminium; so it carried a green message as well as one reading Made in GB. The designers emphasised that they wanted the torch to have a strong narrative and to represent the best of British manufacturing and design.

Carrying the torch on the final stage of its journey was a special mark of public recognition, and there was considerable media speculation as to which Olympian was to get the honour. Then, when it finally arrived at the stadium for the opening ceremony, the torch became a bearer of Olympic heritage as it was ritually handed from senior athletes to representatives of the younger generation who carried it on to light the cauldron. So here the torch first metamorphoses into a medium of fame, and then of inter-generational solidarity within the Olympic family.

In the course of its journey the torch is thus made to tell many different stories and pass through a multiplicity of media and economies of worth. The 2012 torch had to be designed so that it could be lit and carried in a way commensurate with its ceremonial function, serve as a stage prop in a public performance of the Olympic Myth as well as a vehicle of ritual observance, and both enact a host city/nation narrative and constitute a dramatic moment of its staging within a global media spectacle. These successive iterations enmesh the torch-bearers in a web of power relations of which they are scarcely aware. Yet these different usages and meanings do not simply nest neatly inside one another like so many Chinese dolls; they constitute lines of tension within the mega-event structure itself, between the operatic and bureaucratic dimensions of the Spectacle. Their terms and conditions could be spelt out as follows:

Torch bearing as a ritual: This belongs to a class of practices which construct a model or map of a possible world according to some normative ideal internal to the ritual itself, and in a way that releases the participant from any individual responsibility for interpreting its meaning. Such rituals are performative in so far as they enact the symbolic worlds they model: the Olympic oath, or the declarative statements of opening and closing the Games in the first case; rituals of initiation into sporting fraternities in the second. No need, then, for David Beckham or famous Olympians within this Para-Olympic economy of worth. However the addition of an explicit commentary is still required for the proper translation of the ritual into Olympic myth. That task was assigned to the high priests of the Olympic movement or their representatives on earth, the Olympic mediocracy installed in the International Broadcasting Centre. So at this point a moralised or mediatised economy of worth comes into play.

The torch relay as dramatic performance: This requires rehearsal (and not simply re-iteration, as with ritual) as a condition of passage to the act. The torch ceremony has to be studied and practised before it can be properly performed. The structural gap between intention and act creates a potential space for measuring and appreciating performance. How far did the 2012 Torch Relay express or achieve the creative intention of its designers? Enter cultural commentators and media analysts to pass judgement.

The ceremonial torch: The ceremony institutionalises ritual practice and embeds it in a stable narrative and organisational framework, providing a public stage for its performance. Olympic protocols require officiates – officials whose role is to actively supervise their implementation, not just ritual observants or performers. The Olympic torch has to be delivered into the stadium in a certain manner and, as they say nowadays, on budget and on time. The bureaucratic imperative here imposes its own norms on the theatricality of the occasion.

The torch as narrative relay: Here the torch is a key actor in the host city/ nation story, and assembles around itself an array of actors, technologies, media, transport systems, etc. How far does its design facilitate these logistics? Does its handling make it easy to function as a baton to be handed on? Is it safe for disabled users? Is the flame 24/7? Does the medium adequately convey the Olympic message? These were the main concerns of LOCOG and those responsible for organising the relay.

The torch as part of the Olympic Spectacle: The Olympic Spectacle not only incorporates the ceremonies, the performances and the ritual interactions of athletes and spectators, but subsumes them within a co-ordinated display and relay of the Olympic message. The embodied aspects of torch bearing are now abstracted into a purely scopic, photographic or televisual, format, which can then be manipulated to stage-manage public impressions of the event and its broadcast worldwide. Cue for David Beckham and the Famous Olympians to pick up the torch.

Although it is possible to distinguish these different elements analytically, in practice, in the key moments, from the initial lighting of the flame at Olympia to the final igniting of the cauldron in the stadium, they coalesce to constitute a single statement about human solidarity magically transcending all divisions of age, race, gender, and class. This ideology to end all ideologies invites us to shed the second tear of kitsch, to be moved by the spectacle of the world at one with itself, and to be moved by our own sudden feeling of benevolence towards all man and womankind which this inspires. But kitsch has other, perhaps more important, work to do in relaying the Olympic message.

Hyper kitsch

Olympic mascots and souvenirs have long been a primary medium of kitsch, and the 2012 duo of Wenlock and Mandeville were no exception (^33/4). They were cuddly-cute robots designed as 'interactive play toys' (alias teddy bears) for 5 to 15 year olds, with a single cctv camera lens set in the middle of their face for an eye; their bodies were made of shiny metallic material designed to reflect the people they meet, and they spent quite a lot of time texting each other. One commentator described the duo as the product of a drunken one-night stand between a dalek and a teletubby; others have seen a more sinister dimension. Certainly it is difficult to imagine any self-respecting fifteen year old bonding with them, although younger children apparently did. Essentially, the mascots are props for phantasy games in which a national mythography of the modern Olympics – the British, it turns out, invented a Ruritanian version of them at the village of Much Wenlock in Shropshire – can be invested with elements belonging to children's own imaginative worlds. In this way they too get to live the dream.

To aid this process, the couple were embedded in a story which follows their adventures as they travel on a rainbow, meet famous athletes and try their hand at various sports; they also get to visit their spiritual homes at Much Wenlock and Stoke Mandeville hospital – where the Paralympics originated. Despite being so cool and media savvy, Wenlock and Mandeville still embody the traditional British – and Olympic – values of 'fair play'. In the story, Wenlock is having a go at the 110 metres hurdles when he sees a fellow competitor fall, so he stops running to help him up – an act of generosity which costs him the race but wins him the plaudits of the crowd. Children who expected to see similar displays of chivalry in the real Olympics were in for a big disappointment, but kitsch is all about creating an artificial paradise, a country of those who are blind to such realities, and where even a one-eyed robot can be king.

It is in the opening and closing ceremony, however, that kitsch takes centre stage. It is well suited as an idiom for creating an artificial paradise and giving it a spectacular form. The pastiche encouraged by the format generates an iconography that weaves together otherwise irreconcilable messages to create a multi-accented narrative that plays as well to its internal audience – which recognise the cultural references – as it does to outsiders, who simply appreciate the kaleidoscopic effect. Given such versatility, these formats provide a powerful device for mediating between the requirements of a global branding strategy and the cultural heritage claims of local stakeholders.[50]

Kitsch formats come in different flavours, each with its own distinctive design logic. *Ethno-kitsch* draws on motifs from the local ethnoscape, including elements of urban folklore and national-popular heritage; these are morphed into a strongly choreographed multi-culty spectacle, featuring spectacular costume design, flag rituals, dance, folk tunes, etc. *Retro-kitsch* draws on motifs from the re-staging of key moments in a nation or city's history, usually through the medium of dramatic performance, and pageant, supplemented with interactive crowd choreography and music in the form of national-popular anthems. *Techno-kitsch* places emphasis on the use of lasers, strobes, multiple screens, LED technologies and special effects to produce a multimedia extravaganza evoking science fiction and a futuristic digital age. Increasingly these idioms are merged into a form of hyperkitsch; for example in Beijing elements of popular patriotic pageant associated with a nation-building story were choreographed within a carefully historicised ethnoscape and presented in 'cinemascope'.

Kitsch formats are good at generating a 'high' of celebratory sensation and thrill, but because bathos has been substituted for genuine pathos, they tend to produce a climacteric that lacks genuine catharsis, and a narrative that is superficially complex but lacks perspective depth. Instead, the build-up of tension and its final release is orchestrated through choreography and punctuated by pyrotechnics.

Choreography has always played a central role in the staging of Olympic ceremonies; it is the main medium through which its vision of 'communitas' is both enacted and conveyed.[51] Increasingly though, the traditional ritual components – the parade of athletes, the swearing of the Olympic oath, the lighting of the Olympic flame, the release of doves, the official speeches of welcome – have been overshadowed by the presentation of the host-nation story, where mythography and choreography are spectacularly merged. Kitsch facilitates the merger, because although it may involve a ritualisation of aesthetic experience, it also de-ritualises performance, and enables it to take on a suitably 'pyrotechnic' form. The format reinforces the power of audio-visual ideology over the text, and gives the digital 'son et lumière' full rein. It makes for a show full of fireworks from beginning to end.

The active spectator

Debord and Vaneigem's s analysis is most prescient in defining the distinctive features of Spectacle as a mode of cultural production in their emphasis on how it has reorganised the sensorium of spectatorship.[52] The traditional role of spectators at sporting events is to bear collective witness to athletic endeavour and support their home team, which they do through various rituals of identification (cheering, chants, songs, flags, scarves, wearing the team colours, etc). Within this framework there are those whose investment is primarily emotional and who follow the game histrionically, and others whose appreciation of the event is more laid-back, attending to the pattern of play or strategic moves within it.[53] But in both cases all eyes are fastened on what is happening on the field of play.

Increasingly, though, sports fans want to do more than just observe the action; they want to be part of it. For those who feel they are merely spectators of their own lives there is some compensation in being able to actively join in the Spectacle as a performer. This has been achieved by creating a new kind of choreography through which the crowd can be dramatically present to itself, and thereby challenge the passivity associated with watching. It began with the Mexican wave at the World Cup in 1986, but now extends to a whole repertoire of activity, from the constant blowing of horns to the use of banners, placards and hand signs; from playing with balloons, 'zorbing' balls and other outdoor toys to the wearing of fancy dress. The effect has been to produce a carnivalesque atmosphere without, for all that, generating the shared narrative that gives the masking and costuming of actual Carnivals their efficacy as forms of symbolic action. For example men dress up as nuns, or children go as gorillas to the football or cricket match, but the act of transvestism, however imaginative, is purely for exhibitionistic or comic effect; it is about having a laugh with your mates or showing off, not turning the world upside down. And the idiom is predominantly camp or kitsch.

This renewal of creative energy and fun on the terraces has partly been made possible by changes in the way sport is presented to live audiences.[54] The provision of giant screens on which the action is shown in close up, coupled with the fact that spectators can often listen to running commentaries on their mobile phones, means that their attention is divided and no longer has to be focused exclusively on what is happening on the field of play. Athletes, who now have to compete with these distracting media for the spectator's attention, have responded by adopting grandstanding tactics, playing to the crowd, and using special body language to create personal signatures and summon up support. So, too, event organisers redouble their efforts to orchestrate the crowd's response, through the use of fanfares, countdowns and announcements to punctuate every key moment of the play. It is a kind of hyperactive consumerism, and the more spectacular the presentation, the more likely that the fan's interest will be held. Cue for the introduction of kitsch elements directly into the sporting setting: cheerleaders, drum majorettes, marching bands, mascots, all kitted out in garish costumes to add Hollywood production values to the occasion. But there is a catch. The more spectators are impelled into the seductive immediacy of these shows, the more distracted and distant they are likely to become from the sporting action, and the more strenuously they then have to re-engage their attention in what is still for most of them the main event. Meanwhile, back on the field of play, the more exhibitionistic or individuated the athletes' behaviour, the greater is the level of public attention directed towards their body language and work rate – that is, on those very mundane features of their performance they are trying to transcend.

Some commentators have detected in these trends – which for obvious reasons are most developed in mass spectator sports – the symptoms of a 'post-modern' turn in sporting culture, and even the potential for an emancipatory politics.[55] Yet the fact is that although the sporting action is now no longer the sole generator of memorable incident, its power of attraction remains embedded in quite 'old-fashioned' forms of appreciation, and not in these more recent add-ons. A counter example will help to make the point. The Olympics lend a special aura to watching sport which makes the field and track events the highlight of the games, while football remains a sideshow. In other words the Olympics creates its own distinctive culture of spectatorship which subsumes and to some extent over-rides traditional forms of partisanship.

By the same token, it is quite transient in its effect. The dominant distribution of sports fandoms quickly reasserts itself. No matter how many track and field medals Team GB win, the day the games are over, athletics reverts to being watched by very few.

As for the political dimension, it is certainly the case that sport is the only theatre where the audience routinely intervenes to influence the outcome of the drama. Its cheers can lift a team to victory, its jeers demoralise and precipitate defeat. In that sense it offers a simulacrum of the plebiscitary forms of direct democracy; but it also serves as a substitute for their development in the political arena itself. It *dissimulates* active participation in the public realm. Equally, in the volatility of its prejudices the sporting crowd may be a facsimile of King Mob, but in its actual passage to the act of rioting its focus is on rival fans, not the apparatus of the spectacle in which it has an all too material stake.

In this context it is worth noting that the actual forms of participation offered to the Olympic spectators in 2012 involved minimal and mostly conventional kinds of interaction that were strictly orchestrated: singalongs, Mexican waves, manipulating pre-programmed LEDs. Eighty thousand people biting apples all at once might make for quite a good collective crunch, but the Paralympic opening ceremony, where this happened, for all its trenchant assertion of human rights, did not prefigure a popular assembly of citizens and workers convened to enact them. The most significant structural aspect of the ceremonies was that the athletes were both actors in the ritual performance and onlookers in the Spectacle, and in combining these two roles overcame the great divide between those who do, and those who merely watch.

In contrast to the 'post-modern' thesis, the present analysis has located the Olympic sporting spectacle within Carnival Capitalism and its regime of envisagement; the argument has concentrated on the various modalities of kitsch, and their linkage to the idioms of camp and cool within 'high culture', as a mechanism through which a special effect of institutionalised ecstasy is created. I have stressed the regulatory and repressive aspect of this development rather than its emancipatory potential, for example in mainstreaming gay culture.[56] But perhaps the real test is how far the new media which the Spectacle has helped to bring into being have created a platform for the dissemination of alternative values in a way that short-circuits the dominant organisation of appearances. Or has the medium itself indeed become the message? This is a question brought into especially sharp focus by the Olympic ceremonies, and it is to a detailed reading of these cultural politics that we must now turn.

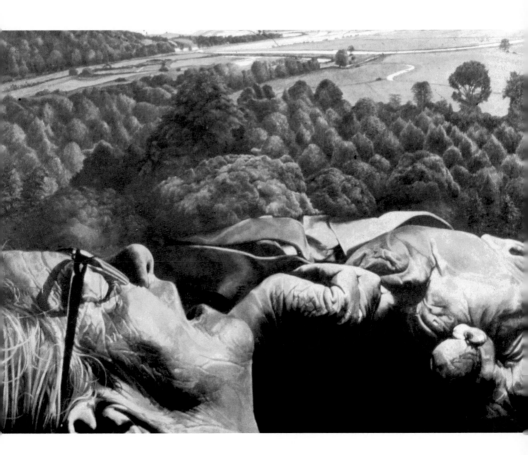

Dreaming England

8. Signs taken for wonders: the politics and poetics of staging a grand project

Be not afeard. The isle is full of noises,
Sounds and sweet airs that give delight and hurt not.
Sometimes a thousand twangling instruments
Will hum about mine ears, and sometime voices
That, if I then had waked after long sleep,
Will make me sleep again; and then, in dreaming,
The clouds methought would open, and show riches
Ready to drop upon me, that when I waked,
I cried to dream again

Caliban, in Shakespeare's *The Tempest*

I am not in any ordinary sense a master
as this savage thinks,
but rather the conductor of a boundless score:
this isle,
summoning voices, I alone,
and mingling them at my Pleasure
arranging out of confusion
one intelligible line.
Without me, who would be able to draw music from all that?
This isle is mute without me.

Prospero, in Aimé Césaire's *A Tempest*

I've seen a lot of strange things in this wood. I seen a plague of frogs. Of bees. Of bats. I seen a rainbow hit the earth and set fire to the ground. I seen the air go still and all sound stop and a golden stag clear this clearing. Fourteen-point antlers of solid gold. I heard an oak tree cry. I've heard beech sing hymns. I seen a man they buried in the churchyard Friday sitting under a beech eating an apple on Saturday morning … Ghosts. I seen lots of ghosts. I seen all the world pass by and go. Laughing. Crying. Talking to themselves. Kicking the bracken. Elves and fairies, you say. Elves and fairies.

Johnny 'Rooster' Byron, in Jezz Butterworth's *Jerusalem*

The Olympics are a stage on which the host nation performs its identity to the world.[1] The Department of Culture, Media and Sport confidently announced that 'the Games will provide a focal point for national identity, representing Britain and British culture to the world and creating civic and national pride that inspires new attitudes and behaviour'.[2] The notion that the Olympics would trigger a wave of popular patriotic fervour and help rebuild a nation in recession was one of the dreams of the 2012 Olygarchs. So what imaginative resources were available to those whose task was to construct an inspirational story about Britain for the 2012 Olympics? This chapter begins by looking at some of the implications of the choice of a theme from *The Tempest* for both the Olympic and Paralympic ceremonies in relation to recent debates about multiculturalism and British identity. It goes on to discuss some alternative interpretations of the play in search of principles that would enable the comic and tragic dimensions of Britain's story to be told, and considers some of the constraints imposed by the aesthetics and protocols of Olympic Spectacle on what could be represented about both people and nation.

Starting points: defining the national-popular

It was a spectacular remake of Britain's island story, drawing its inspiration and strap line from Caliban's famous speech. Danny Boyle's 'Isle of Wonders' opening ceremony conjured up a vision of contemporary Britain as an enchanted place, a post-modern Illyria, where Caliban's children danced triumphantly on its industrial ruins, celebrating a popular patriotism that enabled them to enjoy the benefits of a national health service while feeling immensely relaxed about the lack of any coherent national identity, and to rule the global airwaves with their music while living the Olympic dream. And, seemingly, not a Prospero in sight to spoil their fun.[3]

Shakespearean scholars who have read the play through the lens of post-colonial theory see it as a parable about the all too material dreams of maritime Empire harboured within the sceptred isle, against which Caliban's voice and vision protest.[4] This is the basic premise of Aimé Césaire's famous rewrite of the play. They may have been somewhat bemused to learn that the Tempest theme had been chosen because it encapsulated the 'heritage, diversity, energy, inventiveness, wit and creativity' that defines the post-imperial, multi-national society Britain has become.[5] Even more to hear Caliban's lines being read by Isambard Kingdom Brunel, one of the official heroes of the Industrial Revolution, who, the media briefing told us, embodied 'the inventiveness and entrepreneurial spirit that made Britain great'. Much thus depended on how the theme of Caliban's speech was contextualised; some at least of Britain's back story had to be told in the opening ceremony, and this had to be about roots as well as routes. But how much of the old Churchillian version of the island story could survive its post-colonial translation?[6]

In the event there was perhaps just enough to satisfy the Tory Party and its cultural establishment that invented traditions of British 'Islishness' are still part of the national heritage, if not yet back at the heart of the school curriculum – even if its backwoodsmen were predictably affronted by the absence of traditional pageantry. When the statue of Britain's Greatest Man came to life to send a cheery wave as the helicopter bearing Her Majesty and James Bond flew past to the strains of the 'Dam Busters' on their way to open the Games, it must have seemed for one hallucinatory moment as if the wartime adventure story of Britishness-for-Boys was having a make over. What a shock then to discover that it was all an elaborate wind-up: Pomp was trumped by Punk, and Sid 'God save the Queen' Vicious was to have the last word after all. Her Majesty, judging from the look on her face when she arrived in person, was distinctly unamused at being outqueened as she watched her subjects disporting themselves to a sub-Wagnerian soundtrack from the electro-trance group, Underworld.

The challenge taken up by the ceremony's creative team was to find an Olympic idiom that celebrated the creative spirit of the People but in a way that was neither nationalistic nor populist in content. Antonio Gramsci, the great theorist of the 'national-popular', defined the task as being to find dynamic, or at least unfossilised, elements within the cultures of all the subaltern classes so as to unite them around a progressive concept of the world and their place in it. This was not about an artistic avant garde imposing its taste on the masses, but an ecumenical project 'rooted in the humus of popular culture as it is, with its different tastes and tendencies, its moral and intellectual world, *even if some of these are backward looking and conventional* (my emphasis)'.[7] For Gramsci, writing in the Italy of the 1930s, the national-popular was embodied in folk song and opera, in children's and genre literature. For Danny Boyle and his team, children's literature was still cutting edge but opera, contemporary 'classical' music, jazz and folk were out. His taste was Radio One not Three; the creative spirit of the digital age was to be sampled through rave music and youth multi-culture, and, politically, in a heritage of democratic struggle for trade union and women's rights, not in the operas of Harrison Birtwhistle or the reforming agendas of the political class.

In his book *The Progressive Patriot*, Billy Bragg, the musical voice of Britain's cultural left, has argued that 'establishing space rather than race as our foundation, we can imagine a Britishness which is the sum of every building, field, road, path; every food, custom, belief, culture; every person – in fact everything that is in Britain today, a Britishness that can only be truly appreciated by understanding how and why these things came to be here'.[8]

Boyle's model of cultural inclusivity was much the same as *The Progressive Patriot*'s, although inevitably he had to be more selective in his references, and here his lack of a fully worked out political rationale told. There was no problem about the nation – all the creative work showcased was home-grown. Barcelona might have needed Freddie Mercury to write their civic anthem, while China's Olympic ceremonies team brought in Stephen Spielberg to give their unmake of the Cultural Revolution a gloss of Hollywood production values, but the Isle of Wonders was strictly Made in Britain. Its mix'n'mash of cultural ingredients might have been anarchic but it was very much a case of Anarchy in the UK.

The definition of the popular was much more confused, veering between the demotic and the demographic, the signature tune and the top of the pops hit list. This is not a new difficulty, however. It has never been easy to reconcile the political and cultural dimensions of the national-popular. In Britain, popular patriotism has historically flown a distinctly religious and ethnic flag.[9] The Gordon Riots may have been a cause célèbre for radical Jacobins, and they certainly canalised discontent amongst London's poor and outcast, but King Mob was more anti-Catholic than anti-ruling class. More recently on the cultural left, the ambition has been to wrest the national-popular away from its capture by Thatcherism by creating a rainbow coalition linking the labour movement to feminist, environmentalist and minority rights agendas as well as to campaigns around issues of civil liberty. Yet while these cultural politics may have had some success in radicalising students and professionals they have had little wider impact on the electorate and almost no implantation within the manual working class – indeed they may have intensified its alienation from progressive politics.[10]

This vacuum has been filled by a frenetic ideological eclecticism and mix-and-match cultural politics, and this was reflected in Boyle's approach. His musical tastes went well beyond the restricted code of Britpop and his sense of cultural heritage was equally catholic, although decidedly idiosyncratic. One could thus easily imagine Boudicca and Hereward the Wake getting to audition for walk-on parts as freedom fighters against imperial oppression; and there could have been a cameo role for Robin Hood (alias that puckish trickster Robin Goodfellow or Jack-of-Green) and his Merrie Men, as eco-warriors, pioneers in the defence of England's Green and Pleasant land against property developers and their municipal Sheriffs. But other traditional elements in the story of England – Bede and Beowulf, the Adventus Saxonum, and the history of the English as a chosen people – were less likely to make the cut. Did spectators really want to see a lost tribe of Israelites, crossing the channel as if it was the Red Sea and discovering they are back home in Canaan? Perhaps Merlin might have been asked to conjure up the Arthurian legends as the basis of an alternative Anglo-Celtic foundation myth; the old wizard could then have insisted, with Geoffrey of Monmouth, that Britons were the descendants of Brutus, the well known ex-Trojan, grandson of Aeneas, and organiser of a popular uprising against the King of Rome, who no sooner discovers 'Albion', as his very own white and promised land, than he re-names it after himself; and, then, as a bonus, he finds time to found a city on the banks of the Thames called New Troy, to which his successor, King Lud, will in turn affix his name.[11]

If these sources seemed just too obscure and anglo-centric to be reclaimable, there were a lot of other potential members of the cast who were also off the cultural radar: Britannia made a brief guest appearance in the closing ceremony, though she found herself upstaged by some roller skating nuns, but King Alfred burning the cakes and Canute demonstrating the futility of monarchs trying to hold back the tide of history did not get the call; Drake, Raleigh, Nelson and the crew of HMS Britannia, not to mention Gloriana, Queen Victoria, Florence Nightingale and all the other folk heroes who used to populate the school history books when the map was still coloured red, all had to resign themselves to the fact that they were surplus to requirements and had been pensioned off.[12] In the event it was left to Elgar's Nimrod overture and James Bond to act as standard bearers for the 'island race', a sly reminder that the iconography of Empire can still play well to a global audience if it is served up with Royal approval and taken with a dose of the proverbial Epsom salts. And then, of course, there was Mr Bean and Monty Python to reassure the world that the British have not lost the famous sense of humour that once upon a time was supposed to make them fit to govern more than half of it.

What, though, of Magna Carta, 1066 and all that? Surely the legacy of the freeborn Englishman could be stretched to include others under the ancient shade of Liberty's tree? Here a story about popular democratic struggles might well take root. Inexplicably, the Thames flythrough that overtured the Isle of Wonders completely overlooked Runnymede Island with its monument to the end of feudal absolutism and President Kennedy. Instead we were shown a river that ran softly, but wordlessly and very fast, pausing briefly at Temple Island in Henley to hear the Eton Boating Song (music to the ears of all those Tory old Etonians, no doubt), and get a glimpse of the classical eighteenth-century folly designed by James Wyatt, who built many a country house in the Thames valley where today Russian oligarchs and Arab oil sheiks have taken up residence, ensuring them best seats at the famous regatta. Further downstream, we did not hear from T.S. Eliot whose working river 'sweating oil and tar' has long since vanished; there were certainly no 'empty bottles, sandwich papers/Silk handkerchiefs, cardboard boxes, cigarette ends/Or other testimony of summer nights' to be seen on this eco-cleansed river. No time or space either for Fred D'Aguiar's tone poem in which the iconic figure of Bob Marley is transformed into a river god, the street sounds of reggae transmuted into an elemental tidal force, as the rastaman's locks merge with waves, 'roping off into strand/that combine to make a fat rope/breaking on mud banks and turning pebbles ...'.

Instead the signifiers that were allowed to float downriver – the Pink Floyd's pig flying at half mast over Battersea Power station, the *EastEnders* signature tune, symbolised the fact that Old Father Thames, ex-eighteenth century multicultural waterfront, ex-artery of Empire, ex-white dockland, was now fully rejuvenated as a trope for going with the capital's global information flow. Not so much liquid history as liquid modernity, compressed into a space/time capsule. En route we briefly sampled a more personal past, as we saw Ratty and Mole messing about in a boat, although no wind of change was allowed to disturb this childhood memory of Arcadian bliss, which offered us a brief respite from the onward rush of images of modernity (^69). Nor was there any hint in the subsequent celebration of children's literature that, behind this famous moral fable of the eternally adolescent Toad finally assuming the social responsibilities of *noblesse oblige*, there lurks a political message which Kenneth Grahame (secretary to the Bank of England) was anxious to convey to his young Edwardian readers – and which continues to resonate in these politically disenchanted times: only an alliance between the middle classes, played by the Riverbankers (or the Lib Dems), the gentry, represented by Badger (or Lord Coe), and a reformed aristocracy (cue Toad or Boris Johnson) could prevent the lumpen proletariat or King Mob (alias the Wild Wooders and the 2011 rioters) from stealing the show.

If we were not about to witness a rewrite of Britain's island story from the vantage point of the stoats and weasels, could we at least expect an update of Cool Britannia? For there were Caliban's children joyfully celebrating their capacity to make a song and dance – and joke – about the fact that they no longer had to carry the burden of representing anything other than their own eccentric selves. Yet Boyle's ambitious attempt to forge new links between people and nation in the form of the Olympic rings, while it generated some stunning visual metaphors of community cohesion, inevitably begged a whole lot of questions about the genealogy of British identity and its contemporary memory politics, questions which bear directly on its deeper class articulations.

Rebirthing the nation

Nations never stop giving birth to themselves, and the island – the land no land may touch, in the powerful image struck by the first Elizabethan poets – provides a natural symbol of autochthony.[13] In Churchill's *The Island Race*, written after the second world war, he portrays Britain, for most of its history, as standing defiantly alone in the world, and attributes this proud and sturdy independence to the facts of its physical birth. He talks of 'an original seismic convulsion' which separated the country from the continent, and 'made the straits of Dover and the English Channel the beginning of our island story'. Britain is in fact a continental not a volcanic island, but Churchill's need was to find an image of violent rupture to mark the founding moment. And what was being founded is given a very precise local habitation and a name: the English Channel and the white cliffs of Dover.

For despite the facts of physical geography it was the English who imagined themselves to be an island race, not the Celtic nations.[14] England may have needed Wales and Scotland before it could be said to inhabit an island at all, yet it recruited these countries only as sites for the projection of its own imagined 'islishness'. The island was not only a rhetorical device to enable the English to feel at home and alone with themselves; from the outset this principle of insularity underwrote an imperial strategy. It was the English navy's domination of Britain's coastal waters which facilitated the subjugation of the Celtic nations, and the penetration of Anglophone culture across the whole archipelago;[15] yet the great fear of this 'little England' has always been that without such maritime power, the safeguard of the sea and coastal defences would not suffice to protect the country from invasion; to this was added the anxiety that such an introspective identity would not be strong enough to survive the 'culture shock' of having to accommodate so many different peoples, once they landed on its shores.[16]

John of Gaunt's iconic evocation of the 'sceptred isle' in Shakespeare's *Richard II* maps out both sides of the island story. The speech begins with images of paradisal self containment and fecundity associated with the body of the young virgin queen, whose precious stone (a conventional symbol of virginity in the religious iconography of the period) and potentially 'teeming womb' is protected from foreign invasion (and the dynastic schemes of France and Spain) by 'this fortress built by nature for herself'. But then the mood changes. This 'blessed plot' is besieged by envy and 'bound in with shame' as well as by the 'triumphant sea', so that 'this England that was wont to conquer others, hath made a shameful conquest of itself'.

The sea, as both protector and threat, as a source of wealth, power, and adventure but also of ruin and shipwreck, has been a continual refrain in the many and various iterations of the island story, and this dualism has also shaped the pattern of its inhabitation. Some little Englanders went to market and got to travel, taking their cultural insularities with them as they established a Greater Britain overseas through a global network of trading and settler colonies – the other little Englands; some little Englanders stayed at home and set about busily circumnavigating the island to survey its distinctive features and inscribe them in a nation building narrative. Again these two activities were closely related. Daniel Defoe, a keen supporter of settler colonialism, first plonks Robinson Crusoe down on a tropical island where his castaway hero can display the spirit of enterprise the author so admired in the English; then Defoe himself sets off, following in Crusoe's footsteps, to survey home territory and write his *Travels around the Island of Britain* in which he details the deployment of these very same qualities on native soil.

The fashion for journeys around the coast which began in the eighteenth century as a home grown version of the European Grand Tour was sometimes inspired by curiosity, but more often by anxiety about the 'condition of England'.[17] For the coast was both the front line of defence against foreign incursion, and a weak link in the chain of national governance. There were many coastal communities where the writ of law scarcely ran, and smuggling and wrecking were integral elements of the local economy; as the enclosure movement gathered strength, eroding customary rights in land, so the shore and coastal waters came increasingly to be seen as 'commons' and their harvest, whether of fish or contraband, to be regarded as part of the freeborn Englishman's natural inheritance and right of plunder.[18] So while seafarers might at one moment be regarded as the backbone of the nation, hearts of oak who manned the nation's fleets and sustained its far flung Empire, they might at the next be treated as a 'race apart', belonging to a lawless fringe. For many city dwellers at this time the littoral was also the liminal, a place of cultural edginess; it is no coincidence that the dream that cast the most decisive spell over what it meant to be forever England took place in midsummer in an enchanted wood, out of sight and sound of the unreliable sea (^157).

Little Englanders felt a similar ambivalence about ports. For they were not only arteries of trade, but of cultural commerce with the outside world; their waterfronts were conspicuously cosmopolitan in character, teeming with sailors from overseas and hence suspected of harbouring an alien population who might serve as the conduit of 'foreign' ideas. It was not until the Victorians discovered the seaside as a recreational resort that the coastal periphery was finally rehabilitated and fully integrated into national life, as a healthy member of the body politic.[19]

Even so, in the age of Industry and Empire, when Britain became the workshop of the world, Little England continued to be plagued by a sense of insecurity.[20] At a moment when Britain's sea power was supposedly at its zenith, Matthew Arnold could stand on Dover Beach and hear only its 'melancholy long withdrawing roar'. It was at this point that the island story, as such, was invented as a way of shoring up the sense of superior moral purpose associated with Britannia's civilising mission.[21] It was Tennyson who first coined the phrase, in his line about 'Not once or twice in our rough island story,/the path of duty was the way to glory'; but it was Henry Newbolt in his *Island Race* (1897) and H.E. Marshall's *Our Island Story* which popularised the theme, drawing together the narrative threads of people, nation and Empire into a single historical pageant.[22] For the next fifty years in school rooms up and down the country children learnt to recite Kipling's 'The Steamers' as an object lesson in the logistics of imperial trade and, when Empire day came round, to compose themselves into tableaux vivants, celebrating the link between nautical routes and native roots. Millais's *The Boyhood of Raleigh* (^158), one of the most reproduced paintings of all time, dramatised the Island Story as a boy's own adventure.[23]

For the Victorians and Edwardians, character building was an essential part of nation building and these textbooks continually stress the link.[24] H.E. Marshall portrays William Blake as 'standing alone in Britain's heritage, representing no tendency, belonging to no school, pursuing his solitary path with heroic single mindedness'. As such he is fit company for Nelson, who is 'a single minded and determined fighter with little regard for his own or others' safety', and Florence Nightingale, 'a lamp of reform shining like a single and lonely beacon of hope in a sea of medical ignorance'.

Children's literature was an important platform for the dissemination of this message.[25] While the Imperial imagination offered up the tropical island as a safe haven for staging boy's own adventures in encountering natures and cultures other than their own, there were also home grown islands that offered similar opportunities. Arthur Ransome's famous sailing stories set in the Lake District and the east coast give a rather neat twist to the colonial plot, for now it is the adults who are treated as 'natives', some of whom may be friendly (parents), but the majority of whom are essentially regarded as an alien species, belonging to a quite separate world and not to be trusted. The Swallows and Amazons not only have their own forms of greeting and other rituals, but also give exotic faraway names to all the real places that feature in the story – a local peak becomes Katchenjunga, a local town (Coniston in real life) becomes Rio and so on. These little Englanders display all the anglo-islish qualities – sturdy independence, resilience, fortitude and pluck, as well as a deep love of all things nautical.

Adventuresome reading flourishes best when the world has already been made safe, in this case by Pax Britannica. In times of political turbulence the island story falls back on its default mode: it becomes a story about Fortress Britain, the threat of invasion from the sea and the defence of the realm by the 'English' navy.[26] The geography of risk has always been centred on the Dover Straits, the South and east coasts and the Thames Estuary. For example, the proposal to build a tunnel under the Channel, to reconnect the island to its continental origins, first mooted in the 1890s, produced a flurry of panicky xenophobic reactions: Parliament heard that the French army might disguise itself in ladies' clothes and travel to Dover incognito, before disrobing and marching on London; feral cats and rabid dogs might also take the opportunity to cross the Channel and infect the nation's domestic pets.[27] P.G. Wodehouse lampooned these invasion scares:

> while Germany was landing in Essex, a strong force of Russians, under the Grand Duke Vodkakoff, had occupied Yarmouth. Simultaneously the mad Mullah had captured Portsmouth, while the Swiss navy had bombarded Lyme Regis … China, at last awakened, had swooped down on that picturesque little Welsh watering place, Lllgxtplll … a boisterous band of young Turks had seized Scarborough. And at Brighton and Margate respectively, small but determined armies, the one of Moroccan brigades, under Raisuli, and the other of dark-skinned warriors from the distant isle of Bolly Golla, had made good their footing.[28]

Yet fact followed fiction. Yarmouth was bombarded by the German navy during the first world war while Zeppelins crossed the channel to give the population of southern England a foretaste of the blitz to come. The airship and the sea plane were transitional technologies, and they pointed to a future in which controlling the skies was to be as important as ruling the waves in defending the island home. If the defiant Dunkirk spirit and the rescue of a defeated British army by an armada of small boats was straight out of the 'stand-alone' story script, the Battle of Britain added a new chapter, one which despite its different element could still be assimilated to the safeguard of the 'blessed plot'. In his novel *Waterland* Graham Swift describes the conjuncture as follows:

> In the late summer of 1941, while over southern skies history inscribes itself in white scrolls and provides ample material for the legends of the future, he (the future history teacher) rummages amongst the books his mother left behind and embarks on the two volumes of Hereward the Wake. While the inhabitants of London and other large cities are forced to take refuge within the solid fabric of air raid shelters, he takes refuge in the fanciful fabric of Kingsley's yarn in which, in misty fenland settings, history merges with fiction, fact gets blurred with fable.[29]

A similar blurring occurred in the response of little Englanders to post-war immigration from what was now beginning to be called the New Commonwealth.[30] With the docking of the Empire Windrush in the Port of London in 1948, with its Caribbean passengers eager to make a new home for themselves in what they had been taught to regard as the 'mother country', another island story landed on these shores, one whose telling could not be articulated through the narrative grammar of assimilation which had hitherto been applied to the Vikings, Saxons and Normans, or to refugees fleeing persecution abroad. Sir Roy Strong in his *Story of Britain* (1996) reiterates the principle of assimilation clearly enough:

> The country was invaded piecemeal by those resilient enough to brave the rough waters of its encircling seas. Because of that difficulty small numbers came and once here were absorbed into its existing population.[31]

For Strong, the rites of sea passage, preferably in a storm-tossed boat, function as a principle of natural selection ensuring that only the fittest, those with salt in their blood and iron in their soul, survive, and as true islanders, can be welcomed aboard HMS Britannia.

Strong, and other modernisers of the Island Story have always insisted, with Billy Bragg, that it is about space not race, nation not ethnicity, Britishness not Englishness.[32] Yet its most powerful post-colonial restatement insisted in precisely making the second set of connections, in focusing on the immigration issue. In his infamous 'Rivers of Blood speech' Enoch Powell, taking his cue from John of Gaunt, laments thus:

> At the heart of our vanished Empire, amidst the fragments of its demolished glory, the British are able to find, like one of her own oak trees, standing and growing, the sap still rising from her ancient roots to meet the spring, England herself, the continuity of her existence unbroken, when looser connections, which had linked her with distant continents and strange races, fell away.[33]

In his quest for a 'deep' Englishness, Powell recommissioned an old trope, but then goes on to revive an even older one when he invokes the Tiber, which as an ex-classics professor he well knew linked the founding myth of Rome with that of Albion.[34] For the river is named after Tiberius, King of Alba – the 'white city' founded by Trojan refugees before Romulus arrived on the scene to inaugurate its imperial destiny as Rome. The dockers who marched in his support may not have picked up on Powell's classical allusions or the connections he tried to make between the Roman and the British Empire. But they certainly recognised his appeal to cultural insularities that were already ensconced within their own isolated communities, perched on the cusp of economic redundancy as the Thames, their Alba/Tiber, surrendered its imperial role as an artery of world trade to other, foreign, ports of call. They had to wait until Mrs Thatcher's triumphalist restaging of the island story in the Falklands before this particular mix of fact and fable would become once more part of the national-popular discourse: Fortress Britannia, as the last bastion of England's no longer white but increasingly unpleasant land, summoned to make a final defiant gesture at ruling the waves so that its emblematic oak, now split at the root, could be replanted in a faraway island as a simulacrum of Liberty's Tree.

Order in variety: multiculturalism and England's midsummer dream

The central issue raised by this brief history is the extent to which it is possible to decolonise the island story without it unravelling altogether. Can any of its tropes be recommissioned to tell us about what we were, who we are and what we want to be, without also summoning up a whole history of colonial exploitation? Is there another, less toxic version of the septic isle waiting to be described?[35]

The conventional answer is that it is possible to show that from very early on Britain has been a multicultural society, and 'the English' a mongrel people; the sea, far from being a 'moat defensive', has carried traffic between these shores and the rest of the world from the time of the Romans onwards, and this fact has been registered in the interior of the country's narrative landscape.

The formulaic principle underlying this view of British history was first spelt out by Alexander Pope in the early eighteenth century, in his poem *Windsor Forest*:

Not chaos like together crush'd and bruised
But as the world, harmoniously confused
Where order in variety we see
And where, tho all things differ, all agree.[36]

Pope here enunciates the classical concept of concordia discors – the composition of discordant elements (earth, air, fire and water) into a harmonious universe – and restates it as an aesthetic principle that should (and indeed did) govern English pastoral poetry and landscape painting.[37]

The Augustan poets and painters emphasised order, in both nature and society, over variety. For them art should reflect these pre-established harmonies. The advocates of the picturesque and the sublime introduced the principle of variety – or asymmetry – to unsettle what was otherwise for them a too predictable and even monotonous picture of an ordered world.[38] One way of doing this was to compose the picture around a striking topographical feature: a ruined castle, a fallen oak, a waterfall or river, some human figures at work or play. For this purpose it was necessary to find a commanding view over the countryside, a prospect, as it was called, from which vantage point the pictorial space could be so organised. Into Wordsworth's self enclosed valley of Arcadian bliss – 'all blinded holiness of earth and sky, made for itself, and happy in itself/perfect contentment, unity entire' – certain contrastive features were thus allowed to intrude, thereby adding a new and more dynamic element to the landscaping of Englishness. The 'land no land may touch' now had to recognise that it could not insulate itself from the differences that were in play within it. Indeed it was this very principle of variety that constituted its unique character, its peculiar genius for order. It offered a more inclusive model of insularity.

A good example of how this programme was applied in artistic practice comes from the work of William Daniell, who, in 1823, embarked on the first, and until recently most comprehensive, land-based visual essay in circumnavigating Britain's coastline (^166/7). Daniell had a strong instinct for the coastal sublime. He concentrated on depicting dramatic scenes: the rugged coast, ruined castles standing silhouetted on jagged cliffs, storms lashing against harbour walls. But he is careful to interpose these with scenes of calm:

open armed bays, neat little harbours and bustling quaysides. He is quite explicit about the overall design of the work:

With regard to the selection and arrangement of works ... they will be so disposed as to relieve each other by variety and contrast without too rigid an adherence to the actual order in which the views were taken.[39]

Using this rule of thumb, in which the principle of variety imposes its own order on the peripatetics of the text, he searches for prospects that sum up for him the essentially romantic nature of the island home. The same aesthetic governs the depiction of both sea and landscape. Under this protocol, the littoral and the pastoral dimensions of Englishness, its coastal sublime and rural picturesque, cohere into a single all-embracing vision.[40]

Translated from the field of aesthetics to that of governance, the implications of the principle become clear. It is the English ruling class who will provide the order, the commanding view which organises and composes the political and social scene of nationhood, while their organic intellectuals furnish the symbolic frame that universalises its own rules of representation; meanwhile it is the Others, the People, of whatever description, who will furnish the variety, the diversity, the peculiarities that provide the dramatic element of contrast within it. This is the essential formula of English multiculturalism and its model of insular inclusivity, an intelligible line of first tolerance, then celebration, of difference. Yet for all that this 'genius' for recognising cultures other than its own was solidly rooted in English soil, the need to sustain a social order based on an organic sense of nationhood, where 'tho all differ, all agree', increasingly comes up against the demand for a space of popular representation that opens it up to the not always harmonious confusion of the world, where cultures can become incommensurable and chaos reign.[41]

Multiculturalism as a national-popular project has always pivoted on the tension between these two poles of order and variety, but the contradiction came to a head in the second half of the twentieth century, when the growth of Celtic nationalisms and the proliferation of diasporic communities, each with its own distinct local/global ethnoscape, meant that 'little England' could no longer exert a hegemonic influence over the island story. Order in variety was translated into a plea for unity in diversity, to preserve the territorial integrity of the British nation state against all the centrifugal forces ranged against it.[42] Now the appeal to the facts of a shared physical geography was to an explicitly de-racialised space, and one in which the English could no longer stake a proprietorial claim to be the 'best' of British, even if they secretly still cherished the ambition to be first amongst equals.

Notions of culture as a principle of order and variety have always existed in some kind of tension, and in his *Story of Britain* (1996) Sir Roy Strong offered an ingenious explanation for this fact. We read that the British 'cherish their island as a domain separate and inviolate from the rest of the world', but that at the same time this defended and crowded space can become claustrophobic, and impel the Brits to explore (and, though he does not so much as mention the word, conquer) worlds other than their own.[43] But whether landlubbers and home boys, or seafarers and adventurers, they share, according to him, certain common characteristics: innate conservatism, pragmatism, an ability to compromise, a respect for differences and the ability to engage in revolutionary voyages of the mind.

Strong is, of course, an arch conservative, for whom cultural order is always more important than variety. For liberals the priority is reversed. But what happens within this framework if variety is allowed to develop unchecked, and diversity becomes regarded as a principle of *dis*order? In the 1930s Edward Upward wrote a short story 'The Railway Accident', in which he describes the journey taken by some typical well bred English types to the country for a weekend house party. It begins in familiar enough territory but then goes increasingly off the rails. The Mortmere Express is full of soldiers whose boisterous behaviour begins to get out of hand, as they break down the bulkhead separating the first and third class compartments. As the journey and the story progresses, it becomes clear that the 'Mortmere Express' is a figment of the narrator's imagination and is following in the tracks of a similar train that ran into a collapsed tunnel several years previously, killing everyone on board. No-one is in a position to avert a repetition of the disaster, but at the last minute the narrator and his companion manage to jump clear. They find their way to Mortmere Manor, where an elaborate game of hide and seek is taking place as the centre piece of the weekend party. The game also begins to go off the rails, bringing to the surface the sadism underlying its civilities. It too ends in an act of violence that no one can avert. Here is the narrator's description of the garden in which the game is played out:

> The arum colocasia, lupines, lentils, the pomegranate sycamore, date palms, yew, beech and privet, fenugreek, meloukhia, carob tree, mimosa habbas, lemon verbena, nasturtium, rose and lily. Snakes hung from the elm branches, pigeons rose from the black curtains of leaves, startled by the engine of a car. Across the waters of the sun-white marshes, alligator fishermen punted their raft. Blue-tiled houses which had grown like bushes out of the ground ... Odours of chimes of croquet hoops, tango of views of choirboys through the rustling privet.[44]

There is nothing harmonious about this confusion. It is a picture of chaos, crushed and bruised. The traditionally picturesque English garden, with its carefully arranged interplay of exotic varieties designed to set off by contrast the native blooms, has given way to another, wilder, landscape, where strange weeds and hybrids flourish, date palms and carob trees mingle with yews and beech, and croquet lawns run down to alligator swamps. Even the image of organic community takes on a menacing aspect: blue-tiled houses grow like bushes out of the ground. Variety has become the voice of anarchy. The incommensurable rules OK. English multiculturalism has gone mad.

Yet there is another possible version of the island story, in which signs that not everything in the garden is lovely might be not only recognised, but taken as the focal point for re-imagining the nation ...

The greening of the island story

For an Olympics which was as keen to stress its environmental credentials as its multicultural ones, the greening of Britain's island story which has taken place over the last decade offered an obvious opportunity to portray the country as isle of natural wonders, albeit one whose copy book is beset by 'inky blots' in the form of manifold polluting agents. The popular success of the BBC TV series *Coast*, where each programme takes a stretch of the coastline and explores its geo-history, indicates that this is a re-visioning of the nation's boundaries whose time has come.

Previous coasting expeditions had been on a mission to discover the essential islishness of the Anglo-British character, or to make a statement about the moral and social condition of the nation and what united or disunited its population; the coastal topography is here merely used as a visual stimulus for these peripatetic speculations.[45] In contrast *Coast* is content to let the seaboard itself do most of the talking. The dominant discourse of the series is environmentalist: geologists, archaeologists and naturalists get most of the air time, and only once the ecology has been firmly established are the local historians allowed on site to add their mite of human interest. The programme gives a gloss of circumstantial evidence to the proposition that we are an old country which has continually updated itself and consequently been long at ease with the differences that new populations and cultures have brought to our shores – differences which are less than visible precisely because they have blended so harmoniously into the overall lie of land and seascape.

In presenter Nick Crane's book, *Coast: Our Island Story*, based on the series, the same perspectives are adopted.[46] His opening chapter, entitled provocatively enough 'Precious stones, set in a silver sea', is about the geophysics of coastal formation rather than Gloriana's body. His approach opens up physical geography to deeper inspection, but this mole's eye view of history induces a form of selective blindness when it comes to considering some of its less pleasant aspects. Thus for example he discusses Bristol's international role as a port, including its involvement in piracy and smuggling, but without once mentioning its connections with the slave trade.

At first sight, this perspective seems to remove from the picture almost everything that once made the island story a source of popular imperial pageant. But, on closer inspection, the effect is to literally *naturalise* its narrative features, so they become taken for granted elements in the common sense of what it means to be British today. Take for instance Crane's treatment of the white cliffs of Dover. Having established their geology and noted the fact that the reflective properties of chalk make them a boon to sailors in search of a landmark to steer by, he discusses their symbolic role. He quotes Mathew Arnold's description of them 'glimmering and vast, out in the tranquil bay', but wonders why the cliffs should have become a national trademark with an importance beyond their physical scale. He writes: 'this blinding curtain of chalk veils us from outsiders, but tells us who we are. Dover's white cliffs are where we advance closest to the continent and where we mark our perimeter. They are our first and last sight of home'. The elision between

England and the (British) nation, which is, of course, a trademark of the traditional island story, is here accomplished by the iterative use of the complicit 'we' and 'us', while behind the mixed metaphor of the veil/mirror, the history of the cliffs as a natural symbol of island race-ism entirely disappears, leaving behind only their chalkiness as the material trace of their problematic role. So while Dover itself is described as 'a portal to England' and a 'preface to foreign adventure', its historical role in shaping the *cultural* geography of Anglo-Britishness remains quite obscure.[47] *Coast* is more interested in describing strategies for interacting with (while conserving) the environment than in questioning its modes of depiction.

Safely decontextualised, the coast can then be freely celebrated as an adventure playground – somewhere to walk, climb, swim, surf, dive, fish, hang-glide, sail, go camping, play golf and generally commune with Nature. *Coast* is enthusiastic about the Great Outdoors, and also has a taste for the sublime and the picturesque. Crane's book imposes a more strictly ecological order on the variety it describes, grouping cliffs or bays together, for instance – though he too is awed by Fingal's cave and the tidal power of the Severn bore.

Crane is excited by the fact that the British are heading for the coast in unprecedented numbers, and, in his words, 'have rediscovered the fact that they are islanders' – without any of the ideological baggage that used to accompany the term. In his introduction to the book he argues that the coast plays an important role in forging our identity, but this has 'less to do with nationality than being islanders'. Islishness, once uncoupled from Anglo-Britishness, thus becomes a metaphysical principle of organic community linked to the sea, the source and site of a new environmental populism.

Coast certainly has its heroes and villains. On one side are the small band of conservationists who have ensured that large areas of Britain's coastline are protected habitats for wildlife as well as providing public amenity. The villains of the piece are all those who are despoiling the coastal commons: the property developers who want to build on greenfield sites, the farmers who are destroying wetland ecologies with their pesticides, and the trawlers which have over-fished the coastal waters to the point where stocks are near extinction. At this point some of the old tropes again re-surface, offering us a 'paysage moralisé' of sin and redemption, in which greedy opportunism as represented by smugglers, wreckers and polluters is counterposed to the selfless courage and devotion to duty exemplified by life-boat crews, lighthouse keepers and eco-warriors. Even the sceptre'd isle makes a guest appearance in the image struck of a glittering necklace of forts, ports and resorts strung around the silver sea. And in the background is the long shadow of industrialism, the unacceptable face of capitalism, which capitalism itself has now transcended.

There is, however, more than one way to green an island. In his book *The Luminous Coast*, Jules Pretty writes back a whole natural and cultural history occluded by the eco-picturesque; in his journey on foot he unearths and connects the hidden traces of industry and empire, life and labour, that have silently shaped the contemporary littoral; he makes the process of erosion stand for the loss not just of land but of liberties associated with its maritime edge.[48] And there is another possible metaphor, equally historically grounded and even more organic in its references: silt. Graham Swift, or rather the historian narrator in his novel *Waterland*, describes its vector of meaning thus:

> Silt, a word which when you utter it, letting it slip thinly between your teeth, invokes a slow, sly, insinuating agency. Silt, which shapes and undermines continents; which demolishes as it builds, which is simultaneous accretion and erosion, neither progress or decay. What silt began, man continued. Drainage. Land reclamation. So forget your revolutions, your turning points, your grand metamorphoses of history. Consider instead the slow arduous process, the interminable and ambiguous process of human siltation ... repeatedly, never endingly retrieving what is lost. A dogged and vigilant business. A dull yet valuable business. A hard inglorious business. But you shouldn't go mistaking the reclamation of land for the building of empires.[49]

Here is a post-imperial island story being deliberately built on shifting ground, albeit one still rooted in familiar soil – the fenlands that offered a legendary refuge to Hereward as leader of popular resistance to the Norman yoke. But what happens when the slow tug of tides reshaping land turns into the threat of an engulfing flood, as global warming takes hold, sea levels rise and coastal defences are overwhelmed? Siltation is then no longer as available as a reassuring evolutionary metaphor linking our past, present and future.

One solution is to move the story offshore, into ever more miniaturised and surrogate versions of itself. An advert for a well-known brand of rum asks rhetorically 'Who needs an island when you've got Malibu?'. Perhaps a smarter move is to de-materialise the island altogether so that it occupies a purely virtual space. Britannia then no longer has to rule the waves, because the waves which carry the most vital cultural traffic across this Atlantic archipelago no longer break on any shore.[50] In the global information economy, the virtual island is merely a set of attractors for conveyancing news to people who make use of it tactically as a platform that has no claim on who, or indeed where, they are.

In the twenty-first century, islands have stayed in business as places where people go to imagine they can escape from the worst excesses of modernity. Their attraction has been strongest for those, like the Little Englanders, who have never aspired to be modern, not only because they advance into the future with faces turned resolutely towards the past, but because, living in an old country, they have never fully grasped the brutal historical fact that the present belongs most to those who live in it.[51] Yet islands not only pander to the regressive, solipsistic desire to be home and alone without the burden of having to recognise or represent the Other; they also answer to the need for a less encumbered form of human solidarity, in which no man or woman is an island and everyone on it is from somewhere else. It is this 'heterotopic' function that makes the island such a powerful device for articulating the

Olympic ideal and its imagined community of sporting nations.[52] It is also what has finally transformed it into a major site of investment for multicultural capitalism.

Globalisation, contrary to what many of its critics suppose, is not only a homogenising force. It also articulates differential, even disjunctive, moments of history and culture into a consensual, commodified nexus of 'ethnicities'. Ethnicity becomes a source of social and cultural capital for minorities and hybridity becomes *à la mode* for the affluent middle class at precisely the point when it is pressed into service to sustain the penetration of market relations into every nook and cranny of economic life. Once capitalism moves on from one-size-fits-all methods of mass production and consumption, it needs to operate through the diversification of brands. One way to do this is to 'ethnicise' commodities by associating them with an 'authentic' mode of local fabrication and a community of labour supposedly insulated from the globalisation effect: Shetland pullovers knitted by commuting crofters, genuine Irish malt whisky which tastes of its native heath courtesy of EU subsidies, Welsh lace knitted by the wives of ex-miners amidst the dreaming spires of long abandoned pits – these are the heraldic commodities of the contemporary consumerfest. Capitalism may be indifferent as to the colour of the hands it sets to work provided they are industrious, but it needs to create niche markets around difference. It is still the Others who provide the variety and add the value that sells the goods.

The green movement itself is, of course, strongly anti-globalisation, but it is much keener on small-is-beautiful capitalism. It has given a big consumer boost to organic farming, and farmers' markets, herbalism and naturopathy, ethnic arts and crafts; it has also spawned a new genre of eco-literature, which has taken a leaf out of the books written by the radical urban pedestrians, and by combining the methods of natural and cultural history unearthed the hidden narratives of this country's rivers and mountains, woodlands and off-the-beaten tracks.[53] The vision of Britain's landscape which emerges from these various literary endeavours often echoes Alexander Pope's formula for order in variety, translated into the contemporary discourse of bio-diversity. Implicitly, and sometimes explicitly, the quest is for a deep England, liberated from the burden of having to represent 'race' or Empire, rooted in an aesthetic appreciation of Nature, and a culture that celebrates this elemental identity. But such a proposition can be difficult to sustain when this insular ecology is perceived to be under threat.

In the Stour Valley, in the heart of Constable Country, where the picturesque is something of a cottage industry, they have established a local forum on 'invasive, non-native plant species'. From the newsletter we learn that such species, including Himalayan Balsam, Japanese Knotweed, the Hottentot Fig, Pygmy weed and the killer Brazilian Giant Rhubarb are 'squeezing out our native British plants and unbalancing the natural biodiversity of the river'. These unwelcome foreign immigrants, having evaded border controls at the ports of Harwich and Felixstowe, have entered the countryside illegally and are now busily propagating to the point where they are driving our home-grown dandelions, daisies and buttercups from the land. Those few non-native plants which manage to establish an ecological niche for themselves can be 'naturalised', and become honest citizens in our gardens. But the rest are now regarded as a threat to British horticulture, second only to global warming. The threat may be real enough but it is what its imagination conjures up for some people that is the problem. As Richard Mabey, the ethno-botanist, has shown us, the classification of weeds, those plants out of place, draws on taxonomies which draw the line between Nature and Culture and create a metaphorical language for describing wilderness in such a way as to ascribe alien status to all those who inhabit it.[54] Weeds represent variety in *dis*order and as such they can be recruited to symbolise all those 'foreign' elements in society or the environment that cannot be assimilated under the protocols of 'concordia discors'.

It is in the unregulated borderlands between country and city that these alien species flourish most extravagantly. These edgelands have increasingly replaced the rationally recreationalised coastline as the locus of the liminal; it is where those who are ensconced in the wilder reaches of Englishness, who still pursue the ancient arts and crafts of pastoral, or who want to reclaim the commons and practise rural self sufficiency, cohabit with social outcasts whose lives and livelihoods have been rendered eccentric by the onward march of hyper-modernity. Here Tory backwoodsmen and New Age Travellers can find common cause in campaigning against factory farming or GM crops. It is here too that Johnny 'Rooster' Byron, the anti-hero of Jezz Butterworth's recent remake of Blake's Jerusalem, hangs out with his band of fellow wild-wooders, creating an updated version of 'Merrie England' that includes plenty of wassailing and rough music, mischief and mayhem. He may be a Falstaff without his Prince, but he is not a rebel without a Cause as he battles to defend the right of the freeborn Englishman not to pay taxes while consuming large amounts of real ale.

The paradox of the Isle of Wonders was that it invoked the spirit of Blake and challenged any narrow chauvinistic interpretation of Britain's history. Yet it paraded its riot of references in such a way as to endorse the principle of insular inclusivity that underwrites the basic plot of the island story. So the question arises: to what extent was this double take licensed by *The Tempest*? How far were Shakespeare's poetics subverted in the process of their Olympification?

Calibanalities: the comic and the tragic in *The Tempest*

In principle *The Tempest* theme introduces a dimension of meaning that goes beyond the artifice of kitsch and what I have called 'High' Culture (at least in so far as it is understood as a tragi-comedy rather than a romance).[55] In Harold Bloom's interpretation, the play is about how the power of the imagination (as exemplified by Ariel) is corrupted by the imagination of power (Prospero's seductive magic).[56] As such it would seem to have something very pertinent to say about what has happened to the Olympic Dream. Still, the play remains a tricky point of reference, open to multiple interpretations. Caliban may have become a hero of post-colonial literature, but in his fury and abjection he cuts a tragic as well as comic figure, cursing the language that Prospero taught him and reducing it to guttural cries and groans. Ariel, who is adept in the subversive art of mimicry, is perhaps a better guide to the delicate manoeuvres through which colonial subjects seek to extricate themselves from their cultural predicament, although he hardly represents a realistic strategy of political liberation.[57]

W.H. Auden, in *The Sea and the Mirror*, his long poetic commentary on the play, emphasises the complementarity of Caliban and Ariel, each occupying a different element, their destinies so intertwined that in death they will become 'one evaporating sigh'. The poem was written in 1944, after Auden had emigrated to the USA, leaving behind an embattled island, fighting to keep its sea supply lanes open and survive the German blockade. It is not surprising, then, that he uses Shakespeare's enchanted isle to nostalgically evoke one of his own, a little England which furnished the memoryscape of his childhood, at once ancient and modern, mythical and real. In a prose soliloquy addressed to the audience he has Caliban say:

Carry me back, Master, to the cathedral town where the canons run through the water meadows with butterfly nets ... an old horse tramway winds away westward through suave foothills crowned with stone circles ... to the north, beyond a forest inhabited by charcoal burners, one can see the Devil's Bedposts quite distinctly, to the east the museum where for sixpence one can touch the ivory chessmen.[58]

In most of the poem Auden is concerned to explore what he sees as Shakespeare's Manichaean vision, and how the play struggles to reconcile its oppositions in a final redemptive statement of Shakespeare's art; he traces these binaries to the influence of Christian theology, although perhaps he might have done better to look closer to home, in what we have discerned to be the split representation of our island story.

The poet who wrote that 'we must love one another or die' would probably have been amazed and delighted by Derek Jarman's 'queer' version of *The Tempest*, set in a crumbling gothic mansion on the bleak and windswept Northumbrian coast. Despite moments when it becomes a gay gothic romp – one critic described it as 'Carry on Camping meets Frankenstein' – the film is a serious attempt to explore the play's imaginative hinterland of desire and power, in cinematic rather than theatrical terms. The Hegelian master/slave relationship and triangular interplay of Prospero, Caliban and Ariel becomes an allegory of homo-erotic, rather than colonial desire, with the suggestion that both Caliban and Ariel are split off and repressed aspects of Prospero's own personality – his Jungian 'shadows'. The gothic setting is emphasised by the use of a blue filter, and adds an appropriately sinister dimension to Prospero's role as necromancer, mad scientist and scholar recluse.

In putting together the 'Isle of Wonders', Boyle's main point of aesthetic reference was undoubtedly cinematic, and Philip Greenaway's *Prospero's Books*, with its glossy hi-tech look, lavish crowd scenes and kaleidoscope of digital images, was a key influence. The central conceit of Greenaway's film is that Prospero is not only the main character of the play but its author and producer: all the other characters are his creation and he gives each his own voice, until the very end when Ariel asserts his separate identity. From the isolation of his cell this Prospero tries to control the world through books and the knowledge they contain. It is only when he comes to realise that reason, the empire of the mind, left to its own devices engenders monsters, that he can discover the true power of the imagination to create other possible worlds *without* controlling them, and so welcome Caliban as his true heir. This ending can perhaps be regarded as the starting point for Boyle's Isle of Wonders.

In all these interpretations Prospero remains the central figure around which the drama revolves. But in Robert Browning's long poem *Caliban upon Setebos* (1864) the roles are reversed.[59] Caliban 'plays at being Prospero in a way', not only through 'letting the rank tongue blossom into speech', but through mixing 'his mirth with make believe'. Through the device of a third-person soliloquy, Caliban engages in philosophical speculation about the role of religion and science as alternative explanations of creation, the first associated with a God (Setebos) who is ill at ease with himself and the second with Darwin's theory of evolution. He refers to himself as 'Caliban, a bitter heart that bides its time and bites', but spends most of his time in the poem elaborating a natural theology and pondering the vicissitudes of the struggle for survival on his island. It is Caliban, not Prospero who is now the true philosopher of Nature.

Aimé Césaire's radical rewrite of *The Tempest* develops this theme, but replaces theology with politics, as he transforms Caliban into the voice of the wretched of the earth.[60] The play was written in the late 1960s at the height of the black power movement, and is inspired by Frantz Fanon's work, especially his critique of Octave Mannoni's analysis of the psychology of colonialism.[61] Césaire follows Fanon in tracing out the dialectics of power; just as lordship is the reverse of what it wants to be, so bondage will pass into the opposite of what it immediately is and become transformed into true and real independence. This reversal is inscribed in the genealogy of 'Calabanality' itself. The first syllable refers us to the original name of the Caribs (kallingo) *and* to the Greek word for beautiful (kallos). For black read beautiful. The second syllable represents the other side of the story and refers to the performative power of language to interdict through naming. The old English *bannan* means 'to summon, command, proclaim, forbid' and thence to curse and banish. So it refers us directly to Prospero, who has himself been banished, and spends much of the time on his island of exile summoning, commanding, proclaiming and generally cursing his lot.

And there is another sense of ban, as in 'ban, ban, caliban' which is linked to the notion of banality, and implicates the slave, not the master: it is a feudal term which signifies belonging to a manor, designating common things that serfs could own, like ovens or mills, or else the compulsory military service they had to undergo. So too Caliban having been dispossessed, has to perform menial service like a serf, but also, as a slave, is a mere chattel, a common thing belonging to his master. In the play Caliban spells out his rejection of his name to his master:

> Every time you call me it reminds me of the basic fact that you've stolen everything from me, even my identity ...

> Prospero, you are a great illusionist
> you know deception well ...
> you've ended up imposing on me
> An image of myself:
> underdeveloped, as you put it
> a sub-capable,
> that's how you make me see myself,
> and I hate this image. And it's false.

Instead he insists on being called (after Malcolm) X. Whereas Shakespeare's Prospero uses his linguistic power to silence, distort or ignore Caliban's attempts to devise speech, in Césaire's version Prospero becomes little more than a foil for Caliban's new-found command of political rhetoric. There is a lack of mediation between Prospero and Caliban, and this ultimately opens up a space, not just of dialogue but of mutual recognition. At the end of the play Prospero vows that it is his duty to stay on the island when the others depart; even though he has been reduced to automatic gestures, and is almost lost for words, he manages to summon up a last-ditch appeal: 'Well, Caliban, old fellow, it's just us two now here on the island ... only you and me. You and me. You-me. Me-you!'. But Caliban refuses the invitation to play at elisions. He wants and gets the last word, and that word is Uhuru – Freedom.

At the very end of the play, then, Césaire offers us the prospect that Prospero and Caliban might, after all, recognise they are tragic transformations of one another and their destinies are intertwined. From this standpoint *The Tempest*'s 'other scene' could well feature a black Prospero and white Caliban. But this 'trading places' is no sooner mooted than it is cancelled by the political imperative to reassert the absolute incommensurability of their essential roles. It is this issue of how, and how far, antagonistic realities can be brought together within the same frame of reference without reducing them to the lowest common denominator of kitsch, that forms the central problematic of the 2012 Olympic ceremonies – and which informs the detailed reading of them in the next chapter.

Damien Hirst flies the flag: 2012 closing ceremony

9. London Babylon 0, New Jerusalem 0: a Para-Olympic analysis of the 2012 ceremonies

Ceremonies are grist to a wide range of academic mills, some of which grind exceeding fine.[1] Thus, for example, it is possible to treat the Isle of Wonders and Enlightenment ceremonies as elaborate pieces of multimedia machinery, and take them apart to see how they work to produce their special effects; but a purely mechanistic approach to understanding what was going on is unlikely to capture the niceties of either form or content. Alternatively, these shows could be read as multi-layered texts, paying attention to the key tropes that configure their core meanings, and what remains implicit or unarticulated by these means; but, although we saw taxis and houses made out of newsprint, people walking around dressed as the *Guardian* or the *Mail*, and giant books that turned into water wheels or seagulls, the hypertextuality that was on display was part of a richer mediascape than could be grasped through the methods of literary criticism alone. The Isle of Wonders was also a feast for the semiologist, in weaving together so many different idioms, of dress, dance, music, drama, etc, to convey a multi-accentuated message that can still be decoded bit by bit; but no amount of decoding will tell us where this extravaganza was coming from in terms of how its chosen concepts or themes were selected and developed. Cue then, perhaps, for the deconstructivists to sharpen their pencils into philosophical axes and hack their way through the undergrowth of ideas to get at the axiomatic principles which underlie and subvert the best authorial intentions.

While all these approaches have something to offer, they miss the central point: we are dealing with *stories* and how they are put together; the ceremonial narrative is delivered through specific strategies of emplotment and topicalisation that determine what is chosen to be placed next to, or alongside what, in space and time within the unfolding performance; this placement establishes a certain logic of connotation that offers us a preferred reading of the imagery, highlighting certain chains of association and focusing the process of interpretation around certain key motifs. These principles of contexture not only govern the unfolding of the story line, linking sequences to one another, but within each sequence they organise the interplay of elements and idioms.

Aesthetic choices always have political implications and vice versa.[2] For example the decision to omit the jingoistic second verse of the national anthem – with its imprecation to the Almighty to 'scatter our enemies/And make them fall!/Confound their knavish tricks/Confuse their politics' – was undoubtedly taken on the grounds that it might not be quite in tune with the Olympic spirit; while having 'God Save the Queen' sung by a choir of deaf children was clearly designed to elicit kitsch's second tear.[3]

If politics is the art of the possible, art is the politics of the impossible: it is a utopian proposition about a world in which imagination has come to power. In 2012, however, the first axiom countermanded the second. What if Her Song had been sung – or rather croaked – by a choir made up of people who had had tracheotomies because they had developed throat cancer as a result of being exposed to a lethal gas leak at the Bhopal plant? Perhaps the red, white and blue spotlights might have homed in on the directors of Dow Chemicals sitting in the VIP seats, proud 2012 Official Worldwide Olympic Partners but also owners of Union Carbide, the company responsible for the Bhopal disaster. Such an intervention would, of course, have created a public uproar, and not just because of raising a taboo political subject in what was supposed to be a 'non-political' occasion, but on aesthetic grounds as well; for what could be uglier than these unmusical notes, so reminiscent of Caliban's own guttural cries – except perhaps the indifference of a multinational company to the plight of its local workforce, and a community whose lives have been wrecked by its criminal negligence of health and safety standards?

In Olympic ceremonies political and ideological conflicts become sublimated in aesthetic and ethical ones, which also means that they continue to exercise a subliminal effect, operating just below the threshold of creative and moral perception, foreclosing the options and the decisions taken. For all that, the poetics and the politics of the ceremonies cannot be simply read off from one another; they are mediated by an audio-visual ideology that acts as an independent variable. In the 2012 ceremonies it was chiefly through the medium of kitsch that their politics of inclusive insularity were articulated to an aesthetics of cultural mash-up. It was this order-in-variety rhetoric that persuaded us to suspend judgement or disbelief. We are dealing here with fables or fabula that take their own signs for wonders, and have been artfully contrived to sustain a beautifying lie about their ideological roots and routes. In the analysis that follows I have tried to reconstruct both.

The Enlightenment revisited

Let us begin the story with the opening ceremony of the Paralympics. Themed around the concept of 'Enlightenment', it ambitiously set out to make connections between the history of human rights and scientific reason, Tom Paine and Isaac Newton; it did this by associating the world of books, and their capacity to adventure into other possible worlds, here represented by

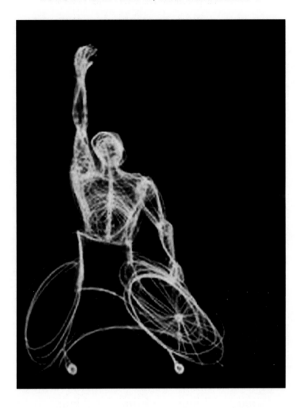

Reaching for the sky: an image from 'Enlightenment'

Prospero, with the world of the disabled and their capacity to transcend physical limitations, embodied by Miranda and all the paraplegics who took part in the performance as dancers, singers and acrobats. Gravity in all its diverse connotations provided the narrative thread linking the discoveries of Newton with those of Stephen Hawking, who now occupies his chair at Cambridge. Hawking was the star of the show, and definitely out-Prosperoed Sir Ian McKellan; for despite what the BBC commentator described as his 'entombment' by motor neurone disease, Hawking has explored the furthest reaches of the universe in search of a 'theory of everything' *without* the prosthetics of Power. The performers also defied gravity and in a double sense; they were shown triumphantly overcoming their often severe physical handicaps *and* the fear of flying, as they swam, ran, danced and tumbled through the air on wires. And then Ian Dury's 'Spastic Autisticus' rang out across the arena, with its defiant lyrics: 'Hello to you out there in Normal Land/You may not comprehend my tale or understand/As I crawl past your window give me lucky looks/You can be my body but you'll never read my books'.

So far so inspiring. But then the kitsch factor kicked in as the show became fixated on the big Apple. Performers dressed in green leaves, in the guise of wodewose or wildwooders, started tossing giant apples to one another as if they were medicine balls, while the spectators, possibly inspired by the old adage that an apple a day keeps the doctor away, or by childhood memories that this was the way to keep the glint in your mother's eye, bit into one as part of their five a day. This was all supposed to remind us that an apple helped Newton discover the laws of gravity, and that Adam's curiosity about the natural world, egged on by the temptress Eve, led him to eat the forbidden fruit of knowledge and get himself expelled from the Garden of Eden. At this point we might have expected to see some dramatic re-enactment of the collision of values that the programme hinted at – between traditional Christian theology with its hostility to science as implicated in the Fall and the eighteenth-century Enlightenment with its deification of reason and campaign against religion as bastion of primitive superstition. This could have been the cue for Browning's Caliban to pour scorn on Calvinistic theories of predestination and creationist mythology. Unfortunately Caliban was busy elsewhere, being played ventriloqually by Winston 'island race' Churchill (as impersonated by Timothy Spall). So everything in this Garden of England was sweetness and light – not to say apple blossom – as spectators and performers joined together to celebrate the legacy benefits of healthy exercise and diet – just what Lord Coe ordered.

The logic of connotation might have extended as far as Steve Job's corporate Apple image, but it stopped well short of making any link between the company logo and Alan Turing, father of the algorithm and computer science, who committed suicide by eating a poisoned one following his prosecution for homosexuality, an act which has subsequently turned him into a gay icon. There was simply no role for Turing, or his machine, either in the Paralympic context or in the Olympic opening ceremony alongside Tim Berners-Lee, even though the inventor of the Internet would not have been there without him. And while the bucolic applefest might have evoked Laurie Lee's *Cider with Rosie*, there was not even the faintest of musical nods in the direction of William Tell, Robin Hood's alter ego, whose campaign on behalf of oppressed peasants against a tyrannical feudal Lord put him in double jeopardy of decapitation, but who saved the day by his skill in marksmanship as he shot the apple on his son's head. Perhaps that story was just not home-grown enough, given that all the ingredients of the show had to be locally sourced.

These were not casual oversights, but symptomatic of the ceremony's whole strategy of emplotment. When Miranda famously exclaimed: 'How beauteous mankind is! O brave new world, That has such people in't!', she was 'innocently' putting Aldous Huxley's dystopian science fiction under erasure as a potential counter-narrative. In Huxley's *Brave New World*, society has been stratified along eugenic lines, with the bright, tall, good-looking alphas and gammas running the show, while the short, fat, ugly epsilons do the shit jobs. A regime of universal happiness reigns through the mass consumption of 'soma', a drug which induces a blissed-out state rather like 'ecstasy'; sport, too, with games such as Obstacle Golf plays its opiate part. In Huxley's dystopia, blind faith in science and technology has replaced individual conscience, while the artificial paradise of 'High' Culture has become institutionalised in and by a state ideological apparatus. In some respects this anticipates the post-modern critique of enlightenment values; *his* brave new world shows science and technology proceeding by its bad side.

In contrast to all this, the Enlightenment ceremony determinedly ignored the dark side of the moon. Its theme may have been gnoseological, but its narrative was mytho-poeic. Its Prospero was scientist as showman, magus and story-teller – not the worrier after truth. Miranda was enjoined to be curious, and invited to marvel at the wonders of science and its ability to render the world strange but not to adopt the scientific attitude of scepticism towards all knowledge claims, including its own. But what kind of Enlightenment project is it that enables wonder and disables critical faculties? There is a word for it: kitsch science.

Adorno, whose critique of kitsch and mass culture was influenced by Huxley's novel, even though he denounced it as one-sided, was the first to explore the intricate connection between the worship of instrumental rationality and the promotion of regimes of happiness intolerant towards the sorrow and distress that form an integral part of the human condition. He thought that such fugues were a powerful tendency in contemporary culture but not inevitable: 'however surely the unselfconscious concept of total enlightenment may move towards its opposite – irrationality – it is nevertheless impossible to deduce from the concept itself whether this will occur and if so, whether it will stop there'.[4]

Adorno's scepticism about the emancipatory power of science and popular pleasure extended to their convergence in sport, whose benefits he saw as contradictory:

> Sport is ambiguous. On the one hand, it can have an anti-barbaric and anti-sadistic effect by means of *fair play*, promoting a spirit of chivalry, and consideration for the weak. On the other hand, in many of its varieties and practices it can promote aggression, brutality, and sadism, above all in people who do not expose themselves to the exertion and discipline required by sports but instead merely watch: that is, those who regularly shout from the sidelines.[5]

The most curious aspect of the Enlightenment show was the questions about science and sport and their inter-relation that it did *not* ask, the ambiguities it could not explore. Instead we were invited to shed tears of gratitude for the benefits both have bestowed on humankind, rather than worry about their frequent misappliance as a means of private profit or national aggrandisement. Even curiouser in a show devoted to celebrating the work of Stoke Mandeville hospital, and in particular the role of Ludwig Guttmann, the neurobiologist who pioneered the Paralympics, was the focus on physics as the paradigmatic science of nature. For, of course, it is biology that has been at the forefront of new developments in both medical and sports science. If there was no place in this version of the Enlightenment for Charles Darwin, or for Crick and Watson, if the Hadron Collider was preferred to the double helix as an audio-visual template for the final sequences, then it was perhaps because cosmology is far less controversial, far less of a bone of contention between religion and science, than the theory of evolution. Creationists are relatively relaxed about the Big Bang theory, because the origins of the universe can now be ascribed to a singular act of Divine Intervention, while the black hole is a neat enough description of Hell as a bottomless pit to satisfy even the most determined Christian eschatologist. Darwinian theory is quite another matter. Natural selection goes entirely against the grain of traditional Christian theology, with its providential view of human nature and the origin of species. The recent controversy over the teaching of creationism in schools, and the militant atheism preached by Richard Dawkins and other Darwinists poses a stark choice: either evolution is the result of intelligent and divine design or else God, if she exists, is an almost blind matchmaker – who at the very least needs to get some NHS glasses if she is to supervise the reproduction of species. Of course Darwinism has not always been a good advertisement for scientific enlightenment. It has some skeletons in its own cupboard, notably the dalliance with eugenics, and with theories of inherited intelligence that rationalised racial inequalities. Today, however, the nature versus nurture debate has moved on, and there is a new kind of biopolitics centred around genetic engineering. Although no-one has yet discovered an Olympic gene, there are some troubling ethical issues around the use of new reproduction technologies and the attempt to create athletic supermen.[6]

All of this adds up to making the discourse of biology problematic in a way that physics is not. Perhaps understandably, then, the Enlightenment show shied away from exploring a subject area where such vexed questions would have been difficult to avoid. It was on the side of the angels, the paraplegic cosmonauts who performed their spectacular aerial ballets free from the weighty questions posed by philosophers of science. Seemingly it was enough for the ceremony to lighten the burden of public misapprehension placed on their shoulders, without picking up the Olympic torch to shine light on its own dark places. Yet even so the issues could not be entirely avoided. The basic message was the sky's the limit or as, Stephen Hawking put it 'there should be no boundaries to human endeavour'. What was being preached, and actively promoted in the branding of the Paralympics, was a super-humanism couched in the aspirational rhetoric of 'High' culture (^182). Yet it is precisely this hubristic impulse that has driven athletes to experiment with performance-enhancing drugs, in order to push themselves beyond the limits of physical endurance in the bid to strike gold.[7]

In this context the language of aspirationalism and the theme of triumph over adversity is indeed double-edged. It is one thing for Miranda to fly up into the night sky to pierce an invisible glass ceiling with her NHS walking stick, quite another to conjure up the figure of Icarus as a role model for disabled athletes. The athletes were enjoined to 'lift the cloud of limitations', but in fact such is the collapse in public expectations that the ambition to get closer to the sun is today more likely to be associated with an increased risk of skin cancer than with any Olympian enterprise.

Meanwhile politics proceeded subliminally and by indirection. When a 17 year old Royal Commando whose legs were blown away by a Taliban bomb in Afghanistan zip-wired from the Orbital tower carrying the paralympic torch into the stadium, we were not only invited to contemplate the universal human tragedy of war, but to shed a second tear at how moved we felt at the spectacle of a young life shattered and rebuilt. What remained unthought, unfelt, unsaid, in this poignant moment was any sense that we were witnessing the aftermath of a catastrophe that was entirely avoidable (as was the huge terrorist tax on this Olympics due to the cost of the security measures required after 7/7). Of course to raise such questions about foreign policy, military adventures and their domestic consequences appears to be introducing an external 'politics' into a sporting occasion designed to transcend them; in fact this expulsion of the Political with a capital P from Olympic discourse only leads to its return by the back door. From the opening choreography, which provided a dazzling visual umbrella under which a myriad of plots could be hatched, to the radical solipsism of the closing anthem, with its rousing hymn to identity politics 'I am what I am', this hiding of the darker side of Reason in the light it sheds on the world ran like an invisible thread through the proceedings. This indeed was the Enlightenment without its dialectic. As such it offered us a spectacular pendant to Adorno's concern that intellectuals might simply recoil in shock from the Frankenstein's monsters that their own powers of reason had created, and either retreat, like Aldous Huxley, into a defeatist, dystopian vision of the future or else construct a romanticised/sanitised view of past and present. The Isle of Wonders showed us what happens when the second option is pursued.

Pandaemonium

There were three main points of reference in Danny Boyle's conception of the host nation story: *The Tempest*, or rather the Prospero-Caliban dialogue about whose version of the island story is to prevail; Blake's Manichaean vision of British history as a struggle between the forces of darkness, represented by London Babylon and the forces of light engaged in building the

Forging the Olympics: a scene from Pandaemonium

New Jerusalem; and finally, and most importantly, Humphrey Jennings's *Pandaemonium*, which gave its title to one of the key sequences.

Jennings's book provides an imaginative history of the industrial revolution told through the testimony of scientists, artists, rich men, poor men and a great throng of miscellaneous witnesses. It is significant for both its method and its perspective on British history. The book is what Ezra Pound called an 'active anthology'; it establishes a complex network of internal cross-references between its chosen passages, which the author referred to as 'knots in the great net of tangled time and space', in a way that takes an original line of thought for a walk across the great debate initiated by Marx on the origins of capitalism in British culture and society. The book starts with Milton's description of the 'palace of devils' in *Paradise Lost* and traces the development of this image of Satanic power through dozens of transformations.

Jennings was a poet who was involved in organising the first exhibition of surrealist art in Britain in the 1930s and wrote for surrealist magazines. He was also a documentary film maker influenced by Eisenstein's theory of montage. Both influences show in the way he juxtaposes the quotations – which he referred to as 'images' – to illustrate strange paradoxes or conflicting points of view, and also, sometimes, to defamiliarise or problematise them through exploring what he called their 'coincidences'. In that respect *Pandaemonium* is quite close to the method adopted by Walter Benjamin in his Arcades project: 'the tearing of fragments out of their context and arranging them afresh in *such a way as they illustrate one another and develop new connections*' (my emphasis). It also has something in common with the original sense of the musical mash-up – combining elements from two songs in order to generate a third. Was this the method in what many commentators saw as the madness or the muddle of the Isle of Wonders?

Unfortunately, for most of the time, Boyle's modus operandi was closer to the business model of a mash-up – bringing together information from widely disparate sources around a common theme and linking them in a purely opportunistic or instrumental way. For example there was the chaotic synchronicity of his 'people's procession', which had Sergeant Pepper's Lonely Hearts Club band side by side with the Jarrow marchers, the suffragettes, the Grimethorpe Colliery brass band, the Nostalgia Steel band, Chelsea Pensioners, Pearly Kings and Carnival Queens. They might all qualify as signifiers of national-popular culture, but here they were jumbled together in a way that wrenched them out of their political contexts while doing nothing to illustrate their possible connectivity in terms of any wider narrative or argument about the evolution of the democratic process.

There is an important distinction to be made here between collage and montage. Collage is about blending together a patchwork of elements to create an impression of 'harmonious confusion'.[8] Its procedural logic is syncretic. In contrast the method of montage is about representing 'chaos crushed and bruised' through dramatic and often surreal juxtapositions. It is dialectical in its procedures. Max Ernst once described it as 'the exploitation of a chance meeting on a non-suitable plane of two mutually distant realities'. The aim is to produce a disturbing or thought-provoking sense of incongruity that puts in question taken-for-granted assumptions and common-sense definitions.[9]

We can illustrate this distinction by comparing the work of two contemporary artists, Mark Titchener and Peter Kennard, who both draw on elements of national-popular culture but to very different purpose and effect. Titchener's work is inspired by William Burroughs's cut-up technique. He uses fragments of text from a variety of sources, including political manifestos, philosophy, advertising and pop song lyrics, and weaves them into a visual tapestry made up of equally diverse material – heavy metal album sleeves, trade union banners and evangelical pamphlets, all of which suggest for him the popular quest for some kind of utopia (^184). Many of his recent works take the form of banners featuring paradoxical injunctions: 'Be angry but don't stop breathing' or 'You can change your life if you want to'. In a piece entitled *And, waiting, we plunged into dreams* (2012), designed as a comment on the Olympics, he merges William Morris wallpaper designs with contemporary wall hangings sold by ASDA, and overlays this rich visual mix with the words I WANT A BETTER WORLD I WANT A BETTER ME, in a large embossed typeface. This collapsing of the distance between fine art and consumer culture is a well-known Britpop strategy, of course. It appears to be part of a democratising impulse to overthrow class-bound hierarchies of taste, but by reducing disparate cultural practices to a common denominator it serves to smooth away their ideological dissonances. The statement of visual equivalence between handicraft and mass production, socialist utopianism and the Samuel Smiles school of self improvement collapses the critical space in which the tension or contradiction between them could be represented. The two value systems are simply segued together into a single seamless web of associations to an aspirational concept of utopia, as if they were nothing more than equivalent purchases in the market place of ideas. The mash up is free market economics applied to the sphere of cultural representation, it is neoliberalism in symbolic action.

In contrast Peter Kennard's photo-montage *Haywain with Cruise Missiles* (^185), in which he juxtaposes the idyllic pastoral scene of Constable country with the weapons of mass destruction that are used to defend it, produces a shock effect which disrupts the taken-for-granted relationship between the dominant iconography of Englishness and the geo-politics through which the 'island nation' pursues its post-imperial role. The image opens a space in which the dialectic between the work of art as a form of enchantment and its exploitation as a medium of mystification can be properly explored.

The Olympic ceremonies followed the Titchener not the Kennard method. For example 'The Symphony of British Music' featured a medley of famous quotes from Shakespeare, Samuel Johnson, Milton, Blake, Donne, etc, in the form of eye-catching headlines embedded in newspapers wrapped around cars, reproduced as costumes and imprinted on walkways. It was an image of a textually saturated culture, but one in which 'Now is the Winter of our Discontent', 'To be or not be' and 'if love is a thing, it is infinite' jostles alongside 'Gotcha' and 'We are ready' in vying for attention; all are reduced to the same level of banality as a *Sun* front page. The visual effect may have been a homage to punk typography, and even been intended to indicate a process of 'levelling up' rather than dumbing down, but since the quotations were not juxtaposed to any purpose, the effect was not so much an intellectual puzzle or a tease, as a no-brainer.

So too in the Isle of Wonders ceremony. Monarchy and Anarchy, Capital and Labour, Henley regatta and the Yellow Submarine, all were part of the same rich pick'n'mix of Britishness, in which 'tho all differ, all agree'. Boyle's approach to order in variety was vividly illustrated in a short 'four nations' sequence, which started with a choir of children in England singing Jerusalem, and then segued into other national-popular anthems sung by children's choirs from Wales (Men of Harlech), Scotland (Flower of Scotland) and two-tone Ireland (Danny Boy *and* the Londonderry Air); meanwhile we watched their rugby teams scoring tries against England, these contributions being capped and rounded off by returning to 'Jerusalem'. So even though the English rugby anthem 'Swing Low, Sweet Chariot' never got play time, and the team lost at rugby, the famous theme tune of England's green and pleasant land still won the day in providing the integrating framework of the musical medley. If this was a brave attempt at celebrating a four nations version of the island story, the Celts still remained part of the fringe festival, not the main event.

The versatility of Pope's formula was not restricted to the home nations. In the closing ceremony order in variety went global, as the athletes of the world, their national squads all happily jumbled up together, were corralled into different segments of Damien Hirst's 3D Union Jack, which provided a red white and blue armature for their various assembly points. There is more than one way to nationalise an Olympics. The principle could also be reversed. 'Variety in order' is an accurate enough description of the multicultural mash-up of music that composed the Isle of Wonders soundscape, with its incessant drumming and techno-trance syncopation from Underworld. The metachronal rhythms of the Mexican wave found their perfect correlate in the hypnogogic waves of sound and light that washed around the arena, mesmerising the spectators – who were, indeed, for an instant, living the Olympic dream.

The ceremonies team may not have followed the Jennings/Kennard method of composition but Boyle's remake of *Pandaemonium* faithfully followed the original in its reading of British history. Jennings, like Ruskin, Morris and the Guild Socialists, was nostalgic for a lost preindustrial and even pre-scientific world, where yeoman farmers and independent artisans enjoyed the fruits of their labour, and where the commons – common land, laws and customs – safeguard the people's ancient liberties, their traditional ways of life and livelihood. As John Clare put it in his poem about the enclosure movement:

> Unbounded freedom ruled the wandering scene
> Nor fence of ownership crept in between
> To hide the prospect of the following eye
> Its only bondage was the circling sky.[10]

In this scenario industrial capitalism erupts as a demonic force destroying the social fabric of rural communities and concentrating the means of creating wealth and culture in the hands of a tiny elite. But for Jennings, if the means of production remained in the hands of capital, the means of vision might yet belong to labour, and these means were not just those of art but science. Unlike many romantic socialists and retro-modernists, he saw science and technology, as represented by Newton and Brunel, as a potentially progressive force prefiguring a better world to come.[11] You could say he wanted the best of both worlds, but did not quite appreciate the tensions, both ideological and material, between them.

Inspired by this dual vision, the Isle of Wonders opened with a tableau vivant of rural English life in the eighteenth century, as one commentator described it: a prelapsarian age of cows, goats, geese, sheep, a shire horse, a bank of wild flowers, a mill race, a Cotswold stone cottage complete with smoking chimneys, a wheatfield stippled with poppies, a wooden barn, a trio of maypoles, rustic games of cricket and football, a cluster of bee hives, a sturdy oak tree, all topped off with fluffy white clouds tethered to squads of minders slowly circling the arena. We were transported to the land of Cockayne, that mythical world of plenty dreamed up by mediaeval peasants living permanently on the edge of famine. Here:

> There is many a pleasant sight,
> It's always day, there is no night.
> There are no quarrels and no strife,
> There is no death, but always life;
> Food and clothing are never short,
>   You'll never hear a sharp retort ...[12]

Yet Cockayne is also a place of violent contrasts, governed by Lords of Misrule, where the restrictions of society are defied, abbots are beaten by their monks, sexual licence prevails and the skies rain cheeses. Breughel depicts it as a drunken orgy. The Soft Machine as an acid trip. It is indeed a world turned upside down. But none of this turmoil was allowed to leak into Boyle's pastoral idyll. No images of rural poverty, no hint of rough music or riot, no indication that Maypole dancing belongs to a tradition of guising and mumming that was mobilised by the Luddites against the onset of an agricultural revolution that was to destroy the moral economy of rural England for ever.[13] Instead we got a Samuel Palmer landscape, without the unsettling sense that Nature might be about to strike back, and with more than a touch of Kinkade – an ethno-retro kitsch rendition of Merrie England. It was a missed opportunity also to give us another Elgar, whose Cockaigne Suite celebrates a putative link with London as the promised land of the Cockneys. Instead what we were shown was an Arcadian world turned upside down by the brutal advent of Blake's dark satanic mills, as worker/drummers emerged from the bowels of the scorched earth and tore away the grass from under their own feet, literally turfing themselves out of Paradise in a kind of do it yourself version of the enclosure movement, building a towering inferno of smokestack industries as they went.

The explanatory commentary that accompanies this segment is keen to point out the two sides of the story:

The Industrial Revolution was a time of tremendous excitement, but also of fear and hardship. The living standards of ordinary people rose for the first time in history. But their lives were also radically disrupted. Families were split as the young went in search of work in cities that were overcrowded and overrun with disease. Everyone, even children, worked punishing hours. Expansion led to war as well as prosperity.

Auden defined poetry as 'the clear expression of mixed feelings', but unfortunately the Isle of Wonders, for all its visual poetry, was singularly lacking in the double edginess its subject matter demanded. Blake's question, reiterated by Jennings – 'what the hammer, what the chain/in what furnace was thy brain/What the anvil? what dead grasp/Dare its deadly terrors clasp?' – remained unasked.[14] Instead, as giant chimneys reared up belching smoke, and furnaces sent a river of molten metal racing around the arena, we had Kenneth Branagh as Brunel and a posse of lookalike top hats to orchestrate the cacophony with Caliban's beguiling words 'be not afeared'. The choice of Brunel to play Prospero-Caliban was certainly meant to reassure. He is a man for all seasons; as one of the prime movers and shakers of the industrial revolution he is a hero of liberal capitalists, while he gets the socialist vote with his designs for hospitals and other public works. He is a civil engineer in a double sense, building bridges between capital and labour as well as railways connecting otherwise isolated communities. He is one of Saint-Simon's positive intellectuals par excellence.

Led by Brunel, the top hats and the workers engage in an energetic double act in which each mimic the other's gestures in operating the levers of industrial power; through the magic of mimesis, machino-facture is literally transfigured back into manu-facture. The choreography suggested not so much the mutual ruin of the contending classes as their mutual emulation. The top hats were as much 'hands-on' as the workers, who managed their own alienation. In that sense this segment could be read as a premonitory metaphor of the growth of the post-industrial happy clappy economy.

At one point the top hats are shown poring over the ground as if it were a map, plotting and planning their next moves in urbanising/industrialising the country. It would perhaps have been more apposite to have shown Brunel & Co perched atop the hill, alongside the proverbial English oak, giving them a commanding prospect over the Lowryesque landscape below; instead they rushed about hither and thither looking increasingly lost and bewildered by the forces they had unleashed. Perhaps their discountenance is not surprising, given that the map is *not* in fact the territory, and the industrial revolution did more than anything to drive a wedge between the imaginative cartographies of artists and the material world as depicted by the natural sciences and transformed by engineers. However harmoniously they may have been confused, it is in that gap and tension between the designs of Power and the projects of ordinary people where much of the chaos, and the crushing and bruising that characterised the new capitalist society, took place. But again there was no hint of industrial strife in this presentation. We saw chimneys with acrobatic steeplejacks hanging from them, but not a sweep in sight, although it was the soot-blackened faces of child sweeps that so exercised Blake's political indignation and enabled the Chartists and other reformers to make the connection between the exploitation of these 'white negroes' and the slave trade (>57-75).[15]

At times, then, it seemed as if Boyle's nerve failed him and he lacked the courage of his Blakean convictions. We got a lot of cod gothic moments (and a large bell) from the director of the stage version of Frankenstein, including a dream battle in which the giant witch Voldemort (on loan from Harry Potter) was defeated by a gang of Mary Poppinses; yet, strangely, there was no place in this graphic review of British children's literature for the work of Philip Pullman, whose Dark Materials trilogy draws explicitly on the ideas and imagery of both Milton and Blake.

In Pullman's stories, dæmons are his children's imaginary companions, guiding animal spirits, which, like Jungian shadows, accompany them through life and form an inevitable part of the growing up process, changing shape to reflect the volatile moods of their young charges and only settling into a more stable form with the attainment of maturity.[16] These figures could have provided a vivid visual counterpoint to the sick, but remarkably robust-looking children who danced for joy on their beds in a sequence designed to pay homage to the founding of the NHS. Pullman's work is, however, controversial. It offers an entirely secular creation myth, through an implicit critique of the Christian concept of the Fall, and C.S. Lewis's popular Christian mythography Narnia. Is that why it was ignored despite its obvious pertinence? Was it just safer to stick with J.K. Rowling, whose Harry Potter series is uncomplicated by such metaphysical speculations?

Yet the Isle of Wonders could not be accused of always playing safe. It had its carefully calculated transgressive moments – the famous lesbian kiss from Coronation Street, the transvestite scene from Billy Elliot – quoted as part of a collage of film clips from the British cinema of the past thirty years. What was lacking, and what accounts for some of the unnecessary foreclosures, was a properly worked out political argument.

I think this can partly be traced back to the ambiguity in Humphrey Jennings's interpretation of industrialism. In the Miltonic vision of Pandaemonium, industrialism is anything but disorganised. On the contrary, it represents a heroic feat of mining and metallurgy, engineering and large-scale planning. What Milton shows us, as we watch the huge fabrication take shape, is the Devil's energy being harnessed to audaciously constructive ends. This points forward to the productivist and bio-energetic vision of capitalism that was to emerge within the labour movement itself at the end of the nineteenth century: industrial technologies were seen as a progressive force which transformed the worker into a human dynamo, and would eventually liberate the working class from the degrading toils of manual labour.[17] An early champion of this technological utopianism was Dr Ure, whom Marx called the 'Pindar of the factory', and who spoke of it as 'a vast automaton, composed of various mechanical and intellectual organs acting in uninterrupted concern for the production of a common object, *all of them being subordinated to a self regulated moving force*' (my emphasis).[18] It is this auto-poetic dynamism that lends itself to audio-visual spectacle, and was captured so powerfully in the drumming that was such a major feature of the Isle of Wonders soundscape.

Still, this is only one side of the story. Milton and Blake do not allow us to forget that both *animal laborans* and *homo faber*, however magnificent their creations, are still the Devil's handiwork. As Milton succinctly puts it: 'let none admire/the riches grown in Hell'. Capitalism makes work for what might otherwise be idle hands, but also robs them of their skill and their pride in craftsmanship, as well as cheating them of the fruits of their labour.[19] In Boyle's Pandaemonium, this sense of living labour and its struggle against alienation is quite lost. What if the workers in this scenario had pressed the pause button, downed their tools and drumsticks and gone on strike? Or just collapsed into immobilism like the Royle family in front of their TV? Then perhaps we would have had to be shown quite another side of working-class life – what workers get up to when they are not simply recuperating from the physical exhaustion of the production line: not only organised sport and rational recreation, but a myriad of activities in which their imaginative life, everything that is stultified by their conditions of labour, might find creative expression.[20] It was precisely this subversive aspect of working-class culture that so interested Humphrey Jennings and Mass Observation, but which was occluded by Boyle's relentless pursuit of an upbeat version of the national-popular.

For example a more deliberative space for reflection might have cued in Lemn Sissay's Olympic Park poem 'Spark catchers', about the old Bryant and May factory on the edge of the site, where in 1888 Annie Besant organised a famous strike of the 'match girls'. At least its jagged rhythms and angry assonances, its 'sulphurous spite filled spit', and its quotes from Besant's article on 'White Slavery in London' – 'The fist the earth the spark its core/The fist the body the spark its heart' – would have provided a counterpoint to the apparently unstoppable drumbeat of the industrial revolution. As it was, technology became, quite literally, alchemy, as it first created a wasteland, and then transformed it into a wonderland, forging the Olympic rings from a molten river Thames. In this way industrialism was invested with a magical power to synthesise discordant elements and reconcile opposites, so that once again 'tho all differ, all agree'.

The same alchemy was applied to telling the story of the transition from the industrial to the digital revolution. Transition? What transition? One technology and economy simply replaced the other as seamlessly as a stage set being changed. There was no downside to de-industrialiation, no structural unemployment, no legacy of pollution, no communities and livelihoods destroyed. The forward march of labour was not so much halted as redirected to the sports stadium and the dance floor, as the machinery of the nation effortlessly changed gear from being the workshop of the world to being its songsmith. As heavy industry gave way to heavy metal and the culture industry, ethno-retro was replaced by techno-kitsch as Cool Britannia ruled first the airwaves, then cyberspace, and gave the national-popular its digital strap line: 'This is for Everyone', the LED display proudly proclaimed as the young people on the dance floor of the arena thrashed through the hit songs of yesteryear.

Prospero-Caliban rules OK

GrossKultur thrives where virtual identities offer a way of trading places. All the ceremonies portrayed a wonderland where anything and everything is possible, where boy meets girl by finding the mobile phone she's lost and sending her a text on it, and where Prospero (alias Brunel and Churchill) gets to speak Caliban's lines and Caliban is bonkers as well as black and beautiful.

London East's own Dizzee Rascal, who volunteered for this latter role in the Isle of Wonders, portrayed a gum-chewing gangsta rapper who has some of Rooster Byron's attitude, but not his redemptive vision of Jerusalem; his dream, unlike Caliban's, is not of riches but of a perverse kind of profit in macho-manliness: 'I wake up everyday it's a daydream/Everythin' in my life ain't what it seems/ ... A heavy bass line is my kind of silence/Everybody says that I gotta get a grip/But I let sanity give me the slip/Some people think I'm bonkers/But I just think I'm free/I'm just livin' my life/There's nothin' crazy about me.' The lad doth protest too much, methinks, though his philosophy of life certainly bears out Adorno's caustic comment that the problem with contemporary youth culture is not that chewing gum undermines metaphysics, but that it has *become* metaphysics.[21]

These elisions of Prospero-Caliban in the Olympic ceremonies owed nothing to Aimé Césaire's attempt to rework the master/slave dialectic, or even Browning's recasting of the debate between science and religion, but they did pose a series of undecidable questions. Is it Caliban's revenge that 'Prospero' can only speak his lines? Or is it the old wizard's final triumph that he can so easily appropriate Caliban's best speech in which he offers the new visitors a guide to the strange music of *his* island? It is anybody's guess. Nevertheless Caliban did get the last word, as the Olympic cauldron was lit and rose high in the night sky. It turned out that he too had been living the 2012 dream, albeit one that returned us to the land of Cockayne:

> And the rain tossed above us;
> In the garden of the world
> But a flame arrives to guide us;
> Past the gold between the anvils of the stars
> ...

> When the light drives out our fears
> And the joy drives out our pain
> And the nations come to greet us
> Waving open arms of waves of golden corn

The last two words of the song perhaps best describe this rather unfortunate attempt at a techno-trance aria which collapses into Olympic kitsch. Musically the most interesting thing about it was the reprise of the whistling theme first heard during the minute's silence for the war dead which briefly halted the Pandemonium. Throughout the ceremony there were moments like this, amounting to what might be called an inter-ludology, in which there was an attempt to ground the proceedings in a 'low' culture where the tragic and comic could gain a temporary foothold (^112-117). The most genuine moment of pathos was entirely unscripted: the frail figure of Muhammad Ali, sitting in a wheelchair alongside other past Olympians. Because sport, and especially Olympic sport, is so closely associated with the boundless energy of youth, the aging athlete necessarily cuts a poignant figure, representing the transience of human life and the vulnerability of the body to the ravages of time.

Mainly though, the downsizing of GrossKultur was achieved by pressing the pause button, stopping the onward rush of sounds and images so that emotion could be recollected in something like tranquillity. The wall of remembrance sequence which showed photographs of the victims of 7/7 against the soundtrack of Abide With Me was one such moment, although the orchestration of cultural memory is rarely achieved by such opportunistic means. There was no shortage of tearjerkers in the ceremonies, although high emotionality – the spontaneous overflow of powerful feelings (Wordsworth) – was reserved for the Games themselves, and the incoherence of hysterical athletes interviewed in the immediate aftermath of their performance, prompting not poetic utterance but the sporting clichés of triumph and despair.[22]

Poetry made by all? Surrealism, inventiveness and the anti-industrial dream machine

The dominant mood music in the ceremonies was, inevitably, upbeat, and almost entirely disconnected from what Jennings called the 'means of vision by which the emotional side of our nature is kept alive, satisfied and fed'. Nor was the inter-ludology informed by a 'poetry made by all' rooted in the dream life of the masses. This was an important plank in the surrealists' programme and a major influence on Humphrey Jennings, especially in his ethnographic work for Mass Observation, where he set out to investigate the phenomenology of the social unconscious and the 'other scenes' of working-class life. Or, as he put it, 'the shouts and gestures of motorists; the aspidistra cult; the anthropology of football pools; bathroom behaviour; beards, armpits and eyebrows; the distribution, diffusion and significance of the dirty joke'.

Surreal is a greatly overworked adjective, nowadays commonly applied to anything at all bizarre or 'wacky', and it was applied generously by journalists and commentators to describe the Olympic ceremonies. There were many images that would seem to qualify for the epithet and indeed drew on just this repertoire: a giant octopus whose tentacles spread out across the arena, books that took flight like birds, doves made out of bicycles, Morris dancers stomping about wearing oil drums for shoes, crows on stilts. But Dada and surrealism – at least as practised by artists like Max Ernst and René Magritte, poets like Lautréamont, or Paul Eluard, or film-makers like Bunuel – was always more than a collage of oneiric images incongruously combined. It involved a form of montage which explored the chaos of crushed and bruised memories and effected a dialectical return of the repressed in powerful and often profoundly disturbing imagery.[23]

The imaginary machines which were such a striking feature of all the ceremonies illustrate what happens when Dada and Dante go to Disneyland, and the shocking becomes merely the charmingly eccentric. Taxis made out of newspapers, a giant grasshopper grown out of car hubs, a 'clampasaurus rex' welded together out of recycled scrap metal, a half-plane half-tank, an orrery with revolving apples for planets – these hybrid constructions variously evoked Heath Robinson's ramshackle *Machine for Catching Bombs*, Jennings's animal machines and Tinguely's animated sculptured ones, Bruce Lacey's improbably Humanoid Robots and Cesar's assemblages made out of crushed automobiles (^64-74). In the Festival of Flames, the Paralympics closing ceremony, where many of these machines featured, the explicit reference was to *Mad Max*, that dystopian fable of murder and mayhem down-under with its weird 'psychomobiles', and to *Those Magnificent Men in their Flying Machines*. But, whatever their provenance, the ceremonial function of these contraptions was not to represent the infernal 'other scene' of the machine age, but to display the multiform aspects of British *inventiveness*, in a carefully arranged marriage of art and science, craftsmanship and high technology, ingenuity and wit.

Inventiveness is to the creative class what resilience is to the 'uncreative' in 2012 characterology – it signifies an innate capacity to adapt to constraining circumstances without complaint by drawing on extraordinary resources of self reliant artfulness. The Olympic spirit and the blitz spirit once more recombined. Armed with a brief to demonstrate this native ingenuity, the designers produced cannibalised machines which might have been built in a dream factory run by a latter day Heath Robinson. If some of these hybrid automata looked as if they might have escaped from the nursery cum laboratory of a budding Dr Frankenstein, they were nevertheless robbed of their surreal and gothic potential by the fact that they had to perform in a kitsch wonderworld straight out of the Emerald City in the Wizard of Oz (^163).

In contrast to this exercise in whimsicality, Humphrey Jennings, like the dadaists and situationists, was interested in exploring the dislocation of the real *by means of the real*, and how this opens up the possibility of both poetic and political transformation. If the surrealists only wanted to *dream* the impossible, the situationists insisted on *demanding* it, because they wanted to revolutionise or surpass the reality principles of everyday life, to break once and for all with the dominant organisation of appearances.[24] The 2012 ceremonies team wanted to practise an art of the possible by sampling popular culture for what it might contribute to their ceremonial mix; but this also involved distancing or disembedding many of these elements from the real contexts that might have given them their power to disturb the all too easy consciences of the Olympic audience. Instead we were given Festivals of Hope in the Saint-Simon mould, jazzed up with pyrotechnic displays of multi-culture, and with all potentially toxic or discordant features sanitised or screened out. We might postulate a new Boyle's Law – the compression and volume of a Grand Spectacle, its rhetorical scope and scale, are directly, not inversely, proportional. Or to put it another way, the richer the mix the more hyper the kitsch.

Taken as a whole, the 2012 ceremonies illustrate just how little room for ideological manoeuvre there is. The 'inspire a generation/can do' agenda was interpreted within a national-popular framework of insular inclusivity. Order in variety was delivered through an audio-visual mash-up in which elements of retro/ethno/techno kitsch predominated, subsuming the transgressive and inter-ludic moments within a 'feel-good' frame. The two opening ceremonies were structured around grand narrative themes of 'inventiveness' and 'resilience', while the closing events disavowed the fact of closure in favour of a spectacular celebration of carnival capitalism and its 'high' culture. A radical poetics of the impossible was sublimated within a politics of the possible.

Cycling towards Jerusalem?

As an example of this process of sublimation, consider the dove cyclists whose entry into the arena provided one of the most memorable moments in the whole spectacle (^101). At one level this was an imaginative response to one of the more difficult ceremonial protocols. In Ancient Greece doves were released from Olympia to signal the truce, and carry the message home to every city throughout the land. Ever since the holocaust of Seoul, when the doves got incinerated as they flew past the Olympic cauldron, organisers have been chary of using real birds, although, given the continuing popularity of racing pigeons in working-class areas of Britain, some replication of the original ceremony would seem to have been apposite.

The trick that was really missed here was to embed cycling in the history of national-popular culture. The bicycle has been a vital link between labour and leisure in many working-class communities. Before the car and motorbike became affordable they were a means of mass transport to work, and provided the actual tools of their first trade for tens of thousands of lads employed in delivering goods and urgent postal messages. The first world war saw both boy cyclists and homing pigeons used to carry messages between the trenches, and many died en route. Push bikes were also an important vehicle of rational recreation and political campaigning; long before Critical Mass used them to reclaim the streets, the Clarion Scouts got on their bikes to spread the socialist message into the countryside, while for the suffragettes, women pedal power was another step forward for the Great Cause of their emancipation. Today, of course, the BMX has become a potent symbol of the link between extreme sport and urban youth culture.

Boyle and his creative team would not have had to look far to connect with this social history. John Burnside's poem 'Bicycling for Ladies' was one of the

Winning Words commissions for the Olympic Park, and takes its inspiration from Sylvia Pankhurst, who wrote a pamphlet of that name, while campaigning for women's rights within the working-class communities of East London. Burnside portrays the aspirations of the feminist cyclists in terms of a social geography that lays claim to a heritage from which they have historically been excluded, but which is for them very present tense:

> they want to ride for hours, on country lanes
> through Saxon woods and miles of ripening grain
> and end up at some point of no return,
> like changelings, in some faded picture book
> from childhood, going headlong through the dark
> to some new realm, where no mere man is king.

The sudden shift into a mytho-poeic space, conveys, directly enough, the struggle to transcend the material constraints of working-class women's lives – the striving for another possible world not dominated by men, yet where 'no mere man' might still rule OK. A similar metamorphosis occurs in the second part of the poem, which focuses on Sylvia Pankhurst herself, and takes us from the detail of her day to day struggles to the vision of a shared epiphany, evoking Stanley Spencer's painting of the Resurrection in Cookham Churchyard:

> The marches are done with,
> the hunger strikes, danger of death
> forgotten, as the sun cuts through the fog
> and all the world cycles away, like risen souls
> made new and tender for the life to come
> in some lost Resurrection Of The Body.

Cycling as a metaphor of a better life to come, but in this world, rather than the next, offers us a vision of sport as a kind of meta-physical education, the body's own way of transcendence and regeneration, one that is not the prerogative of privilege but open to anyone whenever the sun breaks through their personal fog and a truce is called in the war of attrition that often passes for everyday life.

A scenario constructed around this vision would have shown us a procession of cyclists, past and present, circling the stadium on 'flying' machines of various vintages, Victorian errand boys and modern bike couriers, suffragettes and Clarion scouts, led by a Critical Mass choir singing or whistling along to Billy Bragg's rebarbative version of Jerusalem, as homing pigeons are released to the four corners of Britain and a team of disabled BMX bikers perform high wire stunts.[25] Wouldn't this have been a more inspiring note on which to end the Isle of Wonders rather than the spectacle of a lone BMX biker (borrowed from ET, Spielberg's kitsch fable of innocence lost and regained) riding into the sunset, while down below on the streets of London cyclists were being beaten up as they tried to transform Babylon into New Jerusalem?

The last laugh?

The ceremonies got a good press, most of it focused on the Isle of Wonders. The broadsheets were almost unanimous in their praise, finding the shows 'bold', 'imaginative' and 'wildly eccentric'. The liberal/left leaning *Guardian* found the opening ceremony both 'quietly subversive' and 'breathtakingly politically charged', while the *Independent* thought it showed the best of British creativity and wit. The conservative *Telegraph* was predictably less enthusiastic about the cultural politics, but also praised the creative energy on display. The tabloids thought the whole thing was bonkers but very British, a version of the 'naughty but nice' image that has replaced 'sang froid' as the preferred descriptor on our cultural passports these days. The Tory press that speaks most vociferously for its version of Middle England thought that the Isle of Wonders was naughty but not at all nice in its lack of deference to traditional values, while the *Daily Mail*, ever faithful to the unreconstructed island story, castigated it as 'multicultural madness'. The international media found 'Wonders' wonderful but bewildering; the *New York Times* thought it was 'the most elaborate and expensive in-joke ever'.

If there was one thing that the official commentariat agreed on, it was that the opening and closing ceremonies were unique in displaying the Great British Sense of Humour. For many, it seems, the comedy sketches by Rowland Atkinson (alias Mr Bean) and Eric Idle (alias Monty Python) were the highpoints of the shows. Perhaps Britain is the only country in the world in which the ability to make and take jokes has been enrolled as an exercise in national character building, as yet another sign of the grin-and-bear-it resilience that supposedly distinguishes its people.

The ceremonies team's sampling of British humour was part of their commitment to avoid grandiose statements and ground the spectacle in the idioms of national-popular culture, and it certainly was the single most distinctive feature of the 2012 Olympic shows. They exploited the fact that humour is a powerful way of expressing what is otherwise taboo, and dealing with subjects that cause public anxiety.[26] But, more importantly, the whimsical brand of humour they adopted offered them a way of being irreverent without being disrespectful.

Olympic ceremonies have often been bizarre and sometimes unintentionally hilarious affairs, but humour has never before been one of their distinguishing features. And not just because the IOC don't think the Olympics is a laughing matter. A funny thing may have happened to you on the way to the stadium, but somehow when you get there it can seem not quite so amusing. The difficulty of incorporating an element of humour into the proceedings is not, though, just about the ritual solemnity of the occasion; it has to do with the fact that, however universal the human themes and predicaments it deals with, a lot of humour is very culturally embedded and does not travel well. You won't enjoy a situation comedy unless you understand what the situation is about or can somehow translate it into your own terms – as the Chinese did with *Yes, Prime Minister*. So although it is always possible to embed a few in-jokes that only the home audience will get, it requires a very special brand of humour to do the business worldwide.

There is a historical dimension to this. In the days of Empire, the English upper class always prided itself on having a self-deprecating sense of humour, their ability to laugh at themselves being a measure of their superior humanity and hence fitness to govern, and an antidote to their stiff upper lip. Noel Coward caught the tone exactly in his Mad Dogs and Englishmen/going out in the midday sun. Those subjected to Pax Britannica didn't always see the funny side of it, and thought the joke was at their expense – which it often was. In contrast, the tradition of popular humour from Chaucer and the Mummer's plays to the 'Carry On' films, has always been either bawdy or anti-authority or both. And very non PC. Definitely not on the agenda for the Olympic ceremonies. Equally, the alternative comedy circuit has thrown up many fine, inventive comedians who are acute observers of the social scene, but it is difficult to imagine any of them m/c ing the Isle of Wonders and telling Lord Coe jokes with any success. In fact the 2012 Olympics were pretty much a disaster for the stand-up comic who thrives on bad news. Everything went according to plan, the nation was euphoric at the medal successes, so who would want to be a party pooper?

As for satire, the art of the political lampoon survives in the anti-establishment humour of *Private Eye*, and our political cartoonists continue the tradition of Rowlandson and Hogarth; but the role of satire is to stay outside the official discourse, not to act as its intermediary. The TV 'mockumentary' *Twenty Twelve* showed what happens when that line is crossed. Owing more to *Yes Prime Minister* than Ricky Gervais's *The Office*, the series was essentially a sit-com in the Ealing Comedy tradition, sending up some of the more obviously ludicrous aspects of Olympic bureaucracy, marketing and security culture. In addition to giving Lord Coe a walk-on part, the programme was soft-centred in its choice of targets: a panic about bio-diversity and saving the stag beetle in the Olympic Park; an Algerian threat to boycott the games because the Shared Belief Centre did not face towards Mecca; the head of Deliverance who is shot in the foot with a starting pistol banned as an offensive weapon – these were sometimes hilarious skits, but – unlike *The Office* – there was no cringe factor, no hitting below the belt, just yet another demonstration that the Brits can see the funny side of themselves.

Fortunately there is an altogether wilder and more absurdist streak in British humour that is decidedly home-grown, from Lewis Carroll and Edward Gorey to Spike Milligan and Monty Python. Its surreal brand of slapstick comedy, part conceptual pantomime, part circus burlesque, is as much visual as verbal; and it can sometimes transcend national boundaries. So it was well equipped for the task of gently sending up the more OTT aspects of Olympic protocol and generating at least one of the ceremony's few genuinely transgressive moments. The figure of Mr Bean, in his entirely dysfunctional egocentricity, was a perfect foil for Sir Simon Rattle and the London Symphony orchestra; his one man ostinato rendition of the 'Chariots of Fire' signature tune (which was used to accompany *every* medal ceremony) provided an exact metaphor for the all-on-one-keynote triumphalism that marked most of the subsequent BBC commentary. When Mr Bean gets bored with repeating the same note and falls asleep, his dream does indeed represent the return of the repressed, as he imagines defeating his athletic rivals by foul means that are the very antithesis of the British – and the Olympic – sense of fair play.

But was this really a situationist moment, a ludic deconstruction of the Olympic Spectacle? It was too easily recuperated into a charming gesture of British (or English) eccentricity for that. Monty Python suffered the same fate in the closing ceremony. Although their famous 'Silly Olympics' sketch is certainly the funniest send-up ever made, it was not quoted. Perhaps it was too near the athletic bone. Instead we had Eric Idle as a wannabe human cannonball, singing 'Always look on the bright side of life'. As anyone who has seen the *Life of Brian* will remember, the song is sung by a man on a cross near to Brian's, who is gradually joined by a group of crucified followers of the eponymous hero, and is an ironic comment on happy endings – whether in religion or in Disney films. The song contains the verse:

> Life's a piece of shit
> When you look at it
> Life's a laugh and death's a joke, it's true.
> You'll see it's all a show
> Keep 'em laughing as you go
> Just remember that the last laugh is on you.

The song as performed on the night completely lost this gallows sense of humour, and became simply a pastiche of the upbeat 2012 message, on a par with 'I'm for ever Blowing Bubbles', the song West Ham United fans sing to persuade themselves that this season they are not going to be relegated.

Of course humour has its cruel streak. The marginalised and vulnerable often find themselves the butt of jokes that make fun of their difference, because their very claim to belong within the ranks of society and common humanity is felt to be threatening, especially by those whose own tenure there is fragile. Drawing the line under your own feet is the oldest trick in the deviancy amplification business. That was no doubt why the ceremonies that opened and closed the Paralympics were so signally devoid of humour. Yet this precautionary measure was entirely unnecessary. It was to ignore the fact that the disabled community, like all subcultures, has evolved its own distinctive brand of tough humour and indeed its own comedy circuit, some of which was sampled by Channel Four, which televised the Paralympics.

The Tempest also has its comic touches but Caliban is not one of them. He is not one of Shakespeare's rude mechanicals (that part is played by the drunken Stefano and his foil Trinculo), and he is definitely *not* amused by Prospero; he wants to murder him. Nor would he have found it funny to have his best lines stolen by Prospero's deputies in the shape of latter-day builders of bridges and empires. Yet once he is left to his own devices, and Ariel's, we may still hope Caliban will recover his sense of humour now that he is back in charge of his beloved isle. For him, at least, its spell remains unbroken. But it is a bitter sweet transformation. Even though he may be king once more, he has learnt the limits of his powers. If, in his speech, he 'wakes and cries to dream again', it is because he realises the riches that he sees ready to drop from the skies exist only in his imagination. If he has now been enrolled for our version of the Olympic legacy dream, it may be as well to remember that fact.

All that is solid melts...

When Shakespere's Prospero takes his leave of the island, and relinquishes his magical control over its affairs, he also famously recognises that his legacy may disappear with him:

> ... melt into thin air:
> And, like the baseless fabric of this vision,
> The cloud-capp'd towers, the gorgeous palaces,
> The solemn temples, the great globe itself,
> Yea, all which it inherit, shall dissolve
> And like this insubstantial pageant faded,
> leave not a rack behind.

For Prospero plc and the Olygopolists this is not an option. They are in it for the long haul, and for them an enduring legacy is paramount. So what is to become of us now that the 30th Olympiad of modern times is over? Will we live happily ever after?

Boyle included the future in his prospectus but here the lack of a political rationale in his pageant tells. He may wave a wand and magically turn Prospero into Caliban, but the minute the Olympic flame is extinguished the old sorcerer is back in town with his whole posse, and up to his corporate neck in post-Olympic schemes. His mission now is to make sure the cloud capped Orbit Tower, the solemn temple of the stadium, and all the other 'gorgeous palaces', are put to profitable use, so that the 2012 vision, far from being baseless, becomes firmly embedded in the urban fabric. And, as we have seen, when it comes to telling the official story of the Games, it is he who will have the last word again, not Caliban.

In the make-believe islands we inhabit as children, legacy is not a problem. These are once upon a time places where people go to become castaways, have adventures, discover treasure, and then come home again to get on with tea and the rest of their lives.[27] The Olympics also used to be like that, once upon a time, but now that they have grown up and become serious business they go on for ever. Soaps are made for people who no longer believe in happy endings and so don't want the story to ever stop. But the Olympics seemed to promise us an opportunity to enter an enchanted world where we can go on and on living the dream and so live happily ever after. That is their beautifying lie. There may yet be a bitter awakening.

Nevertheless, for all the hype and kitsch, there was something genuinely moving – and that means both tragic and comic – about the excess of ambition, the refusal to compromise with reality, the sacrificial expenditure of energy, the asceticism and excess that the whole project entailed. The Olympics are gratuitously *absurd* and that is their enduring appeal.

This was summed up for me by one of the projects commissioned as part of the art in the park programme (^141). Akroyd and Harvey's 'History Trees' consists of a series of large tree sculptures planted to mark the entrances to the Olympic Park. Each tree has a brass 'memory ring' weighing half a ton placed in its crown, engraved on its interior face with words and phrases reflecting the area's history. The official handout tells us that 'over time, the tree branches and ring will slowly fuse together, becoming a living memory of the Olympic Park'. All the trees had, of course, to be sustainably sourced, the first three being procured from Belgium. There was considerable concern from local environmentalists that the rings might stunt the trees' growth or otherwise cause them injury, until the Royal Horticultural Society gave the project its blessing. The star of the show will be the last tree to be planted, in ten years time, an English oak whose ring is so positioned as to cast a shadow which will be permanently 'captured' by being inlaid into the ground in bronze. Each year, the handout tells us, the two will momentarily align to commemorate a significant event during the games. Quite how this is to be achieved remains a mystery. The words on the rings are, of course, deliberately unreadable, except by someone bold enough to actually climb the tree. Anyone who does so will discover a series of enigmatic and evocative phrases with a variety of local resonances: It's all about water – Cockles from Leigh – A cormorant, symbol of marsh, etc. Otherwise the story they have to tell is strictly for the birds. Eventually the rings will also be invisible, at least in summer, as they form each tree's 'hollow crown'.

An artwork that is designed to celebrate the living heritage of East London and the Olympics will thus serve as an elaborate visual metaphor of occlusion and forgetfulness, in which cultural memory and local history are overgrown by the hand of nature and the march of time. Plato would have loved the idea of the arbitrary coincidence of two shadows, one permanently inscribed, the other ephemeral. Socrates would have grumbled about the expense to the public purse not to mention the inconvenience of having to hang around in the cold while Clio, in alliance with Mother Nature, gets her act together. Philosophically the project is a no-brainer and its aesthetic rationale – a kind of anti-ruinology – is at best a rather glib double take on Anselm Kiefer's explorations of traumatic memoryscape. Yet it is projects like this which in their very obtuseness and superfluity have made London 2012 worth thinking and laughing about, and, yes, even remembering with something like affection.

Ian F Rogers, Opportunity structure? The Olympic Stadium from the River Lea

10. Speaking out of place:
East Londoners talk the Olympics

So far I have largely discussed the 2012 Olympics by examining the points of view of those who were charged with delivering, reporting or evaluating them. But already in Chapter Five we saw a discrepancy of standpoint between the Olympic Park workforce and the official accounts of the site construction process. In this chapter I want to look at how the working-class communities we encountered in the first part of the book responded to the advent of the Olympics on their doorstep. How far did East Enders own the Games, and identify with the aspirations it represents? What patterns of stake-holding emerged as the grand project unfolded, and how were these affected by its vicissitudes? What light does this shed on the longer-term legacy issues?

For this purpose some research was carried out using focus groups drawn from a representative sample of Newham residents.[1] The initial research was conducted shortly before and after the announcement of the IOC's decision on the bid because I was interested to see whether the outcome would make any difference to people's attitudes, and this work continued at intervals over the next five years into the immediate post-games period.[2]

All of the groups, without exception, saw themselves as East Enders first and foremost, and as Londoners or British a long way second, although this was probably due to the topic under discussion. They thought that the Olympics were about East London and should be judged solely or primarily on that basis. There was initially a marked discrepancy in attitude and response between the generations. The older cohort were much more cautious in their appraisal. They remembered previous promises to regenerate the area that had failed to materialise; they were suspicious of the bid's real intentions, and of the media hype surrounding it. Here are some typical comments from the group about the bid campaign:

> It's very patriotic – all those Union Jacks – but I also found the bid campaign very patronising, like it's saying 'what have you done today to make your country proud of you?' People in the East End are proud, proud of the area, proud of what its struggles have achieved. We don't need people from SW1 coming in telling us what to be proud about! We've got a lot to be proud of as it is without the Olympics (community worker).

I don't agree with all the hype – even if it is very skilfully done, it is very dishonest. Now you see it now you don't. It dodges all the difficulties (social worker and local resident).

Some were worried about the potential disruption that might be caused by the regeneration process, the sudden influx of migrant workers and then the flood of visitors; others that the social character of the area would change with affluent middle-class professionals moving in:

I am worried about the local businesses that are going to be displaced, and also the travellers and homeless people – some of them are people who have lived and worked in East London all their lives and now they are going to lose their livelihoods when they are relocated. Even if they get proper compensation, it won't make up for the disruption (long-term resident).

There will be more overcrowding – the roads will be more crowded. I just can't see the transport being good enough. The system is jammed at rush hour as it is. How are we going to cope with additional traffic? (long-term resident)

And others were concerned about the environmental impact:

There will be a huge impact on the environment, with the draining of Hackney Marshes. Whatever they say, the Olympic Park will change the habitat of wildlife beyond recognition – and it may not be for the better (youth worker).

The park looks plastic to me – it's an artificial environment rather like Mile End Park, and unless it is owned and used by local people it will be unsustainable (local resident).

The younger people were unburdened by such memories and fears and were much more up for it, some wanted to volunteer and most thought it would be good for East London:

We want to have fun. The Youth Culture Festival sounds like making for a good atmosphere – everyone partying and having a good time (16 year old girl)

We could have concerts and shows like in Hyde Park (13 year old girl).

Yet despite this enthusiasm few of the young people thought the Games would make any material difference to their own lives in terms of economic opportunities, or would encourage them to do more sport or adopt a healthier lifestyle. The young Muslims were apprehensive that they would be targeted by the Olympic security operation and seen as a potential 'enemy within':

I am worried the police are going to get heavier, there's going to be more stop and search, and it will be worse for Blacks and Asians – they are really going to have a hard time, especially the youth. It's going to mean more trouble. Some people might just go to cause trouble (18 year old boy).

Nevertheless the general mood of the under-21s was cautiously optimistic. As one of them put it, 'I'm not worried about the Olympics, I'm pleased we got it, but I'm not yet jumping for joy'.

The successful outcome of the bid did not, on the whole, change attitudes, except amongst young professionals – teachers, youth workers and community artists – who initially had been very sceptical, but now saw the Olympics as offering opportunities both for them and the community, especially the young people:

I think that we have to give it a chance, wait and see what is on offer. They are making all the right noises. They needed our support to win the bid, now let's see if they deliver on their promises (community worker).

But others were concerned that false expectations may have been raised:

Children take it all verbatim and, of course, they are excited by the potential of the Olympics. And rightly so. You must never stop young people dreaming, but it is irresponsible to encourage and trade off these dreams without being 100 per cent certain that they can be realised (youth worker).

There was some confusion and disagreement amongst the young people themselves as to who had actually won the bid:

We got it because we backed the bid – we had more people behind it than Paris (17 year old boy).

No, it was down to Seb Coe, David Beckham, celebrities, posh people like that (15 year old girl).

No it was down to us! (16 year old boy).

As for the regeneration potential of the Olympics, here again there was considerable scepticism from the older generation:

I'm 100% for regeneration if it's for East Enders, but we have to make sure that it's not just another name for giving big business carte blanche to make a killing out of the Olympics (long-term resident).

Regeneration can mean spending billions, but it can be a flash in the pan, a short-term bonanza with little long-term lasting effect. They all talk about Barcelona – it was great at first, but now the city has slipped back again by all accounts. The benefits just don't match the costs in my opinion (long-term resident).

A consensus did however emerge around what might be termed 'the good enough Olympics':

A good Olympics would be where nothing bad happened, where there wasn't any terrorist attacks or bombs, where there were no muggings, and people didn't run onto the track to disrupt the races (14 year old girl).

A good Olympics will be a trouble-free Olympics with no security incidents (local resident).

An event that takes place with the least possible danger to athletes and spectators. And with the least damage to the environment (youth worker).

We hope it goes off well, gets a good enough crowd, doesn't have any bombs and doesn't cost the taxpayers of London an arm and a leg (social worker and local resident).

When hopes are wrapped up in official hype, there is a tendency to adopt a stance of cynicism or indifference as a safeguard against manipulation or disappointment:

If we don't get the Games people in the East End will just carry on as usual. And if we do get it then they may be a bit pleased but it won't make a whole lot of difference to them. This is an area which is very down to earth; we're not going to have the wool pulled over our eyes or our heads turned by all the hype (community worker).

There is an important vein of national-popular humour that specialises in deprecating aspiration or downplaying success, and elements of it were in evidence in some of the responses we got:

I was at a Kebab. My mum rang my mobile and said we had got it. She was well excited. I was just watching it on the Kebab TV. It was all in Turkish. The guy there just ignored it – he was too busy making the kebab to take much notice. I was glad, though I wasn't over the moon, if you know what I mean (16 year old boy).

There was a realism about many of these responses to the Olympics, especially on the part of young people, that seemed to augur well for their ability to respond with some resilience to the vicissitudes of the project. But would this be sustained in a severe economic downturn?

When I returned to talk to these groups in 2009, after the banking collapse had ushered in a full-blown recession, I found, predictably enough, that the older group were as pessimistic as ever about the outcome, some of their worst fears having been realised. 'I told you so' was the prevailing response. The young professionals, some of whom had become involved in Olympics-related activities, still thought that on balance the benefits outweighed the disadvantages. Some who had initially been sceptical had been won over, although they were cynical about official motivations. 'They just don't want to put their money where their mouth is when it comes to the community' was the general opinion. Amongst the youth group, however, there was a marked change of attitude. Opinion was now sharply divided between those who strongly identified with the Olympic project, and who were looking forward to becoming its 'ambassadors', and those who, although initially enthusiastic, had become disenchanted and now rejected it as a 'con' or waste of time. Amongst the budding twenty-twelvers were two unemployed boys, one white and one Afro-Caribbean, who took a fiercely local and patriotic stance towards the Games – it was 'their' thing and no-one was going to stop them making the most of it. [3] Amongst the nay-sayers, some were unemployed, some at college, or in work, but they all felt that the Olympics were 'not for the likes of them' – it was about outsiders coming in and exploiting the situation for their own advantage. The influx of East Europeans to work on the Olympic Park was again cited as evidence, thus echoing the fears of the older generation. Interestingly, ethnicity made little difference to these responses. Members of BME communities were as worried about the 'immigrant invasion' as were whites.

Three years later, in the immediate run-up to the Games, attitudes had hardened even further. Those who were most apprehensive about the outcome had become fixated on the security issue:

> We've become a target, that's what's happened. You read all this stuff in the papers about the threat and how much it's costing to fix it, but they'll never succeed in eliminating the risk. Look at 7/7. They might protect the athletes and the Olympic Park, but they can't make a whole city secure (long-term resident).

For some, the security measures were the illness of which they purported to be the cure:

> They were supposed to be the legacy games but now they are known as the lockdown games. It's making life unbearable for the local community. Everyone is very jumpy and the authorities over-react to the slightest incident. I saw a middle-aged woman being stopped because she was carrying a bottle of paraffin – apparently they thought it might be a bomb! Talking about 'living the dream', it's a bloody nightmare. I can't wait for it all to be over so we can get back to normal (unemployed office worker).

One of the community workers had an interesting suggestion about the latent function of the security discourse, based on a counterfactual:

Just imagine 7/7 had never happened and there was no big security issue. Whatever would the papers write about? There would be no tension, no edge to the occasion. The media would have to find some boring scandal about people on the fiddle or doping. As it is everyone is on the edge of their seats – will the Olympics go up in smoke? (community worker).

For some of the older residents the unwelcome changes had more to do with the regeneration process rather than the Olympics per se:

I used to go a lot to Stratford to shop in the market. But it's all changed. The shopping city is too expensive, it's crawling with security, it's very crowded. Stratford is just not the friendly place it used to be (pensioner and long-term resident).

I used to take my dog for a walk down Waterden Road, but, of course it's now all blocked off. They've surrounded the whole site with fences, so it's become one big no-go area. They say that after the games the fence will come down, there will be all these bridges. But will I need a pass, or have to go through security checks every time I want to take my dog for a walk in the park? (postal clerk and long-term resident)

This view was not shared by many of the young people. Here is one typical comment from an 18 year old who worked in a local pub:

Stratford is brilliant. It's so buzzy. There's people coming from all over London to shop and take in the vibe. There's always something happening to do with the Olympics. There's a sense of excitement, you see the countdown clock and you think yeah it's all happening.

But there was a significant minority report, which again focused on the security issue and was voiced strongly by young people, especially by the more marginalised boys:

Stratford? I hate it. I used to go there a lot to hang around with my mates, have a laugh, sometimes we'd get lucky and score, but now you just get moved on. One of the police told me 'we don't want your sort round here during the Olympics, you give the place a bad name.' So now I just don't go near it (17 year old college student).

Bonders and bridgers: some patterns of stake-holding

What explains these positions, given that they are not directly correlated to economic circumstance? I think it has a lot to do with different forms of stake-holding, and I have found Robert Putnam's distinction between what he calls 'bridgers' and 'bonders' very pertinent in making sense of how people go about the business of owning – and sometimes disowning – the Olympics.[4]

In general terms, bridgers are individuals, groups or organisations that have the social capital, the confidence and resource, to engage proactively with the world in which they find themselves, and to create partnerships or alliances with others in furtherance of their ends. Bridgers would see the East End as offering a prospect on opportunities offered by the wider metropolitan economy, a place where people come to get a start in life. If they adopt a Londoner identity it will be as a means to widen the scope and scale of their activities.

Bridgers adopted the Olympics as a platform for personal, professional or organisational advancement, and behaved opportunistically to maximise their competitive advantage. They are strenuous networkers, and their involvement takes the form of rational calculating moves, which do not require any deep emotional investment or ideological commitment to the project, although they certainly do not pre-empt it. In fact bridgers often form pressure groups to leverage resources from public bodies, and some organisations, like London Citizens, have been markedly successful in exacting concessions – in this case on minimum wage rates to be paid to the Olympic workforce – from the authorities.

Bridgers are always on the lookout for new opportunities to further their cause, and they take risks, but if they are not reaping substantive rewards they tend to disinvest and move on to what they see as more interesting or beneficial projects. In other words they behave most of the time according to a market economy of worth. The young professionals in the discussion groups seem to generally fall into this category. As we've seen, several who had initially been very enthusiastic at the prospect later became frustrated at what they saw as a lack of commitment to the local community on the part of the Olympic authorities. This was also true of two members of BME communities who had taken leadership roles but felt that their personal investment in the 2012 project was not being matched by the business opportunities.

In contrast bonders are individuals, groups or organisations that have less social capital, but seek to maximise what they have by using it to maintain their own sense of internal cohesion, identity or integrity. Bonders are good at building niches for themselves in markets and institutions, but by the same token they tend to develop a silo mentality, are risk averse, and are always on the look out for possible refuges from the winds of change. They are reactive rather than proactive, and disposed to feel anxious (and less aspirational) about regeneration projects; they are also more likely to experience and talk about loss of community and urban decline. For them the East End is an area that offers sanctuary and is greatly valued for that, but it is perceived as continually being threatened by invasion from outsiders. If they adopt a Londoner identity it will be as a platform to express these local concerns. Quite a number of the older residents came into this category.

If bonders adopted the Olympics they were likely to have a fierce, proprietorial sense of the Games as 'their thing', by virtue of territorial claims staked over local amenity and resource. They operate according to a moral economy of worth in which civic or bio-political values predominate. However this intense and potentially long-term commitment was only likely to happen if they felt their claims and interests were being recognised and validated. If not, they quickly withdrew into disinterest or even outright opposition, and regrouped around their own local concerns. They could, in any case, be reluctant to share 'their' Olympics or 'their' Stratford with other communities or organisations whom they did not regard as legitimate stakeholders. Bonders were to be found equally within white and BME communities.

Both bonders and bridgers could be signed-up twenty-twelvers; and, equally, there were nay-sayers within both groups. Moreover, it was also possible for the nature of people's stake to shift from bridger to bonder, and vice versa. Interestingly the two unemployed boys who became twenty-twelvers had gained social confidence through becoming involved in a scheme that aimed to encourage leadership qualities amongst young Londoners; this undoubtedly helped shift them towards a 'bridger' role, whilst still remaining strongly bonded to the Olympic project as an East End 'thing'.

The distinction between bridgers and bonders is not primarily one of psychological disposition or socio-economic status, although it may have these as some of its correlates. Rather, it is related to the mode of emotional labour that is employed by potential stakeholders, and the type of social networks – concentrated or distributed – through which communities of interest or affiliation get mobilised around specific issues or stakes.[5]

The classic route from bonder to bridger is often through enrolment as a representative of some local interest group onto a public forum – and the Olympics provided a major conduit for such transitions. One of the local community leaders interviewed illustrated very clearly the nature of the process. She ran a large pub very near to the Olympic site, which was frequented by the workforce as well as being patronised by locals. The Railway Tavern was not, she said, 'one of these plastic pubs you get in Stratford High Street, it's a community pub'. Her parents had run the pub in the 1960s when it served the market traders, and she herself had lived in the area most of her life. She was a member of the local community forum, and sat on a number of committees concerned with representing local interests in connection with the Olympics. She was a fully paid-up member of the twenty-twelvers club, seeing the Olympics and its legacy of sports facilities, housing and the Park, together with Stratford City Development, as 'the best we are ever going to get'. The pub sponsored Newham's water polo team, and she was enthusiastic about the Olympic Pool's potential as a new amenity for water sports. She was unfazed by the possibility that it could turn into a white elephant, because of the difficulty of converting it into a leisure pool for family recreational use. For her the Olympics was also an important business opportunity. She had converted the pub into a small hotel catering for business people and others visiting or working on the site. She was a classic bridger, and described in detail how she used her networking skills to get business from the Olympic site and build partnerships through her committee work:

> I get on well with people from all walks of life. I've found that it pays to put yourself about ... you get known as someone who has strong views on the Olympics and also speaks for the community and that gets you

listened to. At the same time I have developed good contacts over the years with the building industry. The site managers come in here for a drink after work, and we get talking. They often don't realise that we offer bed and breakfast, but as soon as they do, they make use of us.

At the same time her strong proprietorial stake in the Olympics led her to question key aspects of its delivery. She was particularly concerned about the provision of skills training and its accessibility to the local community. This is how she put the issue:

I know I may be talking out of place here, but we're going to get an influx of East Europeans – it's already happened – and we've got to give the locals a chance. There have been so many projects in the borough where this hasn't happened. They said they were going to build a Skills Academy on the Olympic Park to give locals, especially young people, on-site training – electrics, plumbing, bricklaying. But it never happened. They just didn't do it. I really don't know why.[6]

These positions not only relate to different stories about the East End and its immediate prospects, they are about different kinds of stakes that individuals, groups, or organisations may have in the Olympics. Here it is useful to distinguish between material and symbolic stakes, though these can be closely connected, as in the case above where business and community interests were strongly linked. But they can also come into conflict. We can imagine them as two circles that overlap to a greater or less extent. For example if you are employed in the Olympics heritage industry, or in promoting the 2012 brand, then enthusiasm for the project is mandatory. If you become disenchanted about the Olympics you cannot do your job. But if you are working as a brickie on the Olympic Park, you could see it as just another building site, although – as we saw in Chapter Five – many of the workforce did, in fact, regard it as something special, and had a symbolic stake in the success of the Games. The diagram below maps out the field of possible positions:

Figure I: Olympic stake holding

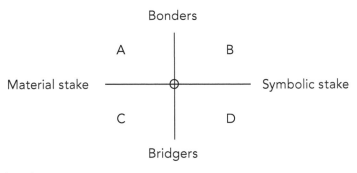

O = The Olympic compact

In the top left hand quadrant (A) are to be found those companies, organisations and interest groups whose immediate economic prospects are directly tied to the games and its legacy, and/or who stake pre-emptive claims over material assets by virtue of contractual or moral entitlement. Companies manufacturing Olympics memorabilia, community organisations in receipt of major funding from the Olympic authorities, athletes whose sponsorship deals depend on outstanding performance and academics whose credibility depends on gaining research contracts for evaluating the games would all come into this category.

In the top right (B) are the twenty-twelvers who are strongly identified with the Olympics and 2012 as 'their thing', and who regard it as a unique, once in a life-time event in which they are actively participating. For them the Olympic Park serves as an important *lieu de mémoire* and the Games themselves are part of an enduring narrative legacy.

In quadrant C we can group all those agencies whose material stake is tactical and time delimited, and/or whose involvement is primarily organised through participation in delivery consortia or via community partnerships. From this position the Olympics may be compared to one another in terms of their material costs and benefits and their legacies. It is also the position from which material disinvestment occurs when assets look like turning into liabilities.

In the bottom right quadrant (D) are those for whom 2012 is but one chapter in a continuing Olympic story, and who compare 2012 to previous Olympiads in terms of their contribution to the Olympic heritage story and the extent to which they have delivered the goods, however defined. It is the position from which symbolic disinvestment occurs when there is a perceived discrepancy between the promises that have been given by the Olympic authorities and the actual outcome.

O marks the Olympic compact, where material and symbolic stakes can be reconciled through a balancing act between strategies of bonding and bridging. It also marks the space where conflicting values of competition and co-operation, commerce and communitas, can also surface, a space of ambivalence and oscillating or contradictory positions.

Like all models, this one is a device to map a set of positions that are empirically found in a variety of strong and weak combinations. Agencies certainly shifted between these positions in the course of their involvement with the Olympics over time, and in response to the project's vicissitudes. For example some East London community organisations that began by staking strong moral claims over the Olympic Park as an exclusively local amenity, found that when they joined partnerships they were expected to partly surrender such claims in the interests of promoting the site's viability as an international heritage and tourist destination, or as an attractive post-Olympic investment opportunity for private developers. Some of these local outfits then disinvested from any stake they might have claimed in the site's material assets, such as housing, while continuing to assert symbolic claims, straddling positions B and C, and becoming strong critics of the Olympic Delivery agencies whilst still supporting the Olympic ideal.

These positions mapped onto the distinctions between different types of legacy and value orientation discussed in Chapter Six. I asked the groups what they hoped they would get out of the Olympics, both personally and for their communities, in the longer term. Bridgers saw legacy in terms of payback, although still couched in the idiom of a moral economy:

> Well, the way I look at it, we've had to go through all this kerfuffle for the past five years, and now it's over I think the community is owed something in return. What we get back should reflect what we've put in, shouldn't it? The legacy is a just reward for all the effort of so many local people to make the Games the success they were' (public service worker).

In contrast, bonders saw the Olympic Park as a windfall, but one which was part of a gift legacy.

> It's like we've been left something by a distant relative, who's very well off. We weren't expecting it, maybe we don't even deserve it, but it's dropped into our lap and we're entitled to it. We've been left this fabulous gift on condition we look after it, and hand it on to our children for their children to enjoy (nursery teacher).

Bridgers were more likely to recognise that the Olympic Park had the potential to continue to attract visitors and money to the area, and was therefore an ongoing investment from which they could expect future material benefits:

> I think we have to recognise that the Park is a fantastic asset and we're very lucky to have a stake in it. If it's handled right I think it will ensure the area's future for many years to come, but we have to make sure it's promoted in the right way and puts East London on the map as a place that has a rich heritage, and the Olympics are now just part of it (local business woman).

Whereas bonders saw it less as a dividend, more in terms of a bequest:

> I think Boris Johnson and the legacy people have to put their money – actually it's our money as taxpayers – where their mouths are and hand the Park over to the Council to run. After all they are always going on about how much they owe East London, how important the community is, and how people should behave generously and give to good causes; well, the East End is a good cause, so how about practising what they preach for once (retired transport worker).

These positions could be summarised as follows:

Table 1 East London legacy values

	Bridgers	Bonders
Gift legacy	Heritage	Heirloom
Payback legacy	Dividend	Endowment

Stake-holding holds definite implications for the way 2012 is remembered. For the bridgers it was a stepping stone in their professional advancement or in the development of the organisations to which they belong. As one of them put it, 'the Olympics were a once-in-a-life-time chance to put ourselves on the big map, and we took it'. For them the Games were primarily a social occasion, rather than a sporting one, a gigantic opportunity to network, to make new social contacts and strengthen old ties. What is memorable for them about the event is not so much the athletic performances, but the Olympic context in which these social encounters took place:

> It was great. We showed all the doubters that we could put on a great show ... the opening ceremony was brilliant. I was so busy I hardly had time to watch the athletics, though I was delighted we got the medals. You've got to be involved to appreciate the amount of effort that went into making the games a success. My feet hardly touched the ground, but when it was all over I had the satisfaction of knowing I'd done my bit to make it work (social entrepreneur).

For Olympic bonders, in contrast, the Games became part of their personal identity kit. Simply being there, being an eye and ear witness to the occasion and sharing the experience with family and friends, was for them of primary importance. It was their way of joining the twenty-twelvers club. But they also had to recognise that if this made the Olympics 'their thing', it was a lot of other people's thing too. Bonders felt comfortable enough in their partisanship of Team GB as the home team, but perhaps a bit less so in a space where almost everyone is from somewhere else, although their sense of hospitality mitigated this effect:

> We were all up for it down our way. We put flags all round the estate to show the world we were the home crew, if you know what I mean ... there was a big party on opening night, everyone came, even people who normally are a bit standoffish. Some people had rented their flats out to visitors from abroad and we invited them as well. Everyone got along just great. I felt proud to be an East Ender, knowing we were so centre stage. The only thing that was a bit off was some of the foreign youth groups that came over, they were walking round like they owned the place, singing their songs and that. I think they should have showed a bit more respect – the Germans were the worst. But the main thing was it was our party and we had a bloody good time (post office worker and local resident).

One of the young people in the group had been a 'Young Games Maker' volunteer and was still thrilled by the experience:

> It was a great honour to be chosen, cos a lot of people applied and only a few got it. I got it through McDonald's – I was working there part-time and they encouraged me to apply ... I got my picture put up on their

website and everything. My friend also went for it but he didn't get it cos he'd been in trouble with the law. We got to meet Seb Coe and some of the Team GB athletes. My job was raking the sand in the beach volley ball arena, which was quite hard work, but I really enjoyed it. In the opening ceremony we got a special mention and everyone clapped. It made you feel you were part of the home team (18 year old unemployed boy).

Others were more sceptical:

Well I reckon that its conscience money with McDonald's. They've made a fortune out of the Games and they get all this bad publicity about the crap they sell, so it just looks good to do their bit for the community, doesn't it? They came round my college asking for volunteers but no-one was really up for it. I mean they got to spend billions on the Olympics so why do they have to rely of people working for them for nothing? The athletes, most of them, don't do it for nothing … (17 year old FE student).

Two of the youth group had managed to get seats to watch events at the Paralympics, one in the Velodrome and the other in the Aquatic Centre. Both of them were fully paid up members of the twenty-twelvers club, and found the whole experience overwhelming, although not always in ways they had anticipated:

I was so excited I didn't get a wink of sleep the night before. It was a long wait before we eventually got inside, but you could feel the atmosphere. We wanted to go up the Tower but there was a long queue so we didn't. It was very hot inside the Velodrome, like a Sauna. My grandad said it reminded him of being in Burma during the war except there weren't no mozzies or Japs. We saw Sarah Storey win gold – everyone went mad. Not all the races were so exciting and I got a headache cos of the noise and the heat. I suppose the athletes are used to it. To be honest, after a couple of hours I was glad to get out and get some fresh air. The Park was amazing when it lit up, it was like something out of fairyland, people walking around smiling, and singing, everyone happy just to be there, just to be part of it (16 year old girl).

We went to see the swimming. It was pretty amazing to see the people. When they were in the water you didn't notice they didn't have a leg or had half an arm missing, they were so fast – I don't know how they did it. But it made me feel uncomfortable, like I didn't have the right to have all my arms and legs because I couldn't swim half as fast as they did without them. I tried to imagine what it must feel like to be one of them, but I couldn't (18 year old boy).

Amongst locals with a direct material stake in the success of the Games, there was a sense of disappointment, even anti-climax at the outcome. One member of the local Chamber of Commerce summed up the mood amongst the small business community:

> Olympics just didn't do the business as far as we were concerned. We were promised a bonanza and it just didn't happen. I normally do well in the summer, but my takings were down. I think a lot of people stayed away because of all the bad publicity about security, the world recession obviously didn't help, and a lot of Londoners left town for the duration thinking it would be over-run by visitors. London was no longer a working city, but it wasn't exactly on holiday either. The Olympics killed London as far as small businesses were concerned. I couldn't wait for them to be over (local shopkeeper).

For some bonders the sense of let-down confirmed their suspicion that they would be the losers and would bear the social costs while the economic benefits went elsewhere:

> London was turned into an Olympic theme park. They had these giant ads for Coca Cola, Gillette and Adidas wrapped around the buildings in Stratford – it was like the Martians had landed and taken over the place. Coe bigged up East London to get the bid but the people who made the money were not the likes of us. Call me a misery guts if you like, but I never had any high expectations that it would be any different (taxi driver).

One issue on which both the youth and adult groups were unanimous was in condemning the decision to relocate the Marathon route from Newham to central London. Indeed it was the only issue through the five years of the research on which there was consensus. But the reasons given were significantly different. Bridgers felt that the decision broke a compact with East London and exposed the fact that, as its local representatives, they were not equal partners in the Olympic project:

> It was a scandal what they did, without consultation. They let a lot of people down, and, frankly, the reasons they gave for the decision just didn't stack up. A really bad show – and it soured what should have been a joyful ending to the Games, as far as we were concerned. The whole point in locating the Games in East London was to put the area on the map, and it went out of the window, just so they could jump to the tune of the Murdochs of this world. I felt ashamed to be associated with the whole thing (social entrepreneur).

Others took a more global and real-politik view:

> Well, the fact is the Olympics aren't just about East London, are they? It's a media thing, there's millions watching around the world, and frankly, if you're sitting in Bombay, Beirut or Beijing watching it, and

you've never been to London, all you'd probably know is Big Ben, Buck House and Trafalgar Square, so unless you see those landmarks you're not going to know it's happening in London. Seeing people running past Stratford Town Hall is not going to ring a bell with them, is it? (part-time child minder).

Bonders took quite a different line. Here is one typical comment from a member of the youth group:

The marathon was a load of bollocks. I was going to watch it 'cos the route was near my house, and me and my mates we were going to do banners and that, but then, when they moved it up West, I thought to hell with it. I'm not gonna watch it on telly, when I should have been out there on the street cheering the runners on. They gave us all the talk about the Olympics being for the East End, but they're taking the piss (17 year old FE student).

There was still plenty to cheer about for most people. The medal successes of Team GB were generally applauded even by some of the miserabilists. One man in his late 70s, who had been one of the most vociferous nay-sayers from the outset, had this to say:

Team GB winning all those medals made me feel proud to be British again. I got a lump in my throat every time the flag went up, I don't mind saying. We're a small country, so coming third after China and the USA meant a lot. It made me think of the war when this country stood alone, a tiny island, against the might of fascism. We made sacrifices then and pulled through together, and the athletes did the same in 2012, they showed us the way (retired postal worker).

The implication for community relations was not lost on the group:

Our Olympic success showed us it don't matter what colour you are, it's the colour of the medal that counts. The whole country was behind Mo Farah. Maybe it shouldn't need the Olympics to teach us this lesson, but if that's one good thing to come out of it, then it will have been worth it (hospital porter).

However opinion was divided as to the longer term impact in terms of the sports legacy. The adult group expressed the hope that it would inspire young people to get involved and deliver health benefits, but many were sceptical that this would actually happen:

The BBC made a big thing about the sport legacy, with all those 'inspire a generation stories', and of course Mo Farah ... but I'm not sure it's going to turn us into a nation of keep-fit fanatics, especially amongst the kind of young people I work with in East London. If they are into

ON THE WRONG SIDE OF THE TRACK?

anything it's football, not athletics, swimming, cycling or rowing. The only difference may be with the black youth who saw Bolt, Farah and all those athletes from Africa and the Caribbean doing so well. But with the Asian kids, they didn't feel they had anything going for them – the Indians and Pakistanis didn't really show up for the Games (youth and community worker).

Others thought that motivations were more complex:

I'm a keen cyclist, have been for many years. I enjoy it, it's good exercise, it doesn't pollute the environment and I fully support the Boris bikes, and cycle lanes. But this has got nothing to do with racing or the Olympics. Cycling's got more popular but not as a sport or because of Bradley Wiggins or Chris Hoy. With the BMX and mountain biking it's a bit different. They are good legacies for the East End (web designer).

For the youth group, the key factor was their identification or lack of it with the athletes, and here issues of 'race' and ethnicity were important. Amongst the black young people there was a definite 'Farah effect': 'he made you proud to be black and British' was the consensus, but this did not extend as far as wanting to actually emulate his success. As one boy put it: 'I do my dancing, I'm not gonna start doing no long distance, just cos Mo do it'. For the girls the success of Nicola Adams in winning a gold for boxing was 'inspirational', but they were not about to follow her example and don the gloves. Most still thought boxing was 'unfeminine', a view shared by the boys who thought it was 'lesbian'.

Role modelling, which is the basis of the 2012 sport legacy strategy, does not necessarily lead to active participation, and in some cases can underpin stereotypical attitudes to athletic performance in a way which actually undermines equal opportunities. The white boys, for example, drew their own lesson from the success of black athletes on the track:

it just shows when it comes to running we just can't compete with them. I mean good luck to them, but it looks like whites are going to have to stick to their own sports, where they stand a chance. Like the long jump or boxing. There it cuts across, doesn't it? Like Luke Campbell, he got gold, he was inspired by Ali, but he's white and he ain't no Muslim (18 year old white boy).

The Bengali young people felt that the absence of their athletes (apart from the gymnast Syque Caesar) in Team GB sent the wrong message and would fuel Islamophobia:

There's this perception that if you're a Muslim, or Asian, you're not interested in sport. You're some kind of wimp. Amir Khan has shown the world that's not true, but people have short memories. We are good at many sports, not just boxing or hockey, but cricket, swimming. We have our own Asian Games (20 year old Bengali boy).

Gender was also important. The girls were predictably keen on Tom Daley, Team GB's mascot cum heart-throb, and their interest was, it has to be said, not entirely inspired by admiration for his athletic qualities:

> He's so cute. I mean he's got a gorgeous body and he's got a great personality to go with it. He's so genuine and he's had so many problems, with his dad dying and that. I've got his picture up on my wall and I've got his autograph on a T shirt which I bought on eBay. I was watching him in the Olympics, praying for him to get gold, then he got bronze and he looked over the moon, not at all disappointed. I thought 'well maybe I'll give it a go' so I went to the swimming pool and climbed up on the diving board. I mean I'm quite a good swimmer actually, I can dive in from the poolside, but up there on the board it was terrifying. I just ain't got a head for heights, if you know what I mean (17 year old FE student).

When it came to the regeneration legacy there was an equally differentiated pattern of response. I asked my discussion groups how they envisaged their post-Olympic role. For bridgers it was a matter of calculated choice determined by the opportunity costs as to whether they pursued their interests or cut their losses and moved on. One social entrepreneur put it like this:

> I've had a good Olympics, it's been fun, well most of it has, and a lot of bloody hard work to get people to work together on this thing. It's been worth it but I think the time has come to start a new chapter. You can't spend your whole life going on about the same thing. Being involved has opened up a whole lot of new opportunities for me, career wise, and I'd be daft not to follow them up.

For some, legacy promised business as usual and a chance to re-mix the metaphors:

> The Park is going to be Olympics Mark 2, isn't it? The games were exhausting and didn't perhaps deliver as much as people round here had been led to expect, but with the legacy we can get our second wind. It's a long distance event, not a sprint. Legacy is a chance to have another bite of the cherry, isn't it? Like everyone else I worry about what's going to happen to the stadium, but I think it will all work out, especially if the economy picks up (local business man).

Bonders in contrast saw the Park legacy as an opportunity to re-stake their claim to its use as a local amenity and resource, even if they remained doubtful about the outcome. This was typical of many comments noted for their cautious optimism:

They've done a tremendous job in landscaping the Park, planting all those trees, and the wetlands, getting rid of all the pollution, and I can see how it will be an asset for generations to come. The BMX track is sure to be a hit with the local youngsters and there will be lots of stuff happening to draw our people in. I just worry that in the long run the area will change and that the benefits will not really go to the people who need it most (gas fitter and community volunteer).

One member of the discussion group had been involved in the campaign by the local community at Hackney Wick to preserve the allotments that were eventually lost to the Park. He was still bitter but determined that the promise to reinstate them would be fulfilled:

It used to be a working-class thing, allotments, well nowadays it is everyone's thing. They should make a big feature of it in the Park. They talk about it being ecological and sustainable, but they should make sure that local people can grow their fruit and vegetables there (retired gardener).

Not everyone was so charitable or optimistic. One youth worker who had been involved in a number of Olympic-related projects, and had become disillusioned by the experience, put it like this:

The legacy is a joke. And the worst thing is the joke is on us, especially all the young people who have bought into it. There are all these quotes from local people on the Park benches, and stuff about the local history, but its tokenism, it costs them nothing, or very little, but it looks good to the visitors who know nothing about East London – they look at it and think 'Oh that's nice, the local people are being listened to'. But when push comes to shove, when it's a question of the big decisions, the ones that cost money, then we don't get a look in. It's the commercial interests, the corporates, who call the shots (youth worker and community activist).

One member of the group was a tenant in the Carpenter estate that directly overlooks the Olympic Park. Many of the tenants had been moved off the estate so that the top floors of two of the blocks could be rented out to the BBC as studios for the duration of the games, and there were persistent rumours that a University wanted to acquire the whole site to build a new campus as part of the post-Olympic Development:

We are not against regeneration, we are against the way they are carrying out the regeneration. We have been told so many different things. We want to keep a community together here, but there hasn't been any communication with the council or the tenant management organisation. It's very frustrating. Its like there is two Newhams, the old one, the one where the real community lives, and the other one, the new one that has been dreamt up by the planners and the Olympics people, which is what they imagine the place should be like to attract people with money (local resident and community activist).

Ceremonial readings

I was interested in how far East Londoners' attitudes and stakes were influenced by the ceremonies and their responses to them.[7] For this purpose I took a leaf out of Mass Observation's book and asked my informants to note down their first impressions of the opening and closing ceremonies, immediately after they had watched them, together with any comments by family or friends who were with them. Then a week later I asked them to write an evaluation, focusing on those elements or scenes which they liked, and those they found problematic, whether because they disliked or didn't understand them. As triggers for the discussion groups that met shortly afterwards I used short excerpts from the ceremonies illustrating issues highlighted by my own thematic analysis. In the second half of the session I screened Julien Temple's *London – The Modern Babylon* to provide a counter-narrative to bounce opinions off, and this led into a brain-storming session about what an alternative opening ceremony inspired by that film might have looked like.[8]

In comparing both the immediate assessments and more considered views, two patterns of response stood out, corresponding broadly to different strategies of Olympic stakeholding. Bonders tended to latch on to a particular image or theme that they liked or hated, and use that as the basis for either praising or rubbishing the whole show: a positive or negative halo effect.[9] They were predictably preoccupied with local cultural references, and how far these and the ceremonies as a whole represented East London, their own tastes and those of their communities. Bonders were strongly influenced by the views of family and friends and were concerned to achieve some kind of consensual validation of their opinions. Here are some representative points of view about the Isle of Wonders:

> I loved it, right from the moment when they showed the Queen with the corgies and James Bond and Winnie waving at them at they flew past ... It showed us at our best, the kiddies singing, the NHS. Paul McCartney. I found the bit where they showed pictures of people's loved ones they'd lost very moving. And 'Abide with me'. It made me cry. Mind you I didn't get a lot of it, especially the second half, but my son and grandchildren loved it – it all made sense to them, they were singing along with it. It brought us all together as a family and a nation (pensioner).

> It made me feel proud. Everyone knows East Enders walk to the beat of our own drum, we have our own swagger. It was nothing like any opening ceremony I've ever seen. Miles better than Beijing. It epitomised the nation. This is our country, our history, this is what you're going to get ... All my friends felt the same way (20 year old unemployed chef).

The following exchange illustrates the importance of cultural affiliations in determining how far the ceremony was owned:

> I loathed it. I thought it was cheesy, with the Pearlies, and the Chelsea Pensioners. It had sod-all to do with East London as far as I am concerned. They bigged up Dizzee Rascal, and showed him walking around Bow like he owned the place, wearing a baseball hat saying rebel and E3, but he's not everyone's local hero, not everyone is into his kind of music and he don't live in E3 no more. He's got a big house up west. He don't speak for the whites or the Asians, only the blacks. Another thing … they showed the Beatles and the hippies, but nothing about the skinheads, which started as an East End thing, or Goths. And then there was David Beckham on that boat with the torch, like he was the real James Bond or something, and the TV guy going on about how the East End was his manor. You gotta be joking, mate (19 year old postal worker).

> You're just saying that out of spite, cos they didn't have no Iron Maiden, or Black Sabbath or heavy metal head-bangers in it. I though the best bits were the dance routines, and they did all the different styles of music and dance, my gran started jumping up and down when they had 'My boy Lollipop'. My little brother loved the Harry Potter bit. There was a boy meets girl story … They had something for everyone, except grumpy old sods like you (18 year old office worker).

Cynicism about the personal motives of the ceremony participants sometimes spilled over into how the show itself was perceived:

> The commentator kept going on about how much money these pop stars had earned for the country, but they didn't say nothing about how much they were getting for doing the show. Paul McCartney got a million quid for a ten-minute pub singalong. Dizzee Rascal pocketed trouserfuls of cash for blagging on about his street cred. How much did the Spice Girls get for getting a free taxi ride? With the athletes it's the same thing. I'm not saying they are just in it for the money, at least not to begin with, but the richer they get, the more they are cocooned in it. They say the Olympics are about 'inspiring a generation' but the only thing they are likely to inspire in most young people is envy (20 year old college student).

Some informants changed their minds after giving it more thought, or considering other opinions:

> My first impression was that it was just a muddle, a very expensive muddle and that it was a great waste of money but then I read a few reviews which said, yes, it was a muddle, but a glorious muddle, and a very British one at that. So it made me think maybe that's what it's all about. It doesn't have to add up like a piece of arithmetic, it's more like

a potpourri. And talking to people at work, many of them felt the same way (IT worker).

At the beginning I was very sceptical. There had been all this hype about it, but then when they showed the coming of the industrial revolution – it was just breathtaking ... and there were magical moments, like the children's choirs, the bird bicycles, the Olympic rings rising into the night sky (retired garage mechanic).

Bridgers were more concerned with issues of narrative coherence and connotation, the connections that were made – or not made – between the country's past, present and future. They were also worried about how the ceremony and its image of Britain might be perceived by the wider world. For them cultural inclusivity was to some extent problematised by the question of insularity. The ceremonies were read less as an inside story about city or nation, more as a global media event. Here are some representative quotes illustrating the contrasting views:

I think they tried to pack too much in. More was less, as far as I was concerned. It should have been more focused, perhaps around the history of East London, which as we know is about the history of immigration and people coming from all over the world. Then it might have been genuinely educational. They showed the industrial revolution and how it destroyed our green and pleasant land, but it should have gone on to show the problems we have with pollution today with all the traffic. There was no continuity, or showing how the past has shaped the present (public sector worker).

It was full of little in jokes, like the gag about the weatherman saying there'd be no hurricane and then you see it happening – it was very funny but I worried that people watching in other countries would not get a lot of it. Too much of it needed translating. I think it may just have confirmed stereotypes about the British as laughing at their own jokes, being preoccupied with their own small bit of the world, and being rather smug and self satisfied about their achievements (teacher).

Multiculturalism – and what is meant by it – was highlighted by the ceremonies and much media commentary on the event, and was a focus of considerable comment, being one of the few topics on which bonders and bridgers agreed:

The media go on about multiculturalism as if they just invented it. In East London we've been living it for the past twenty years, just go down Green Street market any day of the week. We didn't need no Olympics to preach at us (market trader).

As far as I was concerned it was liquorice allsorts. I mean it had lots of different colours and sweet flavours on the outside, what the young people call a 'mash up' – the commentators called it multi-cultural. But on the inside it was the same old liquorice stick through and through – which is rather bitter to taste just on its own. It paid lip service to the contribution that immigrant communities have made, the Empire Windrush and so on, but I felt that as a statement about British identity today it just did not put its money where its mouth was. The thing that really stuck in my throat was when the people with the Olympic flag – Doreen Lawrence, people who have spent their lives fighting injustice and oppression, it was good they were recognised – when they handed the flag over to the Armed Forces, who carry out the military policies of the British government which are responsible for a lot of the problems that Britain has at the moment with terrorism. It was just so wrong (local resident and community activist).

I thought both ceremonies were a very good advertisement for British culture today. The opening was inventive, witty, often beautiful to look at and technically very sophisticated. It took risks, like the Sex Pistols and God Save the Queen, and the lesbian kiss. The worse thing about it was the TV commentators – they clearly didn't have a clue what was going on. They should have been properly briefed. The closing ceremony was a great party, maybe it went on a bit too long but some of it was brilliant – like the cars made out of newspapers, the roller skating nuns and John Lennon's face made out of all those pieces (web designer).

One member of the youth group knew someone who had taken part and made an interesting point about the discrepancy between the event as experienced live by spectators in the stadium and the way it was presented on television by the BBC:

I've got this mate who was one of the dancers in the disco scene. I was looking out for him but I couldn't see him. And he was saying how they didn't show everything going on. He said that when he saw the whole thing next day on the telly it didn't look at all like it was in the stadium. You didn't get the excitement, the noise, the drums, the whole vibe, just watching it on the telly (17 year old boy).

When it came to the sports coverage, the discrepancy could cut the other way:

I watched a lot of it on TV, especially the cycling and the swimming. But when I went to the Velodrome to see the Paralympics it was a lot different. There was a lot of waiting around between races, which you didn't get on telly, and you could see all the cyclists warming up or warming down, which they don't show you. I didn't miss the commentary. Some of it was more exciting, like when everyone was yelling for the home team, but it's not like you could just flip a button and get teleported to the swimming, when you got bored (16 year old girl).

Quite a lot of the discussion was focused around the realism, or otherwise, of the ceremonies, as in the following exchange between a 'bonder' and a 'bridger', both of them strongly committed to an East London legacy from the Olympics.

> If they wanted to show a true portrait of modern Britain we should have had rows of unemployed people dancing around the Maypole while being cheered on by a big gang of teenage mothers. Then we could have had a dance version of chavs rioting and looting while being chased by a handful of Beefeaters, and a side tableau of OAPs freezing to death because they can't afford their heating bill (carpenter).

> It's not meant to be about how the country really is. It's meant to be a picture of how we would like to imagine ourselves, and how we would like other people to see us. It's about dreams. Like John Lennon's 'Imagine'. Imagining the world was not divided by race or religion, and all the nations come together, like in the Olympics. The Olympics showed us what this island we live on could be like if we all had a common purpose, and respected each other's differences (social worker).

The screening of excerpts from *London – The Modern Babylon* helped to sharpen perceptions and positions on this as other issues. Bonders and bridgers alike were almost unanimous in their praise for the film, although they gave very different reasons for liking it:

> It showed everything that the Isle of Wonders had to leave out for fear of offending people. It showed the poverty, the everyday struggles of ordinary Londoners and the contrast with the lives of the well-to-do. We heard from real East Enders, dockers, people from the immigrant communities. And it showed us the downside, the brutality and violence, the riots and strikes, the class resentment. Winny (Winston Churchill) was no more Mr Nice Guy, it showed him in his true colours (retired trade unionist).

> I liked the soundtrack. It stayed close to the pulse, showed how the music evolved, how it expressed young people's frustrations and anger, as well as our dreams (youth worker and musician).

Bridgers were especially struck by the film's montage technique:

> I really liked the way the film moved backwards and forwards, between past and present, cross cutting so we could see the connections, the continuities as well as the change. It wasn't at all preachy, there was no talking head telling you what it all meant, it just showed stuff happening and asked you to make a judgment (local business woman).

Finally the Paralympic Opening Ceremony came in for almost universal praise amongst those who watched it:

It was very moving, to see all those people dancing, flying through the air, defying the gravity of their disabilities and then making the link with science, Newton, the discovery of gravity itself, and Stephen Hawking telling us to look up to the stars, not down at our feet ... so the two sides of the story were brought together around the theme of enlightenment, the power of mind over matter, and over prejudice. I thought the whole thing was much more together and worthwhile than the Danny Boyle show (community worker).

I thought the music was wonderful, especially the last bit where everyone was singing 'I am what I am', and the dancing with the umbrellas, and the books that turned into birds. I am not sure about bringing Prospero in yet again. The poor guy must be suffering from an identity crisis, first he is Brunel then Churchill, and now a cross between Merlin and Dumbledore. What really was the point of it? Still, the main message about human rights and disability came across strongly, which was a good thing (primary school teacher).

However over half the group did not watch it, the majority of them men, who produced a variety of ingenious apologetics for the fact. It was clear that the men felt much more threatened by seeing images of disability than women, but these gendered responses were also overdetermined by stakeholding. Bonders, whose emotional investments tend to follow the bias of projective identification, were polarised between positions of empathy (mostly female) and disgust (mostly male):

It made me cry to hear some of the stories, like the boy who had his legs blown off in Afghanistan when he was only 17, and he came down into the arena carrying the flame, and the young people in wheelchairs carrying the flag – it made me think what I'd feel if it happened to me (16 year old girl).

I started to watch it, but frankly I got bored with all the athletes leering at the camera as they went past. It was just like the Olympics except a lot of them were in wheelchairs. It's not like real sport is it – I mean good luck to them if they enjoy it but, sorry, I just don't fancy watching a bunch of guys without legs trying to play football or dance (public house barman).

I watched it but the whole thing freaked me out. It was just freaky watching a legless geezer dancing on his hands, and all those spazzies whizzing around on wires (18 year old boy).

For the bridgers the issue was not whether the Paralympics were a freak show but whether they were a sideshow:

I think they should have had the Paralympics first, because a lot of people just got a little bit fed up with the whole thing. They keep going on about how we're all going to be inspired by it for the next twenty years. But we're not. The hard fact is that none of the big players take this seriously. You don't see Paralympians advertising Adidas or McDonald's or Coca Cola. It's a very worthy cause but that's all (local businessman).

I think the Paralympics were great. The Channel Four coverage was excellent and their strapline 'thanks for the warm up' was just brilliant. It really showed they meant business (local businesswoman).

One of the group, who was disabled himself, was ambivalent about the event, and pointed out the patronising double standards that were being applied to its evaluation as well as expressing scepticism about the long term benefits, a scepticism which the British Social Attitudes survey subsequently showed to be well justified:[10]

It made me proud that we were hosting this, but I'm not really sure how much it will change public attitudes, despite the opening ceremony. The less fortunate you are seen to be, the less you have to achieve before you're labelled 'inspiring'. It was a polite way of people telling us we probably wouldn't amount to much, but had somehow surpassed their low expectations. I'd place a bet that if our Paralympic football team loses in the first round, they will still be described as 'inspirational'; if the regular England team had done the same at Euro 2012 they would be called a bunch of wankers (shop worker).

The evidence from this research seems to confirm the view that 2012 is a story open to multiple interpretations. Although different kinds of stake-holding did relate to social and cultural capital, the positions of bonders and bridgers did not stack up neatly in terms of conventional distinctions between 'rough' and 'respectable', or unskilled and skilled working class. Moreover some people shifted their positions, and their stakes in the Olympics, in response to the vicissitudes of the project. There were specific issues on which factors of gender and ethnicity clearly influenced attitudes and arguments, but just as many questions concerning the regeneration of East London where the positions taken up cut across these divisions. Age was a more significant differential, particularly in respect of the value judgments that were made about the local benefits or disbenefits of the Games.

The overwhelming majority of the over 25s applied a civic economy of worth in reaching their verdicts, although in some cases environmental or marketised criteria were applied to evaluating specific aspects of the legacy. The youth groups, while no less concerned with the community impacts, drew on a wider range of criteria, using aesthetic, or biopolitical frames of reference in reaching their conclusions. It was interesting that even those young people who had signed up for the aspirational agenda, and had become twenty-twelvers did not adopt the 'Olympic family' perspective. Even amongst those who were enthusiastic about the opening ceremony and Team GB's medal successes, there was little support for the notion of the Olympics as a nation-building exercise, let alone as an expression of David Cameron's 'Big Society'. The community activists and nay-sayers drew on a variety of oppositional rhetorics in voicing their disenchantment, but their objections remained rooted in local circumstances rather than any wider critique of Olympism. The Para-Olympic perspective was articulated briefly in a discussion about the pros and cons of West Ham taking over the main stadium but was otherwise conspicuous by its absence. In the final chapter I will consider some of the implications of this material for developing a community-based strategy for the development of the Olympic Park in the years to come.

Adam Dant, Map of the new East End

11. East 20:
towards a good enough legacy

Going for closure

One of the paradoxical impacts of the Olympics on its host cities is to make them more like themselves and consequently less like each other. London is no exception to this rule. The 2012 Games confirmed the shift in the city's centre of gravity from West to East whilst at the same time highlighting the social divisions which that geography has traditionally mapped.

London's Great Moving East show has, as we've seen, being going on since the 1980s. In 2011 the artist Adam Dant asked several 'scouts' to walk from the edge of the city towards the heart of East London, asking individuals they met en route for directions. The route map that he constructed from these randomised instructions finally and prophetically located a dustbin in Westfield Shopping Centre at Stratford as the centre of the new East End (see illustration). If he had conducted the exercise a decade earlier his scouts might have been led to the superloos in Canary Wharf, or two decades before that to a shabby room once inhabited by a reclusive Jewish scholar in Spitalfields since made famous as a site of cultural archaeology (*41).[1]

What has made this latest displacement from inner to outer East London so decisive is not its physical scale – in terms of sheer floor space the Canary Wharf development far outranks Olympic Park and Stratford City – but the epic scope of the narrative landscape that has been put in place. Yet if it is to truly qualify as an epic, East London's Olympic Story has to meet certain classical requirements: it must begin in medias res (the recession) and with an invocation to a muse (Shakespeare's Caliban), show divine intervention in the city's affairs (the IOC and global capital) and contain long and formal speeches (almost any Olympic-related event). Most importantly, epics feature heroes whose traits or feats embody the moral values of their culture as they set out on a dangerous journey or quest, overcoming many obstacles and adversaries en route, including some drawn from the Underworld (Al Qaida) before returning home, transformed and enlightened by the experience.

Epics choose their heroes carefully; they have to be champions of the people, demiurges whose public works and actions embody popular aspirations without offending the Gods. There was no shortage of candidates for the role in 2012, chief among them the mayor of London, Boris Johnson, and Head of Deliverance, Lord Coe, for whom the Games were 'a chance to live like heroes for the rest of our lives', as he put it in his long valedictory speech at the closing ceremony. There was also much talk of the 'Olympic journey' by the London Olygarchs, and an attempt to promote a superhumanism associated with the exploits of the Paralympians.

Despite these strenuous efforts the London Olympics failed the epic test and remained mired in contradictions that were only partly of their own making. In this they were no exception to the general rule. I have suggested that each Games can be defined by its unique nexus of internal contradiction and how it is managed. So what was special to 2012? The tension between public austerity and profligacy, private immiseration and the official celebration of affluence? The double standard that created a security zone which made Stratford a no-go area for many working-class and minority youth while exploiting their presence as a visible sign of London's multicultural diversity? The promise to end East London's legacy of poverty while leaving behind a legacy of gentrification? Whatever the focus, East Londoners are not going to look back on 2012 as a historic moment of renewal when these contradictions were superseded. They will, though, have a rich fund of stories to tell about what happens to a great city when it tries – and inevitably fails – to live out its Olympic dream.

Located within a more immediate frame of reference, it is relatively easy to draw up a balance sheet for 2012. The event had its undoubted successes. The Velodrome was the star of the architectural show. The prognostications of disaster failed to materialise. Instead, the weather improved, the Team GB medals kept coming and then we had the Paralympics. The Paralympics were the great success story of 2012, and it may well be that the London Games will be best and longest remembered as the Olympiad in which disability athletics came of age as an exciting sporting spectacle in its own right, and not just as a sideshow to the main event. Meanwhile enough people entered into the party spirit – lying around getting drunk or stoned in London parks while watching the athletes perform on giant screens – to keep the local health services working overtime for the duration of the Games.

There were also some costly fiascos. The ill named London Pleasure Gardens, sited at the ominous sounding Silo D in the Royal Docks, were meant to revive the culture of popular festivity and recreation in this recession-blighted part of East London; but the project only succeeded in hosting a concert themed around the explosion in a local munitions factory in 1917 and a two-day festival before it was closed down on health and safety grounds, promptly going into administration and sinking without trace, taking a couple of million pounds of public money with it. And there was the last minute relocation of the marathon in a shameful capitulation to the corporate media, recapitulating a history of long duration in which the East End has been a poor relation to the West.

Yet what counts in the long run is not these obvious indicators of success or failure. I have argued that the post-Olympic debate should neither be limited to an inquest into what went right or wrong in the delivery, nor be extended to become a soap opera in which 2012 and its legacy never end. It should be a genuine 'values tournament', in which the criteria we apply to judging such an event become a subject of a public debate that is as much about the kind of society and city we want to live in as it is about the Olympics themselves.[2]

Values, I have suggested, can be defined in many different ways. To a market economist they measure the extent to which something is desired and how much people are willing to forego to get it. Value is measured by market price, and everything – and everyone – has their price. So we can ask whether the Olympics gave value for money in delivering the goods to all those who in various ways bought into it. To a Marxist economist, however, value is to be measured by the amount of labour that goes into the making of something, which is not fully represented in what its producers are paid; the exchange value of commodities, including that of labour, conceals the mechanisms of exploitation through which 'surplus value' or profit is extracted. From this standpoint the Olympics are a gigantic machinery for exploiting the workforces engaged in their preparation, enabling the companies which employ them to sustain their profitability and stay in business at a time of world recession; in terms of consumption they are a bread and circus act distracting workers from the real issues, a form of popular escapism, pure and simple, at best a way of conducting the class struggle by other, more diplomatic means, at worst a poor excuse to declare a truce.

To a sociologist values represent what groups consider to be worthwhile, what represents for them the 'good life' or what they judge to be fitting or normative: these might be values of altruism, co-operation and generosity, or individualism, competition and parsimony, but in every case they are enacted through specific social practices. For an anthropologist value always involves some kind of symbolic investment in an object, person or event that gives it special, often ritual, significance.[3] So the Olympics may be judged in terms of how far they promote the dominant values of the market place or enable alternative economies of worth to flourish.

When the term 'value judgement' is attributed to some proposition about the world, it usually implies that it is biased, or in some way departs from the gold standard of scientific objectivity and truth. This is especially likely to be the case where aesthetic or moral judgements are in question, and where issues of personal taste or ethics are at stake. 'I think Hadid's Aquatic Centre looks like a giant tongue hanging out' is not likely to be taken as an accurate or fair description of this building, but as a statement of distaste for a certain kind of modernist architecture.

The theory of judgement remains a fraught matter of academic disputation, but most philosophers agree that judgements of any kind are always based implicitly on values rather than on some rational calculation or dispassionate weighing of the evidence.[4] In similar vein I have argued that the idea promoted by the Olympic audit culture that the two can be divorced is a nonsense, because some higher order principle of evaluation is always at stake. What counts as a benefit within one economy of worth may be put down as a cost within another. What counts from one standpoint as the creation of new public amenity for Londoners, from another represents the destruction of a fragile but valuable eco-system and local community resource.

Judgements based on evidence about outcomes are always over-determined by expectations. The higher the expectation, the more invested in the Olympic dream, the greater the inclination to turn a blind eye to shortcomings and concentrate on the positives. But also the greater the gap between promise and outcome the more likely it is that disappointment will be tempered by the 'sour grapes' effect.[5] We never asked for the Olympics in the first place! On the other hand, if you have low expectations, you may be pleasantly surprised, while if worst fears are realised then judgements becomes a game of 'we told you so'. As we saw in the discussion of East Enders' response to the ceremonies, the halo effect – the transfer of approval from a single desirable aspect of a phenomenon to other, much less agreeable, dimensions – can be mobilised by those for whom the Games can do no wrong; and, equally, it can always be countered by its reverse – the damning of a whole show because you don't like one of the scenes: a typical strategy of those for whom the Olympics can do no right.

It is against this background that we have to create a forum for a post-Olympic debate as an intrinsic part of its legacy. One of the problems is that there is no precedent for such a long-term public involvement in planning, and no structure has been put in place to sustain it. The forms of community consultation for 2012 looked impressive on paper, but in practice left a lot to be desired. I was able to observe this credibility gap in action when I visited a primary school close to the Olympic Park site, where the children had devised an imaginative and well researched post-Olympic scheme for an urban farm, complete with sheep, goats, rabbits, pigs and horses, to be located on the Park. The school presented the idea to a design team from one of the site developers as part of a local community outreach programme that boasted that it was committed to working with local people and implementing their ideas. The farm would, the children explained, beef up the site's green credentials, whilst providing a major attraction for children whose needs were otherwise scarcely catered for. It was clearly a very good idea, but unfortunately it was not part of the master plan. So, with a few embarrassed mutterings about 'looking into it', the team hastily produced some samples of paving stones and invited the children to say which ones they preferred for the walkways. 'You'll be able to tell your mums you helped build the Olympics', one of the designers said brightly, as the children, somewhat crestfallen at the lack of response to their proposal, looked dubiously at the brightly coloured tiles.

Cynics might argue that these children were learning an important political lesson about the cosmetic aspects of public consultation in a world where what you see is not always what you get. But it is not an educational experience that sits well as part of a project that appealed so directly to the idealism of youth, and spent large amounts of public money to enlist their enthusiasm and support.

So it will be difficult to create a credible and sustainable framework for public deliberation, but not impossible. The delivery of 2012 was a massively top-down operation. Perhaps it had to be, given its scale and complexity, and the chain of command and accountability imposed by the IOC – although it is entirely possible to envisage an alternative, more devolved and democratically accountable delivery structure.[6] But the same constraints do not apply to the Post-Olympics. If I have argued against 'legacy fetishism' it is not because I think that the post-Games reconstruction of the Park or the regeneration of the Lower Lea Valley are unimportant, but because 'legacy' has become a source of magical thinking about what the Olympics can deliver, and has raised public expectations far higher than is realistic, especially in a period of economic recession. And this can only serve to produce public disenchantment or disengagement.[7]

Many of the East Enders I interviewed in the course of my research surprised me by saying that their strongest wish for 2012 was that 'nothing bad happened'. This was as true of those who were enthusiastic at the prospect as those who were anxious about it. At the time I put this down to the fact that the terrorist bombing in London on the day after the announcement that London had won the bid was still quite fresh in people's minds. But this apprehension persisted over the years and caused me to think that perhaps it represented something more than the fear of some catastrophic incident. It might be a defence against raising hopes for something better that might not be fulfilled. We are, after all, living in a period of rising aspiration *and* falling expectation. It might also be a way of saying that a 'good enough Games' would be one which was remembered for the sporting action, or possibly its opening and closing ceremonies, and nothing else. And as such it might be an implicit retort to those for whom what happens after the event is what counts in the long run.

In Chapter Six I suggested that we needed to reclassify legacies, to specify their different domains and discourses in terms of their internal logics. This proposal is motivated by a desire to frame the Olympic story more precisely. As part of this we need to find a rational point of post-Olympic closure, so that London 2012 does not turn into a shaggy dog story in which the tail gets longer and longer and does all the wagging. Short of that it really is a case of Olympics in Wonderland. Like the Dodo's Caucus race, it is never possible to know when it is over or who has won.

Lord Coe attempted to go for closure when, in his final ceremonial address to the Olympic city and nation, he told a story about his meeting with a doctor while travelling on the underground. The medic had treated the victims of the 7/7 attack and had volunteered for the Olympics as a way of coming to terms with that experience. In the Isle of Wonders, that moment was implicitly recognised in the Wall of Remembrance sequence, which showed photographs of the 52 victims of 7/7, even though they were identified generically as 'family and friends who could not be with us tonight'. Subsequently the sequence was re-described as being a memorial to the war dead, or about 'mortality', but this stab at abstract universality, no doubt inspired by fear of stirring up sensitivities amongst the British Muslim community, did not fool Londoners, who got the message without it having to be spelt out. But what kind of closure is it which remains haunted by such a degree of public disavowal?

There were other kinds of denial. Boris Johnson, clown-in-residence of

London's Olympic Circus, recognised that the Big Tent was about to move on and was anxious lest the momentum of 2012 as a civic enterprise be dissipated. Half jokingly he suggested that London should host the Olympics every year. Yet there is a serious problem here. Given that there is no ultimate arbiter – not even the IOC – of the Games's economy of worth, and no final judgement day, how can some conclusion, however provisional, be reached?

If you ask a professional story-teller how they know when to stop, they will reply that every story has its own in-built principle of parsimony. The Olympic story is no exception. The periodicity of the Games furnishes an intrinsic punctuation point: every four years there is a new Olympiad and a fresh chapter to relate. So far as London is concerned, then, 2016 should be the cut-off point for the 'Olympification' process. Any new planning initiatives after that date should be regarded not as part of the 2012 aftermath but as a new beginning, something to be narrated and evaluated within a quite separate frame of reference, so that the regeneration of East London can take new directions. For example, in terms of the future of Olympic Park, its redevelopment plan needs to be finalised over the next three years so that the assets to be transferred to the host community can be precisely determined.

This does not mean, of course, the end of the 2012 story – its narrative legacy will continue to evolve, as will its reputational status, and as long as there is an interpretive community of Olympics researchers to sustain it, the debate about London's Olympic heritage will go on. But it does mean that we put an evaluative frame around the event which allows us to get it in some kind of historical perspective. We need to understand 2012 as a specific moment or conjuncture in a process of longer duration, namely the regeneration of East London, without reducing its legacy effects to a reiteration or facsimile of some grand master plan dominated by nostalgia for the future.

For most Londoners and even for most of the rank and file twenty-twelvers, the Olympics will certainly be a moment to remember rather than a bench-mark against which to measure the rest of their lives. Just as a 'good enough parent' is one who enables children to grow up and embark on life on their own terms with reasonable optimism, so a good enough London Olympics is one that allows the generation of 'twenty-twelvers' to build on their positive experiences and memories of the event and move on to help build a world in which everyone does *not* have to be an athlete or a winner to enjoy the good things in life.[8] The medal-winning athletes, and some of the Olygarchs who have dedicated the last seven years of their lives to making 2012 happen will find it hardest to move on. For the rest of us ordinary mortals it will be good enough to have been there and come away with a story to tell.

The Olygarchs' parade

The post-Olympic debate is inevitably focused in the short term on the transformation of the Olympic Park being co-ordinated by the Mayor's London Legacy Development Corporation (LLDC). It is worth looking at the composition of the Corporation's board of management, for it has its own story to tell about the priorities that are likely to inform the project. The board includes the usual suspects: some of the key players in the 2012 delivery team, a cross-section of civic and corporate interests supplemented by specialists in marketing, and events/venue management, plus the one mandatory local black media business woman. All the members of the board are, in Robert Putnam's terms, bridgers, people who have worked through partnerships in pursuing their individual paths to success. The chairman, Baroness Ford, is from a banking background, and, despite the fact that this is a public sector organisation, the private sector dominates the board.

There is one social entrepreneur, Lord Mawson, whose career and outlook in some ways exemplifies the approach to regeneration which has been adopted. Mawson started out as a clergyman in an East End parish, and subsequently became disenchanted with Labour's welfare statism, which, in anticipation of David Cameron's critique of New Labourism, he saw as creating a culture of dependency amongst the poor and weakening the bonds of civil society. In its place he advocated a form of bootstrap capitalism with a communitarian emphasis, and – unlike Samuel Smiles – he practised what he preached, setting up the Bromley-by-Bow Health Centre, and running training programmes for the local unemployed to help them set up their own small businesses. Mawson specialises in community engagement around large-scale regeneration projects, and – in his effortless bridging what gap there was between Thatcherism and Blairism – was literally and metaphorically entitled to act as a spokesperson for the 'third sector' in the counsels of New Labour. Now, of course, he is a fervent supporter of David Cameron's 'Big Society'.[9]

The Tories' localist policies always sat somewhat uncomfortably within the dirigiste command structure of LOCOG and the ODA, although, of course, the Olympics aspirational agenda was right up their street. But now in the post-Olympics there is an opportunity for them to demonstrate how Cameron-style localism works, how bottom-up regeneration can somehow be achieved through, or despite, a top-down management structure. Unfortunately the LLDC has fudged the issue. It would have been entirely possible to invite representatives from the local Community Forum or the Stratford Renaissance Partnership, the local regeneration consortium, to sit on the board, and this would have sent a message that more than lip service was being paid to local interests. Instead the emphasis has been placed on establishing deeper forms of community consultation. For example there is a Youth Panel drawn from schools in the five Olympic boroughs, whose members get a crash course in architectural, planning and regeneration issues, as well as in advocacy and presentation skills, and who have made substantive inputs into the designing of youth provision for the Olympic Park. There has also been an attempt at building sustained relationships with local community organisations, especially faith communities.

Nevertheless, all the strategic planning decisions about the Park are to be made by the LLDC, yet another unelected quango of the very kind that the Tories promised to abolish – and in the case of the Thames Gateway Plan actually did. The most crucial decision of all – to turn down the Wellcome Trust's offer to redevelop the whole site as an East London Tech City – was taken by the GLA and the government with no public discussion at all.[10]

Instead the GLA decided to sacrifice long-term public benefit to short-term profit and go ahead with selling off the Athletes Village and adjacent plots to the Qatari Royal family, whose track record in UK property development and management includes creating an urban village for the super rich in Knightsbridge, and the rebuilding of Chelsea Barracks, with the blessing of Prince Charles, as pied à terres for the international jet set.

Imagining community, glossing class

The American poet Wallace Stevens once famously said that people live not in places but in the description of places, and since its inception the LLDC has gone in for some strenuous re-description of the Olympic site, drawing on much the same Panglossian vocabulary as the original bid to promote their vision of the Park as offering the best of all possible urban worlds:[11]

> Imagine the best of London, all in one place. Tradition and innovation, side-by-side, in a landscape of quality family homes, waterways, parklands and open spaces – anchored by the London 2012 Olympic and Paralympic venues. The future Queen Elizabeth Olympic Park will offer all of this and more.
>
> It will take the best of 'old' London – such as terraced housing inspired by Georgian and Victorian architecture, set in crescents and squares, within easy walking distance of a variety of parks and open spaces.

Olygopolis 2020: Legacy development flythrough

It will take the best of 'new' London – whether in terms of sport, sustainability or technology – to create a new destination for business, leisure and life. Above all, the Park will be inspired by London's long history of 'villages', quality public spaces, facilities and urban living, learning from the best of the past – to build successful communities for families of the future.[12]

So it's a familiar story of something old, something new, something borrowed, something blue (waterfront development), the tried and tested formula of what has been called 'recombinant' urbanism, which draws on traditional vernacular architectural idioms in conjunction with state-of-the-art construction and design technologies to produce a post-modern mix of built forms.[13] The motif of the 'urban village' is central to this concept:

Five new neighbourhoods will be established around the Park, each with its own distinct character. Some residents will live in modern squares and terraces, others will enjoy riverside living, with front doors and gardens opening on to water. With the right mix of apartments and houses, located close to the facilities communities need to develop and grow, the Park will have the foundations to become a prosperous, vibrant new piece of city.[14]

The urban village is very much an invented metropolitan tradition and refers primarily to working-class neighbourhoods in the inner city that either have become gentrified, or are where the 'gentry' have always lived – or at least since the eighteenth century.[15] Jane Jacobs, the American urbanist who was an apostle of 'spontaneous un-slumming', saw the urban village as a model of piecemeal urban renewal in inner city areas threatened by slash and burn redevelopment – an alternative regeneration strategy led by small businesses rather than large corporations.[16] More recently, environmentalists have adopted the urban village as a symbol of historical individuality threatened by the culturally homogenising pressures of globalisation, as well as a model of local democracy and sustainable community development.[17] Amidst cries of 'there goes the neighbourhood' as yet another Starbucks opens, the 'small is beautiful' school of urbanism has made significant inroads into both popular attitudes and professional planning practice over the last decade.[18]

Even though it is not in fact an appropriate model for the Olympic Park, given the very different circumstances of its conception, something of this philosophy has undoubtedly rubbed off on the Park designers. One of the features that gives the urban village its distinctive cosmopolitan atmosphere is the presence of artists. The Development Corporation has the ambition to make the Olympic Park into a new cultural quarter – 'a bit of Hoxton and a bit of the South Bank' was how one Olygarch described it – and as such a home and workplace for East London's growing creative class of artists, designers, and media folk. These are a relatively new phenomenon, not least in their mode of attachment to place.[19] For although they are global go-getters, constantly on the move, and definitely 'going places', they are as concerned with the cultural assets which make an area desirable as they are with the market value of their property; the aesthetics of a neighbourhood are as important to them as its material amenities, transport connectedness and social status, and their mobile privatism is tempered by their environmental concerns.[20]

The fact that gentrification is very much the name of the Olympic Park game is underscored by its residential strategy. The legacy plan promises a 70/30 split between privately owned housing for affluent professionals and 'affordable housing' that in principle is available to lower-income groups. In fact recent measures introduced by the government have stretched the concept of affordability upwards to include middle-income groups, whilst at the same time hiking rents in social housing up to 80 per cent of market rents, which will put them well beyond the pockets of the poor. And in some cases even the 70/30 cut is qualified by the cautionary 'if viable'. In East Village, the first of the new neighbourhoods, the housing association has promised that it will be 'nearly impossible' to tell the difference between privately rented homes and the social rents, and that its style of management will be 'tenure blind'. Unfortunately the signs and symbols of social distinction are not confined to architecture, and can defy even the most egalitarian housing policy: no amount of 'pepper potting' can prevent the social radar of passers-by from registering the tale that is told by door knockers, cars, prams, gardens, the presence or absence of curtains, and styles of external décor. Finally the eight to ten thousand jobs that it is claimed the Park will eventually create will be overwhelmingly concentrated in the knowledge economy, financial and professional services and the cultural industries, giving a further boost to the gentrification process, while a smaller number of people will be employed in the low-wage, low-skill sectors, primarily in the local hotel, catering and retail trades, or as office cleaners, site maintenance and security staff.

There is a crude enough spatial logic to this dual economy. The professional services class thrown up by the new economy needs another kind of service class to look after it; it needs people to wash, cook and clean for it; to mend its equipment, service its cars, mind its children and pets, minister to its recreational needs, staff its shops, wine bars and restaurants, improve its houses, fix its drains, and populate its neighbourhoods with a little local colour. This is precisely the role assigned to the post-industrial working class for whom the Olympic Park will provide some limited accommodation.[21]

The persistence of class distinctions is glossed over in the LLDC prospectus in a number of ways. Firstly by the reiteration that much of the housing will be for families, and that 'family values' will prevail in the design of public amenities. In fact in the context of the housing market a family home is simply a large house that has three or more bedrooms, and it can just as easily be occupied by a single childless but affluent owner. The possibility that many of the apartments will become company flats, as happened in the Barbican, another prestigious housing development linked to a cultural centre, or that the new housing will become a buy to rent investment opportunity, as has occurred in the Royal Docks, can certainly not be ruled out.

Secondly, there is a great deal of talk about social inclusivity, but what this turns out to mean is that the site will have disability access and housing designed for life-time occupation, including special provision for senior citizens. While this is admirable, it rather dodges the fact that socio-economic status will continue to regulate and restrict access to these facilities; there is no sense in which this project could be regarded as redistributive in its effect on local housing classes. It is wheelchair access, not social access, that is the priority here. The outcome is more likely to be yet another example of 'splintering urbanism', offering a further prospect on global opportunity structures for those who are already fully paid-up members of the network society, while those who are dependent on the local, or informal economy, or the state, remain a marginal, even if not actively marginalised, presence.[22]

The strongest feature of the plan is its neighbourhood structure, which owes more than a little to Ebenezer Howard's vision of the garden city: housing, schools, shops, health centres and public space, including children's playgrounds, all are closely integrated into the urban fabric. There is no doubt that, taken as a whole, it represents a significant advance on any previous post-Olympic site development. The only pity is that the main beneficiaries are likely to be wealthy investors and middle-class gentrifiers, rather than local East Enders.

Itchicoo Park it ain't

Much is made in the LLDC prospectus of the fact that the Park is an important public amenity for locals as well as a tourist destination for visitors to London. Here is how a day out in the Park is imagined:

> A day in the Park might start with a coffee and toast, soaking in the views of the Park and the striking 2012 Games venues. Your morning could feature a trip up the ArcelorMittal Orbit – to see the remarkable panorama across London – followed by some retail therapy at Westfield Stratford City. Lunchtime could include some exercise at one of the sports venues or some street art in the open spaces that will feature an exciting line-up of activities and performance. Your afternoon could be full of sport, whether trying your hand at BMX at the Velo Park or watching world champions at the Aquatics Centre or the Stadium.
>
> And, to finish the day, you could enjoy dinner at one of the Park's restaurants – or head to Brick Lane, Green Street or other East London hotspots to enjoy local music and cuisine.

This 'visitor' is nothing if not an all-rounder, combining the tastes of flaneur, sightseer, sports enthusiast, shopaholic, fitness freak, gourmet and BMX biker all in one! But actually this little scenario is very revealing about what kind of public space is being envisaged. It is what Michel Foucault has called a 'heterotopia', an 'other' space, which juxtaposes in a single place a multiplicity of sites that are in themselves normally incompatible in scale and function and belong to quite different urban realms: the shop, the stadium, the garden, the observational tower, the terraced house, the pleasure ground.[23] Heterotopias can be exciting and fun, but not everyone wants all the different elements of city life compressed – or jumbled up – in one space.

In any case, what most people enjoy doing in a park on a fine summer's day is nothing much: picnicking, sun-bathing, flirting, reading, listening to music, or just sitting around gossiping, while for those more actively inclined throwing a Frisbee or kicking a ball about is the summit of their athletic ambition. There should be plenty of scope for all this relaxed in/activity in the Olympic Park, especially in the ecological Northern Park which includes wetlands, woodlands and meadows, at least until required for commercial development. Still it is a bit worrying – and symptomatic of the aspirational 'get-fit' Olympic agenda the Park is supposed to embody – that none of the promotional videos or artists' impressions actually show people just lying around on the grass. They are either striding purposefully about, doing or watching sport, or jogging, no doubt egged on by Monica Monvicini's giant installation RUN (^187).

There is another sense in which 'otherness' has been given a local resonance in the LLDC publicity. The frequent mention of 'East London hotspots' with their local music and cuisine, and similar references to events which will 'showcase local diversity and heritage', suggests that if East Enders have a walk-on part in the post-Olympic spectacle it is to add a little local colour to the Park 'experience' by performing their cultures for the benefit of passing trade. It is the familiar 'order in variety' formula of British style multiculturalism: a governing elite (here the Development Corporation) provides the order (in this case the planning framework), while the 'ethnics', the 'locals', the 'people', the 'others', furnish the variety in the urban setting.[24]

From a design standpoint the layout of the Park, its configuration of venues, connecting paths and open spaces, draws explicitly on the tradition of English landscape gardening; but here order-in-variety is applied to the overall planning concept . The variety is provided by the sports venues, each of which has a distinctive architectural identity, and the order – or at least the harmonious confusion – is produced by the landscaping (see illustration). The Park's chief design consultant, and now advisor to the LLDC, Ricky Burdett, is quite up-front about the fact that no 'one-size-fits-all' design brief was imposed on the architects, and that they were encouraged to 'do their own thing'. He describes the result as 'fragmented but organic', an aptly post-modern image for the style of urbanism proposed.[25] This architectural melange could all too easily result in what Rem Koolhaas called junkspace, 'a fuzzy empire of blur, a seamless patchwork of the permanently disjointed'. This is a very different kind of spatiality from that order in disorder created when popular do-it-yourself urbanism emerges through grassroots community organisation.[26]

The biggest design challenge in transforming the park from an Olympic venue into a public amenity has to do with its perimeter. The electrified fence that has surrounded the location since 2006 is due to be replaced by a series of bridges and other entry points. But the fence did more than create a physical barrier; it created an edge city of its own, defined in relation to social exclusion. To transform an impermeable boundary into a real borderland, a space of positive interaction between the park and its environs, will take some doing, and is not going to happen without working through some quite sticky demarcation disputes.

Jason Orton, Lie of the land: Olympic Park 2012

In fact the park has been subjected to number of quite distinct landscaping strategies that co-exist in some degree of tension, some pulling it towards strong boundary maintenance and some towards a more open encounter with the wider environment. Some strategies are designed to make the park into a compact, defensible space: clamping strategies seek to enclose the site around itself to meet financing, security, maintenance and sustainability requirements; clustering strategies seek to give spatial articulation to a multiplicity of pathways, traffic flows and facilities, and a new nexus of productivity, investment and capital accumulation. On the other hand scoping – organising the landscape into a distinctive regime of envisagement and traverse – and scaling – positioning it within local/regional/national and global narratives – opens the site out to a wider set of interactions not so easily regulated.

This underlying spatial tension is camouflaged by the carefully modulated alternation of formal and informal design elements, knitted together to give the semblance of environmental 'organicity'. This manoeuvre takes a very concrete form. The biodiversity action plan for 45 hectares of new habitat, including wetlands, is designed to ensure that the fauna and flora disrupted by site remediation is replaced. Yet there will be no re-instatement of the 'alien species' that flourished amidst the richly polluted urban wilderness that was the pre-Olympic site, making it such an important place of pilgrimage for naturalists and ruinologists alike; no reprieve then for Japanese Knotweed, Indian balsam, and other exotic trespassers, not to mention the marijuana plants that flourished so wildly amidst the industrial ruins. The Park will thus offer the visitor an artificial paradise of Nature, an anti-septic isle from whose green and pleasant land all noxious weeds have been banished; it will be a beautifying lie about the cultural and environmental politics that have gone into its making.

In this best of all possible worlds there is no tension between the local and the global. The Park is advertised as a 'global attraction', with the Orbital Tower as one of the 'wonders of London' and a must-see for visitors, while in the same breath, or in the case of the promotional video with the flit of a butterfly wing, we are sitting in a quiet quasi-suburban garden having tea. The possibility that residents may get a little tired of being constantly ogled and photographed as they mow their lawns by crowds of post-Olympic tourists does not seem to have crossed the minds of the site imagineers, or perhaps they consider it a minor inconvenience, part of a price worth paying for being part of such a prestigious development on such a famous site.

Olygopolis revisited

It is not possible to consider the future of this part of East London without setting it in its wider urban context. For example, the proposed International Quarter, which consists of a 'gold-plated' development featuring office blocks, hotels and luxury apartments in Stratford City, will tower over the ex-Olympic village without a backward glance at the claim in the Park prospectus that the commitment to create intimate living space has not been sacrificed to economies of scale. The presence of this new zone will exert its own gravitational pull on the pattern of London's eastwards growth, and as such can be considered to form part of what we might call Olygopolis.

Olygopolis can be defined as an urban centre whose development and demographic has been largely determined by the catalytic presence of Olympic infrastructure, and where a few large companies – such as Westfield – dominate the spatial economy and push up land values accordingly. In terms of place identity, it is a giant theme park, modelled on Disneyland, where the theme is sport and the Olympics. As for the impact on urban ecology, Olygopolis creates a new set of centre/periphery relations. Planners now talk about the 'Olympic fringe' – by which they mostly mean Hackney Wick and the Lower Lea Valley, areas immediately adjacent to the park, rather than Stratford's more extensive hinterland. The Lea Valley has long been the focus of regeneration plans as part of the Thames Gateway, but now that it has been 'Olympified' its future has been redefined: it is to be a green 'pendant' to Olympic Park.

The case of Hackney Wick, the twenty-twelvers' very own edge city, is instructive in this regard. In the past five years 'The Wick' has established a local/global reputation as a counter-cultural quarter. Many East End artists, driven out of the now fashionable areas of Whitechapel, Spitalfields and Bow by rising rents, moved into studios in the area's industrial warehouses; and hot on their heels came a trickle of galleries, bookshops, cafés and wine bars. However, the cycle of culture-led regeneration and its associated gentrification

Graffiti War: Coca Cola mural dogged at Hackney Wick

was not yet complete by 2012; there still remained a critical mass of young and not so British artists who had put down roots and turned the buildings abutting onto Olympic Park into a 2012 version of Democracy Wall. Their dramatic and often ironic visual statements about 'Olympification' drew crowds of spectators, and WickED became the Cultural Olympiad's favourite, unsponsored, fringe festival. Never slow to seize an opportunity to tap into authentic grassroots creative energy, LOCOG then offered some of the better known 'graffers' commissions to produce a mega mural on the side of a local warehouse paid for by Coca Cola, one of their biggest sponsors, to promote their brand. The coca-colonisation of East London – the visual appropriation of public space by private companies, turning whole areas into giant advertising hoardings for their products – quickly became a focal point of creative dissent. This was not what the rebranding of East London was supposed to be about! The 'Cola Wall' predictably divided the local community of artists. There were some who took a 'if you can't beat 'em, join 'em line', whilst others condemned it as selling out to the class enemy. However the ground is all the time shifting under the artists' feet. The development plan for the area envisages it as 'a new creative and high-tech hub for East London with affordable and flexible workspace and residential apartments with supporting retail space and café/restaurants'. This is the cue for estate agents and property developers to start rebranding the area as 'des res' for the better-heeled members of the creative class: The Wick is on its way to becoming another 'happening scene', like Camden Market, Hoxton or Covent Garden. It is a little case study in the geo-politics of Olygopolis.

Place making: from terminal architecture to dwelling place

The most ambitious and problematic aspect of the park legacy project is the attempt to integrate the remaining sports venues within an emergent urban fabric constructed around residential communities, and what are somewhat optimistically called 'employment hubs'. Sports stadia by their sheer physical size, and the fact that they remain empty for much of the time, and then briefly flood an area with a multitudinous and often vociferous population of spectators, exert an unsettling and even uncanny effect on their neighbourhoods.[27] In the case of Olympic Park the fate of the stadium, the biggest material asset (or in some views liability) as well as the symbolic flagship of the whole enterprise, has come to focus public anxieties about the long-term viability of the 2012 project (^132). The difficulty in finding a tenant, and a sustainable post-Olympic use has conjured up visions of other Olympic venues that have turned into ghost towns, haunted by their former glory, their only function to serve as cautionary monuments to the public folly or hubris that built them. The spectacle of the derelict and vandalised remains of the Athens Games is still just too close for comfort. The fact that the Bird's Nest stadium in Beijing is now used for Segway racing at £12.50 a go is hardly an encouraging precedent.

The prophets of doom have an ally in W.G. Sebald who, like Iain Sinclair, takes a jaundiced view of 'grand projects' and belongs to a long intellectual tradition of gloomy prognostication about urbanistic adventures:

> It is often our mightiest projects that betray the degree of our insecurity. We gaze at them in wonder, a kind of wonder which is itself a form of dawning horror, for we know somehow by instinct that outsize buildings cast the shadow of their own destruction before them and are designated from the first with an eye to their later existence as ruins.[28]

For better or worse there is nothing awesome or prophetic about the 2012 stadium. It is a good example of what has been called 'terminal architecture' – a huge oval shed for accommodating spectators and athletes with the maximum efficiency and minimum of fuss; as such it is indistinguishable from dozens of similar structures, in combining the envelope functionality of the aircraft hanger with the palatial uselessness of the architectural folly and the spiritual hydraulics of a cathedral where people come to worship sport.[29] The sports stadium is a hybrid in another sense. It is part Observatory, but without its panoptic vision, and part auditorium, but without its acoustics. It is a non place, a transit zone, a space of flows.[30] But it is a very special kind of non-place, because although it does not in itself generate any sense of local attachment, the stadium was the epicentre of a global mediascape organised around the games, and in the post-Olympics it serves as focal point of public and private memory work as well as a place of pilgrimage for Olympophiles. It cannot not be regarded as a heritage site.

The original plan was for the stadium to be 'deconstructed' after the games, an operation which has nothing to do with its critical appraisal as an urban text but, rather, is a polite name for demolition. It was only subsequently that it was decided to make it into a legacy venue. Undoubtedly it was the primacy given to legacy in the bid that changed the stadium brief. The fact is that the Olympics are a travelling circus, but, because they have to justify their role by establishing permanent assets for the host city, they cannot exploit the opportunity that would otherwise be offered of developing a new style of temporary plug-in architecture. It is entirely feasible to construct large stadia that are fully demountable. British architects lead the world in buildings that can be instantly erected to provide temporary shelter or stage one-off events. From geodesic domes to pneumatic auditoria, such structures have been at the leading edge of new developments in design and engineering. Such structures also feature significantly in the tradition of radical urbanism inaugurated by Constant Nieuwenhuys and the French situationists in the 1960s.[31] Far from being utopian, this style of architecture offers a strategic solution to the major legacy problem that is created by the need to put up buildings that really have little or no post-Olympic use: simply take them down and move them on to the next Olympic venue. The structures could be commissioned and owned by the IOC and leased to host cities as and when required. To 'ephemeralise' the Olympic infrastructure in this way would not only reduce the cost of staging the games and put them within the reach of a far wider range of cities and nations, but it would also restore to them their properly transient, inter-ludic, role. After all, part of the excitement of a travelling circus when it comes to town stems from the fact that it creates an evanescent environment dedicated to transient pleasures.

As it stands, 2012 Legacy Inc is in some difficulties. The purpose built International Media Centre may have to be demolished: the Aquatic Centre (^ 134) cannot be transformed into a recreational swimming pool for local community use. London already has a world-class athletics stadium in the National Sports Centre at Crystal Palace, and numerous other stadia, including Wembley, that can stage large-scale open air events. The LLDC still puts a brave face on the future:

> Everyone's an athlete. The magic and spirit of the world's greatest sporting festival will live on in the Park's five sporting venues. In the South Park, the two main London 2012 venues – the Stadium and the Aquatics Centre – will be at the heart of an exciting new visitor experience.

To place the two premium sites whose futures are the most problematic at the heart of the 'visitor experience' would seem to be inviting trouble, but what is interesting is the way the notion of 'Olympic heritage' is here pressed into service to legitimate the fact that the legacy venues will in practice be monopolised by elite athletes, and with the exception of the BMX and mountain bike tracks, be of little interest to local communities, despite all the rhetoric to the contrary.

Those who come to live and work in what is now designated as East 20 may never be entirely free from its Olympic aura, although this will subsist primarily as a myth of origin, a source of once-upon-a-time stories. The active narrative which will give the park a distinctive place identity will be fabricated slowly over years by those whose lives have become part of it – not so much as the enactment of a legacy, more as the invention of a new tradition.

What is symptomatically missing from the LLDC vision is any recognition that the urban fabric is made up of the stories woven into, around and about it by those who dwell there; yet it is through this protracted process of story-making that spaces become places with a specific local meaning and identity.[32] For example planners may designate a certain space as a 'public square', but it may instead gain a public reputation as a hang-out for drug dealers or youth gangs, and become off limits to children and senior citizens. The proposed 'British Garden' may become, however temporarily, a gay cruising ground: Meet you in the Gold meaning something quite different from 'see you in Bronze'. Particular groups will in any case establish little niches for themselves in Olympic Park, usually in places where planners least expect it. Skateboarders may take up residence in front of the Aquatic Centre, because the street furniture there offers them acrobatic scope. The Stadium may become a magnet for graffiti artists who want to leave their personal mark on the Olympics in revenge for the appropriation of their art form for the 2012 logo ...

The ways in which spaces become places also has a lot to do with different forms of stake-holding. For example there was an ambitious proposal to build a multi-faith centre, a classic exercise in bridging, but this had to be dropped because of vehement objections on the part of some local faith communities – bonders to a man (sic) – to sharing ecumenical premises. For devout Muslims or Christians, their place of worship is a consecrated space which it would be sacrilege to share with non-believers. Football fans feel the same way about their home grounds, and routinely object to sharing them with rival teams. To someone who is not into football, a stadium may look like a giant shed, but to Chelsea supporters, the Shed is their home from home, a focus of their attachment to the club, and a place of shared memories: it gives them a symbolic stake in the club's affairs – even and especially if, in material terms, Chelsea FC becomes the personal fiefdom of a wealthy Russian Oligarch.

By no coincidence, this intimate connection between stake-holding and place-making has had a direct bearing on the fate of the Olympic Stadium. The vicissitudes of the negotiations between the Olympic authorities and West Ham United, East London's premier football club, have already entered Olympic folklore. Their rival contender, North London's Tottenham Hotspur, cried foul to West Ham's original bid and threatened legal action. Second time round West Ham are still, at the time of writing, odds on favourites to clinch the deal with the backing of London's Mayor and the LLDC. The rival bids illustrated just how lean the alternatives were: a Cricket Academy for young Essex hopefuls with the odd 20/20 game played on an imported pitch; a school for football marketing executives; or the wackiest proposal of all – the use of the stadium as a base from which to stage a Formula One event, turning the streets around Stratford into a snarling race track. Anyone for speedway and greyhound racing?

The stadium saga illustrates the distinctions between different types of legacy making discussed in Chapter Six. Located within a structure of conveyancing designed to maximise payback, the stadium can only be 'sold' as an investment opportunity, and a source of future dividends from profit. Yet it is also by definition a heritage site and potentially a popular lieu de memoire. Inscribed within the conveyance of a gift legacy it may be claimed as an heirloom or public endowment by the community.

This latter possibility is, of course, anathema to the champions of free market ideology. The *Daily Mail*, commenting on the decision to make West Ham the preferred bidder, ranted: 'Something for nothing. That is what is presumed West Ham are getting out of the Olympic stadium deal. A free ride. A gift from a grateful nation.'[33] In fact there are numerous strings attached to this 'gift', including a clawback on future profits that will ensure that West Ham's debt, already 80 million, will almost double and whatever the return on their investment that enhanced status as a 'superclub' will bring, they will remain in the pocket of financiers for generations to come.

West Ham's bid in principle reconciles the two economies of worth. Not only is the club able to ensure that the stadium has commercial viability and retains its value as a saleable asset, but it possesses a large, strategically located, supporter base that can adopt it as their home. Hammers' fans are drawn not only from East London but from the Cockney diaspora, so that every home game represents an ingathering of the tribe from Basildon and Brightlingsea to Billericay and beyond. If the club were to take over the management of the stadium, this would give it not only a new lease of life but a distinctive new identity, no longer associated with the Olympics, of course, but as a focal point of East London's major sporting heritage.

Yet West Ham's fans, bonders to a man, woman and child, were reported to be reluctant to make the move. As far as they are concerned the Olympic stadium is not an heirloom but a Trojan Horse; exchanging it for Upton Park, the club's ground for most of its history and hence a site of great sentimental attachment, would, in their eyes, be an act of *disinheritance*, not a dividend or the repayment of a symbolic debt.

New directions home?

Olympic legacies have in the past become the subject of bitter dispute and recrimination.[34] If the assets of Olympic Park are not to turn into a liability, the fact that their transfer is in the gift of the LLDC, and that the community's claim to entitlement remains at best provisional, should not be allowed to interfere with developing a robust ground-up regeneration strategy based on the legacy value of the Park. If 2012 is truly to earn its laurels as the 'Legacy

Games', the creation of a political framework within which its terms of reference and the issues that arise can be continuously discussed, worked through and decided upon by those most directly affected, would seem to be a *sine qua non*. A good enough legacy is one which is actively owned and controlled by its legatees.

What the Stadium story tells us is just how important symbolic stake-holding can be in determining material outcomes. The LLDC plan for the park takes it for granted that the population who move in to live and work there will share their vision. Their imagined community seems to consist of urban pioneers like themselves. Why else would they be there? So, although the park is conceived as an elaborate piece of social engineering, no strategy of community development has been put in place. It is simply assumed that communities will spontaneously arise in each neighbourhood.[35] This may well not be the case. Tenants and residents associations, bringing together all tenure categories, will need to be actively encouraged to counteract the culture of mobile privatism amongst the more affluent and the social divisions that might otherwise surface. The growth of good inter-neighbourhood relations clearly requires more that the provision of concierges who know how to fix bicycles. The setting up of some broader framework that can also address issues relating to the Park's outward-facing functions is essential. But what form should this take?

One of the positives to come out of the Big Society debate was a renewal of interest in mutualism and models of direct or participatory democracy. If the so called 'Red Tories' could so easily steal some of their best ideas from the left, it was because the Left had largely ignored its own home-grown tradition of communitarianism.[36] But at least the debate has meant that the works of G.D.H. Cole and the Guild Socialists have been taken down from the shelves in the Museum of Labour History, dusted off and given a new lease of life as part of a revitalised discussion about redistributive forms of governance. However, if the localist agenda is to be more than window-dressing, it must involve strengthening intermediate institutions between market and state through a real devolution of power to them. In what will eventually become a new township with a resident and working population of nearly 20,000, there is an opportunity to experiment with a new participatory form of urban governance.

For this purpose the delivery of the Legacy Communities Scheme needs to be handed over to a Community Land Trust, a conveyancing structure explicitly designed for public endowment and through which strategic management powers can be vested in an annually *elected* board, with all residents *and* workers entitled to vote. Already there is a proposal that one of the neighbourhoods should be managed in this way, but this needs to be extended to the park as a whole: the Land Trust would decide development policy and its AGM would have a plebiscitary function much more akin to what the Guild Socialists had in mind. Within this scenario the LLDC would retain residuary planning powers related to the development of the park's public profile as an Olympic heritage site and tourist destination, as part of the payback legacy, as well as remaining responsible for the wider aspects of Olympic regeneration. But the essential issues affecting those who live and work on the site would be determined by themselves.

By definition the Olympic Park is unfinished business. Even within the plans already made there is plenty of scope for improvement and new initiatives. Everyone has their own wish list, their own pet projects, and below I have listed some which are indicative of the Para-Olympic approach I have been arguing for, and which at least have the virtue of being feasible, not expensive, and with a good chance of enjoying popular support, in some cases having already been proposed by local community groups.

Hogwarts: a mega adventure playground

Though there may be provision for small play spaces in each of the five planned neighbourhoods, these will be for children who live on site. There is a dearth of provision for children visiting the park, and a mega adventure playground, with special areas for younger children and those with special needs, as well as for teenagers, employing state of the art technologies and themed around the Harry Potter stories, would be a major attraction, as well as being popular with the home team.

Grunts: an urban farm

As we have seen, this has already been proposed by local primary school children, and would be another strong attraction, with the usual complement of pets, farmyard animals and ponies; for the grown-ups it would be somewhere safe to park the kids and enjoy some 'time out', while for children it would offer a chance to learn that there is more to looking after animals than feeding time at the zoo.

The Raphael Samuel East London Heritage and Olympic Studies Centre

Raphael Samuel, the founder of History Workshop and pioneer of the study of popular history, lived in Spitalfields, so East London would be a fitting place for such a centre. Not just a visitors' centre with a shop selling Olympic souvenirs, it would include an archive of material related to the construction of the park, as well as the 2012 event, a reference library containing material on East London's history, and a reading and seminar room. It could be run in conjunction with local universities, oral history projects and the Museum of London.

The Green Triangle Plotland

My most radical proposal is for a 9-acre heirloom site to be set aside for whatever project is decided upon by the incoming residents and workers, to be operationalised in 2016 and in the meantime to be ring-fenced and left alone to grow as meadowland. Such a development platform would provide an immediate focus for community action, and should involve direct inputs of volunteer labour into the planning, design and construction process. People might decide simply to leave it as meadowland, or to build a crèche or a small outdoor recreational swimming pool. Whatever. The important point is that *they* decide. The proposal is named after the unemployed people who occupied unused land in Stratford and set up a camp to create work for themselves after the first world war. The name is also a homage to those doughty East Enders who were blitzed out of their homes and became do-it-yourself urbanists, constructing their own houses and amenities in Canvey Island and Jaywick, during and after the second world war.[37]

The Lansbury Labourhood

This would be an eco-business park, named after East London's leading municipal socialist, which would be developed as the park's major employment hub, or 'labourhood', generating green-collar jobs and connecting the park to similar developments in Thames Gateway. In this way the park might have a genuinely catalytic impact on its hinterland economy, as well as further substantiating its green credentials.

Beyond the host city blues

So far I have discussed the auto-poetic aspects of the Park legacy, its capacity for self-regeneration. But legacy politics are also inevitably allo-poetic: they are about the impact on environments other than their own. One of the most significant but unremarked aspects of this is the culture of hospitality that was generated around the Games, and its impact on the subsequent reputation of the host city and society. Part of this comprises the narrative legacy: the word of mouth reports, the over a million stories of first-hand encounters with the city and its inhabitants carried back around the world by Olympic visitors, and which, however impressionistic, will do more to shape perceptions of Britain and the British than all the urban imagineering and promotional hype produced by the tourist and heritage industries in the run-up to 2012.

Necessarily we are talking about brief encounters, their very intensity a function of their transience. Like one night stands, they celebrate the pleasure of immediate, no strings attached reciprocity, without the need for guilt or the long-term commitment that competitive giving and mutual indebtedness achieves. Sharing a drink or a bed with strangers may be the start of a beautiful life long friendship, or not; hospitality always involves the ritual promise of an exchange but it is not conditional on it. If you invite a Chinese visitor you happen to sit next to in the Stadium home for a roast beef dinner in the sole expectation that they will put you up and show you a good time when you are next in Beijing, then you may or may not be disappointed, but in any case you are not being hospitable, only calculating.

The Olympic hospitality culture is where market ideology is most dependant on the moral economy for its legitimation and where the conflict between the two is most likely to come to the surface. London's bid to host the Games was predicated on the proposition that East London has a long history of welcoming the world to its doors, and, though it may be no Garden of Eden, at least everyone recognises the vital necessity of – in the immortal words of everyone's favourite *Shameless* anti-hero Frank Gallagher – knowing how to throw a paaarty! But just what does it mean for a city to host the Olympics?

For the original Olympians it meant that a pact (xenia) was struck which allowed strangers (xenoi) to enjoy full rights of hospitality for the duration of the Games. In the classical Greek polis, those who were strangers, either because they lived beyond the city limits or spoke a foreign tongue, were admitted to its precincts and protected against abuse, exploitation, harassment or being taken hostage, provided they answered to their name, declared who they were, whence they had come, and for what purpose they were now in the city. The foreigner, thus defined, transformed the citizen into a host: someone who, because they were masters of their own house, and had the power to issue invitations, was both willing and able to invite foreigners into their midst and to share their food and dwelling place with them. In return the host transformed the stranger into a 'parasite' in the original, non-pejorative sense of the word: someone who has a right to a place at the table, to eat alongside his or her fellows, and whose need for nurturance and assistance is recognised without the need to reciprocate.[38]

The 'parasitism' of the host/stranger relation was not based on an unconditional or absolute welcome. It relied on the 'foreigner' respecting the limits and conditions of that status – they were invited to share what the city had to offer provided they did not attempt to usurp, appropriate or become permanently dependant on the host culture, or in any way seek to dissolve the difference which marked their place as that of the Other. To put it another way, this law of hospitality denied the visitor the opportunity to become a predator, and prevented the host becoming a sacrificial victim to their importunate demands. The gift of hospitality did not incur a debt precisely because it was so limited. If foreigners broke these rules, they instantly became the focus of hostility. Those who outstayed their welcome, and/or were regarded as exploiting the generosity of their hosts, gave parasites the bad name they have today.

The protocols of this ancient code of hospitality are occasionally simulated by the contemporary hospitality industry but only to put a gloss on what is a purely contractual relationship with customers or clients, who only outstay their welcome if they can no longer afford to pay. Olympic tourists may like to imagine they are latter day pilgrims in search of the Holy Grail of Olympic Communitas, but in their hearts – and in their blogs – they know that at best they are welcomed as paying guests, at worst they are resented and ripped off by those who say, with some justice, that they never issued the invitation in the first place. And if they do outstay their welcome on account of their indigence, then they are likely to be treated not just as strangers or foreign visitors, but as unwelcome immigrants. The official power to host, and to issue invitations, is also the power to deny entry and exclude.[39]

Within the scenario of hospitality projected for 2012, a peculiar reversal in the power of welcome was achieved. Those who were definitely not masters in their own house, and were not even stakeholders in the project, had a special duty of hospitality placed upon their shoulders: the poor, the have-nots, the marginalised and excluded, the minorities – these were the very people who were supposed to reach out to embrace visitors, to volunteer to share what little they had with strangers, to carry the burden of representing the gift legacy. Why should this be expected of them? Precisely because, according to populist 2012 rhetoric, their very lack of implication in the market economy qualified them to represent the authentic uncorrupted voice of Olympism. So the hospitality story of 2012 centred on the ways in which the contrast between austerity measures and the conspicuous display of public largesse was mitigated by the sacrificial energy of ordinary citizens in welcoming strangers into their midst.

But what if this burden was refused? If some East Enders exploited the opportunities offered by the Olympics to make a few quid, to sell their torches on eBay, rent out their flats or their bodies to the highest bidder? If London's public service workers seized the time to threaten to go on strike for longstanding demands? Why, they would find themselves condemned on all sides, as much by the apologists for neo-liberalism as by Labour politicians, for being parasites, anti-social elements, spoiling the party, being selfish and letting the side down. And yet weren't the bootstrap capitalists of the informal economy merely following the example of the better off and finding their own way in the enterprise culture? Weren't they providing an opportunity for those who lead safer and more comfortable lives to experience the riskiness of being, however briefly, on the wrong side of the tracks? Similarly, if workers wanted to cash in on the promised Olympic bonanza, weren't they following the example of senior business executives who regularly award themselves bonuses for having to endure the stresses involved in making so much money?[40]

Xenophilia costs the well-off very little – indeed in the era of multicultural capitalism it is exceedingly good for business. Elite cosmopolitanism may be a useful counterbalance to the patrician chauvinism that is still evinced by some of the higher echelons of the Tory Party, but it does not engage with the more visceral body politics that play out on the streets of the working-class city. Here acts of limited altruism, conditional generosity and mutual aid involve a greater sacrifice of immediate self interest. As we saw in Chapter Ten there is a very fine line between welcome and rebuff. Yet the culture of everyday hospitality routinely turns bonders into bridgers through the commonplaces of conviviality: the performance of invitation, the welcoming toast, the naming and taking of places, the breaking of bread, the conversational round, the banter and repartee, the sharing of stories and jokes, the chair left vacant for the uninvited guest, the rites of departure. This offers a far richer script than the overblown protocols of official ceremonial welcome, or the lavish entertainment offered to corporate clients and VIPs by the Olygarchy. In 2012 multicultural capitalism hit town in the form of the national hospitality houses, each promoting their own distinctive range of ethno-commodities – the African village in Kensington Gardens, Casa Brasil in Somerset House, the Danish take-over of St Katherine's Docks – these at least introduced some element of variety into the draconian mono-cultural order of Olympic lock down. But they were no substitute for the dense cultural inter-animation of the truly festive crowd.

All the evidence is that most East Enders rose to the occasion and gave the world the best of what they had to offer without asking for any other reward than their own shared enjoyment. For them, if not for the athletes, the Games were not about winning or losing, but taking part. It was through these acts of kindness to strangers that the rank and file twenty-twelvers came to symbolically own the Games, and stake their entitlement to its legacy, not as a payback but as an endowment. For East Enders it was also a way of asserting that the Olympics were happening in their manor, and that they were, despite all appearances to the contrary, masters in their own house.

Is it possible that we might arrive at a different starting point for assessing the difference East London and the Olympics will have made to each other by taking such small acts more into account? By tracking these tentative forays into a world where commodities are not dissimulated as gifts, gifts are not used to create debts, and reciprocities are not logged on a balance sheet of costs and benefits, by following the short-sighted moves through which a host of 'little people' make a multitudinous difference to what is happening in the world around them, without seeking to be enrolled in any grand narrative, and while resisting having their participation reduced to the abstract quantifications furnished by forensic social science, we might perhaps get a better understanding of what actually existing communism means and what it implies for how cities should be governed. Perhaps from such a Para-Olympic standpoint we might learn from those who had ostensibly the least to gain from taking part – the rank and file twenty-twelvers – what it was that made the Games worth staging at all.

Such a study, to which the present work may be considered a prolegomena, might at least yield a good enough definition of what the enduring legacy of 2012 might consist in. The epigraph of the thirtieth Olympiad of modern times is surely not to be found in Sir Henry Newbolt's poetic injunction to 'Play up! play up! and play the game', still less in Tennyson's equally gung-ho motto, 'to strive, to seek, to find, and not to yield' – now inscribed in tablets of stone in the heart of the Olympic village. Nor is it present in Lord Coe's pre-emptive bid for posterity: 'when our time came, we did it right'. Rather we need to attend to Samuel Beckett, a keen cricketer, whose cautionary injunction to the writer might apply as well to those who believe the Olympics can create a better world at the hoist of a flag as to those who think they should be stopped because they can only make things worse:

'Try. Fail. No matter. Try again. Fail better'.

Endnotes

Introduction

1. For an optimistic reading of the Olympics see J. MacAloon, 'The Olympic Idea', *International Journal of the History of Sport*, Vol. 23, No. 3/4, 2004. For a full-blown anti-Olympic rant inspired by pessimism of the intellect see M. Perelman, *Barbaric Sport: a world plague*, Verso, London 2012. For a blow by blow account of the 2012 games, in which a 'nay-sayer' comes round to a more genial view see N. Lezard, *The Nolympics: one man's struggle against sporting hysteria*, Penguin, London 2012. For a nuanced account of the Olympic movement see A Guttmann, *The Olympics. A History of the Modern Games*, University of Illinois Press, Urbana 1992.
2. For an analysis of these changes see T. Butler and M. Rustin, *Rising in the East? The Regeneration of East London*, Lawrence and Wishart, London, 2001; and T. Butler (ed.), *Eastern Promise*, Lawrence and Wishart, London, 2001; see also the contributions to P. Cohen and M. Rustin, *London's Turning: the Making of Thames Gateway*, Ashgate, Aldershot, 2007, and G. Dench, *The New East End*, Profile, London, 2006.
3. See B. Anderson, *Imagined Communities: Reflections on the Origins and Spread of Nationalism*, Verso, London, 2006.
4. On the role of popular historiography see R. Samuel, *Theatres of Memory Vol II: Island Stories*, Verso, London 1998, and R. Samuel and P. Thompson (eds), *Myths We Live By*, Routledge, London 1995.
5. See R. Hewison, *The Heritage Industry: Britain and the Climate of Decline*, Methuen, London 1987.
6. For further discussion see P. Cohen, *Rethinking the Youth Question*, Macmillan, Basingstoke 1998.
7. See V. Turner, *The Ritual Process: Structure and Anti-structure*, Manchester University Press, Manchester 1974.
8. See A. Minton, *Ground Control: Fear and Happiness in the 21st Century City*, Penguin, Harmondsworth 2009; and the discussion in Chapter Four of this book.
9. S. Coe *Running My Life*, Hodder and Stoughton. London 2012. p390.
10. See J. Marriott, *Beyond the Tower: The History of East London*, Yale University Press, London 2011.
11. See N. Elias and J. Scotson, *The Established and the Outsiders*, University

College Dublin Press, Dublin 2008; and J. Short (ed.), *The Social Fabric of the Metropolis*, University of Chicago Press, Chicago 1971.

12. See J. MacAloon, 'The Olympic Idea', op cit.
13. See A. Guttmann, op cit.
14. See J. A. Mangan and M. Dyreson (eds), *Olympic Legacies: Intended and Unintended*, Routledge, London 2010.
15. For a discussion of the Cultural Olympiad and the role of poetry in public culture see P. Cohen 'Carrying the Torch: Poetry @ the Olympics', *Agenda*, Spring 2012. A version of this text is also available online from my website: www.philcohenwork.com.
16. See www.winningwords.com for further information about this project.
17. I am very grateful for being able to draw on the interesting research of Michelle Johansen at the Bishopsgate Institute. See M. Johansen, 'Adventures in the Wild East: The Early Years of the Eton Manor Boys Club': www.villierspark.org.uk.
18. Quoted in Johansen, op cit.
19. For a discussion of the ideological provenance of the 'Big Society' see the contributions to J. Mackay (ed), *The Age of Voluntarism: How we got the 'Big Society'*, Oxford University Press, Oxford 2011.
20. See P. Farley and M. Roberts, *Edgelands: Journeys into England's True Wilderness*, Jonathan Cape, London 2011.
21. See H. Powell, *The Art of Dissent: Adventuring in London's Olympic State*, Marshgate, London 2012.
22. See his memoir *My Time*, Yellow Jersey Press 2012.

Chapter 1

1. See S. Koven, *Slumming: sexual and social politics in Victorian London*, Princeton University Press 2004.
2. See J. Lennon and P. Foley, *Dark Tourism*, Continuum, London 2000; and the contributions to R. Sharples and P. Stone (eds), *The Darker Side of Travel: The Theory and Practice of Dark Tourism*, Channel View, Bristol, 2009.
3. See J. Walkovitz, *City of Dreadful Delight*, University of Chicago Press, Chicago 1991.
4. Much of what follows has been influenced by L. Nead's *Victorian Babylon: People, Streets and Images in 19th Century London*, Yale University Press, London 2000; and *The Haunted Mirror*, Yale University Press, London 2007. P. Ackroyd's *London: A Biography*, Chatto and Windus, London 2004 was also a very useful companion in this journey, as was the *Cambridge Companion to the Literature of London* (edited by L. Manley, Cambridge University Press 2011). J. Marriott's *Beyond the Tower* (op cit) was a further source of useful information.
5. See I. Sinclair (ed), *London: City of Disappearances*, Hamish Hamilton, London 2006.
6. For a mapping of this field see L. Phillips and A. Witchard, *London*

Gothic: Place, Space and the Gothic Imagination, Continuum, London 2010; and A. Robinson, *Imagining London 1770-1990*, Palgrave, Basingstoke 2004.

7. See the discussion in J. Walkovitz, *City of Dreadful Delight*, op cit.

8. See P. Newland, *The Cultural Construction of London's East End: Urban Iconography, Modernity and the Spatialisation of Englishness*, Rodopi, Amsterdam 2008; and J. McLaughlin, *Writing the Urban Jungle*, University of Virginia Press, London 2000. On Orientalism in general see the pioneering study by E. Said, *Orientalism*, Routledge, London 1978; and for a discourse-based analysis see D. Varisco, *Reading Orientalism: Said and Unsaid*, University of Washington Press, London 2007.

9. See J. Barrell, *The Infections of Thomas de Quincey: A Psychopathology of Imperialism*, Yale University Press, London 1991.

10. See M. Kohn, *Dope Girls*, Lawrence and Wishart, London 1987. On the sexual politics associated with East London's gothic image see J. Walkovitz, op cit.

11. Henry Mayhew and many other Victorian urban explorers frequently used the term in this way. See H. Mayhew, *Selections from London Labour and the London Poor*, Oxford University Press, London 1965; and D. Stanley, *London Street Arabs*, Cassell, London 1895.

12. See S. Freud, *The Uncanny*, Penguin, Harmondsworth 2003.

13. See H. Damisch, trans. J. Goodman, *Skyline: The Narcissistic City*, Stanford University Press, Stanford 2001. For a discussion of the urban panorama see the contributions to M. Zerlang (ed.), *Representing London*, Hellerup 2001; and B. Comment, *The Panorama*, Reaktion Books, London 2002.

14. For a general overview of 'ruinology', see C. Woodward, *In Ruins*, Chatto and Windus, London 2001.

15. See M. Berman, *All That is Solid Melts into Air: The Experience of Modernity*, Verso, London 1981.

16. See E. Hobsbawm, *The Making of the Modern World*, Folio Society, London 2005, p34. See also J. Ruskin, 'The Nature of Gothic', *The Stones of Venice*, Faber, London 1981; and Morris's introductory commentary to this text and his lecture 'Art and Labour'. On William Morris see E. P. Thompson, *William Morris: From Romantic to Revolutionary*, The Merlin Press, London 1977.

17. See M. Girouard, *The Victorian Country House*, Yale University Press, London 1979. For a general discussion of the cultural and political role of the English aristocracy see D. Cannadine, *Aspects of Aristocracy: Grandeur and Decline in Modern Britain*, Yale University Press, London 1994.

18. See M. McCarthy and K. O'Neill, *Studies in the Gothic Revival*, Four Courts Press, Dublin 2008.

19. For a discussion of Marx's gothic imagery and its relation to 'voodoo' economics see M. Taussig, *The Magic of the State*, Routledge, London 1997; and M. Neocleous 'The Political Economy of the Dead: Marx's Vampires', in *History of Political Thought*, Vol. 24 Part 4, 2003. On the

more recent use of this imagery see D. McNally, *Monsters of the Market: Zombies, Vampires of Global Capitalism*, Brill, Leiden 2011.

20. See N. Thoburn, 'Difference in Marx: The Lumpen Proletariat and the Proletariat Unnameable', in *Economy and Society*, Vol. 18, No. 2 2002. For a general discussion of class relations and their representation during this period see K. Swafford, *Class in Late Victorian Britain*, Cambria Press, New York 2007.

21. See L. H. Peer (ed.), *Romanticism and the City*, Palgrave, Basingstoke 2011.

22. See L. Phillips and A. Witchard, *London Gothic*, op cit; and M. de Certeau, 'Ghosts in the City', *The Practice of Everyday Life*, University of California Press, London 1988.

23. See D. Trigg, *The Aesthetics of Decay*, Peter Lang, New York 2006.

24. The best account of this process is given in L. Nead, *Victorian Babylon*, op cit.

25. A pioneering study of this development is to be found in G. Stedman Jones, *Outcast London*, Clarendon Press, Oxford 1987. See also H. J. Dyos and M. Wolff (eds), *The Victorian City: Image and Reality*, Routledge, London 1978. See also T. Hunt, *Building Jerusalem: The Rise and Fall of the Victorian City*, Weidenfield and Nicholson, London 2004.

26. See J. Marriott, *Beyond the Tower*, op cit.

27. See *Journey through the Ruins* online essay, images 16-28

28. See E. de Mare, *Victorian London Revealed: Gustave Doré's Metropolis*, Penguin, London 1973.

29. M. Moorcock, *Mother London*, Scribner, London 2000, p35.

30. See C. Dickens, *Our Mutual Friend*, Penguin, Harmondsworth 1978, p87.

31. For a perceptive analysis of the role which smell played in mapping the contours of social division in the city see A. Corbin, *The Foul and the Fragrant*, Harvard University Press, Cambridge Mass., 1986; see also S. Halliday, *The Great Stink of London*, Sutton, Stroud 2001; and M. Wheeler (ed.), *Ruskin and Environment: Storm Cloud of the 19th Century*, Manchester University Press, Manchester 1995.

32. See D. Trigg, *The Aesthetics of Decay*, Peter Lang, New York 2006. For a general discussion of bohemian cultures in this period see C. Grana, *Bohemian versus Bourgeois: Modernity and its Discontents*, Harper and Row, New York 1967.

33. On the symbolic function of the necropolis see M. Davis, *Dead Cities and Other Tales*, I. B. Tauris, London 2002. On the relocation of the uncanny in Edwardian London see L. Neal, *The Haunted Mirror*, Yale University Press, London 2007. For a discussion of edge cities as heterotopic spaces see K. Hetherington, *The Badlands of Modernity*, Routledge, London 1997; and P. Farley and M. Roberts, *Edgelands: Journeys into England's True Wilderness*, Jonathan Cape, London 2011.

34. T.S Eliot, *The Wasteland*, Faber and Faber 1978, lines 60-4.

35. See G. Stedman Jones, *Outcast London*, op cit.

36. See M. Ball and D. Sunderland, *An Economic History of London 1800-1914*, Routledge, London 2001.

37. See T. Bender and A. Cunar, *Urban Imaginaries*, University of Minnesota Press, Minneapolis 2003.

38. See S. Meacham, *Regaining Paradise: Englishness and the Early Garden City Movement*, Yale University Press, London 2001.

39. See the Introduction to S. Schama, *Landscape and Memory*, Harper Collins, London 1995.

40. See L. Nead, *Victorian Babylon*, op cit.

41. For a discussion of the relationship between urbanism and war see P. Virilio, *City of Panic*, Berg, Oxford 2005.

42. See the introduction to R. Elman and A. Friel, *Charles Booth's London*, Hutchinson, London 1971.

43. See S. Lindqvist, *The History of Bombing*, Granta, London 2012.

44. See J. Gardiner, *War on the Home Front*, Carlton, London 2007.

45. See A. Calder, *The People's War*, Panther, London 1986.

46. L. Mellor, *Reading the Ruins: Modernism, Bombsites and British Culture*, Cambridge University Press, Cambridge 2011; on the aesthetic impact of the blitz see M. Zerlang (ed.), *Representing London*, Hellerup 2001.

47. For a historical overview of this tradition of representation see D. Corbett and J. Russell, *The Geographies of Englishness: Landscape and the National Past 1880-1940*, Yale University Press, New Haven 2002.

48. On these continuities see R. Hewison, *Culture and Consensus: England, Art and Politics 1940-1960*, Methuen, London 1995.

49. J. Cooper, *T. S. Eliot and the Ideology of the Four Quartets*, Cambridge University Press, Cambridge 1995.

50. R. Macaulay, *Pleasure of Ruins*, Thames and Hudson, London 1966.

51. See P. Willmott and M. Young, *Family and Kinship in East London*, Routledge and Kegan Paul, London 1957.

52. See E. Bowen, *The Heat of the Day*, Jonathan Cape, London 1954; and her *People, Places, Things*, Edinburgh University Press, Edinburgh 2008.

53. See C. Jolivette, *Landscape, Art and Identity in 1950s Britain*, Ashgate, Aldershot 2009.

54. See P. Virilio's essay on 'Bunker Architecture' in S. Redhead (ed), *The Paul Virilio Reader*, Edinburgh University Press, Edinburgh 2004.

55. See J. Flann (ed), *Robert Smithson: The Collected Writings*, University of California Press, London 1996. On post-industrial ruins see T. Edensor, *Industrial Ruins: Space, Aesthetics, Materials*, Berg, Oxford 2005.

56. See A. Higgott, *Mediating Modernism: Architectural Cultures in Britain*, Routledge, London 2007, for a general discussion of the trends. For an account by an unrepentant modernist which nevertheless recognises the failures see P. Hall, *Great Planning Disasters*, Weidenfeld and Nicholson, London 1980.

57. For a general discussion and critique of the post-modern turn see F. Jameson, *Post Modernism: The Cultural Logic of Late Capitalism*, Verso, London 1991. For its influence on architecture see C. Jencks, *The Language of Post Modern Architecture*, Academic Editions, London 1981.

58. See G. Lipovetsky, *Hypermodern Times*, Polity, Cambridge 2005.

59. On the cultural turn in regeneration see F. Bianchini and M. Parkinson, *Cultural Policy and Urban Regeneration*, Manchester University Press, Manchester 1993.

60. See D. Sudjic, *The Edifice Complex: How the Rich and Powerful Shape the World*, Penguin, London 2005; and L. Sklair, 'Iconic Architecture and Capitalist Globalization', in *City*, Vol. 10, No. 1, pp21-47.

61. See P Virilio, *From modernism to hypermodernism and beyond*, Sage, London 2000.

62. See R. Koolhaas, 'Junkspace', *October*, No. 100, 2002.

63. See O. Hatherley, *Militant Modernism*, O Books, Winchester 2008; and the critique by W. Self, 'The Frowniest Spot on Earth', *London Review of Books*, Vol. 33, No. 9, April 2011.

64. T. Parker, *The People of Providence*, Hutchinson, London 1983.

Chapter 2

1. See K. Worpole, *Dockers and Detectives*, Five Leaves, Nottingham 2008.

2. A short visual history of East London and its transformation is contained in the online gallery 'Journey through the Ruins', especially images 34-65 and 101-12. The gallery can be downloaded from www.philipcohenworks. com.

3. For a historical account of the insularities of English working-class culture see S. Meacham, *A Life Apart: The English Working Class 1890-1914*, Thames and Hudson, London 1977; and for its more recent forms see P. Cohen, 'Rules of Territoriality and Discourse', in *Rethinking the Youth Question*, op cit.

4. See R. Putnam, *Bowling Alone*, Simon & Schuster, New York 2000.

5. C. Ross, *The Death of the Docks*, Author House, Milton Keynes 2010.

6. L. Greenlaw, 'River History', quoted in M. Ford (ed), *London: a History in Verse* Harvard University Press 2012, p712.

7. A. Bonnett et al, *Thatcherism*, Polity, Cambridge 1988; R. Hobbs, *Doing the Business: Entrepreneurship, the Working Class and Detectives in the East End of London*, Cambridge University Press, Cambridge 1989; D. Hayes and A. Hudson, *Basildon: The Mood of the Nation*, Demos, London 2001.

8. J. Goldthorpe and D. Lockwood, *The Affluent Worker In The Class Structure*, Cambridge University Press, Cambridge 1969; and F. Devine, *Affluent Workers Revisited: Privatism and the Working Class*, Edinburgh University Press, Edinburgh 1992.

9. See M. Katz, *The Underclass Debate*, Princeton University Press, Princeton 1993; see also E. Mingione (ed), *Urban Poverty and the Underclass*, Blackwell, Oxford 1996.

10. See K. Hetherington, *The Badlands of Modernity*, Routledge, London 1997.

11. Interview with Ted Johns 2001.

12. See the contributions to H. J. Dyos and M. Wolff (eds), *The Victorian City: Images and Reality*, Routledge, London 1976 and 1978. Cultural historians have been in the forefront of this revision. See, for example, J. Walkovitz, *City of Dreadful Night*, op cit; and L. Nead, *Victorian Babylon*, op cit.

13. See J. Barrell, op cit.

14. For a further discussion of this point see chapter three of Phil Cohen, *Borderscapes: between memory, narrative and imagined community*, Palgrave, Basingstoke 2013.

15. See C. Husbands, 'East End Racism 1900-1980', *London Journal*, Vol. 8, 1982.

16. Ibid, p54.

17. See G. Stedman Jones, *The Languages of Class*, Cambridge University Press, Cambridge 1981.

18. For a version of this argument from a Marxist standpoint see A. Phizacklea and R. Miles, *Labour and Racism*, Routledge, London 1980.

19. J. London, *People of the Abyss*, Pluto Press, London 2001, p78.

20. See *The Independent*, 27.5.93.

21. *Guardian*, 30.5.93.

22. For East End autobiographies concentrating on the pre-war, wartime and immediate post-war experience see, for example, D. Scannell, *Mother Knew Best: An East End Childhood*, Macmillan, London 1974; H. Thorogood, *East of Aldgate*, Allen and Unwin, London 1935; G. O'Neill, *My East End: A History of Cockney London*, Viking, London 1999; D. Farson, *Limehouse Days: A Personal Experience of the East End*, Joseph, London 1991; J. Gross, *A Double Thread: A Childhood in Mile End*, Chatto and Windus, London 2001; E. Litvinoff, *Journey Through a Small Planet*, Penguin, London 2008, and M. McGrath, *Silvertown: An East End Family Memoir*, Fourth Estate, London 2002; R. Mills, *Everything Happens in Cable Street*, Five Leaves, Nottingham 2011.

23. See J. Bourke, *Working Class Cultures in Britain 1880-1960*, Routledge, London 1993.

24. For a discussion of different models of life story telling see P. Cohen 'To seek in the inferno that which is not', *History Workshop Journal*, Vol. 50, Autumn 2012.

25. See G. O'Neill, *Our Street: East End Life in the Second World War*, Viking, London 2003; and *East End Tales*, Penguin, London 2008. On the Second World War see A. Calder, *The Myth of the Blitz*, Jonathan Cape, London 1991.

26. See E. Hostettler, *The Island at War*, Island History Trust, London 2001; and *A Children's History of the Isle of Dogs*, Island History Trust, London 2010.

27. See W. Fishman, *East End Jewish Radicals*, Five Leaves, Nottingham 2004; J. Marriott, *Poplarism and Labour History*; and J. Shepherd, *George Lansbury: At the Heart of Old Labour*, Oxford University Press, Oxford, 2002.

28. I would like to thank the individuals who generously gave of their time to take part in this research. Names and other identifying details have been changed at the informants' request. The interviews were carried out by Iain Toon and Tarek Quereshi under my directions as part of a project funded by the University of East London.

29. Source: Island History Trust, London.

30. See J. Eade, *Local/Global Relations in a London Borough*, University of Surrey, Roehampton 1994. On the politics of representation within the Bangladeshi community see J. Eade, *The Politics of Community: The Bangladeshi Community in East London*, Avebury, Aldershot 1989.

31. See the contributions to J. Staiger (ed), *Memory, Culture and the Contemporary City*, Palgrave, Basingstoke 2009.

32. See K. Mumford and A. Power, *East Enders: Family and Community in East London*, Policy Press, Bristol 2003.

33. See E. Hostettler, *A Brief History of the Isle of Dogs*, op cit.

34. On the rough/respectable distinction between the two areas see G. Morgan, 'Local Culture and Politics in Docklands', *Environment and Planning D: Society and Space*, Vol. 11, 1993; and T. Cole, 'Life and Labour on the Isle of Dogs', unpublished PhD, 1987. Also C. Ellmers and A. Werner, *Docklands Life and Labour*, Museum of Docklands, London 2003.

35. See E. Hostettler, *A Brief History of the Isle of Dogs*, op cit, p13.

36. Ibid, p23.

37. See M. McGrath, *Hopping: An East End Family at Work and Play*, Fourth Estate, London 2010.

38. See A. Calder, *The People's War*, Panther, London 1986.

39. See C. Ward, *Plotlanders*, 1989; and J. Orton and K. Worpole, *350 Miles: An Essex Journey*, Prompt Press, London 2006.

40. See M. Bernard, J. Ogg, J. Phillips, and C. Phillipson, *The Family and Community Life of Older People*, Routledge, London 2001.

41. See P. Willmott and M. Young, *The Symmetrical Family: A Study of Work and Leisure in the London Region*, Routledge and Kegan Paul, London 1973.

42. See T. A. Hutton, *The New Economy of the Inner City*, Routledge, London 2008.

43. For a further discussion of these positions see P. Cohen and N. Rathzel (eds), *Finding the Way Home*, V & R Unipress, Gottingen 2008.

44. On entrepreneurialism and East End cultures see R. Hobbs, *Doing the Business*, op cit.

45. I would like to thank the young people and staff of the schools for their active participation in this phase of the research. Names and other identifying details have been changed to protect the identity of informants, at their request.

46. On the paternal metaphor see J. Lacan, *Language of the Self*, Johns Hopkins University Press, Baltimore 1968.

47. On school counter culture and its relation to youth culture see L. Back, *New Ethnicities and Urban Youth Culture*, Routledge, London 2001.

48. On baptismal naming see S. Kripke, *Naming and Necessity*, Blackwell, Oxford 1980.

49. See D. Roediger, *The Abolition of Whiteness*, Verso, London 1994, for a discussion of white labourism in the USA.

50. On foundation myths see P. Ackroyd, *Albion: The Origins of the English Imagination*, Chatto and Windus, London 2002.

51. See R. Hansen, *Citizenship and Immigration in Post War Britain*, Oxford University Press, Oxford 2002.

52. See M. Hunter, *Race, Gender and the Politics of Skin Tone*, Routledge, London 2005.

53. See R. Frankenberg (ed.), *Dis/locating Whiteness*, Verso, London 2002.

54. See S. Cohen, *Folk Devils and Moral Panics*, Routledge, London 2002.

55. See D. Roediger, *The Wages of Whiteness: race and the making of the American working class*, Verso, London 1999; and for the English working class, Chapter 5 of P. Cohen, *Borderscapes*, op cit.

56. See K. Harmon, *You Are Here: Personal Geographies and Other Maps of the Imagination*, Princeton Architectural Press, Princeton 2005.

57. See J. Fabian, *Time and the Other: How Anthropology Makes its Objects*, Columbia University Press, New York 1982. On invisible pedagogy and its relation to the hidden curriculum of school knowledge see B. Bernstein, *Class, Codes Control Vol 3: Towards a Theory of Educational Transmissions*, Routledge and Kegan Paul, London 1977.

58. M. Hong Kingston, *The Woman Warrior: Memoir of a Girlhood Among Ghosts*, Curley, South Yarmouth, Mass., 1977.

59. See V. Walkerdine, *Schoolgirl Fictions*, Verso, London 1990.

60. See C. Feldman, 'Mimesis – Where Play and Narrative Meet', *Cognitive Development*, Vol. 20, No. 4, 2005.

61. This research project was linked to a critique of moral symbolic and doctrinaire forms of anti-racism and to the development of an alternative pedagogic approach. For further information see 'It's racism what dunnit?', in J. Donald and A. Rattansi, *Race, Culture, Difference*, Open University 1998; and 'Racism's Other Scene', in J. Solomos, *The Blackwell Companion to race and ethnic relations*, Blackwell 1998. The educational materials and other texts related to this project are available to be downloaded from my website: www.philcohenwork.com

Chapter 3

1. J. Gorman, *Stratford: Another East End*, Five Leaves, Nottingham 2010, pp3-4.

2. On post-fordist work patterns see H. Benyon and T. Nichols, *Patterns of Work in the Post Fordist Era*, Edward Elgar, Cheltenham 2006. On patterns of income distribution and their relation to changing opportunity structures see N. Buck et al, *Working Capital: Life and Labour in Contemporary London*, Routledge, London 2002.

3. See N. Thrift, *Knowing Capitalism*, Sage, London 2005.

4. See P. Wright, *Journey Through the Ruins*, Oxford University Press, Oxford 1991, for an account of the impact which Thatcherism had on the social and cultural geography of East London.

5. For a general discussion see D. Massey, *Docklands: A Microcosm of Social and Economic Trends*, Docklands Forum, London 1991. See also the contributions to T. Butler and M. Rustin (eds), *Rising in the East*, op cit, and T. Butler (ed.) *Eastern Promise*, op cit.

6. See R. Hobbs, *Doing the Business*, op cit.

7. R. Williams, *Towards 2000*, Chatto and Windus, London 1983.

8. For an overview of this history see the discussion in Chapter One of this book.

9. B. Bragg, *A13: A Memory Map*, Victoria and Albert Museum; see also Bragg's song 'Trunk road to the sea'.

10. See F. Bianchini and M. Parkinson, *Cultural Policy and Urban Regeneration*, op cit; S. Zukin, *The Culture of Cities*, Blackwell, Oxford 1995.

11. See V. Cattell and M. Evans, 'Place images, social cohesion and area regeneration in East London', *Rising East*, Vol. 4, pp20-51.

12. P. Gustafson, 'Roots and Routes – the relationship between place attachments and mobility', *Environmental Psychology*, Vol. 43, 2003.

13. See A. Murray, *Recalling London: Literature and History in the work of Peter Ackroyd and Iain Sinclair*, Continuum, London 2007.

14. See M. Schaub, *Janet Cardiff: The Walks Book*, Bormessen, Vienna 2002.

15. See D. Cohen, *Jock McFadyen: A Book About a Painter*, Lund Humphries, Aldershot 2001.

16. See the contributions to R. Bond and J. Bavidge (eds), *City Vision: The Work of Iain Sinclair*, Cambridge Scholars, Newcastle-upon-Tyne 2007.

17. See J. Garreau, *Edge City: Life on the New Frontier*, Doubleday, New York 1991; also P. Farley and M. Roberts, *Edgelands: Journeys into England's True Wilderness*, op cit; E. Charlesworth, *City Edge: Case Studies in Contemporary Urbanism*, Architectural Press, Oxford 2005.

18. Iain Sinclair, *Dining on Stones*, Hamish Hamilton 2005, p37.

19. Iain Sinclair, *Ghost Milk* Penguin 2012, pp72-3.

20. S. Graham and S. Marvin, *Splintering Urbanism*, Routledge, London 2001.

21. For a critique of this position see P. Wright, *Journey Through the Ruins*, op cit.

22. For a general discussion of the thinking behind the Thames Gateway by one of its chief architects see P. Hall, *Urban and Regional Planning*, Routledge, London 2011. On the plan itself see ODPM, *The Thames Gateway Planning Framework*, HMSO, London 2001; and ODPM, *Greening the Gateway*, HMSO 2004.

23. See the contributions to J. Allen and D. Massey (eds), *Rethinking the Region: Spaces of Neoliberalism*, Routledge, London 1998; T. Shaw and F. Soderband, *Theories of the New Regionalism*, Polity, Cambridge 2003; and M. Telo, *The New Regionalism in Europe*, Ashgate, Aldershot 2001.

24. See M. Castells, *The Informational City*, Blackwell, Oxford 1991. For a further development of this dual city theory see S. Graham and S. Marvin, *Splintering Urbanism*, op cit; and G. Pflieger, *The Social Fabric of the Networked Society*, Routledge, Abingdon 2008; see also S. Sassen, *Deciphering the Global*, Routledge, London 2007; and *Cities in a World Economy*, Pine Gorge Press, London 2000.

25. See M. Pawley, *Terminal Architecture*, op cit; and A. King, *Spaces of Global Cultures: Architecture, Urbanism, Identity*, Routledge, London 2004.

26. See M. Auge, *Non-places: Introduction to the Anthropology of Supermodernity*, Verso, London 1995.

27. See E. Soja, *Post Metropolis: Critical Studies of Cities and Regions*, Blackwell, Oxford 2000.

28. See T. Sievens, *The In-between City*, Blackwell, Oxford 2002; and H. Shardar, 'The Linear City: linearity without the city', *Journal of Architecture*, Vol. 16, No. 5, 2011.

29. For example it would be entirely possible to organise an annual Thames Gateway festival, synchronising the various summer carnivals, and generating cultural exchanges between communities on both sides of the river, as well as sponsoring a programme of special TG related events. A Gateway football and cricket league, the twinning of schools and colleges in joint TG related projects, a Gateway debating competition, etc, could also help bring people from the fourteen regeneration zones together around areas of common interest.

30. *New Things Happen: A Guide to the Future Thames Gateway*, CABE, London, 2006.

31. See J. Bennett and J. Morris, *Gateway People*, IPPR, London 2005.

32. See P. Cohen, in P. Cohen and M. Rustin (eds), *London's Turning*, op cit.

33. See S. Lukas, *The Themed Space: Locating Culture, Nation, Self*, Lexington Books, Plymouth 2007.

34. J. Orton and K. Worpole, *350 Miles*, op cit.

35. See R. Carson, *The Edge of the Sea*, Houghton Mifflin, New York 2003; and J. Mack, *The Sea: A Cultural History*, Reaktion Books, London 2011.

36. See also R. Giblett, *Landscapes of Culture and Nature*, Palgrave, Basingstoke 2009.

37. See R. Florida, *Cities and the Creative Class*, Routledge, London 1995. The definition of this 'class' has proved as elastic as that of 'creative industry'. See also C. Landry, *The Creative City*, Demos, London 1995.

38. J. Dobson, *The Art of Management and the Aesthetic Manager*, Cass, London 2006, p27. For a discussion of this business culture see K. Salamon, 'Prophets of a Cultural Capitalism: an ethnography of romantic spiritualism in business management', *Folk*, Vol. 44, 2002; and L. Boltanski and E. Chiapello, *The New Spirit of Capitalism*, Verso, London 2005.

39. See the contributions to D. Mackay (ed.), *The Age of Voluntarism*, op cit.

40. See S. Graham and S. Marvin, *Splintering Urbanism*, op cit.

41. See D. Shane, *Recombinant Urbanism: Conceptual Models in Architecture*,

Urban Design and City Theory, Wiley Academic, Chichester 2005; and P. Healey, *Making Better Places: The Planning Project in the 21ˢᵗ Century*, Palgrave, Basingstoke 2010.

42. See D. Dillon and B. Fanning, *Lessons for the Big Society*, op cit.
43. For an example of current thinking on the left see the contributions to *Soundings*, Vol. 49: Who Speaks for England?.
44. See, for instance, the contributions to P. Marcuse (ed), *Searching for the Just City*, Routledge, London 2009. The development of more flexible and mobile forms of governance for Thames Gateway is discussed in the concluding chapter to P. Cohen and M. Rustin (eds), *London's Turning*, op cit.

Chapter 4

1. See LOCOG, *Open: the World in a City*, London, 2008.
2. For a full discussion of this see Chapter Seven of this book.
3. Memoryscape is a term applied to the way places become memorable through the stories that are told about them and/or the events or situations associated with them. For a discussion of how narratives invest places see the contributions to *Narrating Cities*, Eastern Michigan University, MI 2009; R. Finnegan, *Tales of the City: A Study of Narrative and Urban Life*, Cambridge University Press, Cambridge 1998; D. Hayden, *The Power of Place: Urban Landscapes as Public History*, MIT Press, Mass. 1995; and C. Boyer, *The City and Collective Memory*, Harvard University Press, Cambridge, Mass. 1996. See also J. Birsted, *Landscapes of Memory and Experience*, Spon Press, London 2000.
4. For example Paul McCartney walks around stoned and wondering 'oh where are there places to go/Someone somewhere has to know'; the Smiths arrive at Euston station from Manchester and worry if they've made the right decision this time to leave home. Paul Weller gets blisters on his feet/ Trying to find a friend in Oxford Street; Perhaps the track by Kid British 'Lost in London' offers the most comprehensive survey of metropolitan alienation. See the anthology of the 100 best London songs published by *Time Out* for further information.
5. For a prescient discussion of the centrifugal forces in British society and the role of regional nationalisms see T. Nairn, *The Break up of Britain*, Verso, London 1974. For an update see S. Blandford, *Film, Drama and the Breakup of Britain*, Intellect, Bristol 2007. On regional identities, economic disparities and the north/south divide see J. Allen and D. Massey, *Rethinking the Region*, op cit. For an official view see LOCOG, *Nations and Regions*, London 2007.
6. On the cultural history of the Cockney see G. Stedman Jones, *Languages of Class*, op cit; and P. Cohen, 'The Cockney Trickster', *Docklands Forum Anniversary Report*, Docklands Forum, London 1995. For an autobiographical account of contemporary cockney identity see G. O'Neill, *My East End*, op cit.

7. See J. Eade, *The Politics of Community*, op cit.

8. See the discussion in Chapter Six of this book.

9. See the discussion in P. Cohen, 'Rules of Territoriality and Discourse' in *Rethinking the Youth Question*, op cit.

10. See N. Elias, *The Established and the Outsiders*, University College Dublin Press, Dublin 1978, for an account of this process.

11. See first part of this book for a discussion of the contemporary and historical aspects of East London's community relations. See also G. Dench, *The New East End*, op cit; and J. Marriott, *Beyond the Tower*, op cit.

12. See A. Appadurai, *Modernity at Large: Cultural Dimensions of Globalization*, University of Minnesota Press, Minneapolis 2003.

13. See S. Donald (ed.), *Branding Cities: Cosmopolitanism, Parochialism and Social Change*, Routledge, London and New York, 2009.

14. See B. Schimmel, 'Urban Regime Theory and Urban Regeneration in the Late Capitalist Era' in C. Gratton and I. Henry (eds), *Sport in the City: The Role of Sport in Social and Economic Regeneration*, Routledge, London 2000. For a discussion of the impact which the Olympics have on local political cultures see M. J. Burbank, *Olympic Dreams: The Impact of Mega Events on Local Politics*, Lynne Rienner, Boulder Colorado 2001; and on planning cultures see G. John, 'The Impact of the Olympic Games on the Urban Planning Policy of the City' in C. Kennett et al, *The Legacy of the Olympic Games 1984-2000*, op cit. See P. Eisinger, 'The Politics of Bread and Circuses: Building a City for the Visitor Class', *Urban Affairs Review*, Vol. 35, No. 3, pp316-33, for an overview of the urban politics involved in the bidding and delivery phase.

15. Barcelona's exceptionalism is discussed by A. Gavin in 'Barcelona Revisited', in E. Charlesworth (ed.), *City Edge: Case Studies in Contemporary Urbanism*, Architectural Press, Oxford 2005. See also F. Brunet, *Barcelona – the Legacy of the Games 1992-2002*, University of Barcelona, Barcelona 2004; and M. Botteler and M. de Moragas (eds), *The Key to Success: Barcelona*, University of Barcelona, Barcelona 1995.

16. See J. Eade, *Placing London*, op cit.

17. See *London Divided: Income Inequality and Poverty in the Capital*, GLA, London 2002.

18. On the restructuring of London as a dual city see T. A. Hutton, *The New Economy of the Inner City*, Routledge, London 2008. On the impact of globalisation see S. Sassen, *Cities in a World Economy*, Pine Gorge Press, London 2000. On the shift from a manufacturing to a knowledge-based economy see N. Thrift, *Knowing Capitalism*, Sage, London 2005.

19. The distinction between mythological and ideological narratives is developed by Tzvetan Todorov in his book *Genres in Discourse* and informs much of what follows. For further discussion of these terms see glossary of concepts: www.philcohenworks.com

20. See J. Hannigan, *Fantasy City: Pleasure and Profit in the Postmodern Metropolis*, Routledge, London 1998. For a critique of contemporary

forms of 'Carnival Capitalism' see L. Langman and M. Ryan, 'Capitalism and the Carnival Character: the escape from reality', *Critical Sociology*, Vol. 35, No. 4, 2009.

21. See, for example, J. Ryan-Collier and P. Sander-Jackson, *Fool's Gold: How the 2012 Olympics is Selling East London Short*, New Economics Foundation, London 2008.

22. See L. Phillips and A. Witchard, *London Gothic*, op cit; and for East London see Chapter One of this book.

23. J. Andrews, 'Babylon: an angler's journey up the river Lea', J. Barrett et al, *Caught by the River*, Cassell, London 2009.

24. Iain Sinclair, *Ghost Milk*, op cit; and see also his article in *London Review of Books*, September 2012.

25. See online Appendix for an inventory of the relevant literature.

26. For an example of this genre see Lord Coe's autobiography *Running My Life*, op cit. For exceptions to this rule see R. Bannister, *The First Four Minutes*, Sutton, Stroud 2004; J. Carlos, *The John Carlos Story*, Haymarket Books, Chicago 2011; S. Laday, *King of the Road: From Bergen Belsen to the Olympic Games*, Gefen Publishing House, Jerusalem 2008; see also John Bale et al (ed), *Writing Lives in Sport*, Aarhus University Press; and discussion on sporting memoirs in Chapter 5.

27. For examples of the exposé genre see R. Yarborough, *And they Call them Games: An Inside View of the 1996 Olympics*, Mercer University Press, Macon 2000; R. Pounds, *Inside the Olympics: A Behind the Scenes Look at the Politics, the Scandals and the Glory of the Games*, John Wiley and Sons, Bognor Regis 2004.

28. See M. Hollowchak and H.L. Reid, *Aretism: an ancient philosophy for a modern world*, Lexington Books 2011.

29. Barcelona's exceptionalism is discussed by A. Gavin, 'Barcelona Revisited', in E. Charlesworth (ed), *City Edge; case studies in contemporary urbanism*, 2005. See also F. Brunet, *Barcelona – the legacy of the Games 1992-2002*, University of Barcelona; and M. de Moragas and M. Botteler (ed), *The key to success: Barcelona*, 1995.

30. For an account of the 1948 Olympics see D. Betz, 'Welcoming the World's Best Athletes: the 1948 Olympics', *International Journal of the History of Sport*, Vol. 26, No. 6.

31. See Mass Observation Correspondents for September 1948.

32. See A. Blake, *The Economic Impact of London 2012*, Nottingham University Business School, Nottingham 2011.

33. See A. Minton, *Ground Control: Fear and Happiness in the 21st Century City*, Penguin, London 2009.

34. See the contributions to A. Richards et al (eds), *Terrorism and the Olympics: Major Event Security and Lessons for the Future*, Routledge, London 2011; and P. Fussey et al, *Securing and Sustaining the Olympic City: Reconfiguring London for 2012 and Beyond*, Ashgate, Farnham 2011; and see the contributions to A. Tsouris and P. Efstathiou, *Mass gatherings and Public health: the experience of the Athens 2004 Olympic Games*, World Health Organisation 2007. For the impact of security

measures on local youth in East London see J. Kennelly and P. Watt 'Sanitising public space in Olympic host cities: the spatial experiences of marginalised youth' *Sociology* 2011. For an analysis of the 2011 youth riots and the public response see C. Stott and S. Reich *Mad Mobs and Englishman?* Constable and Robins 2011 and for a historical overview of moral panics focussing on working class youth G. Pearson *Hooligans: a history of respectable fears* Macmillan 1983.

35. See I. Illich, *Tools for Conviviality*, Calder and Boyas, London 1973.

36. See P. Virilio, *City of Panic*, Berg, Oxford 2005.

37. See E. Canetti, *Crowds and Power*, Phoenix, London 2000; D. Riessman, *The Lonely Crowd*, Yale Nota Bene, London 2001; *and* P. Stalleybrass and A. White, *The Politics and Poetics of Transgression*, Methuen, London 1986.

38. See M. Jay, 'Scopic Regimes of Modernity', in H. Foster (ed.), *Vision and Visuality*, Bay Press, Seattle 1988. See also J. Crary, *Suspension of Perception*, MIT Press 2001.

39. See D. Bell and D. Blanchflower, 'Young People and the Great Recession', *Oxford Review of Economic Policy*, Vol. 27, No. 2, 2011.

40. See D. Graeber, *Towards an anthropological theory of value*, Palgrave, New York 2001.

41. See S. Sassen *A Sociology of Globalisation*, W.W. Norton, New York 2007.

42. See M. Roche, *Mega Events and Modernity: Olympics and Expos in the Growth of Global Culture*, Routledge, London 2000; and K. Young (ed.), *Global Olympics: Historical and Sociological Studies of the Modern Games*, Elsevier, Oxford 2005. See also contributions to J. Horne and W. Manzenreiter (eds), *Sports Mega-Events*, Blackwell Oxford, 2004.

43. See G. Hayes and J. Karamales (eds), *Olympic Games, Mega Events and Civil Society: Globalisation, Environment, Resistance*, Palgrave, Basingstoke 2012.

44. For a critique along these lines see J. Ryan-Collier, *Fool's Gold:* op cit; and M. Perryman, *Why the Olympics are Bad for Us and How They Can Be*, OR Books, 2012. For an online network of information and analysis from a critical perspective see www.gamesmonitor.org.uk.

45. See the contributions to B. Carrington and I. MacDonald, *Marxism, Cultural Studies and Sport*, Routledge, London 2009.

46. See D. Miller, *The Official History of the Olympic Games and the IOC: Athens to Beijing 1894-2008*, Mainstream, Edinburgh 2008; and A. Guttman, *The Olympics: A History of the Modern Games*, op cit.

47. See A. Tomlinson, *National Identity and Global Sports Events*, New York University Press, New York 2006.

48. For a critique of 'legacy fetishism' see J. MacAloon, 'Legacy as managerial/magical discourse in contemporary Olympic affairs', *Area*, Vol. 41, No. 1, 2009.

49. See J. Carlos, op cit.

50. See S. Brownell, *Beijing's Games: What the Olympics Meant to China*, Rowman and Littlefield, Lanham, MD 2008.

51. K. Marx, *Grundrisse*, Macmillan, London 1980, p87.
52. See G. Pfister, 'Lieux de memoire/sites of memory in the Olympic games', *Sport in Society*, Vol. 14, No. 4, 2009.
53. The confusion this differential time can lead to was well illustrated in an episode of the *Twenty-Twelve* sitcom; this featured a thousand-hour 'countdown clock' that started by displaying the time and date of the opening ceremony and then counted backwards until July 27 2012 when it showed the exact time and date of its inauguration.
54. C. Cleave, *Gold*, Sceptre, London 2012, p82.
55. The distinction between differential and conjunctural or plenary time was first made by Althusser and Balibar in *Reading Capital*, NLR 1970, in their critique of Marxist historicism and its notions of teleological causality.
56. See the next chapter for a detailed discussion of this issue.
57. See A. Vigor et al, *After the Goldrush: A Sustainable Olympics*, Demos, London 2007; and J. Ryan-Collier and P. Sander-Jackson, *Fool's Gold*, op cit.
58. I discuss this distinction in detail in Chapter Six.

Chapter 5

1. See the master plan published by the Olympic Delivery Authority, *Demolish, Dig, Design*, ODA, London 2007.
2. See H. Arendt, *The Human Condition*, University of Chicago Press, Chicago 1998; and B. Gulli, *Earthly Plenitudes: A Study of Sovereignty and Labour*, Temple University Press, Philadelphia 2009.
3. On urban fabric as a social construction see E.A. Gutkind, *Community and Environment: A Discourse on Social Ecology*, Harbell House, New York 1974; and P. Roberts, *Environment and the City*, Routledge, Abingdon 2009.
4. See E. Grosz, 'Bodies-Cities' in H.J. Nast and S. Pile (eds), *Places through the body*, Routledge, London 1998.
5. See the film compilation *Builders and the Games*, directed by Margaret Dickinson, Carmen Valerio, Ilinca Calucageanu and Ausra Linkeviciute, for a fascinating attempt to portray some of the missing political and cultural dimensions of the Olympic construction process.
6. For a further discussion of this concept see Phil Cohen, Chapter 5, *Borderscapes*, op cit.
7. See B. Latour, *Re-assembling the Social*, Oxford University Press, Oxford 2005, for a statement of actor network theory.
8. Jean Lave has suggested that this kind of informal learning process is characteristic of the way situated knowledge is transmitted in face to face communities of practice. See J. Lave and E. Wenger, *Situated Learning: Legitimate Peripheral Participation*, Cambridge University Press, Cambridge 1991; and the contributions to P. Ainley and H. Rainbird, *Apprenticeship: Towards a New Paradigm of Learning*, Kogan Page, London 1999.

9. For some documentation on this see the film *Builders and the Games*; and for a historical overview of the construction industry: L. Clarke, *Building capitalism: historical change and the labour process in the production of the built environment*, Routledge, London 1992.

10. See *Open: The World in a City*, LOCOG, London 2007.

11. See ODA *Dig, Demolish, Design*, op cit.

12. The full interview and a detailed commentary is available at: www.philcohenworks.com

13. This project was undertaken by the Museum of London Docklands in collaboration with local youth group, Tolerance in Diversity. It involved 14 young people aged 16 to 21 working with artist Sarah Carne. The project is part of a new initiative to create a gallery of East London's recent history.

14. On the role of sport in working-class cultures see N. Fishwick, *English Football and Society 1910- 1950*, Manchester University Press, Manchester 1989.

15. See Chapter 5 of *Borderscapes* (op cit) and the online gallery *Body Politics* for further discussion and illustration of the 'two bodies' theory of labour history.

16. For further discussion see J.H. Hoberman, *Mortal Engines: the science of performance and the dehumanisation of sport*, Maxwell, New York 1992.

17. On the relationship between the monitoring of manual work and athletic performance see A. Rabinbach, *The Human Motor: Energy, Fatigue and the Rise of Modernity*, University of California Press, Berkeley 1992; and R. Solnit, *Motion Studies*, Bloomsbury, London 2003.

18. See J.A. Mangan, *The Games Ethic and Imperialism*, Frank Cass, London 1998; M.A. Budd, *The Sculpture Machine: Physical Culture and Body Politics in the Age of Empire*, New York University Press, New York 1997; and the contributions to J. MacAloon (ed), *Muscular Christianity and the colonial and post colonial world*, Routledge, London 2008. On the classical ideal of the male body and its cultivation as an aesthetic in Renaissance and early modern art see N. Mirzoeff, *Bodyscapes: art modernity and the ideal figure*, Routledge, London 1994.

19. On the history of physical culture see M. Budd, *The Sculpture Machine: Physical Culture and Body Politics in the Age of Empire*, Macmillan, Houndsmill 1997; E. Chevinaski, *Incorporations: Race, Nation and the Body Politics of Capitalism*, University of Minnesota Press, Minneapolis 2006 and the contributions to J. Hargreaves (ed.), *Physical Culture, Power and the Body*, Routledge, London 2007.

20. Quoted in S. Coe *Running My Life*, op cit.

21. See T. Magdalinski, *Sport, technology and the body: the nature of performance*, Routledge, London 2009; and J. MacKenzie, *Perform or Else! From discipline to performance*, Routledge, New York 2001.

22. For a general overview of academic research in this field see I. Willard, *Sport, Masculinities and the Body*, Routledge, London 2009; and K. Woodward, *Embodied Sporting Practices*, Palgrave 2009.

23. For further discussion see Chapter Five in P. Cohen, *Borderscapes*, op cit, and the online gallery *Body Politics*.

24. See L. MacDowell, *Redundant Masculinities: Employment Change and White Working Class Youth*, Blackwell, London, 2003.

25.   In the discussion that follows I have concentrated on the issue of masculinity in sport. This is not because I do not think that the position of women in sport is central to its gendered politics, but because the topic has been so well explored by feminist researchers that there is little I could add here that would be of any value. See, for example, the pioneering research of Jennifer Hargreaves: *Sporting females: critical issues in the history and sociology of women's sports*, Routledge 1993, and her *Heroines of Sport: the politics of difference and identity*, Routledge 2000.

26. See K. Woodward, *Sex, Power and the Games*, Palgrave Macmillan, Basingstoke 2012; and R.W. Connell, *The Men and the Boys*, Polity, Cambridge 2000.

27. For further discussion of this point see Chapter Five of P. Cohen, *Borderscapes*, op cit.

28. See D. Hartman, *Race, Culture and the Revolt of the Black Athlete: The 1968 Olympic Protests and their Aftermath*, University of Chicago Press, London 2003; J. Hoberman, *Darwin's Athletes: how sport has damaged Black America and preserved the myth of race*, Houghton Mufflin Boston 1987; and E. Cashmore, *Black Sportsmen*, Routledge, London 1982.

29. See S. Gilman, *The Jew's Body*, Routledge, New York 1991; and A. Breines, *Tough Jews*, Basic Books, New York 1990.

30. See D. Hartman *Race, Culture and the Revolt of the Black Athlete*, op cit.

31. See the critique by S. Timpanaro, *On Materialism*, NLB, London 1975; and contributions to D. Alexander and R. Number (eds), *Biology and Ideology: from Descartes to Dawkins*, University of Chicago Press, Chicago 2010.

32. For an autobiographical account of the role which boxing has played in East End cultures see S. Hicks *The Boxer Speaks*, Basement Writers 1973. For a general analysis of boxing culture and its social role see J.C. Oates and J. Renard, *On Boxing*, Echo Press, New Jersey 2000; and L. Wacquant, *Body and Soul: notebooks of an apprentice boxer*, Oxford University Press 2004.

33. For further discussion of this see Chapters Three and Five of *Borderscapes*, op cit.

34. B. Wiggins, *My Time*, Random House 2012, p201.

35. See J. MacAloon, 'The Olympic Idea', op cit.

36. See J. MacAloon, *The Great Symbol: Pierre de Coubertin and the Origins of the Modern Olympic Games*, University of Chicago Press, Chicago 1981.

37. For a discussion of British youth movements see J. Springhall, *Youth, Empire and Society: British Youth Movements 1883-1940*, Croom Helm, London 1977; and for Germany, W. Lacqueur, *Young Germany: A History of the German Youth Movement*, Transaction Books, New Brunswick 1962. For a general discussion of youth movements in relation

to nationalism see J. Gillis, *Youth and History*, Academic Press, London 1981.

38. On post-war youth cultures see P. Cohen, *Rethinking the Youth Question*, op cit; D. Hebdige, *Hiding in the Light: On Images and Things*, Comedia, London 1979; and S Hall and T Jefferson (eds), *Resistance through Rituals* Hutchison 1978. On black youth cultures see J.C. Ogbar, *The hip hop revolution: the culture and politics of rap*, University of Kansas 2007; and A. Gunter, 'Growing up bad: Black youth, "road" culture and badness in an East London Borough' in *Crime, Media Culture* Vol 4 num 3 2008. On contemporary white working class youth culture see O. Jones *Chavs: the demonisation of the working class* Verso 2011.

39. See the contributions to M. Giardin and M. Donnelly, *Youth Culture and Sport: Identity, Power and Politics*, Taylor and Francis, London 2008; and M. Gatz et al (eds), *Paradoxes of Youth and Sport*, State University of New York, Albany 2002.

40. A. Sillitoe, *Loneliness Of The Long Distance Runner*, Harper 2012, p23.

41. The thesis that organised sport is part of a wider process that involves the inculcation of specific bodily disciplines and the pacification or suppression of carnal behaviour and human 'animality' was first elaborated by Norbert Elias in *The Civilising Process* (1954); and further developed as the basis for a historical sociology of sport by Elias in collaboration with Eric Dunning in their book *The Quest for Excitement: sport and leisure in the Civilising Process* (2002). Elias's thesis was the starting point for Michael Foucault's concept of biopolitics as a set of disciplinary strategies designed to produce docile bodies. For an application of Foucauldian ideas to physical culture see Pukko Markula and Richard Pringle, *Foucault, sport and exercise* (2005). Foucault's theory has been critiqued by Agnes Heller in Agnes Heller and Sonja Puntscher Riekmann (eds), *Biopolitics: the politics of the body, race and nature*, Avebury, Aldershot 1996.

42. On the moralisation of sport and physical education see the contributions to M. McNamee (ed), *Philosophy and the sciences of exercise, health and sport*, Routledge, London 2005.

43. See D. Hartman, *Race, Culture and the Revolt of the Black Athlete*, op cit; and the contributions to A. Heller et al, *Biopolitics*, op cit.

44. See J. de Graaf et al, *Affluenza; The All-consuming Epidemic*, Berrett-Koehler Publishers, San Francisco 2001.

45. For an overview of issues at the intersection of the sociology of health and sport see G. Lueschen et al, 'The socio-cultural context of sport and health', *Sociology of Sport Journal*, Vol 13 No 2 1996.

46. See for example C. Cleave, *Gold*, Hodder and Stoughton, London 2012; and B. Glanville, *The Olympian*, Faber and Faber, London 2012.

47. For a discussion of this point see M. Robson (ed.), *Jacques Ranciere: Aesthetics, Politics, Philosophy*, Edinburgh University Press, Edinburgh 2005.

48. See J. Ruskin, *Munera Pulveris*, George Allen, London 1894, p34.

49. See R. Bannister *The First Four Minutes*, op cit, p39.

50. See H. Gumbrecht, *In praise of Athletic Beauty*, Bellknap, London 2006.

51. See J. Dunmow and P. Price, *Doing the Business – Life Enhancement through Sport*, Athenaeum Press 2011.
52. D. Diderot, *The Encyclopédie of Diderot and D'Alembert: Selected Articles*, Cambridge University Press, Cambridge 1969, p3.
53. See E. P. Thompson, *William Morris: From Romantic to Revolutionary*, Merlin Press, London 1977, in particular the introduction.
54. For further discussion on this point see R Sennett, *The Craftsman*, Allen Lane 2008.

Chapter 6

1. I would like to acknowledge my debt for much of what follows to the work of David Graeber, and in particular his books *Towards an Anthropological Theory of Value* (op cit) and *Debt – the first 5000 years* (Melville House Publishing 2011). Graeber has, amongst other things, opened up a whole new field of ethnographic study into what he calls 'baseline communism', the everyday cultures of mutual aid that exist in capitalist societies, and he has provided some of the conceptual tools we need for this research. For an interesting parallel analysis of gift exchange and its relation to conditional altruism from a psychoanalytic perspective see A. Phillips and B. Taylor, *On Kindness*, Hamish Hamilton 2009.
2. See M. Mauss, *The gift: form and reason for exchange in archaic societies*, Routledge, London 2002. Graeber argues that Mauss's model of the gift has frequently been wrongly assimilated into a general theory of exchange – as for example in C. Levi-Strauss, *Introduction to the work of Marcel Mauss* (Routledge 1987). For a different view Graeber has drawn on the work of the MAUSS group in France, for example, A. Caille's 'Marcel Mauss and the Gift Paradigm', in *Sociologie et Société*, Vol 36 No 2 2004; see also M. Fournier, *Marcel Mauss, a biography* Princeton University Press, Princeton NJ 2001.
3. There is today a further twist to the story. Some parents are so desperate to be loved by their children that they spend large amounts of money on gifts, in the often vain hope that their children will feel sufficiently indebted to reciprocate by getting good grades at school, being kind to animals and Granny – and generally behaving otherwise than the spoilt brats this 'generosity' has turned them into. In the same fashion politicians want to be liked by their electorate, even if it is only cupboard love; and the Olympics were similarly offered as a windfall or bounty.
4. Under planning legislation introduced by Cameron, major infrastructure projects will be decided by the government, not by public planning enquiries or local authorities.
5. For further discussion of this point see J. Forrester, *Planning in the Face of Power*, University of California, Berkeley 1989.
6. S. Coe, *Running My Life*, op cit, p231.
7. See the contributions to J. Mackay, *The Age of Voluntarism*, op cit; and B. Fanning and D. Dillon, *Lessons for the Big Society*, op cit.

8. Just how double-edged apologies can be is illustrated in the famous and no doubt apocryphal story of Trotsky's telegram to the Comintern: 'I was wrong, you were right, I should apologise'. On hearing this delegates were overwhelmed with relief and joy, but then in the midst of all the hysteria a Jewish delegate from Vitebsk got up: 'Excuse me comrades, I hate to spoil your fun but I am not quite sure that Comrade Stalin read the communication from Comrade Trotsky in quite the spirit in which it was intended. It should read "*I* was wrong? *You* were right? *I* should apologise?"'.

9. For a discussion of blood donation as a paradigm of non-reciprocated prestation see R. Titmus, *The Gift Relationship: from human blood to social policy*, Palgrave Macmillan 2002. Titmus draws on both Mauss and Levi Strauss to argue for an absolute distinction between the circulation of gifts and commodities. A similar dichotomy is made in C. Gregory, *Gifts and Commodities*, New York Academic Press 1998. Graeber, in contrast, argues that this is a false dichotomy, and that competitive giving as the enforcement of debt is a prototype of the market economy.

10. The gift which Agamemnon left behind for the city he had been besieging was ostensibly a form of war reparation, as the Greek fleet had apparently sailed off into the sunset. For the Internet generation the Trojan has, of course, been reinvented as a malicious application that masquerades as a legitimate file or helpful programme but whose real purpose is to grant a hacker unauthorised access to a computer.

11. For example in eighteenth- and nineteenth-century English rural society it was customary for the lords of the manor to lay on feasts and give presents at Xmas and harvest time to their tenantry, who in return were expected to 'donate' either labour or produce to the big house. See J. Barrell, *The idea of landscape and the sense of place*, Cambridge University Press, Cambridge 1972.

12. E.P. Thompson, *Customs in Common: Studies in Traditional Popular Culture*, 1991, p76. Thompson's concept of moral economy has been further developed by Peter Linebaugh in *Ned Ludd and Queen Mab: Machine breaking, Romanticism and the Several Commons*, Retort Press 2011; and in *The Magna Carta Manifesto: liberties and commons for all*, University of California Press 2008. A new school of moral economists argues that forms of collective action and mutual aid are the most effective and equitable ways of managing scarce or endangered resources. See for example B. McKibben, *Deep Economy*, Oneworld Publications 2007.

13. On this point see L. Althusser and E. Balibar, *Reading Capital*, op cit; and the discussion in R. Resch, *Althusser and the renewal of Marxist Social Theory*, University of California Press 1992.

14. The fact is without these co-operative practices capitalist enterprises would soon grind to a halt. This is recognised in post-fordist work practice where flattened, hands-off management structures encourage collective problem-solving and team work. See H. Benyon and T. Nichols, *Patterns of work in the post fordist era*, Edward Elgar, Cheltenham 2006. On the

ON THE WRONG SIDE OF THE TRACK?

individualistic demand for job satisfaction and its relation to personal growth ideologies see T. Frank, *One market Under God*, Doubleday, New York 2002.

15. In his discussion of 'bad faith' in *Being and Nothingness*, Sartre cites a café waiter whose movements and conversation are a little too 'waiter-esque': such exaggerated behaviour illustrates that he is play-acting as a waiter. But that he is obviously acting belies that he is aware that he is not (merely) a waiter, but is rather consciously deceiving himself.

16. On community consultation for the Olympics see the discussion in the final chapter in this book.

17. Nudge economics is an attempt to forestall the tragedy of the commons whilst remaining within the framework of rational choice theory. See R. Thaler and C. Sunstein, *Nudge: improving decisions about health, wealth and happiness*, Penguin 2009.

18. This is the weakness of Karl Polanyi's argument in which, having critiqued the autonomisation of market economics, he then assumes that re-embedding the market within a framework of social reciprocity will automatically lead to a socialisation of commodity relations rather than a marketisation of social reciprocities. See G. Dale, *Karl Polanyi – The Limits of the Market*, Polity, Cambridge 2010.

19. Linguistically the subsuming of one discourse under another involves a substitution of terms, often in the form of a synecdoche i.e. the container being used to refer to what it contains. So 'market' refers to all the transactions, or all the produce exchanged, in this way eliding gift and commodity relations. For further discussion see J. Schultz, 'Discourses of Market Capitalism: an enquiry into the ideologies, moralities and grammars of evaluation in the age of Subjective Ideals' (PhD dissertation, University of California Berkeley).

20. When Hancock discovers he is expected to give a pint of blood he is flabbergasted. He can't afford to lose all that blood. How will he ever get it back? He'll need a transfusion himself! And surely, if his blood is so rare a commodity, he'd better save it. It's certainly too valuable to be wasted on any Tom, Dick or Harriet.

21. See E.P. Thompson, 'The Grid of Inheritance', in J. Goody (ed), *Family and Inheritance*.

22. Collecting cultures are discussed in part two of my memoir, *Reading Room Only*, Five Leaves, Nottingham 2013.

23. Stephen Leacock (*The Best of Leacock*, Bodley Head 1957) has a story about this, which begins with a student who is cross-examined intensely by the bank manager before he is reluctantly allowed a small overdraft; who is followed by a small businessman who wants to borrow £100,000 to expand his firm and is also given quite a tough time before the loan is finally agreed. Finally a plutocrat arrives. The manager bows and scrapes, shows him into his private office, and asks him how much he wants to borrow. The sum of three million is casually mentioned, the manager begs the industrialist to ask for more. There is little discussion, no papers to be signed, the manager is profuse in his thanks, and the deal is done in minutes.

24. For what follows I have drawn on the framework proposed by L. Boltanski and L. Thevenot in *On Justification: The Economies of Worth*, Princeton University Press, Oxford 2006. Graeber's *Towards an Anthropological Theory of Value* has the advantage of grounding a critique of evaluation processes in a comparative cultural analysis.

25. The term 'moral entrepreneur' was first coined by Howard Becker in *Outsiders* (Free Press of Glencoe 1966), and was developed further by Stan Cohen in *Folk Devils and Moral Panics* (Routledge 2002).

26. See Charles Rutheiser, *Imagineering Atlanta: the Politics of Place in the City of Dreams*, Verso, London 1996.

27. This perspective is sometimes described as 'aretism' to contrast it with the agonistic model of achievement-oriented competitive sport. For the Ancient Greeks the meaning of arête was close to the Roman notion of virtu, a moral or spiritual quality which any citizen might possess but which was demonstrated by political actions which made them stand out from the crowd. As such it lacked the elitist and aristocratic connotations which 'excellence' has taken on within Olympo-Patriarchal culture. See H. Arendt, *The Human Condition* for a general discussion of this term; and for its take up within the Olympics debate see M. Hollowchak and H.L. Reid, *Aretism: an ancient philosophy for a modern world*, Lexington Books 2011.

28. See Chapter Nine for a detailed analysis of the ceremony.

29. The concept of 'structure in dominance' was first developed by L. Althusser and E. Balibar *in Reading Capital* (op cit) as a theoretical approach to understanding social phenomena as complex totalities without reducing them to a single underlying principle of structural causation, allowing each element a relatively autonomous effect on the whole. In similar vein, in the model of the Olympic compact outlined here I have made a distinction between an *axis of synergy* – in which affinities, affiliations and alliances between different interests are negotiated (and battle lines drawn) – and *the axis of subsumption*, which configures the field of these interactions and overdetermines their outcome. Using this model it is possible to distinguish four relatively autonomous elements of the compact: (1) the discourses and image repertoires that thematise a compact and give it rhetorical coherence; (2) the nexus of relations between economies of worth; (3) the grand narratives that articulate delivery and legacy evaluation; and (4) the critical and oppositional discourses that problematise the compact but elements of which may also be incorporated within it.

30. See J. Sugden and A. Tomlinson (eds), *Watching the Olympics – politics, power, representation*, Routledge, London 2012.

31. On Los Angeles as a pre-eminent city of the American dream see E. Soja, *Third Space: journeys to Los Angeles and other real-and-imagined places*, Blackwell, Oxford 1996; and M. Davis, *City of Quartz: excavating the future in Los Angeles*, Verso, London 1990.

32. See the contributions to M. Tremaine (ed.), *Blogging, Citizenship and the Future of the Media*, Routledge, London 2007.

33. For the role of national-popular ideology in the Olympics see the contributions to A. Tomlinson and C. Young (ed) *National Identity and global sports events*, New York State University 2006. See also the contributions to S. Foster (ed), *Choreographing History*, Indiana 1995.

34. See Christopher Hilton, *Hitler's Olympics: the 1936 Berlin Olympic Games*, The History Press, London 2006.

35. See Chapter Five for further discussion of this issue.

36. See Chapter Eight for further discussion of the role of the national-popular in the 2012 ceremonies.

37. See Susan Brownell, *Beijing's Games: What the Olympics Mean to China*, Rowman and Littlefield, Beijing 2008.

38. See John Hargreaves, *Freedom for Catalonia: Catalan nationalism, Spanish identity and the Barcelona games*, Cambridge University Press 2000.

39. One of the running gags in the *Twenty Twelve* sit com was that the 'Head of Sustainability' is continually being mistaken for the 'Head of Legacy', and it turns out they are doing pretty much the same job.

40. See Richard Cashman, *The Bitter-Sweet Awakening: the Legacy of the Sydney 2000 Games*, Walla Walla Press, Sydney 2006.

41. See *Meta-Evaluation of the Impacts and Legacy of the London 2012 Olympic Games and Paralympic Games*, DCMS, London 2011.

42. For an economistic approach to host city comparisons see H. Preuss, *Staging the Olympics: A Comparative Guide 1972-2008*, Edward Elgar, Cheltenham 2009. A more urbanistic strategy of comparison is offered by the contributors to J. R. Gold and M. M. Gold, *Olympic Cities: City Agendas*, *Planning and the World Games 1896-2012*, Routledge, London 2007. For an overview see H. Hiller, 'Toward a Science of Olympic Outcomes: the urban legacy', in C. Kennett et al, *The Legacy of the Olympic Games*, op cit. For a general overview of legacy studies see M. Dyreson and J. A. Mangan, *Olympic Legacies*, op cit; and M. Smith, *When the Games Come to Town*, University of East London 2009.

43. See J. Raban, *Soft City*, Picador, London 2008.

44. For a discussion of conventional legacy definitions see H. Preuss, 'The conceptualisation and measurement of mega sports event legacies', *Journal of Sports Tourism*, Vol. 12, No. 3/4, 2007.

45. See the online Glossary for a further discussion of this distinction.

46. See for example the contributions to A. Klausen (ed.), *Olympic Games as Performance and Event*, Berghan, Oxford 1995. For a more focused account of the methodology see H. Eichman, 'The Narrative, the Biographical, the Situational: Scandinavian Sociology of Body Culture, Trying for a Third Way', *International Review for the Sociology of Sport*, Vol. 29, No. 1, 1994.

47. For a critique of audit culture see the contributions to M. Strathern (ed.), *Audit Cultures: Anthropological Studies in Accountability, Ethics and the Academy*, Routledge, London 2000.

48. See N. Rose, *Governing the Soul: The Shaping of the Private Self*, Free Association Books, New York 1999.

49. See J. McKenzie, *Perform or Else: From Discipline to Performance*, Routledge, New York 2001.

50. See R. Solnit, *Motion Studies*, op cit for an account of how aesthetic and scientific studies of the body-in-movement converged. See also M. Budd, *The Sculpture Machine: Physical Culture and Body Politics in the Age of Empire*, Macmillan, Houndsmill 1997. For a critique of contemporary 'body politics' see A. Heller et al (eds), *Biopolitics*, op cit; and E. Cherniavski, *Incorporations: Race, Nation and the Body Politics of Capitalism*, op cit.

51. See A. Rabinbach, *The Human Motor: Energy, Fatigue and the Rise of Modernity*, op cit.

52. For a discussion of the relation between techniques of observation, measurement and governance as regimes of capitalist modernity see J. Crary, *Techniques of the Observer*, MIT Press, Cambridge Mass 2002.

53. See M. Strathern, *Audit Culture*, op cit, p22.

54. There is an irony to the fact that impact studies, with their robust image of measuring extrinsic effects, should be the methodology of choice for evaluating auto-poesis, and that an approach which started out life as a means of empowering local communities to defend themselves against large scale redevelopment should now be the main way regeneration agencies manage conflict and achieve consensus. See J. Obliggiato, *From Community Empowerment to Conflict Management: A Short History of Impact Studies*, Gower 2005.

55. See H. Preuss, *Staging the Olympics*, op cit; J. R. Gold and M. M. Gold, *Olympic Cities*, op cit; H. Hiller, 'Toward a Science of Olympic Outcomes', op cit; M. Dyreson and J. A. Mangan, *Olympic Legacies* (op cit); M. Smith, *When the Games Come to Town*, op cit.

56 See for example *The Olympic Games Impact Study London 2012 Pre Games Report* ESRC 2010. This official IOC study is not due to report until 2015.

Chapter 7

1. For an analysis of Olympic Ceremonies see J. MacAloon (ed.), *Rite, Drama, Festival, Spectacle*, Institute for the Study of Human Issues, Philadelphia 1984; and also the contributions to J. MacAloon and M. de Moragas, *Olympic Ceremonies: Historical Continuity and Cultural Exchange*, Centre d'Estudis Olimpics i de l'Esport, Barcelona 1995. The approach adopted here has been influenced by the work of D. Handelman, *Models and Mirrors: Towards an Anthropology of Public Events*, Berghahn, Oxford 1998; and M. Real, 'Super Bowl: Mythic Spectacle', *Journal of Communication*, Vol. 25, 1975.

2. See H. Gombrecht, *In Praise of Athletic Beauty*, op cit.

3. See R. Bowen, *Isolation, Utopia and Anti-Utopia: The Island Motif in the Literary Imagination*, Harvard University Press, Cambridge MA 1974.

4. See G. Beer, 'Discourses of the Island', in J. Amrine (ed), *Literature and Science*, Kluwer Academic, London 1989.

5. See D. Johnson, *Phantom Islands of the Atlantic*, Souvenir Press, London 1994.

6. See G. Perec, *W, or the Memory of Childhood*, Vintage Classics, London 2011.

7. See A. Tomlinson, 'Olympic Spectacles', *Media, Culture and Society*, Vol. 18, 1996; and 'Disneyfication of the Olympics', in C. Gratton and I. Henry (eds), *Sport in the City: The Role of Sport in Social and Economic Regeneration*, Routledge, London 2000. For a discussion of the narrative strategy see M. Dyreson, 'Scripting the American Olympics Storytelling Formula', *Olympika*, Vol. v, 1996.

8. For an analysis of the impact of globalisation on sporting events see M. Roche, *Mega Events and Modernity: Olympics and Expos in the Growth of Global Culture*, Routledge, London 2000.

9. For a visual synopsis of the ceremonies see the online gallery 'Olympic Dreams and Nightmares'. See images 75-110 for the Olympics, and 195-207 for the Paralympic opening ceremony.

10. Greenberg's original essay appeared in 1946. See his *Collected Essays and Criticism*, University of Chicago Press, Chicago 1993. His perspective on kitsch has recently been taken up by T. Frank in *One Market Under God*, Doubleday, New York 2002. For kitsch as an aesthetic experience see C. Obaqquiqa, *The Artificial Kingdom*, University of Minnesota, Minneapolis 2010. For its role as a consumer aesthetic see the special issue of *Home Cultures: The Journal of Architecture, Design and Domestic Space*, 'Reconsidering Kitsch', Vol. 3, No. 3, 2007. The essay on kitsch by P. Wollen in *Paris Manhattan: Writings on Art* (Verso, London 2004) provides a succinct overview of the debate; and T. Kulka, *Kitsch and Art*, Pennsylvania State University Press, University Park 1996 gives the most considered philosophical treatment of its aesthetic.

11. For an anthology of kitsch images related to the discussion which follows go to the 'Olympic Dreams and Nightmares' online gallery: images 3- 35

12. M Kundera, *The Unbearable Lightness of Being*, Faber and Faber, London 1976, p87.

13. For a critique of consumer culture which complements Kundera's concept see C. Lasch, *The Culture of Narcissism*, Norton, New York 1976. For a Marxist critique of these trends see K. Hetherington, *Capitalism's Eye, Culture, Space and the Commodity*, Routledge, London 2008. On urban imagineering see S. Lukas (ed), *Themed Space: Locating Culture, Nation, Self*, Lexington Books, Plymouth 2007.

14. See T. Adorno, 'Bloch's Traces: The Philosophy of Kitsch', *New Left Review*, No 132, 1984.

15. See F. Davis, *Yearning for Yesterday: A Sociology of Nostalgia*, Collier Macmillan, London 1979.

16. On kitsch, pop art and postmodern aesthetics see J. Suarez, *Pop Modernism*, University of Illinois Press, Urbana 2011. For a general critique of postmodernism from a Marxist standpoint see F. Jameson, *Post Modernism: The Cultural Logic of Late Capitalism*, Verso, London 1991; and M. Berman, *All that is sold melts into air*. London, Verso 1983.

17. See D. Beech and J. Roberts, *The Philistine Controversy*, Verso, London 2002.

18. See the contributions to S. Foster (ed), *Choreographing History*, op cit.

19. For a discussion of the aestheticising of contemporary sport and physical culture see R. Rinehard, *Players All: Post Modernity and sport*, 2002; and M. Holowchak and H Reid, *Aretism: an ancient sports philosophy for the modern sport's world*, op cit.

20. See J. Didion, *Where I was From*, Knopf, p73.

21. See O. Nerdrum, *How We Cheat Each Other*, Kitsch AS, London 2008; and J. Pettersson, *Odd Nerdrum: Storyteller and Self Revealer*, Art Data, London 1998.

22. See O. Nerdrum, *How We Cheat Each Other*, op cit, p34.

23. For a discussion of the uncanny in contemporary art see S. Morely (ed), *The Sublime*, MIT Press, New York 2010.

24. See S. Sontag, 'Notes on camp', in *Against Interpretation and Other Essays*, Farrer, Straus and Giroux, New York 1964; and the contributions to M. Meyer, *The politics and poetics of camp*, Routledge, London 1994.

25. For further discussion see S. Lilley et al, *Catastrophism: the apocalyptic politics of collapse and rebirth*, PM Press, California 2010.

26. See T. Eagleton, *Sweet Violence: a study of the tragic*, Blackwell, Oxford 2012.

27. For a statement of the classical Kleinian position, see C. Bollas, *Forces of destiny: psychoanalysis and the human idiom*, Free Association Press, London 1989; and for its associated cultural politics, C. Lasch, *The Culture of narcissism* (op cit).

28. See T. Frank, *The Conquest of the Cool: Business Culture, Counter Culture and the Rise of Hip Consumerism*, University of Chicago Press, Chicago 1997, for a discussion of the origins of 'cool' and 'high 'culture in 1960s counter culture; also R. Pountain and D. Robins, *Cool Rules: Anatomy of an Attitude*, Reaktion Books, New York 1998, for its relation to contemporary youth culture. For a prescient analysis of the social impact of 'Grosskultur' see N. Postman, *Amusing ourselves to death*, Methuen 1984.

29. R. Caillois, *Man, Play and Games*, University of Illinois Press, Champaign 2001, p46.

30. See M. Bakhtin, *The Dialogic Imagination*, University of Texas Press, Austin 1981. On the history of European carnival and its regulation see M. Allon and P. Stalleybrass, *The Politics and Poetics of Transgression*, Methuen, London 1986; B. Ehrenreich, *Dancing in the Streets: A History of Collective Joy*, Metropolitan Books, New York 2007; and the contributions to T. Sebeok (ed.), *Carnival!*, Mouton, New York 1984.

31. Saint-Simon, *Proposal to End the Revolution*, 1817, p23.

32. See E. Hobsbawm, *Primitive Rebels: Studies in Archaic Forms of Social Movement in the 19th and 20th Centuries*, Manchester University Press, Manchester 1959; and P. Linebaugh, *Ned Ludd and Queen Mab*, PM Press, London, 2012.

33. On the English tradition of carnival and its relation to pre-modern popular

culture, especially mummers' plays and practices of guizing or masking, see A. Garner, *The Guizer*, S. J. Hamilton, London 1975. See also C. Humphrey, *The Politics of Carnival: Festive Misrule in Medieval England*, Manchester University Press, Manchester 2001. For a general overview of contemporary research in this field see the contributions to K. Eisenbichler and W. Huschen (eds), *Carnival and the Carnivalesque*, Rodopi, Amsterdam 1999.

34. On the history of new world carnival see, for example, J. Cowley, *Carnival, Canboulay and Calypso: Traditions in the Making*, Cambridge University Press, Cambridge 1996.

35. M. Mauss, *The Gift*, op cit, p124.

36. See G. Debord, *Society of the Spectacle* (trans D Nicholson Smith), Zone Press, New York 2004, p39. Debord's work has been frequently treated by media studies academics as an analysis of the visual culture industries, and by urbanists as an application of psycho-geographical methods. This is to ignore its espousal of direct democracy and critique of cultural and identity politics of the kind that has come to dominate the left.

37. See K. Wright, *The Rise of the Therapeutic Society: psychological knowledge and the contradictions of cultural change*, Washington Academia Press 2011.

38. R. Vaneigem, *The Revolution of Everyday Life* (trans D Nicholson-Smith), PM Press 2012. Vaneigem's work has tended to be overshadowed by Debord's, but his critique of 'survivalism' is a far more penetrating critique of late capitalism than, for example, that in Jameson's *Valences of the Dialectic* (Verso, London 2009).

39. Vaneigem, *Revolution of Everyday Life*, p139.

40. See J. Crary, *The Suspension of Perception: Attention, Spectacle and Modern culture*, op cit.

41. See Crary, ibid.

42. See M. Foucault, *Discipline and Punish*, Vintage Books 1995.

43. See H. Arendt, *The Human Condition*, op cit.

44. Quoted in Vaneigem, op cit, p218.

45. See N. Bourriaud, *Post Production: Culture as Screenplay: How Art Reprogrammes the World*, Lucas and Sternberg, New York 2000.

46. See LOCOG website: *Using the brand*.

47. See A. Rabinbach, *The Human Motor: Energy, Fatigue and the Origins of Modernity*, op cit.

48. On this term see the discussion in Chapter Six; and the online glossary.

49. See the images 144-161 in the online Olympics Dreams and Nightmares Gallery.

50. See S. Donald et al (eds), *Branding Cities: Cosmopolitanism, Parochialism and Social Change*, Routledge, London 2009.

51. For a discussion of the notion of 'communitas' see V. Turner, *The Ritual Process: Structure and Anti-structure*, Penguin, Harmondsworth 1974; and for the role of festivity as its ritual expression see his *Anthropology of Performance*, NAJ Publications, New York 1986.

52. Debord and Vaneigem do not appear to be at all influenced by Adorno and

Horkheimer's critique of cultural industry which has many interesting points of connection with their theory of the Spectacle. The Frankfurt School tended to emphasise the psycho-dynamic aspects of alienation, and its unconscious forms of internalisation through the medium of popular culture, which they deeply distrusted. In contrast the situationists completely rejected Freudian concepts in favour of their notion of 'recuperation', and perhaps overestimated the emancipatory potential of popular cultures. I am indebted to Donald Nicholson-Smith for this point.

53. See H. Gumbrecht, *In Praise of Athletic Beauty*, op cit, for a detailed phenomenology of sports spectatorship.
54. See J. Crary, *Techniques of Observation*, MIT Press, London 1999.
55. See J. Ranciere, 'The Emancipated Spectator', in M. Robson (ed), *Jacques Ranciere: aesthetics, politics, philosophy*, Edinburgh University Press 2005; also R. Rinehard, *Players All: Performances in Contemporary Sport*, Indiana University Press, Bloomington 1998; and the contributions to J. Bale and M. Christie (eds), *Post Olympism*, Berg, Oxford 2004.
56. For a critique of Leftist Kulturkritik and its refusal to see or seize the emancipatory potential of the new mediascape see Hans Magnus Enzensberger, 'Constituents for a theory of the media', *New Left Review* 1/64 1970.

Chapter 8

1. See A. Tomlinson and C. Young, *National Identity and Global Sports Events*, New York University Press, New York 2006; and M. and M. Roga, *Britain and the Olympic Games: Past, Present, Legacy*, Matador, Leicester 2011.
2. Source: DCMS 2012, *Olympics Evaluation Framework*.
3. Images discussed in this chapter are at the online gallery Olympic Dreams and Nightmares, especially the section on the Tempest, images 40-48.
4. O. Mannoni, *Prospero and Caliban* (University of Michigan Press, Ann Arbor 1990) was the first to situate *The Tempest* as a debate about the nature of colonialism, and this theme has been adumbrated in much of the postcolonial literature. See B. Ashcroft, *Caliban's Voice: The Transformation of English in Postcolonial Literatures*, Routledge, London 2009; and J. Bate, 'Caliban and Ariel write back', *Shakespeare Survey*, Vol. 29, No. 3, 1995.
5. For the debate over British identity see, for example, H. Kearney, *The British Isles: A History of Four Nations*, Cambridge University Press, Cambridge 1989; P. Dodds, *The Battle over Britain*, Demos, London 1996; and the contributions to A. Gamble and T. Wright, *Britishness: Perspectives on the Britishness Question*, Wiley-Blackwell, Chichester 2009.
6. See G. MacPhee and P. Poddar, *Empire and After: Englishness in Postcolonial Perspective*, Berghahn, Oxford 2007.
7. See D. Forgacs (ed.), *The Gramsci Reader*, Lawrence & Wishart, London

2000, especially the introduction by Forgacs; for the continuing relevance of Gramsci's analysis, A. S. Sassoon, *Gramsci and Contemporary Politics: Beyond Pessimism of the Intellect*, Routledge, London 1999.

8. B. Bragg, *The Progressive Patriot: A Search for Belonging*, Bantam Press, London 2006, p24.

9. See L. Colley, *Forging the Nation*, Pimlico, London 1994.

10. For a discussion of contemporary cultural politics in Britain see the journal *Soundings* and the contributions to S. Munt (ed), *Cultural Studies and the Working Class*, Cassell, London 2000.

11. For a review of the disparate sources drawn upon in creating the Saxon and Celtic versions of Britain's foundation myth see P. Ackroyd, *Albion: The Sources of the English Imagination*, Collins, London 2002.

12. See M. Dyreson, 'The Olympic Games and the Historical Imagination', *Olympika*, Vol. vii, 1998, for a discussion of the uses of history in Olympic Ceremonies; and S. Foster, *Choreographing History*, op cit.

13. For a discussion of foundational myths see M. Serres, *Rome: The Book of Foundations*, Stanford University Press, Ca. 1991; and see also A. Rojo, *The Repeating Island: The Caribbean and the Postmodern Perspective*, Duke University Press, Durham 1992.

14. See R. Young, *The Idea of English Ethnicity*, Blackwell, Oxford 2008.

15. For a detailed account of the role of the navy in establishing English domination over the rest of the British Isles see N.A.M. Rogers, *The Safeguard of the Sea*, Harper Collins, London 1997; and for the role of Anglophone culture see M. Hechter, *Internal Colonialism: The Celtic Fringe*, Transaction Publishers, New Brunswick, N.J. 1978. On the political dimension see B. Bradsham and J. Morrill, *The British Problem: State Formation in the Atlantic Archipelago*, Macmillan, Basingstoke 1996.

16. See R. Chamberlin, *The idea of England*, Thames and Hudson, New York 1986; and A. Easthope, *Englishness and National Culture*, Routledge, London 1999.

17. On the growth of travel writing see the contributions to P. Dodds (ed.), *The Art of Travel*, Cass, London 1982; and M. Pratt, *Imperial Eyes: Travel Writing and Transculturation*, Routledge, London 1982. See also J. Raban, *Coasting*, Collins Harvill, London 1986.

18. See J. Rule, *Albion's People*, Longman, London 1992.

19. See I. Friel, *Maritime History of Britain and Ireland*, British Museum Press, London 2003; P. Linebaugh, *The London Hanged*, Penguin, London 2002; S. Hughill, *Sailortown*, Routledge and Kegan Paul, London 1967. For seaside resorts see J. Walton, *The English Seaside Resort: A Social History*, Leicester University Press, Leicester 1983; and *The British Seaside in the 20th Century*, Manchester University Press, Manchester 2000. See also contributions to P. Borsa and J. Walton (eds), *Resorts and Ports*, Bristol Channel Press, Bristol 2004. For changing popular attitudes towards the coast see A. Corbin, *The Lure of the Sea: The Discovery of the Seaside in the Western World 1750-1840*, Penguin, London 1995; and D. Mack, *The Sea: A Cultural History* (op cit).

20. See E. Hobsbawm, *Industry and Empire*, Weidenfeld and Nicholson, London 1968.

21. See J. S. Bratton 'The Island Story', in J. MacKenzie (ed), *Propaganda and Empire*, Manchester University Press, Manchester 1984; and J. MacKenzie, *Imperialism and Popular Culture*, Manchester University Press, Manchester 1988.

22. See H.E. Marshall, *Our Island Story: A History for Boys and Girls*, Phoenix, London 2007. The book has been continuously in print since its publication in 1907.

23. For a detailed discussion of this work see Chapter Seven of *Borderscapes*, op cit.

24. See R.B. Singh, *Goodly is our Heritage: Children's Literature, Empire and Certitude of Character*, Scarecrow Press, London 2004.

25. See M. Kutzer, *Empire and Imperialism in Classic British Children's Fiction*, Gardiner, London 2000.

26. See N. Longmate, *Defending the Island: From Caesar to the Armada*, Hutchinson, London 1989; and *Island Fortress*, Hutchinson, London 1991.

27. See M. Spiering, *Englishmen, Foreigners, and the Image of National Identity*, Routledge, London 1992.

28. Source: P.G. Wodehouse, *Nothing Serious*, Everyman, London 2008, p95.

29. Source: G. Swift, *Waterland*, Picador, London 1999, p89.

30. See J. Mander, *Great Britain, Little England*, Penguin, London 1967.

31. Source: R. Strong, *The Story of Britain*, Hutchinson, London 1996.

32. For a trenchant restatement of the anglo-islish thesis see N. Longmate's *Defending the Island* and *Island Fortress* (op cit); and the earlier work of A. Bryant, *The Story of England: Makers of the Realm*, Collins, London 1953. For a discussion of this tradition see J. Stapleton, *Sir Arthur Bryant and National History in 20ᵗʰ Century Britain*, Lexington, Oxford 2005. For a critique of this school see R. Samuels, *Theatres of Memory, Vol. 2: Island Stories: Unravelling Britain*, Verso, London 1998. For a revisionary thesis which rejects the jingoism associated with this school but still insists on the unity of British history, as well as its diversity, see L. Colley, *Britons: Forging the Nation 1707-1837*, Pimlico, London 1994.

33. Source: J. Collins, *The Speeches of Enoch Powell*, Bellew, London 1979.

34. On the Alba/Tiber mythography see M. Serres, *Rome: The Book of Foundations*, op cit. For a discussion of Powellism see T. Nairn, 'Enoch Powell', *New Left Review*, No. 56, 1974.

35. For a discussion of the postcolonial island story and its relation to multiculturalism see P. Cohen, 'Who Needs an Island?', in B. Schwarz (ed), *New Formations: Front Lines Backyards*, Vol. 33, 1998.

36. See A. Pope, 'Windsor Forest', in B. Dobree (ed), *Collected Poems*, Dent, London 1975, lines 165-9. For a discussion of the poem's aesthetic programme see P. Rogers, *The Symbolic Design of 'Windsor Forest': Iconography, Prophecy and Pageant in Pope's Early Work*, University of Delaware Press, Newark 2004. On its political implications see J.C.

Pellicer, 'The politics of Alexander Pope's "Windsor Forest" and the dynamics of literary kind', *Huntingdon Library Quarterly*, Vol. 71, No. 32, 2008; and S.M. Cleary, 'Slouching Towards Augusta', *Studies in English Literature*, Vol. 50, No. 3, 2010.

37. For the discussion that follows I am greatly indebted to the pioneering studies of J. Barrell, *The Dark Side of the Landscape: The Rural Poor in English paintings 1730-1840*, Cambridge University Press, Cambridge 1980; and *The Idea of Landscape and the Sense of Place*, Cambridge University Press, Cambridge 1972. See also S. Daniels, *Fields of Vision: Landscape, Vision and National Identity in England and the USA*, Polity, Cambridge 1992.

38. See S. Copley and P. Garside, *Politics of the Picturesque: Literature, Landscape, Aesthetics since 1770*, Cambridge University Press, Cambridge 1994; and R. Giblett, *Landscapes of Culture and Nature*, Palgrave, Basingstoke 2009. See also contributions to G. Budge (ed.), *Aesthetics and the Picturesque 1795-1840*, Thoennies, Bristol 2001.

39. See W. Daniell, *A Voyage Around Great Britain 1814-25*, Tate, London 1975, p6. The most influential contemporary exploration of this aesthetic practice was that of U. Price, *An Essay in the Picturesque as Compared with the Sublime and the Beautiful*, Hereford, London 1794.

40. See M. Andrews, *The Search for the Picturesque*, Scolar, Aldershot 1991; and A. Wilton, *Turner and the Sublime Coastline*, Tate, London 1980. For a general historical overview see D. Corbett and F. Russell, *The Geographies of Englishness: Landscape and the National Past 1880-1940*, Yale University Press, New Haven 2002.

41. See R. Young, *The Idea of English Ethnicity*, op cit.

42. See T. Nairn, *The Break up of Britain*, Verso, London 1974, for a prescient analysis of the 'deconstruction' of Britishness.

43. Source: R. Strong, *The Story of Britain*, Hutchinson, London 1996, p67.

44. Source: E. Upward, *The Railway Accident and other stories*, Penguin, Harmondsworth 1972, p45.

45. On traditions of coasting see J. Raban, *Coasting*, Collins Harvill, London 1986; and D. Mack, *The Sea: A Cultural History*, op cit.

46. See N. Crane, *Coast: Our Island Story*, BBC, London 2010.

47. For a discussion of the role which geology played in the Romantic movement see D. Dean, *Romantic Landscape: Geology and its Cultural Influence in Britain 1750-1832*, University of Michigan Press, Ann Arbor, 2007.

48. See J. Pretty, *The Luminous Coast*, Full Circle, Woodbridge 2011.

49. Source: G. Swift, *Waterland*, Picador, London 1999, p178.

50. See A. Rojo, *The Repeating Island*, op cit.

51. See P. Wright, *On Living in an Old Country: The National Past in Contemporary Britain*, Verso, London 1985. On the peculiarities of 'retro-modernity' in British culture see E. Hobsbawm, *The Making of the Modern World*, Folio Society, London 2005.

52. See C. Ginzburg, *No Island is an Island: Four Glances at English Literature in a World Perspective*, Columbia University Press, New York 2000. For a definition – and defence – of Olympianism as a

uchronic ideal see J. MacAloon, 'The Olympic Idea', op cit. For a discussion of Foucault's concept of heterotopia see T. Sieben, *Heterotopia: Postmodern Utopia and the Body Politic*, University of Michigan Press, Ann Arbor 1994.

53. See, for example, R. Macfarlane, *The Old Ways*, Hamish Hamilton 2012; and *Wild Places*, Granta, London 2007; R. Deakin, *Wildwood: A Journey Through Trees*, Penguin, London 2008; and *Waterlog*, Vintage, London 2000; K. Jamie, *Findings*, Sort of Books, London 2005.

54. R. Mabey, *Weeds: The Story of Outlaw Plants: A Cultural History*, Profile, London 2010.

55. For further information see online Olympic Gallery, images 40-48.

56. See H. Bloom's introduction to his *William Shakespeare's The Tempest*, Eurospan, London 2011.

57. See H.K. Bhabha, 'Signs Taken for Wonders', *The Location of Culture*, Routledge, London 2004, for a discussion of mimicry as a strategy of cultural subversion. See also J. Bate, 'Caliban and Ariel write back', op cit.

58. See W.H. Auden, *The Sea and the Mirror*, Princeton University Press, Woodstock 2003, p18.

59. See R. Browning, 'Caliban upon Setebos' in *Poems*, Baydell Press, Ipswich 1973.

60. See A. Cesaire, *A Tempest*, Ubu Repertory Theater Publications, New York 1992; and J. Dayan, 'Playing Caliban: Cesaire's Tempest', *Arizona Quarterly*, Vol. 48, No. 4.

61. Mannoni reads Hegel's master/slave dialectic in psychoanalytic terms: the colonist is suffering from a 'Prospero complex', driven by an unconscious sense of inferiority to lord it over his native subjects, who in turn are suffering from a 'Caliban' complex, unable to break free from their emotional and cultural ties of dependence on the 'mother country' and its 'founding fathers'. Against this double bind, Fanon insists that the experience of colonisation brutalises both coloniser and colonised, but that only the latter has an objective need as well as subjective desire to end the relationship.

Chapter 9

1. For a wide selection of images of the ceremonies see the online Olympic gallery: 76-117 (Isle of Wonders), 194-207 (The Enlightenment), and 64-74 (The anti-industrial machine). A video of the Isle of Wonders and other Olympic ceremonies has also been released, directed by Danny Boyle.

2. For a general discussion of this point see J. Ranciere, *The Politics of Aesthetics: The Distribution of the Sensible*, Continuum, London 2006.

3. On kitsch see the discussion in Chapter Seven.

4. See T. Adorno, 'Aldous Huxley and Utopia', *Prisms*, MIT Press, Cambridge, Mass. 1991, pp96-119.

5. See T. Adorno, 'Education after Auschwitz', *Can One Live After Auschwitz?: A Philosophical Reader*, Eurospan, London 1993.

6. See M. Shildrick, *Leaky Bodies and Boundaries: Feminism, Postmodernism and Bio-ethics*, op cit; and also the discussion in Chapter Five of this book.

7. This issue has been explored in depth in J. Hoberman *The Olympic Crisis: sport, politics and the moral order*, A.D. Caratzes, New York 1986; and *Mortal Engines: the science of performance and the dehumanisation of Sport*, Maxwell Macmillan, New York 1992.

8. See T. Brockelman, *The Frame and the Mirror: On Collage and the Postmodern*, Northwestern University Press, Evanston, Il. 2000. On the theory of montage see S. Eisenstein, *Selected Works*, I. B. Tauris, London 2010. For a discussion of the principle of harmonious confusion see Chapter 8.

9. Quoted in W. Spies (ed), *Max Ernst, Life and Work: An Autobiographical Collage*, Thames and Hudson, London 2006, p78.

10. 'The Enclosure of Commons', lines 67-71, J. Clare, *Collected Poems*.

11. On this point see the discussion in K. Robins and F. Webster, *Times of the Technoculture: From the Information Society to the Virtual Life*, Routledge, London 1999.

12. *The Land of Cockayne*, lines 17-24

13. See E. Hobsbawm, *Labouring Men: Studies in the History of Labour*, Weidenfield and Nicolson, London, 1986; E. P. Thompson, *The Making of the English Working Class*, Gollancz, London, 1980, and P. Linebaugh, *Ned Ludd and Queen Mab*, op cit.

14. W. Blake, 'The Tyger', *Songs of Innocence and of Experience*, Cambridge University Press, Cambridge 1990.

15. See the discussion in Chapter Five of P. Cohen, *Borderscapes*, op cit.

16. See P. Pullman, *His Dark Materials*, Scholastic, London 2001; and A. Bradley, *The New Atheist Novel: Fiction, Philosophy and Polemic after 9/11*, Continuum, London 2010.

17. See A Rabinbach *The human motor: energy, fatigue and the rise of modernity*, op cit.

18. Quoted in the Introduction to H. Jennings, *Pandaemonium: The Coming of the Machine as Seen by Contemporary Observers 1660-1886*, The Free Press, Glencoe 1986. For a discussion of Jennings's work and its relation to the surrealist movement see M. Remy, *Surrealism in Britain*, Ashgate, Aldershot 1999; and for its relation to Mass Observation see R. Menghan 'Bourgeois News', *New Formations*, Vol. 44, 2001; also K. Robins and F. Webster, *Times of the Technoculture: From the Information Society to the Virtual Life*, Routledge, London 1999.

19. See H. Braverman, *Labour and Monopoly Capital: The Degradation of Work in the 20th Century*, Monthly Review Press, New York 1974; and R. Sennett, *The Culture of the New Capitalism*, Yale University, London 2006.

20. On this point see J. Ranciere, *Les Nuits des Proletaires*, Maspero, Paris 1994.

21. T. Adorno, 'Aldous Huxley and Utopia', *Prisms*, op cit, p46.

22. For a discussion of the relationship between poetics and athletics see P. Cohen 'Carrying the Torch?', op cit.

23. See the discussion in E. Sellin, *Reflections on the Aesthetics of Futurism, Dadaism and Surrealism*, Edwin Mellin, Lampeter 1993.
24. See in particular R. Vaneigem (op cit).
25. See the alternative scenario for the Opening Ceremony online: www. philcohenworks.com.
26. The classic theory of humour as a psychological defence mechanism is S. Freud, *Jokes and the Relation to the Unconscious*, Penguin, Harmondsworth 1976. For an overview of perspectives see J. Morreal, *Comic Relief: A Comprehensive Philosophy of Humour*, Wiley-Blackwell, London 2009.
27. See F. Spufford, *The Child that Books Built*, Faber and Faber, London 2002.

Chapter 10

1. The groups were drawn from residents in the London borough of Newham using stratified random sampling. The initial youth group was aged 15-21 and the adult group from 22-70. The groups met on five occasions: two weeks before and two weeks after the outcome of the Olympics bid in 2006; in January 2009; one week before the opening ceremony of the Olympics and one week after the closing ceremony of the Paralympics. The core membership of the groups remained unchanged over the years, but as some people dropped out, most notably from the youth group, they were replaced by people who as far as possible kept the initial demographic constant in terms of age, gender, ethnicity and socio-economic status. On the methodological problems of conducting longitudinal research using focus groups see J. Holland, *Qualitative Longitudinal Research: A Discussion Paper*, London Southbank University, London 2006; and M. Unger et al, 'Can focus groups be used for longitudinal evaluation?', *International Journal of Multiple Research Approaches*, Vol. 5, No. 1, 2011. My thanks to all those who took part in this project, to George Fuller and Henrietta Clarke for carrying out some of the individual interviews, to Iain MacRury for conducting the initial focus groups in 2006, and to Paul Dodge and Mary Kennedy for the subsequent ones.
2. For a full report of this initial phase of the research see *Carrying the Torch*, University of East London 2007.
3. See the online glossary for a definition of this term.
4. For further discussion of these concepts see R. Putnam, *Bowling Alone*, Simon & Schuster, New York 2000; and online glossary.
5. There are in fact a range of intermediate positions which depend on whether the medium of stake-holding is institutional or inter-personal. For example, power brokers (or *machers* in Putnam's Yiddish idiom) accumulate bridging capital within the framework of project partnerships; fixers (or *schmoozers*) on the other hand do their bridging business through strenuous socialising.
6. Local skills training was delivered through the National Construction

College in East London, as well as a variety of other local agencies. See Chapter Five for further discussion.

7. Research into the reception and impact of Olympics ceremonies has been dominated by two traditions: ethnographic analysis, where the focus is on the interaction between athletes, performers and spectators in the arena; and sociological studies of the role of TV and social media in relaying the event to a global audience. Neither approach pays much attention to the interplay of aesthetic form and cultural content in shaping the narrative and hence audience responses, or the mediating role which the regeneration politics of each host city plays in the design and delivery of the ceremonies themselves. John MacAloon has made the most suggestive proposal for such a study. See J. MacAloon (ed), *Rite, Drama, Festival, Spectacle*, op cit; and J. Sugden and A. Tomlinson (eds), *Watching the Olympics: Politics, Power, Representation*, Routledge, London 2012; and the contributions to M. Tremaine (ed), *Blogging, Citizenship and the Future of Media*, Routledge, London 2007.

8. For details of this alternative scenario see my website: www. philcohenworks.com.

9. For a discussion of the halo effect see L. Leuthasser et al, 'Brand Equity: the halo effect in audience perception', *European Journal of Marketing*, Vol. 29, No. 4, 1995.

10. There were initially high expectations amongst the disabled community that the Paralympics would improve their public image and change social attitudes. However research carried out after the games for the British Social Attitudes survey showed that for the first time since the beginning of the recession the number of people who supported an increase in welfare benefits to the disabled had dropped to under 30 per cent.

Chapter 11

1. See R. Lichtenstein and I. Sinclair, *Rodinsky's Room*, Granta, London 2000.

2. Values tournament is a term coined by Max Weber to refer to events whose latent meaning or function is to stage a confrontation between competing belief or value systems. For the application of this concept to the Olympics see A. Guttmann, *The Olympics: A History of the Modern Games*, op cit, and for further discussion see the online glossary.

3. For a discussion of different theories of value see D. Graeber, *Towards an Anthropological Theory of Value*, op cit.

4. On the debate about the moral and epistemological bases of judgement see R. Rorty, *Philosophy as Cultural Politics* Cambridge University Press 2007; and A. MacIntyre, *After Virtue: a study in moral theory*, University of Notre Dame Press 2007.

5. See L. Festinger, *Conflict, decision and dissonance*, Tavistock, London 1964.

6. See the interesting proposals outlined by M. Perryman, *Why the Olympics Aren't Good for Us and How They Can Be*, OR Books 2012.

7. See J. MacAloon, 'Legacy as managerial/magical discourse, op cit.

8. See D. W. Winnicott, *The Child, the family and the Outside World*, Penguin, London 1991.

9. See the contributions to J. Mackay (ed), *The Age of Voluntarism*, op cit.

10. The Wellcome plan included the International Broadcasting Centre being transformed into a multi-university of science, technology and innovation, a Museum of the Life Sciences, a large amount of social housing, and a Community Endowment Scheme for the public management of the rest of the park; it offered a commercially viable solution to the legacy problem with maximum feasible planning gain: its East London version of silicon valley would have created a new green hub for the knowledge economy in a way that linked the local and global dimensions of economic growth within a democratic framework of accountability.

11. For a discussion of post-Olympic urbanism see C. Rutheiser, *Imagineering Atlanta*, op cit. On urban imagineering in general see S. Lukas, *The Themed Space: Locating Culture, Nation, Self*, Lexington Books, Plymouth 2007; and K. Hetherington, *Capitalism's Eye: Cultural Space and the Commodity*, Routledge, London 2008.

12. Source: Legacy Development Corporation website: www.londonlegacy.co.uk.

13. See D. Shane, *Recombinant Urbanism*, op cit.

14. Source: Legacy Development Corporation website: www.londonlegacy.co.uk.

15. See T. Butler and G. Robson, *London Calling: The Middle Classes and the Remaking of Inner London*, Berg, Oxford 2003. See online glossary for further discussion on gentrification.

16. J. Jacobs, *The Death and Life of Great American Cities*, Penguin, London 1974; and for a positive appraisal of her approach, A. Alexiou, *Jane Jacobs: Urban Visionary*, Rutgers University Press, London 2006.

17. See A. Magnaghi, *The Urban Village: A Charter for Local Democracy and Sustainable Development*, Zed Books, London 2005.

18. See the contributions to E. Charlesworth (ed), *City Edge: Case Studies in Contemporary Urbanism*, op cit.

19. See R. Florida, *Cities and the Creative Class*, Routledge, London 1995. See also C. Landry, *The Creative City*, Demos, London 1995.

20. The term was coined by Raymond Williams. See J. Higgins (ed.), *The Raymond Williams Reader*, Blackwell, Oxford 2001.

21. See N. Buck et al, *Working Capital: Life and Labour in Contemporary London*, Routledge, London 2002; and T.A. Hutton, *The New Economy of the Inner City*, op cit.

22. See S. Graham and S. Marvin, *Splintering Urbanism*, op cit.

23. See M. Foucault, 'Heterotopia', in P. Rabinow (ed), *The Essential Works of Michel Foucault Vol II: Aesthetics*, Penguin, London 2000; M. Duhaene, *Heterotopia and the City: Public Space in a Postcivil Society*, Routledge, London 2008; and online glossary.

24. See P. Cohen, 'A Beautifying Lie? On Kitsch and Culture @ the Olympics', in *Soundings*, Vol. 50, 2012.

25. See D. Shane, *Recombinant Urbanism*, op cit; and R. Burdett, *Endless City*, Phaidon, London 2007.

26. See R. Sennett, *The Uses of Disorder*, Penguin, Harmondsworth 1973; and C. Ward, *Cotters and Squatters*, Five Leaves, Nottingham 2002.

27. For a general discussion of the role of the stadium in urban regeneration see the contributions to J. Bale and O. Moen (eds), *The Stadium and the City*, Keele University Press, Keele 1995.

28. See W.G. Sebald, *Austerlitz*, Hamish Hamilton, London 2001, p108. See also A. Vidler, *The Architectural Uncanny*, MIT Press, London 1996.

29. See M. Pawley, *Terminal Architecture*, op cit. The term is used to describe structures whose design is entirely determined by their function of containing large numbers of people or goods. See also A. King, *Spaces of Global Cultures: Architecture, Urbanism, Identity*, Routledge, London 2004; R. Trumpbour, *The New Cathedrals: Politics and Media in the History of Stadium Construction*, Syracuse University Press, New York 2007; R. Sheard, *The Stadium: Architecture for the New Global Culture*, Periplus, Singapore 2005.

30. See M. Auge, *Non Places: An Introduction to the Anthropology of Hypermodernity*, Verso, London 2005.

31. Nieuwenhuys spent twenty years creating models of his nomadic city, which he called 'New Babylon', where Homo Ludens rules OK, and 'play' and creativity, no longer the preserve of a social elite, are part of the texture of everyday life. Many of Nieuwenhuys's ideas were subsequently taken up by the British Archigram group, in their project for an 'instant city' built out of a throwaway architecture; and their influence can be seen in Heneghan Peng's versatile bridge for the Olympic Park that instantly converted from games time to legacy use.

32. For current research on place making and narrative landscapes see the contributions to S. Daniels et al (ed), *Envisioning Landscape, Making Worlds: Geography and the Humanities*, Routledge, London 2011.

33. *Daily Mail*, 5.12.12.

34. See for example the discussion of Atlanta in C. Rutheiser, *Imagineering Atlanta*, op cit.

35. See B. Elliott, *Constructing Community: Configurations of the Social in Contemporary Philosophy and Urbanism*, Lexington Books, Plymouth 2010.

36. See P. Blond, *Red Tory: How the Left and Right have Broken Britain and How we can Fix It*, Faber and Faber, London 2010. On Guild Socialism see G.D.H. Cole, *Guild Socialism*, Fabian Society, London 1934; and J. Vowls, *From Corporatism to Workers' Control: The Formation of British Guild Socialism*, University of British Columbia 1980.

37. See C. Ward, *Plotlanders*, op cit.

38. For a discussion of this point see M. Serres, *The Parasite*, Johns Hopkins University Press, Baltimore 1982.

39. See J. Derrida, *Of Hospitality*, Stanford University Press CA. 2000.

40. See S. Henry and M. Heyman, *The Informal Economy*, Sage, London 1987; and for its role in East London see R. Hobbs, op cit.

Thinking through the Olympics

Online resources available at www.philcohenworks.com

The field of Olympic Studies exists at the intersection of many disciplines, each of which has its own angle, its own story to tell: the historical sociology of sport; media and cultural studies; the anthropology of performance; urban and community studies; political science, and so on. The field is also traversed by what might be called hyper-disciplines – theories and methodologies that claim to provide general paradigms of understanding for the human sciences, viz Marxism, feminism, post-colonial studies, post-structuralism, each of which has its own strategy for topicalising the field, its own preferred reading of the issues, centred variously on class, gender, ethnicity or discourse analysis. It is not easy to bring these different approaches into any kind of productive dialogue, let alone concordance, yet that is the challenge and excitement of working in this field.

I have compiled some online resources to inform, provoke, amuse and entertain. I hope they will be useful companions to readers who want to set out on this adventure for themselves.

This material includes:

- A list of key 2012 players

- The legacyspeak machine

- The twenty-twelver's rough guide to useful post-Olympic expressions

- Map Readings: a select list of resources for further study.

- A glossary of concepts, consisting of a series of short essays on some of the key terms used in developing the book's argument, contextualising them in relation to current debates in the human sciences.

- London New Jerusalem 2012, a scenario for an alternative opening ceremony based on ideas brainstormed with East London focus groups.

- Three on-line galleries which comprise visual essays on themes related to the book. Further information on these can be found under the list of Illustrations.

- Gary's Olympic Game. The full transcript of this interview, discussed in Chapter Five, with comments designed to be useful in classroom discussion.

- A course outline for an undergraduate studies programme based on the book: *London Olympic Cultural and Urban Studies* (Locus).

To access this material simply go to my website: www.philcohenworks.com and click on East London and the Olympics.

Notes on contributors

Phil Cohen grew up with Steve Ovett and Jean-Paul Sartre as his teenage heroes and has been trying to get them into the same book ever since. He is author *of Knuckle Sandwich: Growing up in the working class city* (with Dave Robins); *Rethinking the Youth Question; Finding the Way Home* (with Nora Rathzel) and *London's Turning: The making of Thames Gateway* (with Mike Rustin). A collection of his recent work, *Borderscapes: between memory, narrative and imagined community* is forthcoming. His poetry has been published by *Critical Quarterly, Agenda*, and *Soundings*. His memoir *Reading Room Only* is published by Five Leaves in 2013. He is Emeritus Professor in Cultural Studies at the University of East London. Further information from www.philcohenworks.com.

John Claridge started his career in photography at the age of 15, working at McCann-Erickson in London. It was during a two-year period there that he had his first one-man show. In 1963, at the age of 19, he had his own studio in the City of London, after assisting American photographer David Montgomery for two years. Since then he has been commissioned by and worked for most leading advertising agencies and clients worldwide. His work has been exhibited all over the world, as one-man shows and collectively. He has been presented with over 700 awards for photography, both editorial and commercial. His work is held in museums and private collections worldwide, including The Arts Council of Great Britain, Victoria & Albert Museum, National Portrait Gallery and The Museum of Modern Art. He has published six books: *South American Portfolio* (1982), *One Hundred Photographs* (1988), *Seven Days in Havana* (2000), *8 Hours* (2002), *In Shadows I Dream* (2003) and *East London* (2007).

Adam Dant studied at the Royal College of Art, London and the MS University Faculty of Fine Arts, Baroda, India (1988), and now lives and works in East London. He has acquired a reputation as a creator of 'mockuments', works based on floor plans to create a psycho-history of the institution being anatomized. Mishap and folly proliferate in his work, and he has been described as someone who 'delights in serious craziness that pokes fun at our contemporary media by proposing charismatically strange alternative perspectives'. He recently curated *Hackney Hoard* (Galerie8, London, 2011), an idea that formed after a mysterious golden coin was found near his home in Hackney. Selected solo shows include Hayward Gallery (London), Adam Baumgold Gallery (New York), Hales Gallery (London), Galerie Brighi (Paris). In 2002 he received the Jerwood Drawing Prize for his *Anecdotal Plan of Tate Britain*.

Peter Dunn is lead artist and Director of ART.e @ the art of change which he founded in 2001 as a new departure in the relationship between Art, Regeneration, Technologies and environment (hence the name ART.e), and as a legacy organisation of The Art of Change and the Docklands Community Poster Project, both of which he co-founded with Loraine Leeson. He has written articles for many publications in this country and abroad on themes related to art, constituencies, communities and regeneration, and more recently on the implications of digital media and the Network Society. He has major public artworks in: Portsmouth, Stevenage, Gravesend, Bournemouth, Oxford and London Boroughs of Tower Hamlets, Newham, Camden & Islington, Hackney, Southwark and Lewisham. For further information see www.arte-ofchange.com.

Jake Humphrey studied architecture at The University of Liverpool (BA Hons). Part of Unit 11 at The University of Greenwich (Dip Arch) taught by Ed Frith and Patrick Lewis. The image reproduced in this book, 'Destruction', is the first of three key narrative images from the 'Reprise and Fall' series (with Leo Robert). In this series the myth of Icarus and Daedalus is transplanted to the Thames Gateway, a strangely pliable, shifting landscape particularly soaked in myth, both historical, and more recently, draped in the pycho-geography of writers like Ian Sinclair.

Aldo Katayanagi was born to two creative professionals, and was encouraged from a young age to study medicine. He instead graduated from the School of Visual Arts in New York with a degree in illustration. He is at peace with this, and currently lives in Chicago. His art often combines light-hearted and disconcerting elements that play off of and redefine one another. His work has been exhibited at the Society of Illustrators, and can be viewed on his site at aldo-art.com.

Peter Kennard and **Tarek Salhany** are both artists living and working in East London producing images that attempt to counter the dominant visual culture and ideology of capital. They try in their work to visualise the contradictions within late capitalism by showing that the domination of the majority by the few and the ruthless exploitation of both people and global resources inevitably leads to wars and systemic crises of the economy and the environment. They have created a book together, @*earth* (Tate Publishing, 2011), which is a story without words. Told in the language of photomontage, it is a visual narrative of global destruction exposing the current state of the earth, the conditions of life on it and the need to resist injustice. Peter Kennard teaches at the Royal College of Art and Tarek Salhany at Queen Mary University of London. Peter Kennard's work is held in numerous public collections in Britain, Europe and North America.

Loraine Leeson is a visual artist specialising in community-based practice around a variety of issues, particularly regeneration of the urban environment. Loraine is particularly known for her work on *The Docklands Community Poster Project* of the 1980s, which involved the production of photo-murals, exhibitions, photography and events in support of the campaigning communities of London's Docklands. Current projects include *The Young Person's Guide to East London*, involving hundreds of teenagers in representing their city for a wider public, which has received an Olympic *InspireMark* and a Media Trust *Inspiring Voices* award. *Active Energy* is an interdisciplinary and intergenerational collaboration developing renewable energy initiatives for East London. She is a Fulbright scholar, lecturer at Middlesex University, associate researcher at University of Creative Arts and runs the arts charity cSPACE.

Jock McFadyen was born in Glasgow and came down to London at the age of 15. He was educated at Chelsea School of Art and taught one day a week at the Slade between 1980 and 2005. His paintings from the early 1980s were populated by the waifs and strays of pre-Canary Wharf London, based not on inventions but sightings of individuals and events of the time. In 1991 he was commissioned by the Artistic Records Committee of the Imperial War Museum to record events surrounding the dismantling of the Berlin Wall, and in 1992 he designed sets and costumes for Kenneth MacMillan's *The Judas Tree* at the Royal Opera House. In 2005 he collaborated with his wife Susie Honeyman to create The Grey Gallery, to work with artists, writers and musicians on a project by project basis with the aim to work across all disciplines. Jock currently lives in Bethnal Green. He has had over 40 solo exhibitions and his work is held by 30 public collections as well as private collections in Britain and abroad.

Jason Orton studied Politics and Industrial Relations at Essex and Warwick University. After working for several years as an educational researcher he returned to college to complete a Diploma in Photojournalism at the London College of Communication. He has worked as an editorial photographer for newspapers such as the *Daily Telegraph*, *Financial Times* and *Guardian*. In 2005 he published the book *350 Miles - An Essex Journey*, a collaboration with the writer Ken Worpole. For the past seven years he has been documenting the changes that are taking place in an area east of London often referred to as the 'Thames Gateway'. In 2010 he was commissioned to document the development of the 2012 Olympic site. He contests that it is not enough to consider the Olympic site in isolation, which is why his photography explores the surrounding land and riverscapes.

Ian F. Rogers was born in London and was given his first camera, a 120mm Rolleiflex at the age of 12 by his dad, who ran a successful photography business in Saint Vincent & the Grenadines. Since then he has been attracted to the light like a moth and has published photo books on the Caribbean, Norway and Newham. 'From Old to Newham', which contains photographs depicting the urban gentrification of East London, can be accessed at http://www.blurb.co.uk/bookstore/detail/1436067. He lives with his wife Heidi in Stratford. Further information: ianrogers@hairoun.eu.

John Wallett is an artist and graphic designer with over twenty years experience of living and working in the East End. Since the early 1990s he has worked with a wide range of writers, artists, photographers and activists, community groups, arts education and campaign organisations. A founder member of the Common Knowledge collective, he divides his work time between their offices at 18 Victoria Park Square, Bethnal Green and his current home in Wivenhoe, Colchester. He has also worked with the author

Roger Mills on the map for 'Everything Happens in Cable Street' (Five Leaves) and is currently working on 'The Schengen Principle': a book of images and texts by photographer Anthony Lam exploring the social territories around Poplar and Canary Wharf. Further information from john@idz.info and www.commonknowledge.org.uk.

Julian Wood was born in the London and educated at Exeter University and the University of London. He emigrated to Australia in 1992 and now lives and works in Sydney. Julian is a sociologist by training but has also had a portfolio career involving work in the film industry and the arts and film criticism as well as academia. He is currently teaching and researching in sociology at the University of Sydney. Julian has published in the area of youth studies and the sociology of the media in various academic journals and books. He has also illustrated and published cartoons. His cartoons appeared in the *East London Review* 2005-2007.

Index

Entries for notes refer to page number followed by chapter and note numbers (e.g. 385n5(41) refers to note 41 on chapter 5, page 385). Entries in *italics* refer exclusively to illustrations, figures or tables.